LIBRARY OF HEBREW BIBLE/
OLD TESTAMENT STUDIES

426

Formerly Journal for the Study of the Old Testament Supplement Series

T&T CLARK • LIBRARY OF BIBLICAL STUDIES

Alan R. Millard

Writing and Ancient Near Eastern Society

Papers in Honour of Alan R. Millard

Edited by
Piotr Bienkowski (University of Manchester),
Christopher Mee (University of Liverpool) and
Elizabeth Slater (University of Liverpool)

t&t clark

NEW YORK • LONDON

T & T Clark International, Madison Square Park, 15 East 26th Street, New York, NY 10010

T & T Clark International, The Tower Building, 11 York Road, London SE1 7NX

T & T Clark International is a Continuum imprint.

Library of Congress Cataloging-in-Publication Data

Writing and ancient Near Eastern society: papers in honour of Alan R. Millard / edited by Piotr Bienkowski, Christopher Mee, and Elizabeth Slater.
p. cm. – (Journal for the study of the Old Testament. Supplement series ; 426)
Includes bibliographical references and index.
ISBN 0-567-02691-4 (hardcover)
1. Writing–History. 2. Middle East–Civilization–To 622. I. Millard, A. R. (Alan Ralph) II. Bienkowski, Piotr. III. Mee, C. (Christopher) IV. Slater, Elizabeth. V. Series.
P211.W716 2005
411'.09–dc22
2005014969

Printed in the United States of America

05 06 07 08 09 10   10987654321

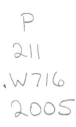

CONTENTS

Preface

Alan Ralph Millard epitomises the rounded, 'holistic' scholar, bringing together expertise in Semitic languages, archaeology and biblical studies, and never allowing himself to become a narrow specialist. His boyhood fascination with British archaeology and ancient coins led him to biblical archaeology—through his father's friendship with the Assyriologist Donald Wiseman and his own strong Christian faith—and eventually to Oxford where he studied Semitic languages under Professor G.R. Driver. After Oxford he travelled around the Middle East for a year on a travelling scholarship, spending time in Iraq and Petra among other places. Then he worked in the Western Asiatic Department of the British Museum, and for seven years was Librarian at Tyndale House, the library for biblical research in Cambridge. In 1970 he came to the University of Liverpool to succeed William Martin as Rankin Lecturer in Hebrew and Ancient Semitic Languages, eventually being awarded a personal chair. During that time he participated in archaeological excavations in Iraq and Syria, most recently as epigrapher to Peter Parr's excavations at Tell Nebi Mend, ancient Qadesh on the Orontes. He retired in 2003.

This volume of papers in Alan's honour is a slightly unusual approach to a *Festschrift*, in that it includes a paper by Alan himself. Two of the main threads that have run through his career have been an interest in the uses of writing in the ancient Near East and in relation to the Bible, and a deep desire to communicate the fruits of his research to as broad a public as possible: he regularly organised extremely popular day schools and wrote many readable and authoritative books on aspects of biblical archaeology. The stimulus for this volume was an attempt to combine these interests of Alan's, with a public colloquium in his honour held in Liverpool in April 2003, consisting of papers on various aspects of writing and ancient Near Eastern and Mediterranean society given by colleagues from Liverpool and elsewhere. We felt it would be interesting and appropriate for Alan too to give a paper, an opportunity, as it were, to provide an overview of particularly important aspects of a topic he has spent his whole life researching. This paper is included here, fittingly closing the volume.

Understandably, not all the contributors to the colloquium felt it appropriate to submit their papers for publication—David Hawkins' and Irving Finkel's papers are not included here. However, the publication of the volume provided an opportunity for other colleagues across the world, who had been unable to attend the colloquium, to submit papers in Alan's honour.

The resulting volume of essays on the broad topic of writing and ancient Near Eastern (and Mediterranean) society is, we hope, a fitting way to express our appreciation to Alan for what he has achieved, for his subject and for us all. As a scholar, teacher, colleague and friend he has always been careful, considered, objective, wide-ranging, generous—and an inspiration.

ABBREVIATIONS

AASOR	Annual of the American Schools of Oriental Research
AB	Anchor Bible
Act.Sum.	Acta Sumerologica
ADAJ	Annual of the Department of Antiquities of Jordan
AfO	Archiv für Orientforschung
AHB	Ancient History Bulletin
AION	Annali dell'Istituto Universitario Orientale di Napoli
AJA	American Journal of Archaeology
AK	Antike Kunst
AOAT	Alter Orient und Altes Testament
AoF	Altorientalische Forschungen
AMI	Archäologische Mitteilungen aus Iran
ANES	Ancient Near Eastern Studies
ANET	Pritchard, Ancient Near Eastern Texts
AntClass	Antiquité classique
Arch.Anz.	Archäologischer Anzeiger
ARM	Archives royales de Mari
ARV2	J.D. Beazley, Attic Red-Figure Vase Painters (second ed.: Oxford 1963)
ASAtene	Annuario della Scuola Archeologia di Atene
AS	Anatolian Studies
ATD	Acta Theologica Danica
ATSAT	Arbeiten zu Text und Sprache im Alten Testament
AV	Archäologische Veröffentlichungen
BA	Biblical Archaeologist
BagM	Baghdader Mitteilungen
BAI	Bulletin of the Asia Institute
BAR	British Archaeological Reports
BASOR	Bulletin of the American Schools of Oriental Research
BN	Biblische Notizen
BMECCJ	Bulletin of the Middle East Culture Center in Japan
BO	Bibliotheca Orientalis
BZAW	Beihefte zur Zeitschrift für die alttestamantliche Wissenschaft
CAD	The Assyrian Dictionary of the Oriental Institute of the University of Chicago (Chicago: Oriental Institute 1956–); N2 refers to the second volume of two devoted to the letter 'N', published in 1980
CRAIBL	Comptes rendus de l'Académie des Inscriptions et Belles Lettres
CBQ	Catholic Biblical Quarterly

CHLI	Corpus of Hieroglyphic Luwian Inscriptions. Volume 1: J.D. Hawkins. The Hieroglyphic Luwian Inscriptions of the Iron Age. UISK 8.1. Berlin and New York: Walter de Gruyter, 2000.
COS	W. W. Hallo & K. L. Younger, eds, The Context of Scripture, 3 vols, Leiden & New York: Brill, 1997–2002
CQ	Classical Quarterly
CTN	Cuneiform Texts from Nimrud
DDD	Dictionary of Deities and Demons in the Bible (eds K. van der Toorn, B. Becking and P.W. van der Horst, Leiden 1995)
DJD	Discoveries in the Judaean Desert
DNWSI	Dictionary of the North-West Semitic Inscriptions (Leiden 1995)
EI	Eretz-Israel
ESV	English Standard Version (Bible)
FOTL	The Forms of the Old Testament Literature
HAR	Hebrew Annual Review
HSAO	Heidleberger Studien zum Alten Orient
HSS	Harvard Semitic Studies
IrAnt	Iranica Antiqua
IEJ	Israel Exploration Journal
IOS	Israel Oriental Studies
IstMitt	Istanbuler Mitteilungen
JA	Journal Asiatique
JAOS	Journal of the American Oriental Society
JBL	Journal of Biblical Literature
JCS	Journal of Cuneiform Studies
JHS	Journal of Hellenistic Studies
JHS Suppl.	Journal of Hellenistic Studies, Supplementary Series
JJS	Journal of Semitic Studies
JNES	Journal of Near Eastern Studies
JQR	Jewish Quarterly Review
JRS	Journal of Roman Studies
JRGS	Journal of the Royal Geographical Society
JSNTSup	Journal for the Study of the New Testament, Supplement Series
JSOT	Journal for the Study of the Old Testament
JSOTSup	Journal for the Study of the Old Testament, Supplement Series
JSPSup	Journal for the Study of the Pseudepigrapha, Supplement Series
KAI	Kanaanaische und Aramaische Inschriften (Wiesbaden 1966–69)
KTU	Die keilalphabetischen Texte aus Ugarit
LACTOR	London Association of Classical Teachers, Original Records
LIMC	Lexicon Iconographicum Mythologiae Classicae (Zürich 1981–97)
MCS	Manchester Cuneiform Studies
MDOG	Mitteilungen der Deutschen Orientgesellschaft
MDAIA	Mitteilungen des Deutschen Archäologischen Instituts, Athen
NABU	Nouvelles assyriologiques brèves et utilitaires
NAB	New American Bible
NAS	New American Standard Version

NAWG	Nachrichten der Akademie der Wissenschaften zu Göttingen
NCB	New Century Bible
NEA	Near Eastern Archaeology
NICOT	The New International Commentary on the Old Testament
NIV	New International Version (Bible)
NJB	New Jerusalem Bible
NLT	New Living Translation (Bible)
NRSV	New Revised Standard Version
OBO	Orbis Biblicus et Orientalis
OLA	Orientalia Lovaniensia Analecta
Op.Ath.	Opuscula Atheniensia
PEFQS	Palestine Exploration Fund, Quarterly Statement
PCPhS	Proceedings of the Cambridge Philological Society
PNA	S. Parpola, K. Radner, H. Baker (eds), The Prosopography of the Neo-Assyrian Empire Helinski: The Neo-Assyrian Text Corpus Project, 1998–
QDAP	Quarterly of the Department of Antiquities in Palestine
RA	Revue d'Assyriologie
RB	Revue biblique
REA	Revue des études anciennes
REB	Revue des études byzantines
REJ	Revue des études juives
RlA	Reallexikon der Assyriologie und vorderasiatischen Archäologie
RIMA	Royal Inscripitions of Mesopotamia: Assyrian Periods
SAA	State Archives of Assyria
SAAS	State Archives of Assyria Studies
SBJT	The Southern Baptist Journal of Theology
SBLDS	Society of Biblical Literature Dissertation Series
SHCANE	Studies in the History and Culture of the Ancient Near East
SRAA	Silk Road Art and Archaeology
STDJ	Studies on the Texts of the Desert of Judah
SVT	Supplement, Vetus Testamentum
SVTP	Studia in Veteris Testamenti Pseudepigrapha
TOTC	Tyndale Old Testament Commentaries
TA	Tel Aviv
UF	Ugarit-Forschungen
UT	Ugaritic Textbook
VT	Vetus Testamentum
VTSup	Vetus Testamentum, Supplements
WBC	World Biblical Commentary
WO	Die Welt des Orients
ZA	Zeitschrift für Assyriologie
ZAH	Zeitschrift für Althebräistik
ZAW	Zeitschrift für die alttestamentliche Wissenschaft
ZPE	Zeitschrift für Papyrologie und Epigraphik
ZDMG	Zeitschrift der deutschen Morgenländischen Gesellschaft
ZDPV	Zeitschrift des deutschen Palästina-Vereins

List of Contributors

Pierre Bordreuil, CNRS

Alasdair Livingstone, University of Birmingham

Dennis Pardee, University of Chicago

M.C.A. Macdonald, University of Oxford

Wolfgang Röllig, Eberhard Karls Universität, Tübingen

John F. Healey, University of Manchester

David T. Tsumura, Japan Bible Seminary, Tokyo

Graham Davies, University of Cambridge

K.A. Kitchen, University of Liverpool

Daniel I. Block, Southern Baptist Theological Seminary, Louisville

Christopher Tuplin, University of Liverpool

K. Lawson Younger, Trinity International University, Deerfield

George J. Brooke, University of Manchester

John Davies, University of Liverpool

Alan Millard, University of Liverpool

MIGRAINES D'ÉPIGRAPHISTE

Pierre Bordreuil

La migraine figure certainement au nombre des maux dont ont souffert les premiers déchiffreurs de langues oubliées. Par bonheur, tous n'ont pas connu la fin prématurée d'un Champollion dont les découvertes abrégèrent sûrement la vie. Au contraire, disposant aujourd'hui de voies connues, les épigraphistes seraient immodestes de comparer leur sort à celui de 'déchiffreur-défricheur' qui fut imparti à leurs grands anciens. Et pourtant, qui parmi ceux qui ont reçu la charge de faire connaître des documents vraiment dignes d'intérêt, c'est à dire des documents dont la difficulté pimente le contenu, a jamais échappé à cette sorte de gravidité, à cet état d'âme en ciel d'orage qui précède à plus ou moins long terme l'élucidation?

Grâce aux circonstances, en contact fréquent depuis plus de trente ans avec des inscriptions ouest-sémitiques du second et du premier millénaire, connues le plus souvent, mais parfois aussi méconnues ou même ignorées, je connais bien cette affection devenue plus ou moins chronique et maintenant familière. Ce qui suit entend seulement répéter quelques conseils de bon sens, illustrés d'exemples et visant à éviter, ou à réduire les effets de cette forme de céphalée. Le plus souvent imprévue, elle peut se manifester dans la quiétude feutrée d'un musée ou du salon d'un collectionneur, dans la pénombre d'une échoppe battue par la rumeur du Souq ou encore *in situ*, sous la lumière et dans le vent d'un ciel d'Orient. En d'autres termes, la migraine de l'épigraphiste sémitisant peut se contracter partout où ce dernier est mis en demeure de se mesurer avec des *ipsissima verba* vieux de deux à trois mille ans.

Le sémitisant de l'Ouest se trouve en effet dans une situation qui ne peut se comparer ni à celle du bibliste ni à celle de l'helléniste ou du latiniste. Tandis que le bibliste dispose d'un texte comportant certes des variantes, mais aussi de plusieurs versions grecque, syriaque, latine et surtout de l'incomparable fixation *ne varietur* du texte hébreu nanti d'une vocalisation par les Massorètes, l'helléniste et le latiniste disposent non seulement d'une documentation épigraphique très abondante mais encore du support de textes de tous genres et de toutes époques, rédigés de surcroît dans des langues bien connues. En revanche, le sémitisant de l'Ouest qui se consacre à l'épigraphie du premier millénaire dispose d'une documentation singulièrement appauvrie. Rédigée sur des supports périssables, la littérature phénicienne a complètement disparu et il en est de même pour l'essentiel de la littérature araméenne ancienne. Quelques papyrus et ostraca ressortissant à des archives privées ont été conservés par la sécheresse des climats d'Egypte et de Judée, mais l'épigraphie phénicienne et araméenne, disséminée pour la première entre l'Anatolie et l'Egypte, entre la Mésopotamie et la Méditerranée occidentale et, pour la seconde, entre l'Afghanistan et l'Asie Mineure, entre Teima et Eléphantine, reste encore surtout lapidaire.

La situation de l'épigraphiste qui entend se consacrer à l'épigraphie ouest-sémitique du second millénaire peut paraître différente au premier abord. En effet, les tablettes rédigées au moyen du système cunéiforme alphabétique découvert à Ougarit, au nombre de plusieurs centaines, se situent à l'intérieur d'un laps de temps qui est peut-être inférieur à un siècle et elles proviennent de la même ville. Leurs graphies et leur langue sont par conséquent bien plus homogènes que celles du premier millénaire. Pourtant, en dépit des caractéristiques propres à chacun de ces systèmes, les mêmes recommandations sont valables pour l'épigraphie sémitique en cunéiformes alphabétiques du second millénaire et pour l'épigraphie sémitique linéaire du premier millénaire et l'on verra au moyen de quelques exemples que les mêmes erreurs d'appréciation y sont aussi à éviter.

La conviction constante qu'il conviendrait de ne jamais oublier—valable aussi bien pour le cunéiforme alphabétique du second millénaire que pour les trois grandes variétés d'écritures sémitiques alphabétiques du premier millénaire, à savoir le phénicien, l'araméen et l'hébreu épigraphiques—peut s'exprimer en deux constatations:

I) Notre connaissance des graphies est encore incomplète

II) Le contact avec l'original est indispensable.

I) Notre connaissance des graphies est encore incomplète

A) Ayant entrepris il y a quelques années de relire l'ensemble des tablettes alphabétiques découvertes par la mission archéologique française de Ras Shamra-Ougarit et conservées dans les musées de Damas, d'Alep et du Louvre, j'ai vu passer plusieurs centaines de tablettes de tous genres et d'états de conservation fort divers. J'étais pendant tout le temps de cette recherche très attentif aux différentes formes prises par chaque lettre de l'alphabet d'Ougarit et simultanément, je notais les textes dont la copie et la reproduction photographique n'étaient pas encore publiées.

Ayant remarqué parmi les tablettes mises au jour pendant la 23e campagne de 1960 un abécédaire qui était demeuré inédit (RS 23. 492) (Dietrich *et al.* 1995: 5. 19), je décidai d'y consacrer une note (Bordreuil 1982: 9–10), car la fin de l'alphabet me paraissait présenter un phénomène

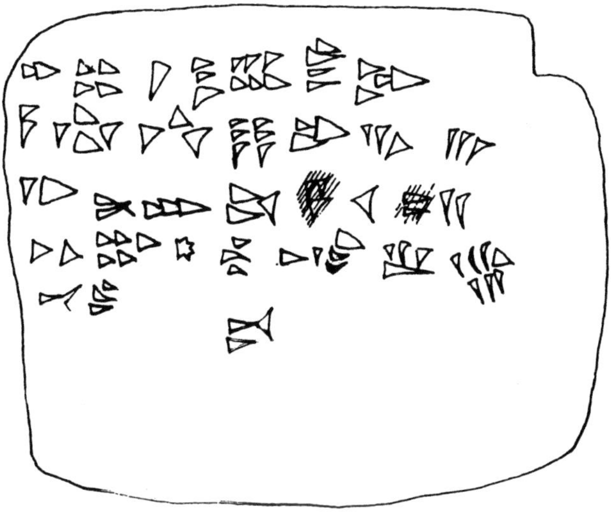

Fig. 1. L'abécédaire RS 23. 492 (d'après Bordreuil 1982: 9).

intéressant (Fig. 1): il s'agissait d'un clou vertical assez court qui était plaçé immédiatement après la lettre /*t*/ et avant le /*ỉ*/. Dans la lettre suivante on pouvait considérer que le clou vertical avait été absorbé par le clou horizontal inférieur, ce qui permettait de lire un /*ỉ*/ (Ellison 2002: II, fig. 782). Cette dernière lettre se révélait alors d'une certaine importance puisqu'on pouvait légitimement en déduire que les créateurs de l'alphabet d'Ougarit, adaptant à l'argile un alphabet antérieur se terminant par /*t*/, avaient voulu marquer la séparation entre l'alphabet antérieur et leur propre innovation qui consistait à ajouter trois lettres supplémentaires après le /*t*/. Cette observation était satisfaisante pour l'esprit et, si elle n'apportait rien de nouveau, elle confirmait ce qui semble aujourd'hui admis sur la place de l'alphabet d'Ougarit dans l'évolution de l'alphabet sémitique. De plus, fort de mon expérience épigraphique des tablettes d'Ougarit, j'aurais affirmé sans hésitation que ce clou vertical ne pouvait appartenir au /*ỉ*/ qui suivait puisqu'un tel type présentant le clou vertical à la gauche des trois clous horizontaux superposés me paraissait alors sans exemple.

C'est une découverte épigraphique, encore inédite, faite en 1983 par la mission archéologique conjointe franco-syrienne de Ras Ibn Hani qui m'a mis sur la piste de cette forme particulière du /*ỉ*/ composé de trois clous horizontaux précédés d'un clou vertical de dimensions variables,[1] alors que de manière constante, le clou vertical est situé immédiatement sous la tête du clou horizontal inférieur (Fig. 2). La lecture du /*ỉ*/ étant ici incontestable étant

[1] R.I.H.: 83/17+19+38+41 ligne 21': *bt .ỉl*ʹ*ḏn*ʾ *àḥd*; l. 30': *bt . ỉl š* ; l. 37': *bt . ỉl* ʹ*dn*ʾ *[.*

Fig. 2. Tablette cunéiforme alphabétique inédite R.I.H. 83/17+19+38+41, l. 12–21.

donné le contexte, j'étais alors contraint d'abandonner la proposition pourtant bien séduisante formulée l'année précédente, à savoir que les scribes de l'Ougarit auraient voulu séparer la fin d'un alphabet antérieur se terminant par /*t*/ et les trois lettres qui étaient propres à l'alphabet local. En l'absence d'étude exhaustive sur la paléographie des textes cunéiformes d'Ougarit j'ai trouvé quelque excuse à mon erreur. Ce type d'erreur sera dans peu de temps inexcusable puisque une thèse remarquable a été soutenue en 2002 à l'Université de Harvard par John Lee Ellison: 'A Paleographic Study of the Alphabetic Cuneiform Texts from Ras Shamra/Ugarit' (Ellison 2002). Ellison a noté l'existence de trois types de /*ì*/; il appelle celui-ci 'Type C /*ì*/'[2] et il l'a identifié dans deux textes: RS 18. 102: l. 1, 8 et RS 24. 284 (Fig. 3). La première attestation avait été remarquée par Ch. Virolleaud comme étant 'une forme particulière unique jusqu'à présent'.[3] La seconde attestation n'a pas été notée dans l'*editio princeps* (Milik 1968: 136 l. 9), mais elle est correctement lue dans *CAT* (Dietrich *et al.* 1995: 1. 130 l. 9) et dans l'ouvrage de D. Pardee (2000: 729–37 et fig. 26 (l. 22)) qui propose de retrouver ici le théonyme *ìlìb* (2000: 731) (Fig. 4).

Il avait donc fallu attendre la 18e campagne en 1954, soit vingt ans après les premiers déchiffrements, pour voir attestée cette forme de lettre qui ne devait être identifiée que onze ans plus tard en 1965, plus de trente ans après les premiers déchiffrements. A ce jour, elle n'est connue que par quatre textes: RS

[2] Ellison 2002: I, 228s. II, figs 807–8, p. 196.

[3] Virolleaud 1965: 34, p. 48s. = Dietrich *et al.* 1995: 4. 381.

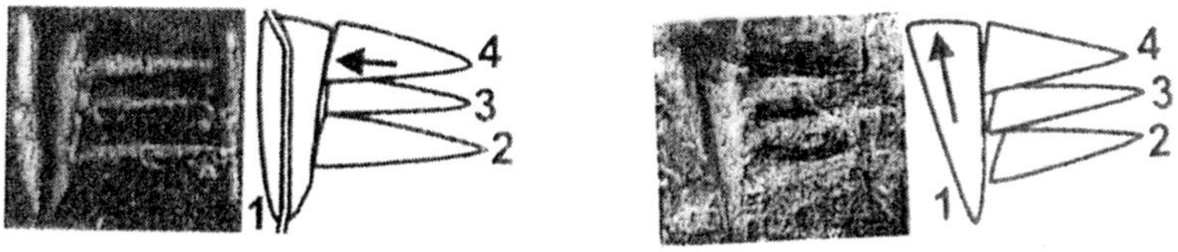

. . . .

ilm[

*tś*ʿ. ʿ*ś*[*r*

bn ʿ*dr*[

ḫmś ʿ*l*. *bn*[

ḫmś ʿ*l r*ʿ*l*[

ḫmś ʿ*l ykn*[

ḫ[*mś*] ʿ*l abǵ*[*l*

ḫmś ʿ*l ilb*[ʿ*l*

ʿ*śr* ʿ*l* [

Fig. 3. Tablette cunéiforme alphabétique R.S. 18. 102.

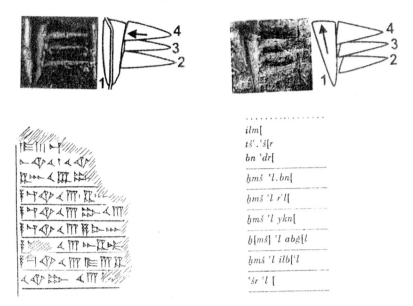

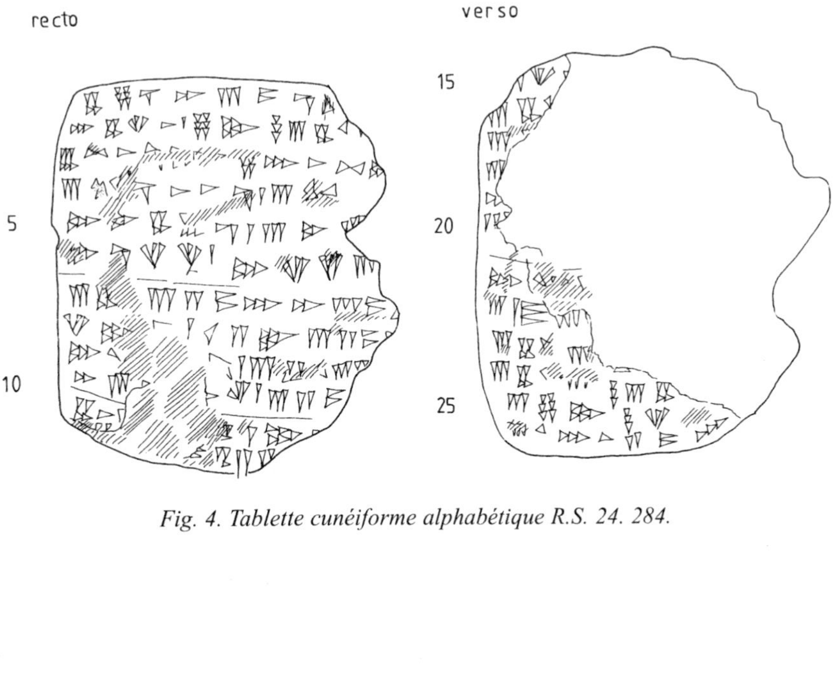

Fig. 4. Tablette cunéiforme alphabétique R.S. 24. 284.

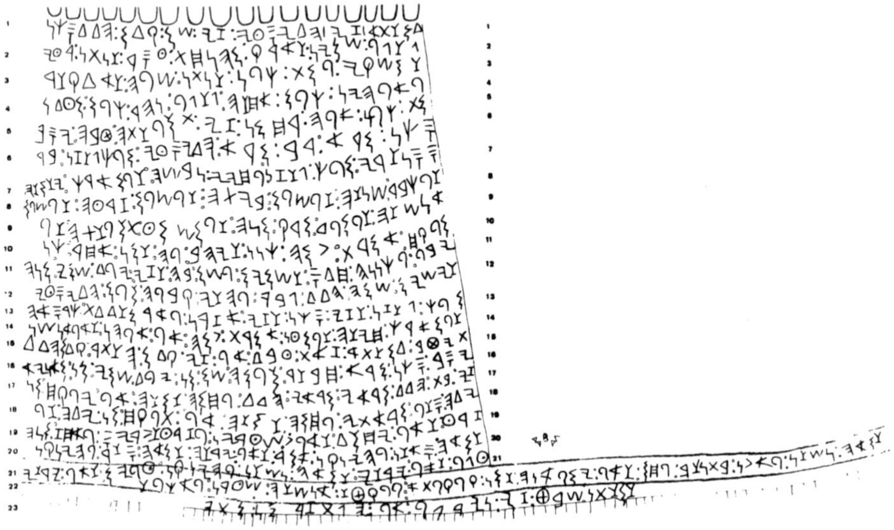

Fig. 5. L'inscription araméenne de Tell Fekheryé.

18. 102, RS 23.492, RS 24.284 et RIH 83/17+19+38+41 sur un total approximatif supérieur à quelque deux mille textes alphabétiques connus à ce jour.

B) Voici maintenant deux notes relatives à un texte important que j'ai eu le bonheur de publier il y a 21 ans en association avec notre ami et collègue Alan Millard que nous fêtons aujourd'hui: il s'agit de la statue de basalte de Tell Fekheryé (Fig. 5). Celle-ci est entrée désormais dans le cercle hélas! trop étroit des inscriptions en araméen ancien qu'on peut qualifier de majeures. Elle vient de trouver place dans le premier volume de la cinquième édition de *KAI* (Donner and Röllig 2002: n° 309) et tout récemment, une page presque complète lui a été dédiée dans un volume intitulé 'The Ancient aramaic heritage' (Brock and Taylor 2001: 65). Depuis notre publication, peu de modifications ont été apportées à la lecture du texte que nous avions établie. La seule proposition qu'on puisse noter dans le domaine de l'épigraphie se trouve à la ligne 20 où Dennis Pardee (1998: 145–47) a proposé, là où nous avions lu un /H/, soit /YRWH/, de lire un /Y/ final, soit /YRWY/ à vocaliser *al yirway*: 'qu'il ne soit pas rassasié'. En raison de la présence de cette dernière forme /YRWY/ répétée deux fois à la ligne suivante, nous avions proposé de considérer le /H/ de la ligne 20 comme une erreur de scribe à corriger en /Y/ (Abou Assaf, Bordreuil, Millard 1982: 54). En réalité, et Pardee a bien fait de le signaler, nous avons à faire ici à une maladresse matérielle et non pas à une faute d'orthographe qui aurait été commise par le lapicide et c'est bien un /Y/, de forme inattendue qu'il faut transcrire ici.

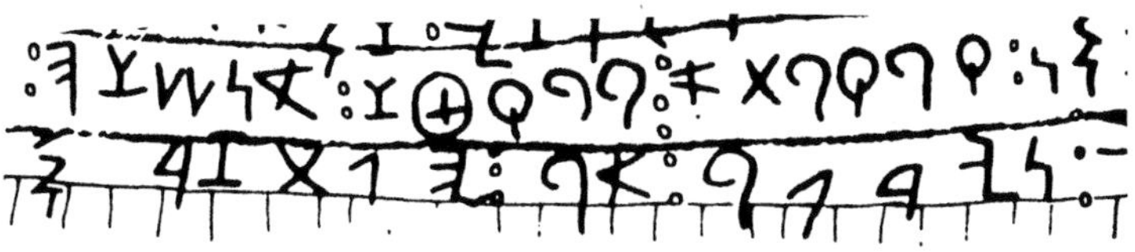

Fig. 6. Ponctuation de l'inscription araméenne de Tell Fekheryé, l. 22 et 23.

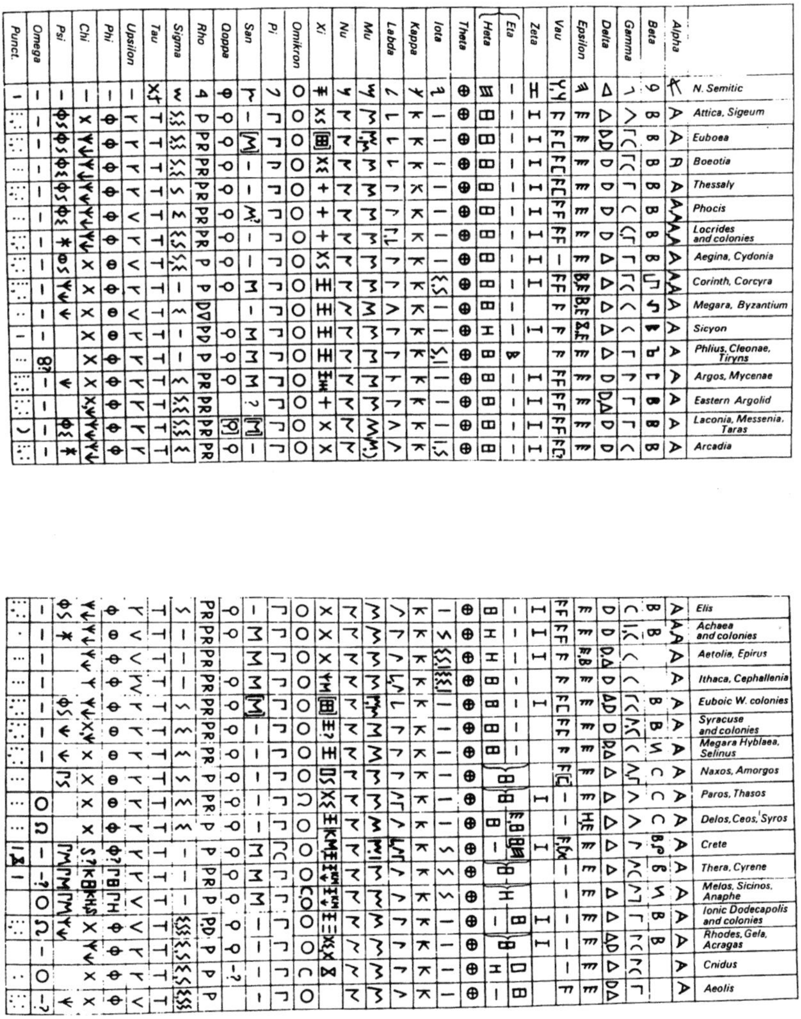

Fig. 7. La ponctuation des plus anciennes inscriptions grecques (d'après L. Jeffrey, The Cambridge Ancient History *III, 1 Cambridge 1982 p. 820).*

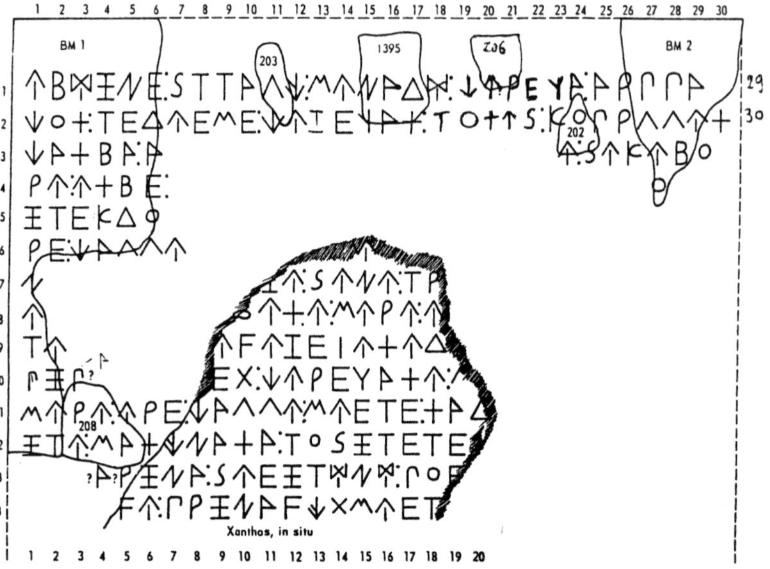

Fig. 8: L'inscription de la face sud du pilier de Xanthos.

Je dois encore relever une importante donnée que nous avions omise: il s'agit de la ponctuation de cette inscription. Les mots sont séparés les uns des autres par deux ou trois points incisés verticalement (Fig. 6) et nous n'avions pas noté que ce phénomène apparaît dans quelques autres inscriptions alphabétiques plus récentes. Ce sont de brèves inscriptions grecques parmi les plus anciennes connues (Jeffery 1982: 820s; Bordreuil 1993: 263). L. Jeffery a recensé la ponctuation de ces inscriptions grecques provenant de trente-deux sites ou régions différentes, dont les plus anciennes datent des environs de 750 av. J.-C. (1982: 823) (Fig. 7). Quatorze d'entre elles présentent la caractéristique d'alterner les séparateurs composés de deux ou de trois points verticaux, c'est-à-dire exactement le même procédé que sur l'inscription araméenne de Tell Fekheryé. Sur quelques inscriptions lyciennes on retrouvera les séparateurs formés exclusivement de deux points disposés verticalement, par exemple sur la version lycienne de la trilingue de Xanthos qui date du IVe s. av. J.-C. (voir Dupont-Sommer *et al.* 1979: pl. XIV), sur la face sud du Pilier de Xanthos (Bousquet 1992: 170, fig. 4) (Fig. 8) et sur la face étroite lycienne de la Base d'Arbinas.[4] De ce point de vue, l'inscription paléo-phrygienne T-03 provenant de la Tyanitide, c'est-à-dire de la région de Tabal (Egetmeyer 2002: 23), est peut-être au VIIIe s. av. J.-C. un *missing link* entre le Levant et la côte lycienne. Par conséquent, il est difficile d'échapper désormais à l'idée

[4] Bousquet 1992: 182, fig. 5 et pl. 79, 1.

Fig. 9. Les lettres /M/ et /Ṣ/ de l'inscription araméenne de Tell Fekheryé.

que l'alphabet sémitique n'a pas seulement été transmis vers l'occident par le canal tyrien auquel Qadmos, fils d'Agénor et frère d'Europe, a attaché son nom, ou par le canal giblite, comme on pourrait le penser à partir des inscriptions d'Aḥirom et de ses successeurs. La présence de ces séparateurs ponctuels verticaux dans un texte phrygien, dans une inscription autochtone découverte en Lycie, puis dans les inscriptions des îles grecques proches de l'Asie mineure donne à penser que l'Asie mineure est à prendre désormais en considération parmi les relais de transmission de l'écriture alphabétique ouest-sémitique vers le monde grec.

La bilingue de Tell Fekheryé est caractérisée aussi par l'apparition de graphies nouvelles, phénomène qui se retrouve encore de temps en temps sur des inscriptions ouest-sémitiques du premier millénaire. Le spécialiste devrait être ici encore plus circonspect puisqu'ainsi qu'on l'a vu, la pauvreté de la documentation et sa grande dissémination spatio-temporelle rendent plus probable l'apparition de telles nouveautés. Il existe pourtant des cas où toutes les précautions d'usage sont de peu d'utilité: qu'on en juge!

La version araméenne de cette inscription bilingue de Tell Fekheryé (Abou Assaf, Bordreuil, Millard 1982) présente un exemple caractéristique de ce phénomène. Les formes de /K/ et de /*ayin* / sont inattendues au IXe siècle ou même nouvelles comme le /Ṣ/ et le /W/. L'identité de cette dernière lettre ne pouvait faire de doute en raison de sa position de copule et de *mater lectionis*, mais la forme du /Ṣ/ allait faire problème comme l'a montré malencontreusement la publication prématurée de Ali Abou Assaf qui a proposé la lecture /M/ (Abou Assaf 1981). En effet, le /Ṣ/ en zig-zag vertical rappelle le /M/ dont il ne se distingue ici que par une oblique supplémentaire située dans la tête de la lettre (Fig. 9). La valeur de cette forme nouvelle m'avait échappé dans un premier temps, d'abord parce qu'inattendue, ensuite parce que peu lisible à première vue sur le basalte, enfin parce que la lecture /M/ donnait une signification pertinente aux trois mots dans lesquels elle semblait apparaître.

La première attestation de cette lettre équivoque se trouve à la 5e ligne (Fig. 10a) où, lue /M/, elle contribuerait à former le mot *TMLTH. Vocalisé *temiluteh*: 'sa parole', ce mot conviendrait parfaitement au contexte, ʾLH RHḤMN ZY TMLWTH ṬBH: 'le dieu clément dont la parole est bonne' étant une eulogie des plus banales.

Cette même lettre semblait apparaître encore à la 16e ligne (Fig. 10b) comme initiale d'un mot de trois lettres MLM+ H suivi de ŠM: 'il (=le roi) a mis son MLM'. On pouvait alors considérer sans difficulté que MLM tran-

Fig. 10a. Ligne 5 de l'inscription araméenne de Tell Fekheryé: ʾLH: RḤMN: ZY: TṢLWTH: ṬBH: '..dieu clément qu'il est bon de prier...'.

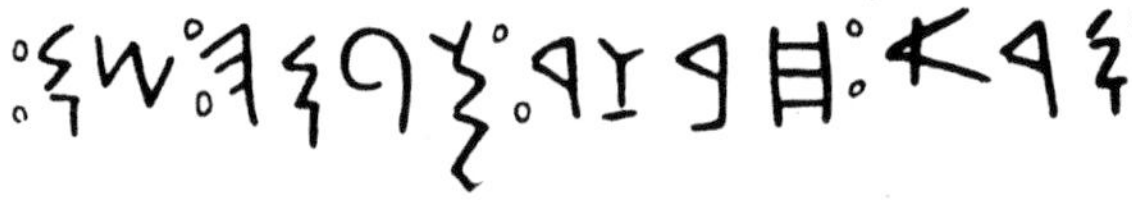

Fig. 10b. Ligne 16 de l'inscription araméenne de Tell Fekheryé: YSB: SKN: MRʾ: ḤBWR: ṢLMH: ŠM '...qui demeure à Sikan, le Seigneur du Khabour, il a plaçé sa statue...'.

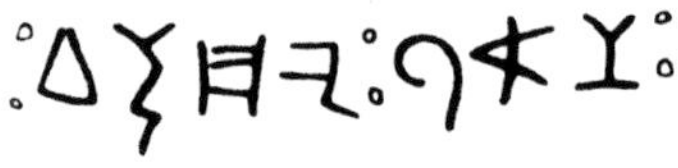

Fig. 10c. Ligne 19 de l'inscription araméenne de Tell Fekheryé: WʾL: YḤṢD: '...et qu'il ne moissonne pas...'.

scrivait le *melammu* mésopotamien, sorte d'auréole nimbant rois et divinités. Pourquoi même ne pas aller jusqu'à faire de cet attribut une sorte d'hypostase placée en ce lieu par son titulaire royal?

La troisième attestation à la 19e ligne (Fig. 10c) permettant de lire WL ZRʿ WʾL YḤMD: 'Qu'il sème et ne rende pas grâce!' paraissait convenir au contexte puisque la malédiction proférée ici entendait priver le profanateur de la joie consécutive aux semailles.

Ces premières lectures /M/, cohérentes et non dénuées d'intérêt, devaient être rapidement et complètement ruinées à partir du terme correspondant à MLM, à la 26e ligne de la version assyrienne. Ce mot, qui est *ṣalam*: 'statue', ne pouvait être l'équivalent de MLM (=*melammu*) mais suggérait de lire son propre équivalent araméen qui est ṢLM dans la version araméenne.

A partir de la nouvelle lecture ṢLM de la 16e ligne, il devenait aisé de corriger à la 19e ligne la lecture du verbe YḤMD par celle du verbe YHṢD, d'où WL ZRʿ WʾL YḤṢD: 'Qu'il sème et ne moissonne pas!', substituant aux réjouissances des semailles la succession semailles-moisson. Le terme TMLWTH de la 5e ligne pouvait dès lors disparaître lui aussi et de subjectif: 'le dieu dont la parole est bonne', le sens de la phrase devenait objectif: 'le dieu qu'il est bon de prier' (TṢLWTH).

L'erreur avait pu être réparée à temps, mais qu'aurait-on fait, sans l'existence de la version assyrienne, d'une lettre ressemblant fortement à un /M/, encore complètement inconnue en tant que /Ṣ/ et contribuant à former des mots déjà connus tells que TMLWT, ḤMD et MLM, transcription très

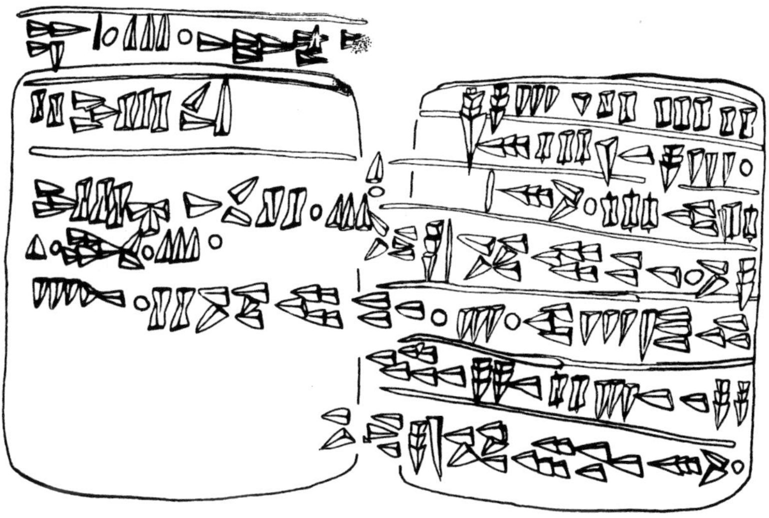

RS 22-03

Fig. 11. La tablette alphabétique sénestroverse RS 22.03 (d'après Bordreuil 1981: 303).

acceptable du *melammu* assyrien. La présence du mot ṢLM donnait certes le point de départ, mais il n'aurait pas emporté à ce point la conviction si un examen minutieux de la pierre ne m'avait au préalable fait noter—sans d'ailleurs en tirer immédiatement les conséquences qui allaient s'imposer un peu plus tard—l'oblique supérieure supplémentaire qui en réalité distingue paléographiquement le /Ṣ/ du /M/. Ce rappel des circonstances de l'établissement du texte sur la statue elle-même amène à une seconde recommandation.

II) Le contact avec l'original est indispensable

D'une grande banalité, le bien-fondé de cette constatation peut être minimisé aujourd'hui pour les tablettes en cunéiformes alphabétiques, en raison de l'apparition de procédés de reproduction nouveaux. Un badigeonnage de silicone sur l'ensemble de la tablette entraîne la formation d'une pellicule qui en séchant forme une sorte de sac reproduisant fidèlement à l'intérieur le relief cunéiforme du texte. L'introduction de plâtre liquide permet en séchant d'obtenir la reproduction d'un texte intact, pratiquement à l'identique. Le recours à l'original par les soins d'un spécialiste reste pourtant indispensable pour les documents altérés auxquels seul un oeil exerçé pourra peut-être arracher encore quelques signes. En revanche, on pourrait admettre qu'une tablette en parfait état de conservation soit directement étudiée sur des moulages de ce type qui sont vraiment des fac-similés. Il y a seulement quelques années un tel procédé n'existait pas et l'exemple qui va suivre illustre bien les mécomptes auxquels pouvait aboutir l'utilisation de moulages insuffisamment fidèles.

A) La tablette ougaritique RS 22.03 découverte en 1960[5] (Fig. 11) porte sur ses deux faces un texte en cunéiformes alphabétiques incisés de droite à gauche, contrairement au sens habituel qui est orienté de gauche à droite, à l'instar des cunéiformes babyloniens. L'éditeur du texte, Charles Virolleaud, n'a jamais tenu en mains l'original, demeuré à Damas, mais seulement un jeu de photos et de moulages réalisés par simple application de chaque face de l'original sur une abaisse de plâtre fraîchement gâché. Cette opération a permis de réaliser des moulages séparés pour chaque face et pour chaque tranche inscrites. L'absence d'une véritable reproduction de l'ensemble du document en trois dimensions explique à mon avis le piètre résultat épigraphique auquel était parvenu l'éditeur et son ahurissante bévue consistant à faire de la face partiellement inscrite le début et de la face complètement inscrite la fin du message. Or, il est de simple bon sens de considérer qu'une face complètement inscrite constitue le début d'un message et que ce dernier peut se terminer sur une face incomplètement inscrite. Une telle erreur n'aurait évidemment pas été commise si le spécialiste avait pu travailler à partir de l'original en trois dimensions ou d'un 'positif' en plâtre exécuté, comme on l'a vu plus haut, à partir d'un 'négatif' fidèle.

Le dessin de la planche 2 reproduit à plat l'ensemble du document et il permet d'évacuer à la 5e ligne toute possibilité de boustrophédon que proposait l'*editio princeps*. En réalité, le scribe au lieu d'aller à la 6e ligne en fin de recto a continué d'écrire la 5e ligne en mordant sur le verso avant de reprendre normalement au recto la 6e ligne. On voit que les principaux apports à l'intelligence de ce texte—à savoir l'identification du recto et du verso et la reconnaissance de la poursuite de la 5e ligne sur le verso—présentés plus de vingt ans après celle de Charles Virolleaud n'auraient pas pu se faire jour sans un examen direct prolongé 'en mains' de la tablette alphabétique sénestroverse RS 22.03.

Ayant résolu ces quelques questions épineuses, il ne reste plus qu'à attendre la prochaine migraine!

[5] Virolleaud 1960, Dietrich *et al.* 1995: 4. 710, Bordreuil 1981.

Bibliographie

Abou Assaf , A.

1981 'Die Statue des HDYS'Y, König von Guzana', *MDOG* 113: 3–4.

Abou Assaf, A., P. Bordreuil and A.R. Millard

1982 *La statue de Tell Fekheryé et son inscription bilingue assyro-araméenne* (Paris: ADPF).

Bordreuil, P.

1981 'Cunéiformes alphabétiques non canoniques I: la tablette alphabétique sénestroverse RS 22.03', *Syria* LVIII: 301–10.

1982 'Quatre documents en cunéiformes alphabétiques mal connus ou inédits' *Semitica* XXXII: 5–14.

1992 'Contrôleurs, peseurs et faussaires', T. Hackens et Gh. Moucharte (eds), *Numismatique et histoire économique phéniciennes et puniques*, Studia Phoenicia IX (Louvain-la-Neuve): 13–18.

1993 'Statue masculine à inscription bilingue assyro-araméenne au nom d'un personnage de Guzana', *Syrie, Mémoire et civilisation* (Paris): 260–63.

Bousquet , J.

1992 'Les inscriptions du Létôon en l'honneur d'Arbinas et l'épigramme grecque de la stèle de Xanthos', *Fouilles de Xanthos*, tome IX vol. 1, sous la direction d'Henri Metzger (Paris): 155–88.

Brock, S.P., and D.G.K. Taylor (eds)

2001 *The Hidden Pearl, the Syrian Orthodox Church and its Ancient Aramaic Heritage*, Volume I, *The Ancient Aramaic Heritage* (Roma).

Dietrich, M., O. Loretz and J. Sanmartin

1995 *The Cuneiform Alphabetic Texts from Ugarit, Ras Ibn Hani and Other Places (KTU: second, enlarged edition)*, Abhandlungen zur Literatur Alt-Syrien-Palästinas und Mesopotamiens Band 8 (Münster).

Donner, H., and W. Röllig

2002 *KAI* Bd 1. 5., erweiterte und überarbeitete Auflage (Wiesbaden).

Dupont-Sommer, A., E. Laroche and H. Metzger

1979 'La stèle trilingue du Létôon', *Fouilles de Xanthos*, tome VI (Paris).

Egetmeyer, M.

2002 'La crise: le sud louvite', *Dossiers d'archéologie* 276: 20–23.

Ellison, J.L.

2002 *A Paleographic Study of the Alphabetic Cuneiform Texts from Ras Shamra/Ugarit*, 2 volumes, Dept of Near Eastern Languages and Civilizations (Cambridge, Massachusetts: Harvard University).

Gordon, C.H.

1965 *Ugaritic Textbook*, Analecta Orientalia 38 (Rome).

Jeffery, L.H.
1982 'Greek Alphabetic Writing', *The Cambridge Ancient History*, III, Part 1, *The Prehistory of the Balkans; and the Middle East and the Aegean World, Tenth to Eight centuries* BC (Cambridge).

Milik, J.T.
1968 'Quelques tablettes cunéiformes alphabétiques d'Ugarit', *Ugaritica* VII (Paris): 135–46.

Pardee, D.
1998 'Deux brèves remarques épigraphiques à propos de l'inscription araméenne de Tell Fekheryé', *Semitica* XLVIII: 145–47.
2000 *Les textes rituels*, fascicule 2, Ras Shamra-Ougarit XII (Paris): 729–37.

Virolleaud Ch.
1960 'L'alphabet senestrogyre de Ras Shamra (Ugarit)', *CRAIBL*: 85–90.
1965 *Le palais royal d'Ugarit* V (Paris).

TAIMĀ' AND NABONIDUS: IT'S A SMALL WORLD

Alasdair Livingstone

Of all the regions of the ancient Near East it is probably North-west Arabia that displays some of the most complex relationships between different types of writing and writing systems and the people and societies that used them. Here, various forms of the North-west Semitic alphabet rubbed shoulders with local alphabets of Old South Arabic character on rock faces and on the sides of mountains (Winnett and Reed 1970). At the heart of the region lies the oasis town of Taimā', where there are fine examples of monumental Imperial Aramaic lapidary script as well as inscriptions illustrating various phases in the development of the Nabataean script (Gibson 1975; Donner and Röllig 1973; 1976; 1979; Beyer and Livingstone 1987; 1990; Livingstone 1995). As is well known the Neo-Babylonian king Nabonidus somewhat mysteriously resided in Taimā' for a decade leaving his son Belshazzar as regent in Babylonia and indeed there is a significant body of Babylonian and later written material relating to his sojourn at the oasis and activities in North-west Arabia, although to date none of this has been recovered at Taimā' itself. W.G. Lambert has summarized and discussed the content and implications of most of the pertinent written material apart from the local inscriptions from in and around Taimā' itself (Lambert 1972), while the cuneiform Nabonidus 'corpus' has recently been drawn together by Schaudig (2001). P.-A. Beaulieu's history of the reign of Nabonidus offers a detailed discussion of the chronology of the Taimā' adventure (1989: 149–69). Various suggestions have been made as to why Nabonidus chose to reside for such a long period in such a remote place. Lambert points out that even if control of the desert trade routes through Taimā' was important, this would not require the personal presence of the king for such an extended period. The most plausible reason for Nabonidus' personal interest in Taimā' is in connection with the cult of the moon god that flourished there as is known from the inscriptions and iconography published and discussed in the works referenced above. Nabonidus' own dedication to furthering the cult of the moon god Sîn in Mesopotamia is well known and even extended to some quite complicated mystical and theological material in his inscriptions (Livingstone 1986: 47). Recently a group of Taimanitic[1] inscriptions has been published that relates directly to the king's sojourn at the oasis. There is also other textual material from or relating to Taimāʾ that has come to light since Lambert's article of 1972 and the purpose of the present contribution will be to discuss this material, placing it where appropriate into the perspective of writing and its place in society. It is hoped that this contribution will be of some interest to Alan Millard, whose own research has ranged from the history of the alphabet, and the early civilizations that invented and used it, to Mesopotamia and cuneiform studies.

We owe our knowledge of the new Taimanitic inscriptions in the first instance to the work of Khalid M. Al-Eskoubi, a researcher at the General Department of Antiquities and Museums in Riyadh. Working in the vicinity of Taimāʾ, Al-Eskoubi photographed, studied and interpreted 309 rock face inscriptions, of which over three quarters proved to be previously unknown, and published them in a book in Arabic in which he offered colour photographs of the inscriptions as well as transliterations, translations and commentary (Al-Eskoubi 1999). This publication met with a rapid response in print from scholars in Germany, Italy, Jordan and Saudi Arabia, three articles or papers appearing in close succession all in the same year and without knowledge of each other. A short note was written based entirely on Al-Eskoubi's work and emphasizing the use of a word translated 'friend' in connection with individuals associated with Nabonidus (Gentili 2001). A much longer and more detailed study with extensive philological and cultural historical commentary appeared almost simultaneously (Hayajneh 2001). At the same time further work was being carried out in the field. Said F. Al-Said of the Department of Archaeology and Museology of the King Saud University, Riyadh, had deemed it advisable to travel to Taimāʾ and collate the newly discovered inscriptions, concentrating on those with references to Nabonidus and his entourage. He achieved more accurate copies, and with these, and a series of photographs, worked intensively on the material with W.W. Müller of the Philipps-Universität Marburg (Müller and Al-Said 2001; 2002). These authors publish autograph copies of the inscriptions concerned, based on autopsy of the original rock faces, and these can be compared very instructively with the not always clear photographs published by Al-Eskoubi. While in the jointly authored part of their work Müller and Al-Said were not aware of the work of Hayajneh, in the 2002 article Müller was able to include an addendum in which he reacted to some of Hayajneh's interpretations, especially in so far as they had not been in the mean time eclipsed by the new collations.

The texts of the inscriptions as established by Müller and Al-Said are as follows:

[1] For this terminology and classification see Macdonald (2000).

I

1. *ʾn mrdn ḫlm nbnd mlk bbl*
2. *ʾtwt mʿ rbsrs kyt*
3. *nm bfls tlw bdt lʿq*

II

1. *sktrsl bn srtn ʾtw*
2. *mʿ rbs[rs]*

III

1. *ʾn ʾnds sdn mlk bbl nśrt*

IV

1. *ʾn ʾnds ḫlm nbnd mlk bbl*

The interpretation of this sort of material is of course ridden with uncertainty. It is somewhat as if, for English, one had no literature and no English dictionaries, but only colloquial graffiti which one was endeavouring to understand with the aid of French, German and Latin lexical material. An attempt will be made here to determine what is reasonably certain and to discuss its implications. *Nbnd mlk bbl* is without question Nabonidus, king of Babylon, and in this connection the *rbsrs* is without doubt the high official or commandant, Babylonian *rab ša rēši*. The consonantal shifts agree with what one would expect from a transmission of the word through Aramaic.[2] The two words that directly express relationships to the king of Babylon, namely *ḫlm* and *sdn*, are not Babylonian. Both have meanings in Classical Arabic that are likely to be etymologically relevant to the passages here, although one cannot be sure to have captured the exact nuance. The word *ḫalīm* means 'friend, one favourably disposed to another'. However, with regard to this expression the absolute autocracy flaunted by Mesopotamian monarchs cautions one against the nuances 'friend' or 'companion'. One is far away from the world of Alexander and his companions, or indeed the Prophet and his. It could well be remembered though that Nabonidus had a substantial army in the field in the vicinity of Taimāʾ and was about to, or already had, killed the king of Taimāʾ, if we are to believe the 'verse account', taken his place, and also dispatched a large section of the population in the process. Given the nature of the terrain and the vast difference of local conditions from what Nabonidus and his agents were used to in Mesopotamia and Syria, it seems unlikely that he would have been able to do or contemplate this without high level local support. That there were Taimanites settled or resident in Babylonia who then accompanied Nabonidus to Arabia is by no means improbable (Livingstone 1989). It seems perfectly plausible that different factions existed and that a

[2] For the vexed matter of the Arabian sibilants see Beeston (1962).

leading member of a faction favourable to Nabonidus would potentially style himself *ḫlm nbnd mlk bbl*, 'one favourable to Nabonidus, king of Babylon'. One notes that the one individual *ʾnds* is both *ḫlm* and *sdn*: it would not be unthinkable for one individual to have the post of *sdn* and the political position of being favourable to Nabonidus. As pointed out by Hayajneh, *ḫlm* could also be understood as corresponding to the Arabic word *ġulām*, 'servant'. Against this interpretation could be argued that the king's personal servants were most likely to be Babylonians.

Müller in his addendum to his joint article with Al-Said (Müller and Al-Said 2002: 121) draws attention to some biblical passages in connection with the concept 'the friends of Nabonidus', namely 1 Macc. 3: 38, 2 Macc. 1: 14, the Septuagint text Daniel 3: 91 and the passages Daniel 3: 24 and 3: 27 in the Massoretic text of the Hebrew Bible, and at least with the implication that these could be relevant to the phrase *ḫlm nbnd*. In the case of Maccabees where the Seleucid Antiochus speaks to his 'friends', this is a post-Hellenistic world very different from that of the sixth century BC. Comparison of the Daniel passages is however instructive. While the Septuagint has Nebuchadnezzar speaking to his 'friends' (φίοι), the Massoretic passages have the word *hadabā́r*, which designates a high ranking royal official and is a loanword from Old Persian (Beyer 1984: 559).[3]

Müller and Al-Said (2002) translate *sdn* as 'der (Leib)wächter (oder: Kämmerer)', words which like '(body)guard' or 'chamberlain' carry purely secular connotations. They concede, however, that *sādin,* the active participle of the root *sdn*, denoted in early Arabic the guardian or protector of a shrine. The *Encyclopaedia of Islam* (1995), s.v. *sādin,* points out that the nuance of the root 'veil, curtain' is relevant to the function of the *sādin*. Further, for Pre-Islamic Arabia this source maintains that there existed a clear distinction between the *sādin* on the one hand as guardian of a shrine, and the *ḥājib* as the palace door-keeper or chamberlain on the other. Perhaps one should postulate for the *sdn* a religious role in connection with the cult of the moon deity in Taimāʾ. One could think then that this individual was the custodian of a symbol of the moon that was carried at the head of the army.

The personal names in the inscriptions present a problem since apart from Nabonidus himself none of them are obviously—or even conceivably—Babylonian and only one is likely to be of Arabian origin, Māridān, attested in both Sabaic and Safaitic (Müller and Al-Said 2002: 107). For *sktrsl* Müller and Al-Said look to Asia Minor, and in particular Caria, while for *ʾnds* Müller prefers to see the name as Greek Onaidos, while Al-Said points out that a personal name *Andāsu* is attested in Assyrian. Hayajneh however throws a spanner in the works by pointing to some Elamite name forms and it is

[3] For a detailed prosopographic and documentary study of the φίλοι see Savalli-Lestrade [1998] where the author has sought to define the originality of this Hellenistic institution.

perhaps best to hold judgement in reserve. Müller describes the final name, *srtn*, as a *crux interpretum*, pointing out that although Cilician and Lycian offer personal names beginning in *seri* and *sari-* these are not however attested with the affix *–tn*. He then brings forward Greek Στρατῶν for consideration, defending the loss of the first dental phoneme by referring to Arabic *ṣirāṭ* as a loanword from Latin (*via*) *strata*. Here one could suggest though that Arabic has simply reacted to the triple consonant cluster with an emphatic for the first two phonemes separated by an anaptytic vowel from the third.

In the first inscription *'n* is clearly the first person singular pronoun and *'twt* the same voice of the non-prefix verbal form of the amply attested Semitic root *'tw*, 'come'. The word represented by the single consonant *k* as pointed out by Müller and Al-Said is most likely to be a conjunction answering to Arabic *kay*, 'so that, in order to'. The verbal form *ytnm* is plausibly understood, as suggested by Müller and Al-Said, as a prefix conjugation form of the root *nmy* with a meaning such as would be shared by the corresponding Arabic verb 'to climb or progress from one place to another'. Hayajneh takes the *k* with the *t*, understanding the expression as corresponding to the Syriac particle *kīt*, 'that is to say'. Müller and Al-Said's suggestion results in better sense. What follows is more difficult. Al-Said would understand *bfls* as referring to a geographical region: 'in *fls*', while Müller suggests that it is an appeal for assistance from Fals, that is the deity of Ṭaiyi' known only from the *Kitāb al-'aṣnām* of Ibnu 'l-Kalbī. The word *tlw* is plausibly taken as a verbal noun from the Arabic root meeting 'to follow, come after'. The word *bdt* is understood by Müller and Al-Said as a collective of the root from which the word Bedouin comes, and they point out that this has in Classical Arabic the broken plurals *buddā'* and *buddā* as well as the more familiar *bawādin*. This is put forward by the authors in the spirit of 'kann kaum anders als … erklärt werden'. The present writer would prefer to see clear epigraphic evidence before accepting the existence of the concept or word 'Bedouin' at this period. The two authors disagree in their interpretation of the final term in the inscription. Al-Said sees *lʿq* as a tribal or personal name while Müller thinks of the Sabaic expression *wṯnn wʿwqhw*, 'the boundary stone and its defender', where the corresponding root in Arabic is *ʿwq*, with the meanings 'hinder', 'hold back'. In the second inscription the only real problems are the personal names, already discussed. In the third inscription there is an epigraphic problem. Al-Eskoubi took the final character as *ṭ* and understood the word as from the common West Semitic root *nṭr*, 'guard'. Müller points out that this is not possible epigraphically and suggests that the character is *ś* and that its somewhat aberrant shape could be the result of influence by the Old Aramaic Sameḵ letter. Müller would then understand the term as belonging to the military terminology of Sabaic and referring to the activities of an advanced guard. Müller's suggestion is corroborated by other material in Taimanitic that he draws attention to, where reading the same character as *ś* rather than *ṭ* improves the sense. The final inscription is free of problems and all four can be rendered as follows:

I

1. I am Māridān, a supporter of Nabonidus, king of Babylon.
2. I came with the commandant in order to
3. advance .... to hold (the enemy) back.

II

1. Skrtrsl, son of srtn: he came
2. with the commandant.

III

1. I am ʾnds, the shrine guardian of the king of Babylon; I lead the advance.

IV

1. I am ʾnds, a supporter of Nabonidus, king of Babylon.

These inscriptions are remarkable for a number of reasons. Seen from the point of view of writing and society the most significant feature of the Taimanitic inscriptions, and indeed the Thamudic inscriptions in general, is that they stem from the general populace; almost uniquely in the ancient Near East they are a record of the minor doings and thoughts of private individuals grazing their animals, being lovesick and engaged in trivial undertakings. The present inscriptions, however, as elucidated above, are with one exception not due to individuals whose names belong to the well documented ancient North-west Arabian onomasticon. There is also the feature that their inscriptions relate to a momentous event, the arrival of a Babylonian army accompanied by the Babylonian king himself. The manner and execution of the inscriptions deviates in no way from the norm for Taimanite inscriptions, but there is a difference in style. They draw attention to the subject of the inscription by beginning with the first person singular pronoun, a feature not found in Thamudic inscriptions but common in royal and monumental inscriptions throughout the ancient Near East.

In what ways is our understanding of Taimāʾ and the involvement of Nabonidus in its history different than it was when Lambert collected and discussed the evidence thirty years ago? The inscriptions presented above provide the first local evidence for Nabonidus' involvement in the affairs of Taimāʾ. The fact that these inscriptions are securely dated to a particular period in the reign of this king must prove to be a valuable chronological benchmark for the study of the Thamudic scripts, which share with much of the epigraphy of Pre-Islamic Arabia seemingly insoluble problems of dating.

Since Lambert wrote in 1972, Taimā' has lost some of its previous obscurity. Serious attempts have been made by the Saudi General Department of Antiquities and Museums to identify and delimit the archaeological areas in the town and commence excavation, although often with inconclusive results. There seems, however, to date no reason to link any of the recently exposed architectural features with Nabonidus or the sixth century BC (Parr 1989). The only monument with such a link is the Aramaic Taimā' stela now in the Louvre which has on its edge what was once probably part of a Neo-Babylonian relief. While the most recent discoveries raise the possibility that other Thamudic inscriptions also date to as early as the sixth century BC, two other sources, from Syria and Mesopotamia respectively, make it necessary to posit the status of Taimā' as a place of some importance already in the eighth century BC. Inscriptions of Yariris, king of Carchemish, record his knowledge of foreign languages and scripts, remarkable but also understandable in the case of the ruler of a cosmopolitan city such as Carchemish. One inscription refers to 'the script of the City, the script of Sura, the script of Assyria, and the script of Taiman'. Greenfield (1991: 179–80) suggested that Sura should be understood as Tyre (*ṣūr*) and Taiman as Taimā'. This, as the major West Arabian urban centre nearest to Carchemish, would then stand for the Old South and West Arabic scripts. It is well known that Taimā' has a by-form Taimān, this being *inter alia* commonly used in the *nisbah* formation. The passage was discussed in detail by Livingstone (1995: 134–38), where a series of arguments is put forward that Taiman is to be understood in this inscription as the Arabian town of Taimā'. One would then have four geographical indices, each standing for one of the great scripts in use in the eighth century BC: Carchemish for Hieroglyphic Luwian, Tyre for the Phoenician alphabet, Assyria for cuneiform and Taimā' for the Old South and West Arabian script types. It should be noted however that Hawkins (2000: 131 and 133) refers to Greenfield's suggestion without taking a position. Starke (1997: 390–92) agrees with Greenfield that it would be surprising if Taiman were to refer to the Aramaic script, since the Aramaic script of this period was indistinguishable from the Phoenician. He refers, however, to the Aramaic script of the Tell Fekherye bilingual first published by A. Abou-Assaf, P. Bordreuil and A.R. Millard (1982). This differs from other Aramaic inscriptions of the period in that *s* is used for /*ṯ*/ and the use of *matres lectionis*. His suggestion is that although this form of writing is known to us only from this monument it may have been much more widespread and regarded by Yariris as a distinct type.

The point that traders from Taimā' ranged widely at this period has been brought home by the discovery of an archive of tablets from Suḫu in central Mesopotamia (Cavigneaux and Ismail 1990: 321–456). These include a report by Ninurta-kudurri-uṣur, governor of Suḫu and Mari, concerning a trading caravan of Taimanites and Sabaeans that he had attacked, confiscating its goods, including 200 camels and their loads, blue Tyrian wool and 'all kinds of things one could wish for' (*mim-ma mi-reš-ti* DÙ.A.BI). On the topic of contact between western Arabia and Mesopotamia at such an early date another recently discovered archive of cuneiform tablets must also be mentioned. This archive belongs to a community settled in the vicinity of Nippur in the eighth century BC (Cole 1996). A significant number of individuals mentioned or represented in the archive have names that point to the Dedan and Taimāʾ area generally and there are also other elements that point to Arabia. All this material provides a certain background to the concerns of both Assyrian and Babylonian kings with matters Arabian from the ninth century onwards (Ephʿal 1982).

Returning to the new Taimanitic inscriptions there are still questions to be asked. Why should two individuals with names that appear to identify them as foreigners be so keen to make their mark locally in the form of rock face inscriptions in Taimanitic: not only Taimanitic writing but also language? This question must be posed whether or not one believes that each hammered out his inscription on the rock face himself, or had another do it for him. If either or both were Greeks, why did they not write in Greek? Or in another language and script if they were not Greeks? Gibson (1975: 148) has, on the basis of personal names and cult, drawn attention to the cosmopolitan nature of Taimāʾ in the period about a century later than Nabonidus' sojourn there. Assuming the names are foreign, then whether *ʾnds* and *skrtrsl* the son of *srtn* were in fact 'naturalized' Taimanites (whatever that involves) or whether they had come from abroad, as seems to be suggested by *sktrsl*'s own testimony, the fact that they chose to write their inscriptions as they did shows that they, like Yariris, considered that Taimanitic language and script had a certain prestige.

While the new discoveries do not of course mean that Taimāʾ was not a remote and unexpected place for a Babylonian king to spend a decade, they do show various types of contact and mutual awareness between Taimāʾ and its environs and Syria and Mesopotamia. The ancient world was perhaps a smaller place than we sometimes think.

Bibliography

Abou-Assaf, A., P. Bordreuil and A.R. Millard
1982 *La Statue de Tell Fekherye et son inscription assyro-araméenne*, *Études Assyriologiques* 7 (Paris).

Al-Eskoubi, K.
1999 *An Analytical and Comparative Study of Inscriptions from the "Rum" region, Southwest of Tayma* (Riyadh). [The book itself offers this title in addition to the main Arabic title.]

Beaulieu, P.-A.
1989 *The Reign of Nabonidus King of Babylon 556–539 BC* (New Haven and London).

Beeston, A.F.L.
1962 'Arabian sibilants', *Journal of Semitic Studies* (Manchester): 222–33.

Beyer, K.
1984 *Die aramäischen Texte vom Toten Meer* (Göttingen).

Beyer, K., and A. Livingstone
1987 'Die neuesten aramäischen Inschriften aus Taima', *ZDMG* 137/2: 285–96.
1990 'Eine neue reichsaramäische Inschrift aus Taima', *ZDMG* 140/1: 1–2.

Cavigneaux, A., and B.K. Ismail
1990 'Die Statthalter von Suḫu und Mari im 8.Jh. v. Chr.', *BagM* 21: 321–456.

Cole, S.
1996 *The Early Neo-Babylonian Governor's Archive from Nippur*, Nippur IV (Chicago).

D'Agostino, F.
1994 *Nabonedo, Adda Guppi, il deserto e il Dio luna: storia, ideologia e propaganda nella Babilonia del VI sec. A.C.* (Pisa).

Donner, H., and W. Röllig,
1973 *Kanaanäische und Aramäische Inschriften* (Wiesbaden), Band II, Kommentar.
1976 *Kanaanäische und Aramäische Inschriften* (Wiesbaden), Band III, Glossare und Indizes, Tafeln.
1979 *Kanaanäische und Aramäische Inschriften* (Wiesbaden), Band I, Texte.

Ephʿal, I.
1982 *The Ancient Arabs* (Jerusalem and Leiden).

Gentili, P.
2001 'Nabonidus' friends in Arabia', *NABU* 2001: 90.

Gibson, J.C.L.
1975 *Textbook of Syrian Semitic Inscriptions*, Volume II, *Aramaic Inscriptions including inscriptions in the dialect of Zenjirli* (Oxford).

Greenfield, J.C.
1991 'Of scribes, scripts and languages', *Phoinikeia grammata*, *Collection d'Études* 6 (Namur): 173–85.

Hawkins, J.D.
2000 *Corpus of Hieroglyphic Luwian Inscriptions*, Volume I, *Inscriptions of the Iron Age*, Parts 1, 2, 3 (Berlin and New York).

Hayajneh, H.
2001 'First evidence of Nabonidus in the ancient North Arabian inscrip-

tions from the region of Taymā'', *Proceedings of the Seminar for Arabian Studies* 31: 81–95.

Lambert, W.G.
1972 'Nabonidus in Arabia', *Proceedings of the Seminar for Arabian Studies* 5: 53–64.

Livingstone, A.
1986 *Mystical and Mythological Explanatory Works of Assyrian and Babylonian Scholars* (Oxford).
1989 'Arabians in Babylonia/Babylonians in Arabia: some reflections à propos new and old evidence', in T. Fahd (ed.), *L'Arabie préislamique et son environment historique et culturel* (Strasbourg): 97–105.
1995 'New light on the ancient town of Taimā'', in M.J. Geller, J.C. Greenfield and M.P. Weitzman (eds), *Studia Aramaica, New Sources and New Approaches* (Manchester): 133–43.

Macdonald, M.C.A.
2000 'Reflections on the linguistic map of pre-Islamic Arabia', *Arabian Archaeology and Epigraphy* 11/1: 28–79.

Müller, W.W., and S. Al-Said
2001 *Biblische Notizen, Beiträge zur exegetischen Diskussion, Heft 107/108* (Munich): 109–19.
2002 'Der babylonische König Nabonid in taymanischen Inschriften' , in N. Nebes (ed.), *Erstes Arbeitstreffen der Arbeitsgemeinschaft Semitistik in der Deutschen Morgenländischen Gesellschaft vom 11. bis 13. September 2000 an der Friedrich-Schiller-Universität Jena* (Wiesbaden): 105–22.

Parr, P.J.
1989 'Archaeology of North-west Arabia', in T. Fahd (ed.), *L'Arabie préislamique et son environment historique et culturel* (Strasbourg): 39–66.

Savalli-Lestrade, I
1998 *Les Philoi royaux dans l'Asie hellénistique, hautes études du monde Gréco-Romain* (Geneva).

Schaudig, H.
2001 *Die Inschriften Nabonids von Babylon und Kyros' des Grossen samt den in ihrem Umfeld entstandenen Tendenzinschriften. Textausgabe und Grammatik* (Münster).

Starke, F.
1997 'Sprachen und Schriften in Karkamis', in B. Pongratz-Leisten, H. Kühne and P. Xella (eds), *Ana šadî Labnāni lū allik*, Fs. Wolfgang Röllig (Kevelaer and Neukirchen-Vluyn): 381–95.

Timm. S.
2004 'Jes 42, 10ff. und Nabonid', *Schriftprophetie. Festschrift für Jörg Jeremias zum 65. Geburtstag*. ed. F. Hartenstein, J. Krispenz, and A. Schart (Neukirchen-Vluyn): 121–144. [Note that this article has been reprinted in an omnibus edition of esssays by Stefan

Timm: '*Gott kommt von Teman...*' Kleine Schriften zur Geschichte Israels und Syrien-Palästinas, eds C. Bender and M. Pietsch, *AOAT* 314 (Munster 2004): 238–59.]

Winnett, F.V. and W.L. Reed
1970 *Ancient Records from North Arabia* (Toronto 1970).

Dresser le bœuf à Ougarit

D. Pardee

L'existence du nom commun *malmād* en hébreu, signifiant 'aiguillon de bœuf', aussi bien qu'un passage où la racine LMD s'emploie en rapport avec des bovidés (Os. 10:11), pouvaient laisser prévoir l'usage en ougaritique de cette racine pour exprimer le dressage d'animaux domestiqués. Cela semble désormais démontré à Ras Shamra—Ougarit par un petit fragment de la 18e campagne. Cette bribe de texte n'est pas passée totalement inaperçue jusqu'ici, puisque le fragment fut enregistré dans la *TEO* (Bordreuil et Pardee 1989: 194), mais elle est néanmoins restée inexploitée. Il s'agit de RS 18.[565],[1] déposé au musée de Damas sans numéro d'inventaire.[2] Quoique de dimensions médiocres, ce fragment comporte trois nouveautés pour notre connaissance de l'ougaritique : (1) l'emploi de LMD en rapport avec *ảlp*, [ʾ 'bœuf', pour exprimer le dressage des bœufs ; (2) les premières attestations en ougaritique de la racine NZQ, 'souffrir d'un mal' ; et (3) une nouvelle variante de la formule comportant le verbe YDʿ, 'savoir', par laquelle l'auteur du message souligne l'importance de ce qu'il dit.

Les détails matériels

Dimensions : hauteur 36 mm ; largeur 53 mm ; épaisseur 26 mm.
État : partie inférieure de tablette dont la surface est assez usée, surtout au

[1] Les crochets signifient que nous avons attribué cette partie du numéro à cet objet lors de la préparation de la *TEO* alors que ni le fouilleur (C. F. Schaeffer) ni l'épigraphiste à l'époque (Ch. Virolleaud) n'ont fait entrer ce fragment de tablette dans la série d'objets découverts à Ras Shamra en 1954.

[2] L'étude actuelle se situe dans notre projet de (re)publication des documents épistolaires en langue ougaritique entrepris en 1980–81 lorsque nous avons revu les textes de ce genre connus à l'époque ; entretemps, nous avons accordé la priorité à plusieurs autres projets de sorte que l'étude globale des lettres n'est pas encore terminée, quoiqu'elle soit bien avancée. Nous avons étudié RS 18. [565] pour la première fois le 25 mai 1981 et l'avons revu le 17 juin 1993 pour en faire le facsimilé, le 4 juin 1996 pour en vérifier certaines lectures et de nouveau en 2003 pour exécuter la photo qui accompagne cette article. Nous remercions le personnel du musée de Damas, en particulier Mme Muyassar Yabroudi, conservatrice du Département Oriental, M Robert Hawley et Carole Roche qui ont effectué la photographie en 2003, et M Pierre Bordreuil qui a lu, corrigé et approuvé le manuscrit de cet article.

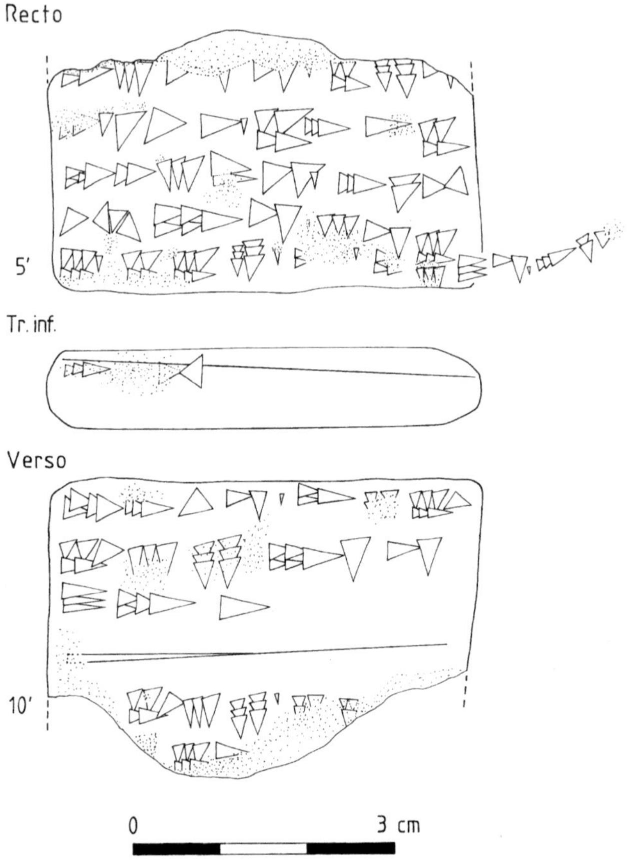

Fig. 1. RS 18. [565] facsimile.

recto. L'orientation *recto*/*verso* est décidée (1) par la courbe de la tablette (le *verso* est plus plat que le *recto*) et (2) par le sens du texte (si on inversait cet ordre, la lettre aurait commencé sans formules—ce dernier fait est attesté, mais la combinaison des deux facteurs ne laisse guère de doute sur la bonne orientation du fragment).

Lieu de trouvaille : comme nous l'avons indiqué dans la *TEO* (p. 194), ce fragment se trouve aujourd'hui dans un petit carton portant l'inscription suivante : 'RS 1954 non inventorié, fragm de lettres'.[3] Il est donc probable qu'ils proviennent des fouilles du palais royal, plus précisément des Archives Sud-Ouest, mais cela ne peut être qu'une supposition.

[3] Il y avait quatre autres fragments dans ce carton ; l'identification comme fragments de lettres s'est avérée plausible pour tous les quatre.

Fig. 1. RS 18. [565] photograph.

Texte

Recto

1’) ⸢k⸣l ⸢—m .⸣ b y⸢-(-)⸣[…]
2’) ⸢w,⸣ . gʿt . b ntb
3’) w alpm . nzq
4’) ʿšrm ⸢. l⸣md
5’) d . bdy ⸢. w⸣ . ⸢k⸣lhm . nz⸢q⸣[ ]

Tranche inférieure

6’) ⸢n⸣[-]q

Verso
7’) w nʿm . k ⸢y⸣dʿ
8’) bʿly [.] rgm
9’) hwt

10’) [-] bʿly . y⸢s⸣[…]
11’) [ ]d⸢-⸣[…]
…………………

Traduction

Recto
1’) tout ? […]
2’) et (il y avait) des mugissements en route ;
3’) et les bœufs ont souffert des maux,
4’) les vingt (bœufs) dressés
5’) qui étaient sous ma supervision : tous ont souffert.

Tranche inférieure

6’) Ils ont so[uf]fert

Verso
7’) et il est bon que
8’) mon maître tienne compte de ce
9’) fait.

10’) [ ] mon maître fera [X …]
11’) [ ] […]
…………………

Texte vocalisé
1’) kullu ? […]
2’) wa gaʿâtu bi natībi
3’) wa ʾalapūma nazaqū
4’) ʿašrāma lummūdu
5’) dū bîdiya wa kulluhumu nazaqū
6’) nazaqū
7’) wa naʿīmu kī yidaʿu
8’) baʿlīya rigma
9’) huwata

10') [ ]baʿlīya [...]
11')

....

Commentaire

Ligne 2'. On connaissait déjà le nom commun *gʿt* par la légende de *Kirta* où le bruit de plusieurs animaux, y compris le mugissement des bœufs de labour, empêche le futur beau-père du héros de dormir (*CTA* 14 iii 122, v 225–26 *gʿt alp ḥrṯ*). La racine étant *tertiae infirmae*, il s'agira du même nom ici et la phrase est donc nominale.

La fonction de *ntb* dans ce message semble être de signaler que les bœufs qui sont l'objet de la plainte déposée par cet auteur ont souffert en route,[4] soit qu'ils aient été surmenés par le responsable de leur transport, soit qu'ils aient subi un accident ou une attaque quelconque. En l'absence du début du texte, il est impossible de déterminer la source de la souffrance dont il est question aux lignes 3'–6'.

Lignes 3', 5'–6' *nzq*. Le fait que la ligne 6' ne porte qu'un seul mot et que le scribe n'a pas complété la ligne, semble ici marquer une sorte d'insistance de la part de l'auteur et du scribe sur l'importance du mot qui s'y trouve. La restitution de {n[z]q} paraît indiquée d'après le contexte. En accadien le verbe exprime la souffrance psychologique,[5] en hébreu et araméen plutôt la souffrance physique.[6] Le sens de ce texte fait préférer la seconde de ces acceptions.

Ligne 4'. La racine LMD est assez bien attestée en ougaritique, mais on ne connaissait auparavant aucun texte où elle exprimait le dressage de bœufs.

[4] Comparer I Sam. 6:12 où il est question de bovidés sur un chemin : *wayyiššarnā*^{h} *happārō*^{w}*t badderek ʿal-derek bê*^{y}*t šemeš bimsillat ʾaḥat hāl*^{ə}*kū*^{w} *hālōk w*^{ə}*gāʿō*^{w} *w*^{ə}*lōʾ sārū*^{w} *yamī*^{y}*n ūś*^{ə}*mō*(ʾ), 'Les vaches prirent tout droit le chemin en direction de Beth Shemesh. Elles gardèrent la route principale, meuglant en marchant, sans dévier ni à droite ni à gauche'. Même si le contexte et le message des deux textes sont bien différents, l'un illustre l'autre parce que dans les deux il est question de bovidés qui meuglent en cheminant.

[5] Voir *CAD N*$_{2}$: 136–39 ('to worry, to be upset, to have worries').

[6] La racine n'est pas typique de l'hébreu biblique, où n'est attesté que le nom commun *nēzeq*, 'injury, damage' (*BDB*: 634) et cela dans un texte tardif (Est. 7:4). En araméen biblique, le verbe est intransitif au Peal ('suffer injury' [ibid., p. 1102]) et transitif au Haphel ('injure' [ibid.]). Dans la littérature juive, un éventail plus large de formes est attesté dans les deux langues (voir Jastrow, 1903: 892–93) ; on remarque qu'en araméen le Peal a pris la force d'un verbe transitif. Le verbe est déjà attesté dans l'une des inscriptions phéniciennes de Zindjerli (*KAI* 24: 14 *yzq*, probablement au Yiphil, exprimant le fait de 'mutiler' une inscription) et assez rarement dans les inscriptions araméennes (voir Hoftijzer et Jongeling, 1995: 724). La racine est absente du syriaque.

En hébreu biblique, le verbe n'est attesté qu'une fois en rapport avec des bovidés : selon Os. 10:11, on dresse les génisses pour fouler la récolte de grains à l'aire (*ʿeglā^h^ m^ə^lummādā^h^* [part. Pual] *ʾōhabtī^y^ lādū^w^š*, 'génisse dressée, qui aime à fouler l'aire'.[7] Que l'usage du racine ait dû être plus répandu dans cette langue est prouvé par l'existence du mot *malmād* dans la formule *malmad habbāqār*, 'aiguillon de bœufs' (Juges 3:31).[8] Il est bien connu qu'à Ougarit les bovidés étaient dressés à tirer la charrue,[9] et LMD doit ici désigner ce genre de dressage, que l'objet tiré soit la charrue, le traîneau servant à dépiquer la récolte (comme en Os. 10:11) ou le char. L'objet de l'auteur de la lettre ougaritique en ajoutant cette précision était sans doute de souligner la valeur des animaux estropiés. En hébreu, on connaît l'adjectif *limmūd* ; la forme dans le texte ougaritique était vraisemblablement celle de l'adjectif substantivé, au singulier selon la règle lorsque le nom désignant l'objet compté suit le nom de nombre 'vingt' (Tropper 2000: 400–1 (§ 69.152)).

Lignes 7'–9'. On rencontre ici deux variations du *topos* dont YDʿ est le noyau et qui exprime le désir de la part de l'auteur de la lettre que son correspondant tienne bien compte de ce qu'il dit.[10] C'est seulement ici que YDʿ est introduite par la formule *w nʿm k*, 'il est bon que'. C'est aussi la seule fois que le texte qui précède est résumé sous la forme *rgm hwt*, lit. 'cette parole'.

Conclusions

Quelqu'un qui était responsable d'un nombre important de bœufs dressés écrit à un supérieur comme à son 'maître' au sujet d'un événement où vingt de ces bœufs ont été l'objet d'un traitement nuisible par une ou plusieurs personnes qui ne sont pas nommées dans la partie conservée du texte. Il s'agissait d'animaux dont la valeur était accrue par le fait d'être dressés pour le travail. L'auteur ne décrit pas le mal que ces animaux ont subi mais répète le verbe signifiant 'souffrir d'un mal' trois fois, signe sûr de son accablement devant la situation. La mention de mugissements en route indique peut-être que ces animaux furent surmenés au cours d'un transport quelconque. Autre signe de son état psychologique : l'invitation au personnage supérieur de se rendre bien compte du message, telle qu'on la

7 Cette pratique est décrite en détail par Whittaker 2000: 62–69.

8 En *Jér.* 2:24 et *Job* 11:12, la racine est employée en rapport avec le *pereʾ*, 'l'onagre'. La nuance dans le premier cas semble être celle du dressage en tant que domestication alors que, dans le second, l'allusion est plutôt aux 'habitudes' de la bête sauvage.

9 Voir le texte de la légende de *Kirta* cité plus haut. On trouvera d'autres textes cités chez Bordreuil et Pardee 1993: 23–58, en part. p. 23–32, et Olmo Lete et Sanmartín 1996: 181.

10 Par exemple, la lettre que porte la tablette RS 19.011 se termine par la formule *w dʿ dʿ* /wa daʿ daʿ/, lit. 'sache(-le) ! sache(-le) !' (Virolleaud 1965: 137, no 114).

connaît par d'autre textes, est ici élargie par une introduction (*w nʿm k*) et par un renvoi explicite au récit de l'auteur (*rgm hwt*). Ainsi, mine de rien, ce fragment portait des petits trésors insoupçonnés pour notre connaissance de la langue et de la culture ougaritiques. C'est un honneur pour nous de les déposer aux pieds d'Alan Millard.

BIBLIOGRAPHY

Bordreuil, P., and D. Pardee
1989 *La trouvaille épigraphique de l'Ougarit.* 1 *Concordance* (Ras Shamra—Ougarit V/1; Paris: Éditions Recherche sur les Civilisations).
1993 'Textes ougaritiques oubliés et "transfugés"', *Semitica* 41–42.

Brown, F., S.R. Driver, and C.A. Briggs
1907 *A Hebrew and English Lexicon of the Old Testament* (Oxford: Clarendon).

Donner, H., and W. Röllig
1996–9 *KAI* (Wiesbaden: Harrassowitz).

Hoftijzer, J., and K. Jongeling
1995 *Dictionary of the North-West Semitic Inscriptions* (Hadbuch der Orientalistik, Erste Abteilung: der nahe und mittlere Osten, Einundzwanszigster Band; Leiden: Brill).

Jastrow, M.
1967 *A Dictionary of the Targumim, the Talmud Babli and Yerushalmi, and the Midrashic Literature* (Brooklyn: Shalom).

Olmo Lete, G. del, and J. Sanmartín
1996 *Diccionario de la Lengua Ugarítica* I (Aula Orientalis Supplementa 7).

Tropper, J.
2000 *Ugaritische Grammatik* (Alter Orient und Altes Testament 273 ; Münster, Ugarit-Verlag).

Virolleaud, Ch.
1965 *Textes en cunéiformes alphabétiques des archives sud, sud-ouest et du petit palais* (Palais Royal d'Ugarit V; Mission de Ras Shamra 11. Paris : Imprimerie Nationale; Klincksieck).

Whittaker, J.C.
2000 'Alonia and Dhoukanes: the ethnoarchaeology of threshing in Cyprus', *NEA* 63.

Literacy in an Oral Environment

M.C.A. Macdonald

> In discussing the question of the use of the early alphabets we are looking at icebergs: visible to the sailor is one third or less of the icy mass. The surviving examples of ancient West Semitic alphabets are only a small proportion of what was written with them in the Levant. It is easy to assume that what we see truly represents the situation in antiquity, yet such an assumption is quite wrong; rather, we can assume there was a far wider use of writing than the range of specimens recovered can suggest. (Millard 1991: 110)

Alan Millard gave this wise warning in his study of 'The Uses of the Early Alphabets' and I quote it not only because it is a caveat which needs constantly to be kept in mind when approaching the subject of this volume, but also because at the heart of this paper I will present what is possibly a very peculiar exception to this rule, a case not of WYSIWYG ('What you see is what you get') but WYSIATW ('What you see is all there was').

For the purposes of this paper, I would define 'literacy' as the ability to read and/or to write at one of a number of different levels. I would define a 'literate society' as one in which reading and writing have become essential to its functioning, either throughout the society (as in the modern West) or in certain vital aspects, such as the bureaucracy, economic and commercial activities, or religious life. Thus, in this sense, a society can be literate, because it uses the written word in some of its vital functions, even when the vast majority of its members cannot read or write, as was the case, for instance, in early mediaeval Europe or Mycenaean Greece, where literacy was more or less confined to a clerical or scribal class.

By contrast, I would regard a non-literate, or oral, society as one in which literacy is not essential to any of its activities, and memory and oral communication perform the functions which reading and writing have within a literate society. Prehistoric and—at least until very recently—most nomadic societies were of this sort. There are, of course, gradations between these two extremes and, just as it is possible to have large numbers of illiterates in a literate society, so, perhaps surprisingly, it is possible to have many people who can read and/or write in an oral society, without this changing its fundamentally oral nature.

When large sections of the population of a literate society cannot read and/or write, they inhabit an oral enclave within that literate society, since their daily lives are usually touched by reading and writing only when they come into contact with the authorities, or when, in relatively rare cases, they need to use long-distance written communication. By contrast, groups of literate individuals within an oral society do not inhabit a corresponding 'literate enclave' for, it seems, they still operate socially as non-literates,[1] even though they can read and write.

In this paper I shall examine a few of the numerous forms literacy can take, some of the often surprising uses which can be made of it, and the overlapping relationships between literate and non-literate communities. In the first section, I shall look at some relatively well-documented attitudes to literacy, and the uses made of it, in the modern and early modern period. In the second section, I shall examine what can be learnt from these cases and, in the third, I shall try to use these lessons in an attempt to understand some examples of literacy in an oral environment in the ancient Near East. I should stress at the beginning that I shall not be dealing with the cognitive consequences of literacy and orality, as discussed by such scholars as Goody and Havelock, nor shall I examine the enormous cultural changes which they ascribe to the acquisition of literacy,[2] fields in which I have no competence. Rather, I shall be studying at a more basic—more mechanical level—the effects on scripts and on the people who use them, of particular types and uses of literacy in literate and oral environments.

I

> Since the Second World War, the accepted model has been to regard it as necessary that reading and writing follow each other closely, that formal school instruction be almost the only conceivable teaching method, and that economic models provide us with a decisive explanation of a functioning literate environment.[3]

Egil Johansson lists these common assumptions—before exposing them as erroneous—in one of his many excellent studies of literacy in Sweden. The superficiality of such views, based on our own narrow experience in the twentieth-century West, quickly becomes obvious when one examines life with and without literacy in other cultures and at other times. Indeed, even a look beneath the surface of our own society reveals evidence that things are not so clear and simple as they might seem.

[1] I use the term 'non-literate' of those who cannot read and/or write within an oral society. I restrict the term 'illiterate' to those without these skills in a *literate* society.

[2] For an excellent summary of the debates on these aspects of literacy, and an important contribution to the discussion, see Thomas 1992: 16–28.

[3] Johansson 1988: 138; repeated with minor differences in 1998: 59.

Societies with no use for literacy

Even today, most nomadic societies in the Middle East have little use for writing. For a start, there are a number of severe practical difficulties. Writing materials are not readily available in the desert and have to be imported from the settled regions. In Middle Eastern deserts, the wind blows fiercely for at least half of most days and nights, with frequent dust or sand-storms, and the rains in winter and spring can be of tropical force. So, those who live in tents do not have much use for materials that can blow away, or be destroyed by dirt, wet and the attentions of hens, goats, dogs and rodents. It is no surprise, therefore, that nomadic societies living in these conditions have developed highly effective ways-of-life and social structures based on the use of powerful memories and oral communication, in which literacy can find no useful function.

Even when literacy is available, individuals and communities can often make the positive choice to remain non-literate. For example, in the 1970s, many Bedouin children in Jordan began to attend the schools which the Jordanian army was setting up in the desert, because it was thought that the ability to read and write would help them find jobs in the towns during years of drought. Unfortunately, however, these schools tried to inculcate a pro-urban and anti-Bedouin ideology and kept the children away from the long and complicated training in camel-herding, which 'can only be learned by doing'. So, after a few years, many children decided their time would be better employed in the traditional manner, looking after the herds and improving their desert skills.[4]

Thus these Bedouin made a deliberate choice to remain non-literate and preserve their oral enclave within the literate societies (Syria, Jordan, and Saudi Arabia) which surrounded them. Within this enclave, reading and writing has no function in the normal operations of everyday life, either at a communal or at an individual level. This does not mean that there are not some Rwala who can read and write—four of their nine shaykhs went to school and university in Europe and America, for instance. As I remarked at the beginning, just as one can have *ill*iterates in a literate society, so one can have literate individuals within an oral community.

In a tribal society there are distinct disadvantages to the use of writing as a means of record. At its most basic, a tribal society is one in which all social and political relationships are conceived, expressed, and explained in genealogical terms. This requires what William and Fidelity Lancaster have called 'generative genealogy' (1981: 24–35). A Bedouin genealogy, for

[4] Lancaster 1981: 102–3. Note that 'it must be pointed out that this is the view of the children themselves. Personal autonomy is so highly prized [among the Bedouin] that such decisions are made by the child, although the parents will advise'. (ibid. 103).

instance, has at the 'bottom' the individuals who make up the particular group of people for whom you are entirely responsible and who are entirely responsible for you.[5] The upper part of the genealogy is what might be called the theoretical 'map' of the relationships between the different tribal sections (represented by the names of their eponymous 'ancestors'). Clearly, the lower part is fixed and the upper part is sufficiently well known that it can only be manipulated with great difficulty. However, between the upper and lower parts is what the Lancasters call a 'conceptual break' (1981: 25) where the joins between the top and bottom parts of the genealogy are extremely hazy and 'no one can 'remember' the genealogy between an individual and the ancestor of the tribal section' (1981: 26), they just 'know' that it must exist because everyone 'knows' that that individual belongs to that section. This circular method of arguing, based on the assumption that 'it must be so because that is how it is', is the basis of the explanation of social and political situations by generative genealogy.

Political or social events, such as the gradual merging of one section with another or hostility between sections of the same tribe, are 'explained' by the (usually unconscious) adjustment of the tribal genealogy. Naturally, this is only possible in a non-literate society which relies on memory. For memory can be questioned and in an oral society a 'historical fact' is only what a sufficient number of people agree they remember. Obviously, the exact structure I have described is by no means the same for all tribal groups. I have taken the Rwala Bedouin as an example, because of the very clear way in which the Lancasters have explained the system. However, this living, protean quality is characteristic of 'working' tribal genealogies and has driven to distraction scholars from urban societies (both Islamic and Western) who have tried to record and fix them in writing. It will be clear, therefore, that non-literacy is fundamental to the functioning of a vibrant, purely tribal society.

Thus, we should beware of the assumption that literacy is always desirable and advantageous. We need also to avoid assuming that reading and writing are inseparable skills.

Writing without reading or schooling

Since the 1960s, numerous studies have shown that the skills of reading and writing are acquired separately[6] and that 'reading and writing are no more closely or necessarily associated than horses and carriages, or lovers and

[5] The *ibn ʿamm* (literally 'son of a paternal uncle') group.

[6] See, for instance, works mentioned in Holdaway 1979: 38–61, plus those of Johansson, Smout, Thomas, etc. in the list of references.

marriages' (Smout 1982: 121). There are many examples of children who teach themselves to write before they can read and who often write at considerable length,[7] both as self-expression, for their own amusement, and, ostensibly, to send messages to others.[8]

It has been suggested that a different sort of 'write-only' literacy can be traced in the Persian period in Egypt where 'there are dockets of various kinds, acknowledgements on tax receipts, names of witnesses accompanying legal contracts, and possibly some mummy-labels, where the impression is hard to resist that the writer is competent in this sort of text, but little else' (Ray 1994: 63). However, I would suggest that, if this was indeed the case, it represents *copying* from memory rather than the ability to write, for which surely the minimum criterion must be the ability to create an original text, however short. For the same reason I would not regard so-called 'signature literacy', that is the ability to write one's name but nothing else[9] as writing-literacy. The example of the unfortunate Petaus, a 'village scribe' in Egypt in the second century AD, who practised over and over again writing his signature, his title and 'I have submitted this' (ἐπιδέδωκα), with minimal success,[10] shows in action the process of someone memorizing a particular sequence of shapes without comprehending the function of each one,[11] and should make us question whether this can usefully be called 'literacy'. I shall not therefore be discussing cases such as these.

[7] See, for instance, Chomsky 1971. When writing English, where there is a large divergence between pronunciation and conventional spelling, they work out for themselves a roughly phonetic spelling system based on the sounds and on the names of the letters. What is particularly interesting is that 'different children independently arrive at the same spelling systems. Systematic features that may appear from the records of an individual child to be idiosyncratic turn out on comparison to be common to all the children. Working with an inadequate number of symbols (26 letters to represent all the sounds of English), the children all reach their solutions to this dilemma in much the same way. They also share an interesting failure to represent certain phonetic features [such as a nasal when followed by another consonant] that they do have the alphabetic means to represent' (Chomsky 1971: 505). On this latter feature see the discussion of 'phonetic writing' in Safaitic, below.

[8] 'They label their drawings, keep diaries, write letters, send notes—all systematically spelled and without their yet being able to read' (Chomsky 1971: 501). For example, Chomsky quotes two 'get well' messages and four messages to his parents written by a five-and-a-half year old boy confined to his room as a punishment, which he wrote on paper darts and launched over the banisters to glide downstairs (1971: 506).

[9] For references see, for instance, Harris 1989: 4, n. 3.

[10] *P. Petaus* 121 (P. Köln Inv. 328). See the photograph in Youtie 1966: 135 and the interesting discussion and references in Hanson 1991: 171–75, especially the comparison with a 'slow writer' who could however draft an original text (174–75).

[11] Hence, his spelling mistakes such as the omission of the initial epsilon in ἐπιδέδωκα in the last eight of the twelve times he practised the formula. Such a repeated mistake would surely have been impossible if he had been aware of the sense of what he was writing. See Hanson 1991: 174 on Petaus' mistakes.

Reading without writing or schooling: Sweden in the 17th and 18th centuries

In Sweden in the 17th and 18th centuries, 90% of the population lived in scattered, mainly agricultural, settlements in the country (Johansson 1988: 135–36). In urban life, literacy could have practical benefits in certain occupations and there were some schools which could provide it (Johansson 1988: 135), 'but on the whole, the rural population believed that, for everyday use, they did not need much bookish education' (Johansson 1988: 136). However, the church held that to read God's word 'with one's own eyes and understand it, was everybody's calling and right according to the Lutheran accentuation of the priesthood of every man', and in this it was backed by the state (Johansson 1998: 123). So, in the reign of King Charles XI, the Church Law of 1686 was passed requiring every man, woman and child in Sweden to learn to read, and this was augmented by further laws at various points in the course of the 18th century.[12]

The Lutheran principle of 'the priesthood of every man', according to which, in the household order, the husband was responsible for education, just as the clergyman was in the parish, also, conveniently, meant that this campaign could be pushed through without the public provision of schools.[13] Children were to be taught at home whenever possible, with parish officers acting as backup if this was insufficient (Johansson 1988: 141). The principal aim was to enable each man, woman and child, to read and memorize Luther's Catechism, the psalms, the biblical readings for the ecclesiastical year, the 'Hustavla',[14] and prayers for home and church. Children were to be taught to read these aloud, clearly and diligently, until 'they shall have become fully aware of the text they are reading and heed its utterance as if they heard it spoken by another. In this manner, the children should gradually acquire a firm grasp of the textual meaning and content, and be able to articulate such in words other than those given in the text'.[15] Thus, reading was regarded not as a *substitute* for memory but, on the contrary, as a means to the end of memorization and understanding.

The campaign was backed up with harsh sanctions. Confirmation was forbidden to anyone who could not read, and no unconfirmed person was permitted to take Holy Communion or to marry.[16] By a decree of 1723,

[12] Johansson 1977: 152, 163 [=1998: 58, 69]; 1988: 141.

[13] Johansson 1977: 152, 163 [= 1998: 58, 69]; 1988: 141.

[14] Luther's *Haustafel*, a plaque to be hung on the wall of every house, with biblical texts outlining the Christian duties and obligations of each of the three sections of the social hierarchy: church, secular government and household (Johansson 1977: 157–61 [= 1998: 62–67]).

[15] An admonition from the Rural Dean to those instructing young children in the parish of Norrbotten in 1720, quoted in Johansson 1988: 142.

[16] Johansson 1988: 137 and see the description by the Scottish evangelist, John Patterson writing of his visit to Sweden in 1807–8 (quoted in Johansson 1988: 137–38).

parents and godfathers who neglected 'diligently to see to it that their children applied themselves to book reading and the study of the lessons in the Catechism' had to pay a fine which would be used for the 'instruction of poor children in the parish' (Johansson 1988: 141). There was also strong social pressure to learn to read. Each year the bishop and rural dean visited every village in the diocese and held rigorous public examinations of all the inhabitants to test their reading abilities (Johansson 1988: 137–38, 141).

This campaign was extraordinarily successful. Already by the mid-18th century, Sweden had well-over 80% reading-literacy in the rural areas and over 90% in the towns. Travellers from both Sweden and from other countries remarked that even the poorest rural house contained books of devotion (Johansson 1988: 137), and this is confirmed by the inventories of property made when villagers died.[17] At the same time, only 25% (at most) of the urban populace (itself only a tenth of the population of Sweden as a whole) and only 10% of those in the country (representing nine-tenths of the total population) were able to write.[18] Writing, after all, brought with it no religious gain comparable to reading,[19] and most people simply did not need it in their daily lives.[20]

In Scotland too in the 1740s—if the Cambuslang records are at all typical—there was very widespread reading-literacy, though here it was taught primarily in schools, with back-up from family or employer when necessary (Smout 1982: 125–27). As in Sweden, this was to enable each individual to read and absorb the Word of God.[21] All those questioned at

[17] 'The books in a rural parish, for example, in Dalecarlia, Rättvik, are listed for each household in the church examination register of the 1720s. In this parish of approximately 600 families, around 400 ABC-books, 650 to 750 Catechisms, more than 1,100 psalters, 29 Bibles, and about 200 other religious books were registered. [Rättvik Church Examination Register, 1723–1759]' (Johansson 1988: 140). By 1800, 'More than three hundred titles ... could at that time be found in the homes in Västerbotten county in northern Sweden. ... A comparable offering of books could also be seen in the other Scandinavian countries' (1998: 121). It seems likely that, as in Scotland, non-devotional books would also have been read, if they were available. However, if they were present in the houses, they were not declared, or perhaps not counted since they were irrelevant to the purposes of the examination.

[18] Johansson 1988: 155–57 (statistics based on Church Examination Registers from two urban and six rural parishes in the deanery of Skytt, Scania, for the years 1702, 1721, 1731 and 1740, covering approximately 1000–1150 individuals each time).

[19] A view also maintained by English Sabbatarians of the late 18th and early 19th centuries who were quite prepared to teach reading in Sunday Schools, but not writing (Smout 1982: 122–23).

[20] Johansson 1977: 155 [= 1998: 61]. Even the representatives of the peasantry in the Swedish *Riksdag* (Parliament) in the 1760s could read but not write (Johansson 1988: 157). There were approximately 150 representatives from the peasantry in every *Riksdag* at this period (Johansson 1977: 161 [= 1998: 67]).

[21] Smout 1982: 122–27, though note that some of those questioned at Cambuslang said that they enjoyed reading ballads and chap-books as well as the Bible (1982: 123, 124). Smout also quotes a contemporary of Burns recalling the first publication of the latter's poems, 'I can well

Cambuslang could read. But although writing was also taught in schools, between a third and three-quarters of the men questioned at Cambuslang could write, and no more than about 10% of the women had learned the skill (Smout 1982: 121, 124). Again, reading and memorization seem to have gone hand in hand, with religious works, particularly the Catechism, the psalms and, later, other parts of the Bible, being used as the texts. One Gaelic-speaking Highlander explained that he was 'put to school' when he was about twelve years old and taught to read the Bible in English (though he was allowed to read the psalms in Gaelic).[22] It was only much later that he learnt to speak and understand English, through contact with English speakers, 'but I could have read most of the English Bible before I knew anything of the sense or literal meaning of what I was rendering'.[23] This contrasts with the general emphasis in Sweden and in Lowland Scotland on *understanding* the religious texts being read.

Practical literacy in an indigenous language and script: Vai

The Vai language[24] is written in a syllabary invented by Duala Bukare in the 1820s or 1830s. Each character in the syllabary represents a consonant + vowel, but there is no way of showing vowel tone, nor is there an established method of indicating vowel length, both of which are semantically significant

remember how that even ploughboys and maidservants would gladly part with the wages they earned the most hardly and which they wanted to purchase the necessary clothing if they might but procure the works of Burns' (1982: 123, n. 29).

[22] The translation of the Psalms into Gaelic was published by the Synod of Argyle in 1694 and was widely available from then on (www.electricscotland.com/history/literat/irish.htm), but the New Testament in Gaelic was not published until 1767 (thus some 25 years after this Highlander gave his testimony), and the translation of the Old Testament did not appear until 1801 (Meek 2001: 521). It had been Scottish government policy since the early 17th century to try to eradicate Gaelic by teaching reading through English (Durkan 2001: 562), and this young man's experience may have been one of the unexpected results of this policy.

[23] Smout 1982: 124. Compare this with Goody, Cole and Scribner's description of the way children in West Africa are taught to read and pronounce written Arabic in order to memorize the text of the Qur'ān, without understanding the meaning of the individual Arabic words (1977: 290–91). See note 29 for more details.

[24] The Vai language is spoken by approximately 105,000 people in western Liberia (89,500) and in Sierra Leone (15,500). About 35% of the Vai people also speak a second language (20% English, 10% Mende [in Sierra Leone] and 5% Gola). About 10% are literate in the second language (English or Mende). [Source: http://www.ethnologue.com/show_country.asp?name=Liberia] and in the 1970s between 20% and 25% of Vai men were literate in the Vai syllabary (Scribner and Cole 1978: 453). Apart from being predominantly Muslim, they are 'virtually indistinguishable from their neighbors in terms of ecology, social organization, economic activities, and material culture' (Scribner and Cole 1978: 453). For a more detailed description of the Vai and their way of life, see Scribner and Cole 1999: 23–4. I am most grateful to Professor John Baines (Oxford) for this reference.

in the spoken language. There is also no word-division, so 'a string of syllabic characters runs across the page without spacing or segmentation. Each character, depending on its semantic function, may represent a single-syllable word, one of several such words differentiated by tone, or a component unit of a polysyllabic word' (Scribner and Cole 1978: 456). As a result, the traditional method of reading is to pronounce, out loud, strings of syllables, varying the vowel lengths and tones until they fit into meaningful units, at the same time keeping the separate syllables in mind until they can be integrated into words and phrases (Scribner and Cole 1978: 456). This is similar to the method of reading the Tifinagh, described below.

Approximately 20–25% of Vai men can read and write in the script, which is learnt informally, not at school.[25] For the Vai, 'their writing and reading are not activities separate from other daily pursuits, nor does learning to read and write require a person to master a large body of knowledge that is unavailable from oral sources' (Scribner and Cole 1978: 453). Writing in Vai is normally used for a variety of practical purposes: short letters, and relatively simple administrative tasks in personal, social and commercial life, etc.[26] But although 'literates are accorded high status' (Scribner and Cole 1978: 454), nothing in Vai life is *dependent* on literacy in the Vai script.

By contrast, English is not simply the vehicular language[27] of Liberia, but is the language and script in which it functions as a literate society. It is not

[25] Scribner and Cole 1978: 453, and see Scribner and Cole 1999: 62–4 for tables showing percentages of literates in the Vai, Arabic and English scripts, and in combinations of the three. For the ways in which the Vai script is learnt, and the motives for learning it, see ibid. 65–68.

[26] A few very skilled individuals have used it to write histories, books of aphorisms and diaries. See for instance the merchant's ledgers and the constitution and membership records of a religious association recorded in the Vai script, described and discussed in the interesting article by Goody, Scribner and Cole (1977). However Scribner and Cole make clear that 'the Vai book is generally intended for the writer himself', though, on occasions, extracts may be read out in public, for instance to settle a dispute. But 'these are relatively rare occasions notwithstanding, Vai books, including those containing literary contents, are not intended for general distribution. They are a private affair, compiled by individuals for their own use and pleasure, and for that of their close friends and kin. *Vai books are not used as part of the process of teaching Vai script, nor are they produced in any quantity*. The few exceptions to this generalization occur, significantly, among people who are close to the Americo-Liberian culture that dominates the captial city of Monrovia and that uses formal schooling in English as its literate base. Thus, we found multiple copies of biblical stories translated into Vai, occasional government posters advocating a policy or candidate for public office, and a section of a newsletter produced by the YMCA office in Robertsport devoted to local news, all written in the script' (Scriber and Cole 1999: 81–2 [my italics]). Compare this with use of the Tifinagh by governments and other political organisations in North-West Africa, mentioned below, and cf. Fig. 5.

[27] I use this calque of the French *langue véhiculaire* rather than the term 'lingua franca' since historically the latter was a specific mixed language used in the eastern Mediterranean, which was based on Italian with the addition of French, Greek, Arabic and Spanish words and phrases. By contrast, a 'vehicular language' is a *single* language used for communication between people whose mother-tongues are mutually incomprehensible.

only taught in the schools but is the medium of all teaching and all official communications. Thus a Muslim Vai, educated at school, will know at least two languages (Vai and English)[28] and possibly three scripts (Vai, English and Arabic).[29] However, the mere existence of the Vai syllabary does not make the Vai a literate society (in the sense of my original definition), either within their own community or within the wider Liberian community. Only *c*. 10% of Vai people are literate in English and someone who knows the Vai syllabary but not the English alphabet will be *il*literate within the literate society of Liberia.

On the other hand, since the Vai syllabary is used by only a small minority of the Vai population and is used only for personal, not for political, bureaucratic or religious, purposes, writing in the Vai script has not penetrated the fundamental functions of the Vai community, which still works as an oral society. When the wider, literate Liberian society impinges on the Vai it does so in English[30] and, as with all non-literates faced with the demands of a literate society, the Vai turn to those who can speak, read and write the language of the authorities, to act as intermediaries.

Literacy for fun: the Tifinagh[31]

As far as I know, the only nomadic desert society in the recent past and today in which literacy is widespread, is that of the Tuareg in north-west Africa.

[28] In some areas, particularly in Sierra Leone, some Vai people also speak Mende which has its own indigenous script known as Kikakui. Mende is a recognized language of education in Sierra Leone (information from: http://www.ethnologue.com/show_country.asp?name=Sierra Leone).

[29] A reading knowledge of the Arabic script, for the purposes of memorizing the Qur'ān is taught to Muslim children. However, Goody, Cole and Scribner comment 'by and large, "learning book" means being taught to find the rough phonetic equivalents of Arabic letters so that individuals can memorize verses of the Koran, the meaning of which may be explained by some learned man who has actually acquired some Arabic or who has memorized a translation or a commentary. ... *However the use of Arabic itself was relatively restricted ... because the number of people who could decode the meaning (i.e. read) as distinct from decode the sound was very limited*' (1977: 290–91, my italics). See also the more detailed description of the acquisition of literacy in Arabic among the Vai, in Scribner and Cole 1999: 52–3, 68–9, and compare the situation of the eighteenth-century Highlander mentioned above, and Olszowy-Schlanger's description of the early stages of teaching the Torah in mediaeval Jewish communities (2003: 68).

[30] One Vai speaker and writer commented to Goody, Cole and Scribner, 'in Africa we need Arabic to help us go to Heaven and we need English to improve our standard of living' (1977: 291).

[31] I have, alas, no expertise whatsoever in the Tifinagh and, in what follows, I have leaned heavily on the fascinating work of L. Galand, P. Galand-Pernet, M. Aghali-Zakara, J. Drouin and N. van den Boogert, who have made comprehensive studies of the script and its uses. I am particularly grateful to Professor Lionel Galand and Professor Paulette Galand-Pernet who read a draft of this paper and made many helpful comments. Naturally, I alone am responsible for any errors in the use I have made of the information with which they kindly provided me.

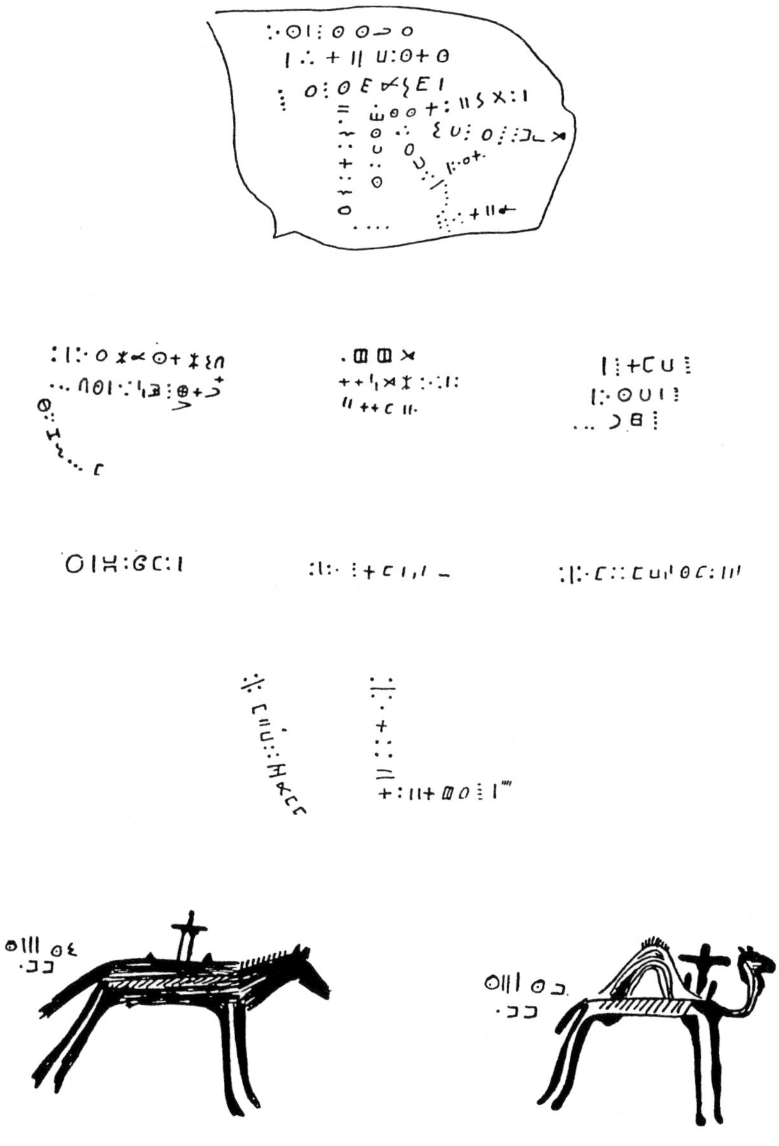

Fig. 1. Tuareg graffiti in the Tifinagh characters (from Reygasse 1932).

They use the Tifinagh characters[32] to write in the sand or to carve graffiti on the desert rocks,[33] and for very little else (Fig. 1). As Lionel Galand has written, 'le berbère offre l'étrange particularité d'être une langue orale pourvue d'une écriture' (1989: 344).

The Tifinagh characters are thought to be descended from letters of the Libyco-Berber script, which was used in North Africa from before the Christian era. However, the latter is still not entirely deciphered and the exact process of this descent is far from clear.[34] The script was traditionally written without word-division, is almost entirely consonantal and does not show strengthening of consonants.[35] As Galand remarks these features, 'en raison de la morphologie berbère, font encore plus cruellement défaut que dans les écritures sémitiques' (2002b: 411).

The Tifinagh are used very widely today in Algeria, Niger and Mali by the Tuareg, an entirely oral society in which memory and oral communication perform all the functions which reading and writing have in a literate society. Their social system is tribal[36] and their way-of-life is, for the most part, nomadic. The Tifinagh are used primarily for games and puzzles, short graffiti and brief messages.[37]

[32] Tafinəq (pl. Tifinagh) is the feminine word which designates specifically a character in the consonantal alphabet used by the Tuareg. The plural, 'Tifinagh', is the term most widely used by the Tuareg for this script (see Aghali-Zakara and Drouin 1973–79: 248).

[33] Although there are large numbers of rock inscriptions in the Tifinagh characters (see, for instance, the *planches* and *photos* in Reygasse 1932), Aghali-Zakara and Drouin say that these are very old and even when legible can no longer be understood by the Tuareg. Indeed the technique used to carve them seems to have been lost and they are said to have been carved 'when the rocks were soft'. There are also some texts carved on a tree at Dafkao (Imannan, Niger), which while apparently less ancient, are not modern (Aghali-Zakara and Drouin 1973–79: 267–68; Aghali-Zakara 1993: 145, figs 2 and 3).

[34] See Galand 1966: 14–16; 1998: 593–94; 2002a: 10. For a comparison of some of the Libyco-Berber signs and the Tifinagh, and their respective values, see Aghali-Zakara and Drouin 1973–79: 254–55; Aghali-Zakara 2001: 5. On the origins of the Libyco-Berber script, see Galand 2001a.

[35] For an interesting study of the implications of this lack of means to represent strengthened consonants see Galand 1996. The Tifinagh characters represent only consonants except for a dot representing [a] at the end of a word. The signs for *w* and *y* can sometimes also be used for [u] and [i] respectively, at the end of words, but never elsewhere (Aghali-Zakara and Drouin 1973–79: 250). Today, young people who have learnt the Arabic or the Latin scripts often use word-dividers when writing in Tifinagh (ibid. 263). See below under the discussion of orthographic developments in scripts used in oral environments.

[36] It is, however, very different from that of the Bedouin of the Middle East, not least in having a very strong 'caste' hierarchy which over-arches the tribal structure. For a brief description, see Prasse 2000: 379.

[37] Aghali-Zakara and Drouin 1973–79: 284–90. Coninck states that the young men of the Kel-Antessar in Mali used the Tifinagh to write down their poems and songs at his request (Coninck and Galand 1957–60: 79). Galand has also identified a few words of a poem mentioned by Père de Foucauld, in a graffito in the Tifinagh (Galand 2001b). I am most grateful to Professor

Aghali Zakara and Drouin have shown in great detail how the Tifinagh characters are learnt informally by children from each other, from older female relations (Van den Boogert 2000: 476) or from servants, but not from those adults with whom they have a relationship which requires respect on the child's part (father, grandfather, maternal uncle, etc.). Indeed, the script is so much associated with playfulness and youth that many older men consider it beneath their dignity to admit to knowing the Tifinagh, and the characters would never even be referred to in an assembly of notables or an important meeting (Aghali-Zakara and Drouin 1973–79: 280, 284–86).

The impetus to learn to read and write the Tifinagh comes entirely from the child and is not imposed in an institutional milieu, as is the study of Arabic or French in those areas where these are taught. The Tifinagh are learnt in the course of games, competitions and jokes among children. The Tuareg say 'it is not something you learn on paper'—paper and pencil being associated with the non-traditional culture—'it is not like the Qur'ān which you learn step by step 'this is this, this is that' nor like French which one learns letter by letter [i.e. systematically]'. They also like to emphasize that they learn the Tifinagh more quickly than they do the Arabic letters. They say that they learn all the Tifinagh characters in a day, simply by watching others and asking them. Aghali Zakara and Drouin conclude that personal motivation is undoubtedly one of the factors which facilitates this learning process (1973–79: 281).

All individuals use the Tifinagh and there is no difference between male and female, young and old, or between social classes. The only differences are degrees of competence, and this has nothing to do with social category, but simply with aptitude and experience. Children use it in games. Young people write each other notes. The latter are often in a sign-code agreed between the two, intended to foil the inquisitive. They are also used in gatherings to which young women go, not with their husbands (if they are nobles) but with an older or younger brother or other male relative. Because these social uses of the script are particularly common among the young, people say that the Tifinagh are 'the business of the young or of children', or they are 'something which young boys use to get in touch with girls of the same age' or 'they are only a game' (Aghali-Zakara and Drouin 1973–79: 285).

Children learn first to write their name in the sand, and then the names of their relations and friends, and then words signifying common objects, etc.

Galand for this reference which I have not yet seen. However, this does not seem to have been normal practice among the Tuareg. See Aghali-Zakara and Drouin who say 'l'écriture ne transpose pas systématiquement le discours oral, en particulier les répertoires littéraires dont la vitalité se fonde sur l'oralité' (1973–79: 292). See also Galand-Pernet who emphasizes the oral nature of Berber literature, even when it is recorded and reproduced on disks, tapes or the radio. 'Dans la société touarègue où la connaissance de l'écriture est ancestrale, le texte littéraire reste purement oral, l'écriture ayant d'autres fonctions sociales que la fixation des textes' (1998: 30, and see 27–31).

Knowledge of the script is extended through competitions, each child thinks of something and writes it on the ground, and the others try to read it. If it turns out to be too difficult to read, they say 'the words refuse you' and the writer gives the solution, the others then laugh at the reader who failed. Thus, learning comes through play, and the prime use of the script is for amusement.[38]

Texts are read letter by letter, each consonant being spelled out in a sing-song voice and combined with each of the vowels in turn until the correct sound of the syllable and the correct word is recognized *aurally*, not visually[39] (cf. the method of reading the Vai script, described above). This seems to be a rite of reading which is observed even when the reader immediately understands a group of characters familiar to him (Aghali-Zakara and Drouin 1973–79: 283). This again is part of the game.

The Tifinagh are occasionally used for practical purposes. Sometimes men will write short messages[40] in them when they are separated by a long distance, and in some areas a simple record of tax returns is kept in the Tifinagh. However, in the latter case the absence of any ciphers in the script means either that all numbers have to be written out in words, or else numerals from the Arabic or Latin scripts used.[41] Artisans, who form a relatively despised class and therefore do not have to maintain their dignity, often use the Tifinagh to write *me fecit* inscriptions, expressed in a semi-magical formula, on objects they have made in wood, stone, or metal, particularly jewellery.[42] In the past, the Tifinagh were used for inscriptions on

38 Aghali-Zakara and Drouin 1973–79: 281–82; Aghali-Zakara 1999: 109–10.

39 Coninck and Galand 1957–60: 79; Aghali-Zakara and Drouin 1973–79: 283, and Aghali-Zakara 1999: 112 where he says that this process is carried out 'à mi-voix'.

40 Early in the second decade of the twentieth century, some members of the Tuareg Kel-Ahaggar addressed a number of messages on scraps of paper and cloth to Père Charles de Foucauld and 33 of these have survived and have now been edited and published by L. Galand (1999). (This total of 33 includes five cases in which two separate messages were written on the same sheet, but excludes no. 27 in the edition, which is not a letter, and no. 29 which was written by Lieutenant de la Roche.) In his section of the introduction, Aghali-Zakara notes that it is extremely rare for messages such as these to be preserved since they are regarded as of no historical importance 'car ils véhiculent un message personnel, généralement intime. C'est pour cette raison qu'ils sont détruits au fur et à mesure dans cette société à tradition orale, où la parole était encore, il y a quelques décennies, l'essentiel réceptacle des Dires. Tout message écrit est éphémère' (Galand 1999: 113–14).

41 In some places local forms of ciphers have been developed but these do not appear to be either very old or widespread. The traditional method of showing numbers is to write them out in words and since, for example, the number 'nineteen' is often expressed as 'two tens from which one is missing', this can be somewhat cumbersome. See Aghali-Zakara 1993: 148–53.

42 Professor Galand has kindly drawn my attention to the fact that bracelets made from a stone which has been identified as serpentine and bearing inscriptions in the Tifinagh used to be worn by Tuareg men, see Foucauld and Calassanti-Motylinski 1984: 70. In this case, the inscriptions in the Tifinagh were sometimes carved by women, rather than by the maker, and would read 'Moi, une Telle déclare : j'ai ma part [d'amour] assurée auprès du possesseur de ce bracelet!' (*ibidem*). Similary, 'virtually everyone engaged in a craft who knows the [Vai] script

shields and also for writing insults on the sand in the path of somebody one disliked (Aghali-Zakara and Drouin 1973–79: 288). However, as Galand points out, when a Berber wishes to write a text of greater length he turns to a foreign alphabet—and often to a foreign language—which he either writes himself, if he is literate in the foreign script and tongue, or gets someone else to write for him.[43]

But as Aghali Zakara and Drouin make clear, by far the most frequent use of the Tifinagh is in games and amusements. Interestingly, the basic rule in these games is to make the reading as *difficult* as possible by encoding the message. The lack of signs for vowels and for strengthening of consonants, and the absence of word-division, make the script difficult enough to read. However, one game involves infixing extra consonants between the syllables of a word. Another consists in mixing up the order of the consonants. These two procedures can be used separately or together. Sometimes failure in these games carries a 'forfeit' such as having to drink twenty glasses of tea in succession. For the maintenance of their dignity, grandfathers, fathers, big brothers, maternal uncles, etc. do not take part in these 'childish games played in the sand' (Aghali-Zakara and Drouin 1973–79: 289–90). On the other hand, adults will often use the script among themselves and full competence in it is usually only gained after long practice in adulthood.[44] The pleasure in setting ever more ingenious puzzles when composing these texts does not end in childhood but becomes more complex and sophisticated.[45] The Tifinagh have remained a pastime and have made no inroads into the non-literate culture of the Tuareg,[46] as represented for instance by its rich oral literature. Indeed,

uses it for work-related purposes, even if in minimal ways' (Scribner and Cole 1999: 82). By contrast, as we shall see below, all the Safaitic inscriptions on manufactured objects known at present are simple graffiti which make no reference to the objects on which they are carved.

43 Galand 1998: 593. Galand-Pernet points out the existence of mediaeval manuscripts in the Berber language 'entièrement rédigés en caractères arabes, avec quelques signes adaptés à la phonétique berbère', and adds that the Arabic script is used today by contemporary authors writing secular works in Berber (1999: 106–7). It is worth noting that the majority of the messages written in the Tifinagh and sent to Père de Foucauld by members of the Tuareg Kel-Ahaggar consist of good wishes, with occasionally a simple request, and would be described by the Tuareg as *tehult* 'salutations' rather than as 'letters' (see Casajus 1999: 97–98).

44 Thus, although most of the Tuareg who sent notes in the Tifinagh to Père Charles de Foucauld were nobles (see Galand 1999), they apparently felt at ease doing so because they were writing to a foreigner.

45 Aghali-Zakara and Drouin 1973–79: 284–89, and see also 261 on old people and women.

46 See Aghali-Zakara 1993: 152–53: 'les parlers berbères, en dépit de l'usage d'une écriture originelle—perdue pour les uns et maintenue pour les autres —, n'ont vraisemblablement toujours été que des parlers non écrits. Aucun document en effet, hormis les inscriptions lapidaires réduites, ne nous est parvenu depuis l'Antiquité et la pratique touarègue contemporaine, excepté les usages modernes très récents, montre bien que cette écriture ne sert ni à la compilation ni aux digressions'.

even where Arabic and French have been taught in schools, the Tuareg still see their own culture as oral.[47] Summing up, Galand writes

> C'est une graphie qui reste proche d'origines où la magie de l'écrit n'exigeait du lecteur—s'il y en avait un—que la reconnaissance de formules rituelles, et non le déchiffrement des combinaisons que la langue peut multiplier à l'infini. Aujourd'hui même, elle fonctionne plus facilement comme un aide-mémoire, permettant de capter une information plus ou moins attendue, que comme porteuse d'un message véritablement imprévu, dont la lecture s'avère toujours assez laborieuse. ... Les emplois restreints dans lesquels l'écriture berbère est généralement restée confinée expliquent sans doute qu'on ait rarement cherché à la perfectionner en séparant les mots, ainsi qu'en notant la tension consonantique et les voyelles.... (2002b: 410–11)

II

This brief description of a few forms and uses of literacy in very different circumstances suggests the following conclusions.

Literacy is not necessarily desirable, as its rejection by the Rwala Bedouin makes clear. Nor is it a homogeneous state. It can exist in many degrees and many qualities. One can be literate in one's second language but not in one's mother tongue, like those speakers of the unwritten Modern South Arabian languages who have learnt to read and write Arabic. Such people inhabit an oral environment within their own community but a literate one in the wider society of which they are also members. However, as we have seen, this can also be true even when the individual's mother-tongue has its own script, as in the case of the Tuareg and the Vai. Their scripts have not penetrated the basic functions of their own communities—which therefore remain non-literate—and are incomprehensible to the wider literate societies in which their communities are encompassed. The uses of literacy can also be restricted by an individual's or a community's way-of-life or environment, as with nomads in desert conditions.

Contrary to the assumption identified by Johansson in the passage quoted at the beginning of the previous section, reading and/or writing do not have to be learnt in a formal environment. The skills can be acquired just as effectively, and often more quickly, through play, as with the children in the West who learn to write before they can read and among the Tuareg, or they can be taught informally at home as among the Vai.[48]

[47] Aghali-Zakara and Drouin 1973–79: 292. See also Aghali-Zakara 1999: 113–14, quoted in note 40.

[48] The teaching of reading at home in seventeenth and eighteenth century Sweden appears from the records to have been formal and imposed by the parents (in response to legal requirements) and so in these respects is more comparable to school-learning than to the informal acquisition dependent on the child's wish to learn, as among the Tuareg and probably among the Vai.

Again, these examples have shown that there is no foundation to the common assumption that reading and writing are simply two sides of the same coin and that if you can do one you must be able to do the other. As we have already seen, there are children who teach themselves to write and who are unable to read what they have written and—at the time—feel no need to learn. In 17th and 18th century Sweden, we have seen an example of almost universal reading-literacy imposed from above, where neither the authorities nor, apparently, the majority of the individuals concerned, felt that there was any need for writing to be learnt.[49] In Scotland too, where there *was* schooling, although all the men and women questioned at Cambuslang could read, and a sizeable percentage of men could write, only 10% of the women questioned had the latter skill. Reading in Sweden, and to a lesser extent in Scotland, was taught for a particular purpose, that is to permit every individual to memorize and understand the word of God. We shall see in the next section another example of reading taught for a very specific reason. In rural Sweden and elsewhere, the authorities felt that no purpose would be served by forcing people to learn to write, and clearly most individuals agreed with them, since in the home education programme there was nothing to stop parents teaching their children, or having them taught, to write if they so wished.[50] Reading and writing are not simply separate, and separable, skills but have quite different uses, and an individual or a community can decide that it is worth learning one but not the other.

This can be seen, for example, in mediaeval England (and many other societies) where the practical skill of writing was clearly distinguished from the art of composition. The ability to write neatly and legibly was an artisanal skill, which though very useful, did not carry much status. An intellectual would normally be *able* to write, but, unless he was a monk,[51] he would use the ability only for personal purposes.[52] Instead, he would dictate to an amanuensis.[53] '"Reading and dictating" [*legere vel dictare*] were ordinarily

[49] See Johansson 1988: 156–60 for a discussion of this.

[50] It would appear that slightly less than 10% of the rural community did feel it was worth learning to write and presumably would have been available to teach the others. The village pastor would also have been able to teach it, had there been a demand.

[51] 'Monks [as opposed to secular clerics] wrote more of their own works because they were expected to be humble and also because some had training in a *scriptorium*' (Clanchy 1993: 126).

[52] For instance, Robert Grosseteste of Lincoln, 'the most academic, conscientious, and efficient bishop of the thirteenth century' in England (Clanchy 1993: 76), wrote notes 'in a fast cursive script' 'like other university masters' (128), on whatever material was at hand, including the margins of manuscripts (120). St Thomas Aquinas composed his earlier works in writing, in a personal shorthand comprehensible only to himself known as *littera inintelligibilis*. He would then read this to a secretary who would take it down in a legible script (Carruthers 1990: 4). Later, he dispensed with the first stage and composed in his head and dictated the works from memory (ibid. 4–6).

[53] The most extraordinary example of this is St Thomas Aquinas who is reported to have dictated three or even four different works to different secretaries at one sitting (see Carruthers 1990: 3).

coupled together, not "reading and writing".'[54] 'Writing was a very necessary activity, but it was not to be done by great ladies' (Clanchy 1993: 193) or gentlemen, for that matter. 'The profits of literacy, in terms of both heavenly and earthly advantage, were therefore best sought in religious reading. Skill in writing (which was taught separately from reading) could be rewarding for scribes working in rich monasteries and professional ateliers ... but such men were the exceptions. Most writing involved repetitive manual labour of the type done by ... the king's clerks' (Clanchy 1993: 194). Thus, reading and writing are not only clearly separable skills, but they can have different social roles and status, according to the availability of materials, technologies and the needs of different societies.

In the modern West, we take the availability of writing materials and the desire to write for granted. But when literacy first becomes available to a society, or to a section of a community, which has previously managed perfectly well without it, the abundance or lack of easily available writing materials may well be the deciding factor in whether or not it is adopted, or the speed with which it comes to be used.[55] As Clanchy has shown, this was the case in mediaeval England where 'neither for reading nor for writing were materials readily available in domestic settings' (Clanchy 1993: 194) and 'the habit of sending missives, conveying ephemeral information about day-to-day matters, developed slowly ... the spoken word of messengers sufficed for conveying the ordinary business of the day'.[56] Up to the reign of King John (1199–1216) 'the spoken word was the legally valid record and was superior to any document' (Clanchy 1993: 77), and this only changed as a result of the demands of the king's government, not public sentiment. After all, written documents could easily be forged or altered—and elaborate precautions were taken to prevent this happening[57]—whereas the word of an

[54] Clanchy 1993: 125. Indeed, as early as the Roman period this practice had become so common that, from the Augustan age onwards, the meaning of the verb *dictare* was extended to cover 'compose, draw up', a semantic development parallel to that which the verb *scribere* had earlier undergone (see *The Oxford Latin Dictionary* (Oxford, 1996) *s.v. dicto* and *scribo*). Indeed, at least by the twelfth century (and probably a great deal earlier) *scribere* could also include dictation, since 'John of Salisbury remarks in a letter to Peter, abbot of Celle, in *c.* 1159: "While I was writing this (*scriberem*), the secretary [*notarius*] was moved to laughter by the greeting at the head of the letter"' (Clancy 1993: 126). By the Middle Ages, *ars dictationis* (i.e. the ability to compose in one's head and then dictate to an amanuensis) was a branch of rhetoric (Clanchy 1993: 125–26).

[55] It is worth noting that Scribner and Cole state that 'one reason for greater facility in reading [than in writing] among the older generation [of the Vai] was the difficulty of finding writing materials' (1999: 68).

[56] Clanchy 1993: 89–90. Clanchy says this was because 'Latin was too formal a medium' for such ephemera, but it must surely also have had to do with the lack of suitable writing materials, the shortage of people who could write and the lack of any compelling need to change the traditional methods of conveying day-to-day communications.

[57] On the extensive forging of documents in mediaeval England see Clanchy 1993: 148–49,

honest man who had taken an oath on the Gospels was felt to be more reliable.[58]

As we have seen with IT in the modern world, the introduction of a new technology is usually greeted with enthusiasm by a few and indifference or resistance by many, until its increasing use (particularly by institutions) pushes all but the most 'die-hard' to accept it. Clanchy's description of the spread of reading-literacy in mediaeval England could apply, *mutatis mutandis*, to the process in many other societies.

> The most important consequence of the proliferation of documents was that it prepared the gentry, the country-keeping knights, for literacy. Documents had to precede widening literacy. They had to have increased by accumulation in central archives and extensive distribution over the country before understanding of them became widespread in the shires. *The gentry were not going to learn to read until documents were available and necessary.* Necessity and availability also made for easy familiarity with writing, and from familiarity stemmed confidence in literate ways of doing business. Traditionally, literate modes had been the preserve of clerics and rulers. It took time, combined with a massive increase in the number of documents, to change traditional habits (Clanchy 1993: 78 [my italics]).

This, and the examples in the previous section, also call into question the linked assumptions, again cited by Johansson, that reading and writing are inherently and universally desirable because they are of practical (and, ultimately, economic) use. There are many situations and many societies in which they are neither desirable nor serve a practical/economic purpose, as we have seen among the Rwala Bedouin. The Tuareg's use of the Tifinagh shows that there are many other reasons for learning to read and/or to write. Similarly in Sweden, the government campaign for universal reading-literacy

170–71, 297–99, 318–27. On methods of reducing the risk of interference with documents see, for instance, ibid. 87–88.

58 Clanchy traces the transition of the verb 'to record', which up to the first half of the twelfth century meant 'to bear oral witness', but by the second half had come to mean 'to produce a document' (1993: 77). A similar semantic shift can be seen in the context of the early uses of the Arabic script. From pre-Islamic times well into the Umayyad period, the Arabic word *risālah* apparently meant 'the oral transmission of a message' and the change in meaning to 'written letter' is not recorded before the reign of Hishām bin 'Abd al-Malik (AD 724–743). See Arazi and Ben-Shammay 1995: 532, but note that the statement in their first paragraph that the term is 'attested at a very early stage, in the inscriptions of Arabia, with the meaning of message or mission' (532) is based on a misunderstanding of the purpose of Harding 1971, which is not a dictionary but an index of names, with Classical and Modern Arabic words given purely for comparative purposes. However, the word *rs¹l* meaning 'messenger, envoy' is found, probably as a North Arabian loan-word, in Sabaic in CIH 541/90, 91 where it refers to the ambassadors of the North Arabian kings of Ghassān and al-Ḥīrah (Beeston *et al.* 1982: 117). See the interesting discussion of Ancient South Arabian words for 'a *written* letter' in Maraqten 2003: 276–77.

was entirely for spiritual,[59] not economic, purposes, for which a far more selective campaign which included writing would have sufficed. In the next section, I shall discuss this in relation to some ancient examples.

As noted above, the Tuareg will occasionally use the Tifinagh to write a short letter or to a keep a record of tax returns, but if they need writing for practical and economic purposes then, either personally or by proxy, they will employ the language and script of the wider literate society, i.e. Arabic or French. English serves the same purposes for the Vai. For both the Tuareg and the Vai, their own scripts do not normally have the functions which *we* associate with literacy, and they have in no way penetrated the basic functions of their societies, which remain fundamentally and proudly oral.

The effects of the use of a script such as the Tifinagh or Vai by an oral society are very marked. Both the Tifinagh and the Vai syllabary are defective scripts which are read slowly and with difficulty even by those brought up with them. In the next section, I shall examine in more detail the effects of this type of use on other scripts.

We have seen that the children who learn to write before they can read develop, without prompting, a 'phonetic script' which in principle, though not in every detail, is more or less universal among children writing in English. This spelling also commonly fails to represent certain sounds (notably the nasals [m] and [n] before other consonants) even though the child knows the signs for them. The Tifinagh, which are learnt informally and used principally for amusement and self-expression are also written phonetically and spellings will vary according to the Berber dialect spoken by the writer.

It is important to remember that scripts like the Tifinagh and Vai, are read *aloud.* Indeed the Tifinagh, at least, are also *written* aloud.[60] In the Tifinagh the reader pronounces each consonant aloud and tries it with different vowels until the correct combination is achieved. In Vai, he pronounces strings of syllables aloud with different vowel length and vowel tone until he finds the right ones. Thus, the recognition of a word is *aural* not visual.[61] In this

[59] In Sweden, 'resistance to costly school systems was great among the rural population. Reading was primarily done as spiritual exercise during the quiet of the Sabbath, not in aid of the everyday struggle. As it had no obvious practical use, naturally it should not cost anything' (Johansson 1998: 121).

[60] 'Écrire nécessite de murmurer des mots pour ne retenir que les sons qui s'écrivent (les consonnes) sans oublier, les aligner traditionnellement sans les séparer en utilisant à bon escient les signes biconsonantiques [monograms] ....' (Aghali-Zakara 1999: 113). It would seem that Galand-Pernet's dictum on the importance of the voice in the composition and reception of manuscripts in the Berber language written in Arabic characters would also apply to texts in the Tifinagh, 'La voix peut précéder, dans la création, ou suivre, dans la diffusion, la mise par écrit de l'oeuvre' (1998: 79). See also note 156.

[61] Scribner and Cole 1978: 456. See also note 156 below. Note that in seventeenth- and eighteenth-century Sweden, children were to be taught to read religious texts aloud until 'they shall have become fully aware of the text they are reading and *heed its utterance as if they heard*

method of reading there is a direct link between sound and sign and it is unlikely that non-phonetic, historical or conventional spellings would develop. This has important consequences for our interpretation of scripts used in similar circumstances in antiquity.[62] However, as M.J. Carruthers has pointed out in her study of the use and training of memory in the Middle Ages, aural-reading (i.e. either reading aloud or sub-vocalization) was also an important tool in memorization (1990: 6–7).

In antiquity and in pre-modern Europe, literacy was the handmaid of memory, rather than its rival. 'The cultivation and training of memory was a basic aspect of the literate society of Rome, and continued to be necessary to literature and culture through the Middle Ages. This privileged cultural role of memory seems independent of 'orality' and 'literacy' as these terms have come to be defined in the social sciences.'[63] A well trained and highly developed memory was considered to be the most important intellectual attribute one could have.[64] Thus, the assumption that, once acquired, literacy automatically leads to a distrust and progressive disuse of memory is entirely false, at least in periods and places before mass printing and mass literacy. This is symbolized by the case of Spensithios the scribe and remembrancer of a community in Crete around 500 BC, whose duties were 'to write down and remember ... the affairs of the city, both secular and divine',[65] and by the ancient and mediaeval scholars who absorbed, classified and catalogued in

it spoken by another' (quoted in Johansson 1988: 142, my italics). Svenbro, à propos of ancient Greek writing, claims that the use of *scriptio continua* 'as experience shows, makes reading aloud a virtual necessity' (1993: 45, but see 166–68 where he modifies this). Gamble makes the important point that 'in reading aloud the written was converted into the oral. Correspondingly, in the composition of a text the oral was converted to the written. In antiquity a text could be composed either by dictating to a scribe or by writing in one's own hand. Yet when an author did write out his own text, the words were spoken as they were being written, just as scribes in copying manuscripts practiced what is called self-dictation. In either case, then, the text was an inscription of the spoken word. Because authors wrote or dictated with an ear to the words and assumed that what they wrote would be audibly read, they wrote for the ear more than the eye' (1995: 204).

62 This aural reading also lies at the basis of the new orthography used for 'texting' on mobile phones and in some advertisements. Phrases such as 'RU' (for 'are you') '2B E10' (for 'to be eaten'), and '2DI4' for ('to die for'), make no sense visually and can only be understood aurally. They can also reveal features of the spoken language, such as 'MENU' for 'me 'n you', rather than the Standard English 'you and I' (UNI?)

63 Carruthers 1990: 11, and see 160–62 on the preference for transmitting the contents of books via a scholar's memory than by 'the ignorant, word-scattering, cloudy-headed idiots who would erase ('denigratum') or otherwise spoil the texts in transmitting them', that is 'the professional copyists and secretaries into whose charge the copying of books for university scholars had now passed' (paraphrasing Richard de Bury (1286–1345) *Philobiblion* VIII.134).

64 Carruthers 1990: 3–7, and *passim*.

65 Jeffery and Morpurgo-Davies 1970: 124–25 (text and translation), 131–33 and 148–51 (on ποινικάζεν δὲ [π]όλι καὶ μναμονεϝ͂εν) and see the discussion in Thomas 1992: 69–71 (whose translation I have used above).

their memories the material they read and then recovered and re-ordered it when they wrote or dictated.[66]

In 'literate societies' where the vast majority of people encountered literacy only at second-hand,[67] where there was no mass production of texts, and where most documents were hard for all but the highly trained to decipher, memory remained the prime means of personal record. The importance of reading, therefore, was that it made available more material to memorize.[68] This is surely one reason why so many more people learnt to read than to write in literate societies, for, as Carruthers puts it, 'reading and memorizing were taught [in the Middle Ages] as they were in antiquity, as one single activity' (1990: 101). Writing, when it was taught at all, was learnt as a separate skill.

This link between reading and memorizing is of fundamental importance. In Sweden, the purpose of learning to read was specifically the memorizing and understanding of the Scriptures and other religious texts. In Scotland and elsewhere, there were occasional accidents where memory and understanding parted company, as in the example of the Highlander mentioned above. Such problems are inevitable, however, when one is required to learn to read a foreign language before one has learnt to understand it, as seen in the example of children in West Africa learning to read and memorize the Qurʾān without knowing Arabic.

Reading which is used as an aid to memorizing requires two distinct but linked skills. These are what might be called 'sight-reading'—that is reading and understanding an unfamiliar text—and 'prompted recitation'—that is reciting a text from memory using the written form as a prompt when necessary. These are skills which are used for specific purposes in most literate environments. There is an almost exact analogy with musicians, who can sight-read a new musical score but, even when they have learnt a piece, will usually still keep the score in front of them as a prompt. Similarly, priests and regular churchgoers know the liturgy off by heart but often still keep the missal or prayer book open in front of them and turn the page at the correct

[66] See Carruthers 1990: 4–10 (summary using the example of St Thomas Aquinas), and *passim*. While Clanchy is obviously correct in saying that 'the practice of making memoranda, whether on wax or parchment, contradicts the common assumption that medieval people had such good memories that they required no notes', I would tentatively suggest that he may be overstating the case when he continues 'once they were literate, they had the same needs as a modern writer' (1993: 120).

[67] That is, public notices or official documents were read to them and, on the rare occasions when it was necessary, a scribe would write and sometimes even sign for them. See Hanson 1991 for a fascinating discussion of illiterates in Ptolemaic and Roman Egypt.

[68] For example, Rosalind Thomas notes that 'Plato's famous description of primary-school teaching, usually cited to show the teaching of literacy, actually says that the children are given poems of good poets to read and learn *by heart* (*Protagoras* 325e)' (1992: 92, her italics). See also the remarks below on the purpose of teaching reading to Jewish boys in Roman Palestine.

place. Politicians making speeches will often treat their notes in a similar way. This does not mean that any of these readers is incapable of instantaneous sight-reading, simply that that is not what the particular situation requires.

Prompted recitation is not the same as learning by heart a text spoken or read by someone else, even if the book is open in front of the learner.[69] It is dependent on the learner being able to sight-read. In an age before silent reading was general, this meant performing the direct conversion of written symbols into sounds. However, for those who have been taught to read solely to enable them to memorize a particular text and who, for whatever reason, have little opportunity to read other material, sight-reading can be a long and painful process. In antiquity—and sometimes today—this involved spelling out the words, aloud, letter by letter or syllable by syllable, as with the Tifinagh characters or the Vai syllabary, a process often not helped by the ways in which the text was presented. But this very difficulty in the initial reading, together with the act of reading it aloud, are in themselves an aid in the process of memorizing. In order to survive, those who live in societies where literacy is not used in daily life, have to have sharp and extremely powerful memories. So, one or two slow and painful sight-readings of the text would have committed not only the words to memory but—at least to some extent—their positions and relationships on the page,[70] so that the 'book' (like a musical score) could thereafter be used as a prompt or a 'security blanket'. As Gamble points out, for public reading it was extremely important that the text be memorized to ensure a smooth performance and to avoid the painful letter-by-letter decipherment of sight-reading (1995: 204–5).

Finally, these examples show that the use of a script within a community does not automatically make it a literate society. As we have seen, both the Tuareg and the Vai have their own scripts but remain oral enclaves within much larger literate societies, which use different languages and scripts. Within these wider societies, Tuareg who cannot read or write Arabic or French are *ill*iterates, even if they know how to use the Tifinagh, and the same is true of Vai who are not literate in English.

However, even communities which share the same language and script as the wider literate society, can remain fundamentally oral (in the sense of my initial definition). Thus, the environment of rural Sweden, in which 80% of people could read (but less than 10% write), remained a largely non-literate one, because literacy was not vital to the practical functioning of these country communities. Young children, even when they have taught

69 This was one of the many ways of reading in mediaeval England. See Clanchy 1993: 194–95.

70 This is an unconscious process which is different from the very deliberate mnemonic processes described by Carruthers (1990: 80–121, 221–57).

themselves to write, remain in an oral enclave within the literate society, because all communication with them is by word-of-mouth. As we have seen, most of the Tuareg and the Vai inhabit oral enclaves, which function perfectly well without the use of literacy, as they always have done, even when large numbers of people use the Tifinagh for pleasure, and small numbers use the Vai syllabary for minor practical tasks.

It will be clear that while the concepts of literate and oral societies are theoretically useful, in practice, both in antiquity and today, there is no clear division between them, let alone between the literate and oral communities of which they are made up. They co-exist and overlap and the same individual may move between them as circumstances require.[71] Thus 'literacy in an oral environment'—far from being a contradiction in terms, as might appear at first sight—has been, and in some places still is, a relatively common occurrence.

In the last part of this paper I will try to apply the insights gained from the situations discussed above to some uses of literacy in oral environments in pre-Islamic Arabia.

III

It is interesting to compare the use of literacy in 17th and 18th-century Sweden with that in the Jewish communities of Roman Palestine. Undoubtedly, the radical Protestant emphasis on individual Bible study in post-Reformation Europe and America, which prompted the literacy campaign in Sweden, owes a great deal to Jewish practice. It is, after all, a religious duty for Jewish men to study the Law and to read it aloud in the Synagogue. In Roman Palestine, it seems that there were large numbers of Jewish schools attached to synagogues where boys were taught to read Hebrew[72] in order to read the Torah.[73] But, as the editors of the new Schürer put it, 'this zeal in the upbringing of the young was aimed at impressing the Torah on their minds and not at providing them with a general education. Thus their first lessons were in reading and *memorizing* the scriptural text',[74]

71 On this see, for instance, Graff 1986: 69–70.

72 It has been suggested that in the diaspora, where the Septuagint version of the Bible was used, similar instruction in reading Greek 'must have been' provided by Jewish communities to their children (Gamble 1995: 7), but as far as I know there is no evidence for this.

73 See Schürer 1973–87, ii: 418–19 and see note 31 there, on the provision of different types of schools. For details of the public reading of the Scriptures in synagogues in the Roman period, see Gamble 1995: 208–11.

74 Schürer 1973–87, ii: 419 (my italics). Josephus, extolling the virtues of Jewish religious education, wrote 'if one of us should be questioned about the laws, he would recite them all more easily than his own name' (*Contra Apionem* 2.19). Note also a letter from a mediaeval Jewish merchant of Fusṭāṭ in Egypt to his wife 'asking her to send their children to school in the

and it is unlikely that for many this skill was transferable to any other sphere. After all, the Hebrew of the Torah was not the common language of everyday life in Roman Palestine[75] and it is very doubtful whether the ability to sight-read, memorize and give prompted recitations of carefully copied manuscripts of the Torah would have translated into an ability to read day-to-day documents in non-calligraphic Aramaic, let alone those in Greek or Latin. If, in the Diaspora, ordinary Jewish boys—as opposed to those from privileged homes—were taught to read Greek in order to study the Septuagint, this may well have enabled them to read other carefully written material in Greek and, with further practice, ordinary hand-written documents. But alas, we have no evidence on this point.

In this context, it is interesting to compare the evidence for the teaching of reading and writing in the Jewish community of mediaeval Cairo, which has been analysed in a recent article (Olszowy-Schlanger 2003). Since Arabic was the spoken vernacular of the Cairene Jews in the Middle Ages, their children 'were initiated to literacy in what was, for them, effectively a foreign language [Hebrew]' (Olszowy-Schlanger 2003: 52). While some seem to have been taught the Arabic script,[76] this was usually for the purposes of general culture and occupational advancement.[77] The vast majority of boys learnt to read only Hebrew, and that for the sole purposes of studying the Torah and fulfilling their Sabbath duties. For most of these children, the only *language* in which they were fluent was Arabic, but (unless they had had special tuition) the only *script* they could read was the Hebrew alphabet. It is therefore not surprising that those who wished to reach the widest audience within the Jewish communities under Arab rule wrote in the Arabic language expressed in the Hebrew script.[78] For the same reasons Yiddish, a dialect of

synagogue in the morning as well as in the evening: "the only esteem we have among fellow human beings is due to what was engraved in our memory when we were children"' (Olszowy-Schlanger 2003: 52–53).

[75] On this see Schürer 1973–87, ii: 20–28. See also a letter to two of Simeon ben Kosiba's lieutenants which contains a much disputed passage which seems to say that it was written 'in Greek as we have no one here who can write Hebrew' (Schürer 1973–87, ii: 79, n. 279; 420, n. 33), though other interpretations are possible.

[76] See the evidence in Olszowy-Schlanger 2003: 49–51.

[77] Olszowy-Schlanger quotes the words of the great Hebrew translator of Arabic works, Yehuda ben Shaul ibn Tibbon, addressed to his son in his ethical will, 'you know well that the great men of our nation would not have achieved their greatness and their elevated position but through their knowledge of Arabic script' (2003: 49, 54).

[78] There is a curious and, at present apparently unique, example of a translation of the Passover Haggadah into a Berber dialect written in the vocalized Hebrew square script. It was found in a school exercise book in a Jewish village in the Atlas Mountains of Morocco. See Galand-Pernet and Zafrani 1970. Given the importance of children in the Sēder, it is customary in most Jewish communities to follow each passage of the Hebrew text of the Haggadah with a translation in the vernacular (ibid. 10–11). Berber is not an habitually written language and it is

mediaeval German used as a vehicular language by the Jews of eastern Europe, was written in the Hebrew alphabet and I would suggest that Karshuni (the writing of Arabic in the Syriac script) originated in similar circumstances among Christians living in Muslim Arab societies.

Moreover, as in Sweden, since the study of the Scriptures was the sole purpose of teaching children to read, there was no impetus to teach them to write.[79] Thus, while large numbers of Jews could read Hebrew (or possibly Greek, in the Diaspora), far fewer could read other languages, and fewer still could write.[80] Roman Palestine as a whole clearly constituted a 'literate society', not because most Jewish men could read the Torah, but because it depended on literacy for its administrative, commercial and religious functions. If I am correct, this would be a case where, for the majority of Jewish men, schooling and literacy were limited to a single sphere of life and in every other sphere these 'literates' would have inhabited an oral enclave, as did those who could read in rural Sweden in the 17th and 18th centuries, as explained above. In the case both of Sweden and of Roman Palestine, I am, of course, speaking of the majority of those who were taught to read. As in any community, a combination of ability and opportunity would have enabled exceptional individuals to extend their literacy and to take part in the functions of the wider literate society of their day.

For the most extreme examples of literacy in an oral environment in the ancient Near East, we need to look at nomadic societies in the Syro-Arabian deserts. From perhaps as early as the eighth century BC, nomads throughout the western two-thirds of the Arabian Peninsula and north into Syria not only learnt to read and write but covered the desert rocks with scores of thousands of graffiti.[81] Of these, the best studied are the Safaitic inscriptions which seem to have been written between the first century BC and the fourth century AD, in the deserts east and south-east of the Ḥawrān. I have written of these many times before[82] and so here I want only to touch on them as an example of literacy in an oral environment. The language of these nomads was an

likely that the Hebrew alphabet was the only script known to the person who wrote down this translation or to the readers for whom it was made.

[79] Gamble 1995: 7; Schürer 1973–87, ii: 420; and note that in mediaeval Cairo, 'for the overwhelming majority [of Jewish boys], learning to write in Hebrew was an aid in the all-important art of reading it. For these pupils, the prime purpose of writing was merely to be able to recognize the shape of the letters and to associate it with corresponding phonemes. Once children were able to identify the Hebrew characters, their training in writing as such all but stopped' (Olszowy-Schlanger 2003: 55, see also pp. 60–66 on the teaching methods). However, see Millard 2000: 168–72 on the extent of the ability to write in Roman Palestine.

[80] A parallel can be found in Byzantine Egypt where at least one Church Reader was apparently unable to write and even to sign his own name. See Lane Fox 1994: 144 for a brief discussion and references.

[81] See Macdonald and King 2000, and Macdonald 1995a; 2000: 43–46.

[82] See for instance Macdonald 1993; 1995a; 2000; 2004.

Ancient North Arabian tongue related to Arabic but distinct from it and the script is one of the 'Arabian'[83] or 'South Semitic' family, of which Sabaic is the most famous ancient example and Ethiopic the only living survivor.

As I noted in the first section, literacy is of little use to nomads and might even have positive disadvantages if used as a substitute for memory. Writing materials have to be imported from the settled areas and are easily destroyed and, unlike paper in the modern age, papyrus outside Egypt is likely to have been expensive for people in a subsistence economy.[84] Pottery, which when broken seems to have provided the everyday writing support for the sedentaries in much of the ancient Near East, was of little use to nomads for the very reason that it was breakable and not easily replaced, and they preferred vessels made of stone, wood, metal and leather.[85] Thus, the only writing materials which were plentifully available to them were the rocks of the desert, but for most people these are not much use for writing lists, letters, or other everyday documents.[86]

We do not know why these nomads learnt to read and write but it does not seem to have been for any practical purpose. For a start, both the language and script would have been incomprehensible to their Aramaic- and Greek-speaking settled neighbours and the script would have confused their literate nomadic neighbours further south, since they used several of the same or similar signs for different sounds.[87] So it would not have helped them in their

83 For this term, which reflects the fact that use of this alphabetic tradition was confined almost entirely to the Arabian Peninsula, see Robin 1996: 1208.

84 T.C. Skeat makes the very valid point that the question of whether papyrus was cheap or expensive 'is purely a modern one' and is entirely absent from ancient sources (1995: 75). However, he also notes that '99.9% of our evidence comes from Egypt and is not necessarily applicable to the rest of the ancient world' (1995: 76). So, we can only speculate. *Prima facie*, it would seem probable that a product which had to be imported from Egypt to inland Syria would not be sufficiently cheap to supplant the free alternatives of oral communication and memory. As Skeat himself says, 'a writing material [or, in this case, an alternative] which costs *nothing* must always be cheaper than a writing material which costs *something*' (1995: 78, his italics).

85 Thus, a number of stone vessels (bowls, beakers and tripod platters) are known. These bear Safaitic graffiti of similar form to those on the rocks of the desert. See, for instance, Ryckmans 1951: 87–91; and see the remarks in note 42, above. I am in the course of preparing a corpus of all known examples of these inscribed vessels. It may also be significant that in the four excavated graves connected with Safaitic inscriptions where we can be virtually certain that the body is that of the person mentioned in the texts, objects in wood, leather and bronze, as well as fragments of textile and beads have been found (Harding 1953: 11, pls III/2, IV), plus other objects in metal, stone and shell (Harding 1978: 243, pl. XL/d; Clark 1981: 244–45, pl. LXIX), but not a single sherd of pottery (note that the sherds found *near* the Cairn of Saʿad were 'probably of mediaeval date', Harding 1978: 243). Naturally, an argument from silence based on so small a number of excavations is not conclusive, but it may be indicative.

86 See the discussion in the previous section of the requirements for the spread of literacy. See note 102 below for some improbable suggestions as to how the desert rocks could have been used for reference works and communication.

87 See the script table in Macdonald 2000: 34; 2004: 496; and note 101 below.

Fig. 2. A Safaitic-Greek bilingual graffito from the Wādī Rushaydah, southern Syria

Fig. 3. Three Greek graffiti from the Wādī Rushaydah, southern Syria.

relations with neighbouring peoples. Instead, those who went to the settled areas often learnt a smattering of Greek which they showed off when they came home, in Safaitic-Greek bilingual graffiti (Fig. 2) or simply in Greek (Fig. 3). The author of the bilingual in Fig. 2[88] had been taught the Greek

[88] The text was found by the Safaitic Epigraphic Survey Project in the Wādī Rushaydah, east of Jabal al-ʿArab. It will be published in the final report which is in preparation. The Greek text reads Μνησθῆ Νασρηλος Αλουου and the Safaitic reads *l-nṣrʾl bn ʿlw*.

alphabet in the manuscript rather than the monumental forms. This is particularly clear in the form of his *ēta*, in which the right hand upper vertical is missing, but also in the forms of *alpha*, *lambda*, and *upsilon* which are characteristic of the script found in papyri of the first and second centuries AD.[89] On the other hand, Fig. 3 shows that this was not always the case. Of the three Greek graffiti on this rock,[90] the first is in the formal register[91] (note particularly the forms of *mu* and *ēta*), while the second and third, like that on Fig. 2, are in the informal (note particularly the forms of *ēta* and *upsilon*). It may have depended on the whim of the informant which register he taught to the nomad, or in one case he may have written out the letters and in another used an inscription as an exemplar.

One of the many interesting features of these texts is the apparent ease with which their authors mastered two very different orthographic systems, Safaitic, which was entirely consonantal with no *matres lectionis*, and Greek in which the vowels were written but some Semitic consonants, such as ʾ, ʿ, *ḥ*, *h*, etc. had to be omitted. This does not seem to have caused any particular

[89] Compare for example the shapes of these letters in the Babatha papyri (Lewis, Yadin and Greenfield 1989: *passim*).

[90] These were discovered by the Safaitic Epigraphic Survey Project at the same point in Wādī Rushaydah but on the opposite side of the wadi. They will be published in the final report, though number 3 has already appeared in Macdonald, Al Muʾazzin and Nehmé 1996: 480–85. The texts read as follows (1) Μααιανης (perhaps compare *Mʿynw* in Nabatean [LPNab 27/2, JSNab 365, CIS ii 990, 3049] and the woman's name *Mʿynʾ* in Palmyrene [Stark 1971: 34, 95–96]); (2) Δηβος (probably the name *Ḏʾb*); and (3) Σααρος Χεσεμανου Σαιφηνος φυλῆς Χαυνηνων (S^{2}ʿr son of Kaḥs^{1}mn, Ḍayfite of the section of Kawnites). Another Greek graffito by the same author in which he gives his grandfather's name (also Kaḥs^{1}mn) has been found in north-eastern Jordan, see Macdonald 1993: 310 and n. 47; Macdonald, Al Muʾazzin and Nehmé 1996: 483–84. The name Kḥs^{1}mn has so far been found only in the Safaitic inscriptions. Kawn is known from Safaitic texts to be a section of the large tribe of Ḍayf, which was one of the two main tribal groupings of the (literate) nomads, east and south-east of the Ḥawrān in the Roman period.

[91] Just as linguists distinguish different 'registers' in the spoken forms of a language, which are used according to the particular circumstances in which the speaker finds himself, so also, I would suggest, there are registers in the form of script which a person will use in different circumstances. Public announcements (such as monumental inscriptions and graffiti) are normally carved or written in a formal register, whereas personal documents are usually hand-written in an informal register. Some (or all) of the letters of an alphabet may have a different form in different registers (e.g. our capitals and lower case), and, depending on his level of competence, a literate person may have in his head a reading and (less often) a writing knowledge of most, if not all, the forms appropriate to the different registers. Thus, as Clanchy remarks, 'the good scribe' (in mediaeval England as in other times and places) aimed 'to have command of a variety of scripts appropriate to different functions and occasions' (1993: 127). Nevertheless, the notorious phrase *lapidarias litteras scio* in Petronius' *Satyrica* (58.7), if it reflects reality, warns us that 'public inscriptions in the Roman world provided a large-scale and abundant (if not richly amusing) reader for any child who learnt his letters informally' (Horsfall 1991: 62) and that, if he had no reason to learn to read handwriting, it was quite possible for a person to be literate in this register alone.

problems for them, at least none are visible in the texts which have been found so far.[92]

If a nomad, literate in Safaitic, went to the settled regions of the Ḥawrān he would have come into contact with a society literate in Aramaic and Greek. In this society, his ability to read and write Safaitic would be irrelevant and he would be an *il*literate until he learnt enough of the local languages and scripts to read (and possibly write) them. However, it is unlikely that he would need, or want, to do so, except in a few, very specific, circumstances. It would be far more important for him to acquire a smattering of the *spoken* languages, for the vast majority of the ordinary villagers and townsmen with whom he would have had dealings are unlikely to have been able to read and write their languages either, and there would certainly have been scribes for the relatively rare occasions when literacy was needed.

Such a situation would be very similar to that of a Tuareg, literate in the Tifinagh, who today comes into contact with the wider society in North Africa, which is literate in Arabic or French, or of a Vai, who can read and write his own script, dealing with wider Liberian society which is literate in English. In all three cases, if the individual wanted to 'better himself' within the wider society, he would do well to learn this foreign language and script, but if he were content to remain in his own non-literate community he would continue to use his own language and script and remain *il*literate in the wider society. Of course, if he was bright and curious, he might bring back from the 'literate society' a knowledge of the foreign script (without necessarily an understanding of the language),[93] as did those who wrote their names in Greek, or Greek and Safaitic, in the desert. In this case, he might use the foreign script to play or to impress, in the same way as he used his own script, within his non-literate society.

The alphabets used by the nomads presumably had their ultimate origin in a settled literate society and, although there is no evidence of the process, the following hypothesis seems to offer a plausible explanation, though I would emphasize that it can be no more than an hypothesis. If, for instance, a nomad in Arabia was guarding a caravan or visiting an oasis and saw someone writing a letter or doing his accounts, he may well have said 'teach me to do that', simply out of curiosity. I and others have had just this experience with Bedouins on excavations. Because the nomad comes from an oral culture he has a highly developed memory and so learns the skill very quickly. In my

[92] They also, of course, mastered the Greek ways of showing relationships and affiliation to social groups and I know of no examples where nomads made mistakes in these constructions. This contrasts with those, relatively rare and usually later, formal texts as, at random, Negev 1981: 55, No. 57/2–3, Piccirillo and Alliata 1994: 249–50, no. 6d, 251–52, no. 8c, which use the construction 'N υἱὸς N' which is much closer to the 'Semitic' formula 'N *bn/br* N'.

[93] Compare the West African school-children, mentioned above, who are taught to 'decode the sound' of Arabic letters, when learning the Qurʾān, but not to 'decode the meaning (i.e. read)' (Goody, Cole and Scribner 1977: 290–91), see note 29.

case, I wrote the unjoined forms of the letters of the Arabic alphabet on the Bedouin's hand and the next day he was writing his name and mine, still in the rather wobbly unjoined forms of the Arabic letters I had written on his palm.

This is probably how the nomads mentioned above learnt the Greek alphabet and just as most of them learnt the manuscript forms of the Greek letters so, I would suggest, the nomad who first picked up the Ancient North Arabian alphabet would probably have learnt the Ancient North Arabian letter shapes used in handwriting rather than those of the formal register which survive in the inscriptions and graffiti of settled societies.[94] These 'manuscript' forms, which had developed through writing with ink on papyrus or leather or cutting with a sharp blade on soft wood,[95] would then no doubt have undergone changes as they were carved on irregular rock surfaces. There would also, almost certainly, have been further changes as, in the transmission from one nomad to another, there were occasional lapses of memory as to which shape represented which sound, and as the phonological differences between one dialect and another rendered one letter redundant or necessitated the creation of another.[96] All these factors and many more may have produced the marked differences between the Ancient North Arabian letter-forms which survive on the one hand in the *formal* inscriptions and graffiti of a settled literate society such as that of Dedān,[97] and on the other can be found in the numerous related scripts used by the nomads.

Although there is, at present, no evidence either way, it would seem likely that once the use of writing had been acquired by one nomadic group, it was then passed on in the desert from one individual or group to another, rather than being repeatedly re-introduced by a succession of independent contacts with the sedentaries. The orthographies of the scripts used by the nomads lack any *matres lectionis* or word-division and can be written in any direction, and are thus in marked contrast to the orthography of Dadanitic, the

94 Graffiti are normally carved or written in what I would call the formal register of a script, rather than the register used for handwriting. As the late Jacques Ryckmans pointed out (e.g. in 1993: 30), one has only to think of graffiti in our own societies which are almost always in 'capital letters', even when written with spray-paint.

95 As was the practice for day-to-day documents both informal and official in Yemen. For a description see, for instance, Ryckmans J. 1993: 20–23; Ryckmans J., Müller and Abdallah 1994: 27–29; Maraqten 1998: 292–93.

96 Compare the different versions of the Tifinagh used by groups of Tuareg speaking different Berber dialects. See also Galand-Pernet 1999: 106, where her summary 'il y a une diversification scripturaire comme il y a une diversification dialectale' could equally be applied to Ancient North Arabian. Aghali-Zakara and Drouin collected ten Tifinagh 'alphabets', consisting of differing numbers of signs, from different regions (1973–79: 251). See the table of letter-forms from different areas in Aghali-Zakara 1993: 144.

97 For the preliminary re-assessment of the complex mixture of registers and types of spirit used in and around ancient Dedān, see Macdonald in press a.

only Ancient North Arabian alphabet definitely to have been used by a sedentary literate society.[98]

Thus, it seems probable that those who wrote the Safaitic inscriptions would have learnt the Ancient North Arabian alphabet from their neighbours further south. The nearest geographically is the Hismaic script[99] which was used by nomads in the Ḥismā desert of southern Jordan and north-west Saudi Arabia, by other nomads in the limestone desert of east-central Jordan, and also by people in central and northern Jordan (e.g. the Kerak, Madaba[100] and Zerqa areas, among others). There are also some 'mixed texts' which contain letter forms from both the Safaitic and Hismaic scripts (see Macdonald 1980: 188). On the other hand, a number of letters in the two scripts have the same form but completely different values, which perhaps reduces the likelihood that it was the source.[101] Another possibility is that Safaitic developed from Thamudic B which was used by nomads throughout the western two-thirds of the Peninsula from Yemen to southern Syria (Macdonald 2000: 72, n. 117, Macdonald and King 2000: 438). However, these can be no more than guesses, for it is highly unlikely that it will ever be possible to trace the processes by which these desert scripts developed, since they are represented only by the handwritings of thousands of individuals for which we very rarely have any secure dating evidence. Thus, unless these circumstances change dramatically, any attempt to trace their development can be no more than sterile speculation.

[98] Whether Taymanitic was another is uncertain. The vast majority of the texts have been found outside the oasis and while they generally use word-dividers, they do not employ unidirectional writing or *matres lectionis*. Only three texts are known in the Dumaitic script, apparently used in the oasis of Dūmā (al-Jawf), and all these read from right-to-left, though, given the small numbers, this is hardly significant, especially since they are all on the same rock-face. Only one employs word-dividers (WTI 23) and the only indication of a *mater lectionis* is in the word *wddy* at the end of WTI 23, which Winnett interprets as 'my love'. However, cf. *s*[1]*ʿd-n* in the same text, where if Winnett's translation 'help me', is correct one would expect *-*ny*. The Dispersed Oasis North Arabian inscriptions (see Macdonald 2000: 33, 42–43) are generally too short, and often too enigmatic, to provide useful evidence in this respect.

[99] The Hismaic script was formerly called 'Thamudic E', 'Tabuki Thamudic' and, misleadingly, 'South Safaitic'; see Macdonald 2000: 35, 44–45. Geraldine King (1990b) first clearly defined the characteristics of the Hismaic script and language. More work is now needed to identify the distribution and background of the texts, as far as this is discernible. See most recently Macdonald and King 2000: 437–38.

[100] See, for instance, Daviau *et al.* 2000: 279–80. The presence of some of these texts on door-frames and other architectural elements of houses is not unfortunately conclusive evidence that they were written by sedentaries, since the texts are graffiti, not monumental inscriptions, have no particular function in their architectural context and contain no information indicating the way-of-life of their authors. See Macdonald, in prep.

[101] It will be seen from the script table in Macdonald 2000: 34 that the Hismaic signs for *g*, *ḥ*, s^2, *ṭ*, *ṯ* and *ẓ* are either identical or very similar to the Safaitic signs for *ṯ*, *ḏ*, *n*, *ḥ*, *ḍ* and *z* respectively. On the other hand, other signs in Hismaic, e.g. those for *ḍ*, *ḏ*, *ġ* and *z* are quite different from their equivalents in Safaitic.

When the nomad returned from the settlement to his tent, he would have found little to write on but rocks. It is therefore not surprising that we have no evidence that any of these nomads used the script for any practical (let alone economic) purpose within their society.[102] Well over 20,000 Safaitic inscriptions are known today, and one stumbles over thousands more whenever one goes into the basalt desert. Almost as many are known in the Hismaic and Thamudic B, C and D and Southern Thamudic scripts.[103] Yet virtually all these texts are graffiti and in none of them is there any evidence that writing served a practical purpose. However, this does not necessarily mean that they were all purely frivolous. The solitary writing of graffiti in the middle of the desert, as well as passing the time, seems often to have served as an emotional outlet for these nomads, just as it can for others in other circumstances.[104]

Nomadic life entails a great deal of hanging around, guarding the flocks while they pasture, keeping watch for enemies or for game, etc. and in most cases this is a solitary vigil. Before they learnt to read and write, these nomads used to carve their tribal marks on the rocks or make drawings, as they still do. Literacy, it seems, added an extra pastime with almost endless possibilities. The writing materials—sharp stones and rocks—were available in infinite quantities and the process of inscribing was sufficiently slow and arduous to fill hours and hours.

Thus, writing in these societies fulfilled a real need in the lives of individuals, not in the practical, material and economic spheres with which

[102] Harris is incorrect in stating that 'precisely because of the nomadic character of the peoples in question, graffiti acquired among them a surprisingly wide range of functions. Circumstances encouraged them to leave written messages in order to maintain contact with each other and to establish rights to wells and camping places' (1989: 189–90, n.79). This unfortunately, betrays a lack of knowledge of the content and distribution of the Safaitic inscriptions. Not one of them contains a 'message' or a private property notice, and 98% of them are carved on stones and rocks amid millions of others in the basalt scatter on the desert floor and so would usually only be discovered by accident. This very 'sedentary' view of the uses of writing also betrays an ignorance of the conditions of nomadic life where the concept of personal real estate does not exist and where 'private property' notices would be incomprehensible and unenforceable. Similar confusions are evident in the hypotheses put forward in Robin 2001: 569–70.

[103] On these see Macdonald 2000: 33–35, 43–45; Macdonald and King 2000.

[104] It is interesting to compare the open tone of the Ancient North Arabian graffiti, and the frankness with which their authors express emotions such as grief, fear and occasionally lust, with the poetic mediaeval Arabic graffiti collected (and only occasionally invented!) by the author of the *Udabāʾ al-ġurabāʾ* (or *Kitāb al-ġurabāʾ*) 'The Book of Strangers' (Crone and Moreh 2000). As the translators say of the content of these texts, 'educated men were trained to be reticent about themselves, but they speak with relative freedom in their informal graffiti. Some positively pour out their hearts to unknown passers-by ... clearly feeling free to do so because they would never meet the readers. Passers-by would often add responses even though the original writer was unlikely ever to see them....' (ibid. 9). It was commonplace for a passer-by to add a note to a Safaitic graffito, saying that he had found it and (usually) was saddened. Often he weaves his text in amongst the letters of the first.

we are accustomed to associate it, but as a creative antidote to hours of solitary boredom. The use of the Tifinagh by the Tuareg serves a similar purpose, as well as having an important additional social function, in play. It should be clear from many of the examples discussed above that these are not merely perfectly valid functions for literacy, but are regarded as entirely sufficient in societies where either the materials and/or the social conditions and/or the external pressures do not exist for the written word to take on a wider range of functions.[105] We need to rid ourselves of the deterministic prejudice that all societies, once they have discovered literacy, will move inexorably towards modern Western concepts of its uses.

The content of these graffiti, when it is more than purely personal names, is concerned exclusively with nomadic life and 98% of them have been found in the desert and almost nowhere else. There is, therefore, no doubt that the vast majority of them were carved by nomads rather than by settled people. This raises the interesting question of why this should be. There is no apparent reason why the Safaitic script should not have been used in towns and villages, just as Greek was occasionally used in the desert.[106] Indeed, there is an unpublished Safaitic inscription, unfortunately of unknown provenance, whose author claims affiliation to the people of the town of Salkhad (Macdonald 1993: 348–49), and my friend and colleague Hussein Zeinaddin has recently discovered 400 Safaitic inscriptions among the villages on the eastern slopes of Jabal al-ʿArab/Jabal al-Druze, overlooking the desert.[107]

However, it is significant that virtually all of the latter were found in areas *between* the villages, and in the upper reaches of the wadis which run down into the desert, in places where animals are taken out to pasture. Thus, the shepherds or herdsmen who, if modern practice is a guide, may often have been nomads hired for their herding skills, would be in the same circumstances as those in the desert and in need of something to relieve boredom.

[105] This does not mean, of course, that, in such societies, writing is not occasionally used for more practical purposes. As mentioned in the previous section, short notes or simple tax returns are sometimes written in the Tifinagh, and Safaitic can be used to inscribe 'markers' identifying the person buried under a cairn. But these exceptions do not alter the principal function of writing in these societies, anymore than the occasional humorous graffito alters the fundamentally practical function of writing in modern Western societies.

[106] See the inscriptions mentioned above. There are, of course, a few graffiti in the desert carved by Greek-speakers from the settled regions. Perhaps the most poignant was found by F.V. Winnett and G. Lankester Harding at Jathūm, in the desert of north-eastern Jordan. It reads, 'Life is [worth] nothing. Diomedes the lyrist and Abchoros the barber, both went out into the desert with the commander of hoplites and were stationed near a place called *Siou* [i.e. the cairn of] *Abgar*' (Mowry 1953, with the reading of the penultimate word corrected by Schwabe 1954; SEG XVI, no. 819; for commentary see Macdonald 1993: 349–50).

[107] Zeinaddin 2000. These account for most of the 2% of Safaitic inscriptions *not* found in the desert as such, though see the next paragraph and Macdonald in press b.

These circumstances were not a normal part of agricultural or urban life, which does not normally require—or indeed allow—long hours of solitary idleness out in the open, and so provides neither the opportunity nor the necessity of carving graffiti on rocks as a pastime.

We have virtually no evidence for the extent of literacy in the countryside, or among the general population of the towns, of southern Syria in the Roman period.[108] Arguments can rage back and forth over the *probability* of whether individual literacy was necessary, desirable or generally achievable for these sectors of the population, but for the moment the debate is sterile since we lack the vital facts. Our ignorance is such that we cannot even be certain what language was in popular use in the towns and rural areas of the Ḥawrān at this time. It is usually assumed to have been Aramaic, though in fact there is little or no evidence one way or the other. The occasional Aramaic, and more frequent Greek, monumental inscriptions set up in the towns and villages of southern Syria are not evidence for the general use of these languages, let alone for general literacy in them, any more than Latin memorials in English country churches are evidence that Latin was widely spoken, or even read, in rural England at the times they were erected.[109]

Regardless of how widespread literacy may have been in southern Syria, these settled populations would have lacked the means and the opportunity to leave large numbers of personal inscriptions on durable materials in places where they would be undisturbed by future generations. So, even if there had been mass literacy in these areas at this period, we would be unlikely to find much evidence of it. The most we have are the signatures of sculptors on statues, reliefs and monumental inscriptions, which represent a handful of names but no other information beyond their professions.[110] Even in these

[108] Horsfall provides a salutary counter to Harris's too dismissive attitude to rural literacy in the Roman empire (Horsfall 1991: 65–66; cf. Harris 1989: 17 ['rural patterns of living are inimical to the spread of literacy'] and 191).

[109] There are innumerable examples from most literate cultures of cases where the symbolic value of monumental inscriptions is clearly more important than accessibility or legibility. The most famous of these is perhaps the great trilingual inscription of Darius the Great at Bīsutūn/Behistun in western Iran, on which see Tuplin in this volume. It was carved, with enormous labour, in Old Persian, Akkadian and Elamite, all cuneiform scripts not easily read at the best of times by the average passer-by. But this gigantic inscription was positioned so high that the text appears as no more than a blur when seen from the road below. Darius had, however, sent copies of the text (in various languages, including Aramaic) to all parts of his empire, so the content was broadcast, but not by the inscription. Henry Rawlinson was probably the first person to read the inscription itself in the two and a half thousand years since it was carved, when in 1835 he made his first descent on a rope from the top of the cliff to copy the texts. A different form of inaccessibility is represented by mediaeval Arabic monumental inscriptions in which the letters are woven into ever more complex calligraphic patterns until it becomes extremely difficult to disentangle the sense from the decoration.

[110] Thus, for instance, on a fragment of a statue base we read 'Shudū the mason' (Musée du Louvre AO 4491, Lyon no. 60/Brussels no. 81), while the base of a sculpture of an eagle bears

cases, we cannot be sure that these inscriptions were composed by the sculptors themselves rather than copied from a text provided by a scribe.

By contrast, the evidence for widespread literacy in the deserts east and south-east of the Ḥawrān and throughout western Arabia is abundant, and has survived because it is on durable surfaces in areas where, until very recently, there has been little subsequent disturbance. It is this, and the complete absence of even indirect evidence that these scripts were habitually used for writing on other materials, that makes them a peculiar exception to Alan Millard's very sensible warning quoted at the beginning of this paper. In these particular cases, one could almost say that the proportions are reversed and we are seeing the iceberg from below, that is, the vast majority of documents which were written in these societies have probably survived and only a relatively small percentage have been lost. At least, this seems to me the most reasonable conclusion to draw from the available evidence, but naturally it is only one possible interpretation and it may well be disproved by future discoveries.

Among these nomads, as with the Tuareg, writing seems to have been used for a very restricted range of purposes, though it will be clear that the particular forms of diversion afforded by the Tifinagh and by the Safaitic script differ. The Tifinagh seems very often to be used for communal amusement such as puzzles and competitions, or for brief messages and billets-doux, and, in the past at least, for solitary graffiti. On the other hand, virtually all the Safaitic inscriptions so far found are graffiti, and we have only a very little evidence that they were sometimes carved in company,[111]

the text carved in relief 'this is the eagle which Rabbū son of Ḥanīpū, the mason, made' (Musée de Suweidā' inv. 196, see Teixidor in Dentzer and Dentzer-Feydy 1991: 148 and pl. 24). The pedestal of a statue with a six-line honorific inscription, has the artist's signature along the bottom ''An'am son of 'Aṣbū the sculptor. Peace!' (LPNab 101, Musée de Suweidah no. 158), while on the arch of a niche another artist has signed his work in a crude *tabula ansata*, this time in Greek: Ταυηλος Ραββου τοῦ Σοχερου ἐπ[οίησεν] 'Tauēlos son of Rabbos son of Socheros made [it]' (Musée du Louvre AO 11079. Lyon no. 43/Brussels no. 71). On the lintel of a mausoleum inscribed in Greek and Nabataean (LPNab 105) the mason's 'signature' is as prominent as the name of the deceased, 'For Ṭaninū son of Ḥann'el [is] the funerary monument. Ḥūrū son of 'Ubayshat [was] the mason.' See Macdonald 2003: 45.

[111] See, for instance, LP 325 (Macdonald, Al Mu'azzin and Nehmé 1996: 467–72) where the author records that his father drew the picture for him while they were waiting, together with his brother, for the rest of the tribe to return from the annual migration. There are also occasions when two brothers each carved his name + *bn* but 'shared' their father's name, which they carved only once (e.g. WH 1754+1755, and in Hismaic KJC 716+716a). There are also the so-called 'joint texts', on which see Winnett and Harding 1978: 17. On a number of occasions, members of the same family have written their names and genealogies one below the other on the same stone. A remarkable example of this is a stone (at present unpublished) from WH Cairn 21 on which a father, his seven sons and his slave have written their inscriptions one below the other and separated by horizontal lines. Each says that he was involved in 'kidding' the goats (*scil.* helping them to give birth) in the same year. WH 1673, 1698 and 1725b (from the same cairn) are by three of these brothers and record the same activity, and the latter two are dated to the same year.

and none for the script being used to write messages.[112] However, the use of the scripts as pastimes is common to both cultures, as—it would appear—is the failure of literacy to penetrate the vital functions of the respective oral societies in which they were employed.

The habitual, informal use of these scripts is also suggested by the ways in which they were/are learnt. As we have seen in the first part of this paper, writing is of little practical use within nomadic societies, and even less if the script is incomprehensible in the world beyond the desert. As the example of the Rwala suggests, if literacy is of no practical use, there is clearly no point in organizing the formal teaching of it. Conventional letter orders, whose original principles of organization (if any) have been lost in the mists of time, and which simply have to be learnt by rote, are typical of school-taught literacy. Because the order is transmitted systematically and universally in formal teaching, it can then be used as a numbering system, either by giving the letters numerical values as in the Greek and in many Semitic alphabets, or by using the letters as a fixed sequence in lists, as we do with the Roman alphabet.

We know, from ethnographic observations, that the Tifinagh are spread via children's games,[113] and we suspect that Safaitic was spread in an equally informal way. There is no conventional letter order for either script, a pretty clear indication of the lack of formal teaching. The Tuareg are proud of this and say 'all the signs are equal' and so one can say them in whatever order one wishes,[114] and, as mentioned above, children tend to pick them up piecemeal in games. However, in two areas, a mnemonic technique for remembering them has been reported. This consists of a formula which contains almost all the letters, those which are missing being learnt later one by one. In Ahaggar the formula is: 'This is I, Fadimata daughter of Ourenis who say: Fadimata, one doesn't touch her hips; her dowry is sixteen horses'. The first phrase contains the formula which normally marks the beginning of a text in the Tifinagh *awa năk* ..., 'It is I, N', which also plays the vital role of indicating the direction of the writing.[115] The mnemonic technique here is similar to that of the phrase 'the quick brown fox jumped over the lazy dog', traditionally used to display all the letters of the English alphabet.

112 Of course, this does not mean that it never happened, simply that, if it did, such messages have not survived, presumably because they were written on perishable surfaces rather than rocks. We also have no references, either in the graffiti or in external sources, to the script being used in this way.

113 See above and Aghali-Zakara and Drouin 1973–79: 280–84.

114 Aghali-Zakara and Drouin 1973–79: 251. There is apparently one exception, in the Dinnig, where the order is said to be fixed, according to a legendary tradition, though Aghali-Zakara and Drouin suspect it is based on a number of different mnemonic techniques (1973–79: 252).

115 Aghali-Zakara and Drouin 1973–79: 282–83; Aghali-Zakara 1999: 109–10; and, on the opening formula, see Aghali-Zakara and Drouin 1973–79: 261–62 and Drouin 2003.

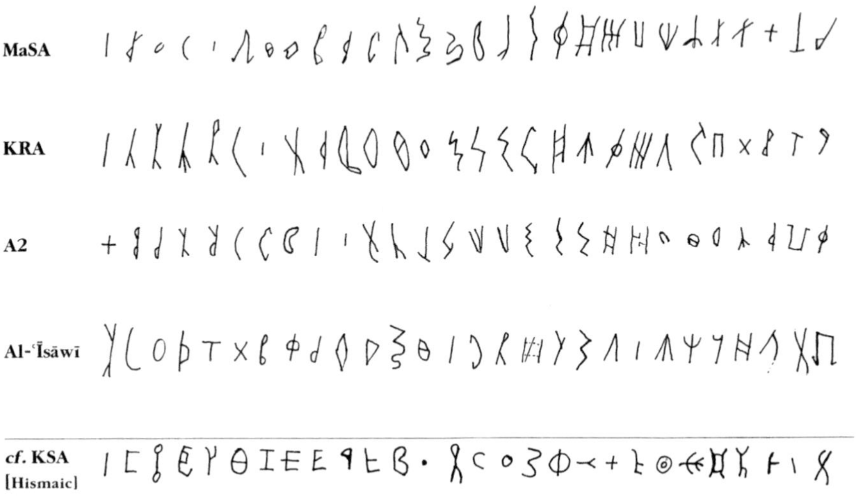

MaSA:	*l ṣ ʿ b n ẓ w g ṯ d r k s^2 f m h ḡ q ḍ ṭ s^1 ḥ ḍ ʾ ẖ t z y*
KRA:	*l h ʾ ḏ ṣ b n ẖ d m g w ʿ s^2 ḡ f r ḍ ḥ q ṭ s^1 k ẓ t ṯ z y*
A2:	*t ṯ y ʾ ṣ b r m l n ẖ h z k ḥ s^1 s^2 ḡ f ḍ ṭ ʿ w g ḏ d ẓ q*
Al-ʿĪsāwī:	*ʾ b {g] d z t ṯ q y m {ʿ} s^2 w l r ṣ ṭ h f s^1 n ḥ ḏ ḡ ḍ k ẖ ẓ*
KSA [Hismaic]	*l b g d h w z ḥ ṭ. y k m n ṣ r ʿ f q s^1 t ḡ ḍ ḏ ṯ ʾ ẓ s^2 ẖ*

Fig. 4. Four different ways of setting out the letters of the Safaitic alphabet according to the shapes of the letters. At the bottom, the Hismaic alphabet in an attempt at the abjad *order.*[116]

We now have four examples of the Safaitic alphabet written out,[117] in each of which the letters have been arranged in a different order, none of them a conventional *abjad* or *hlḥm* (Fig. 4).[118] In each, the letters have been grouped according to the similarities which the particular writer perceived in

116 In order to maintain comparable sizes, the letters have been copied free-hand from photographs of the inscriptions and so give an impression, rather than a precise reproduction, of their exact shapes (for which see the published photographs). The stances of the letters have been reproduced as they appear in the original, allowing for the fact that only A2 was carved in a straight line. The position on the stone of the last three letters of KRA means that they could equally well be read in the order *y z ṯ* or *z ṯ* (as in King 1990a: 62, 76) or *ṯ z y* (as here).

117 These are MaSA (in Macdonald 1986: 101–5); KRA (in King 1990a: 62–63, 74, 76); A2 (in Macdonald, Al Muʾazzin and Nehmé 1996: 439–43); 'al-ʿĪsāwī' (one found by the Safaitic Epigraphic Survey Programme at al-ʿĪsāwī the publication of which is in preparation).

118 The *abjad* is (the Arabic form of) the name of the traditional order of the Phoenico-Aramaic alphabet, from which we get our 'ABC'. For a discussion of the Ancient North Arabian letter-orders see Macdonald 1986 (supplemented by 1992) and, more recently, Macdonald, Al Muʾazzin and Nehmé 1996: 439–43. The *hlḥm* is the traditional order of the 'Arabian' or 'South Semitic' alphabet, now known from several examples in the Ancient South Arabian script, and traces of which are

their shapes.[119] It is interesting that, of these four, two begin with the letter *l*, the introductory particle (the *lām auctoris*) which marks the beginning of 99% of all Safaitic inscriptions, with the letters *b-n* (which spell *bn* 'son of' and form the commonest combination of letters in these texts) following shortly after, i.e. in imitation of a graffito. The *b* is usually open in the direction the text is running and, like the initial identifying formula in texts in the Tifinagh, serves to indicate the direction of the inscription.[120]

By contrast, the only known Ancient North Arabian alphabetic letter order in a script habitually used by a settled, literate society, follows the *hlḥm* order.[121] There is a very interesting example of a hybrid letter order in the Hismaic script, the errors and anomalies in which suggest that it was a joint effort between someone familiar with the *abjad* letter order but not the script and someone who knew the script but not the letter order. This begins with *l*, instead of *ʾ*, and then continues *b-g-d-h-w-z* etc.[122] Similarly, among the Tuareg, we find that when a person literate in French or Arabic lists the Tifinagh letters, he generally follows the conventional order of the foreign alphabet in which he is literate, with modifications for letters which do not correspond (Aghali-Zakara and Drouin 1973–79: 252). The Hismaic *abjad* provides a close parallel to this.[123]

A lack of formal teaching would suggest that there were also no conventional or historical spellings and that the authors of these texts wrote phonetically, as they spoke (see section II, above). This is certainly the case with texts in the Tifinagh characters which reflect the different Berber dialects of their authors (Aghali-Zakara and Drouin 1973–79: 253–55). It is also noticeable in a more subtle way in what Aghali Zakara and Drouin call 'bi-

visible in the traditional order of the Ethiopic syllabary, or vocalized alphabet. See Ryckmans J. 1988; 1992: 316–19, and, for an excellent summary description, see Robin 1996: 1208–11.

119 This is less true of the alphabet from al-ʿĪsāwī, which interestingly begins *ʾ-b-{g}-d*, possibly reflecting a memory of contact with the *abjad* order, if the third letter is indeed *g* not *ʿ*. If this was the case, the memory was apparently very faint since after *d*, there are no further sequences from the conventional order.

120 Occasionally the *b* is turned at 90° in a decorative form of the script, and very rarely at 180° at the whim of the writer, and so does not perform this function.

121 This is in the Dadanitic script (formerly called Lihyanite, see Macdonald 2000: 33). It was first identified in the inscription JSLih 158 by W.W. Müller (1980: 70) and was discussed in more detail in Macdonald 1986: 112–15 (where fig. 5 has been printed upside-down!).

122 KSA from Khirbat al-Samrāʾ in north-eastern Jordan. It was first published in Knauf 1985, see the discussion in Macdonald 1986: 107–12, and 1992.

123 Thus, the letter *ṣ* is in the place of *samekh* (see Macdonald 1992 for an explanation of this) and, very curiously, this is followed by *r*. *S*^{1} is in the place of *šīn*, as is to be expected (see Macdonald 1986: 110; 2000: 45–6, Fig. 5; 2004: 498–500). At the end of the *abjad*, after *t*, come the letters *ḡ ḍ ḏ ṯ ʾ ẓ s*^{2} *ẖ* which had been omitted, either by accident (in the case of *ʾ*) or because there was no traditional place for them in the *abjad* (see Macdonald 1986: 111–12, and 1992).

consonnes', or what might perhaps be better termed 'monograms'.[124] These are not ligatures in the typographical sense, but are representations of two or three consonants by a single sign which is distinct from each of the signs of which it is composed. Only certain consonant clusters are susceptible to being represented in this way and only when the consonants represented are in a *phonetic juxtaposition* rather than simply adjacent in the *scriptio continua* which is normally employed in these texts (see below).[125] Thus, only consonants which, in speech, are not separated by a vowel, are treated in this way, and, given this condition, a monogram can cross morphemic boundaries, for instance joining the last and first consonants of two successive pronominal suffixes on a verb, see the examples in Aghali-Zakara and Drouin 1973–79: 264–67. This shows very clearly the primacy of speech in the use of writing in this society. To repeat Galand's telling description 'le berbère offre l'étrange particularité d'être une langue orale pourvue d'une écriture' (1989: 344), a statement which would hold equally well for the languages of the nomads who wrote the Ancient North Arabian inscriptions.

That those who wrote the Safaitic inscriptions wrote 'phonetically' is neatly illustrated by a text recently discovered in southern Syria[126] in which the author betrays a very different accent from that of the others who wrote these graffiti. He spells the word which elsewhere in Safaitic universally occurs as *q-y-ẓ* (meaning 'he spent the dry season') as *ʾ-y-ḍ* (i.e. with *hamza* for /q/ and *ḍād* for /ẓ/) which is how it would be pronounced today in Damascus, Beirut or Jerusalem. As far as I know, this spelling is by far the

124 Aghali-Zakara and Drouin 1973–79: 255–59, 262–63, 264–67. Galand understandably prefers the term 'ligature' ("caractère représentant plusieurs lettres en un seul signe graphique") 'pour prévenir la confusion, trop fréquente, entre la terminologie de l'écriture et celle de la phonétique' (2002a: 8 and note 5). Unfortunately, however, in English typography the term 'ligature' is used of signs such as æ, œ, fi and fl which are composed simply by removing the space between the two letters, whereas the Tifinagh 'monogram' is a new sign, sometimes consisting of a simple combination of the two characters it represents (e.g. a circle [= /r/] and three dots [= /k/] become three dots within a circle [= /rk/]), but often being formed by the removal of an element from one of the signs (e.g. /j/ is represented by two vertical lines crossed by two horizontals, /nj/ is represented by two verticals crossed by *one* horizontal), or by turning it at 90° (e.g. /b/ is represented by a circle crossed by a vertical line, /mb/ is represented by a circle crossed by a horizontal line). For other examples, see Aghali-Zakara and Drouin 1973–79: 258–59, 262–63. I have therefore, *faute de mieux*, used the not entirely satisfactory term 'monogram' for these composite signs.

125 Aghali-Zakara and Drouin 1973–79: 256. 'il s'agit, pour les Kel Tamasheq [the Touraeg name for themselves], et dans l'utilisation de ces signes, de "lier le sens" et d' "associer des sons"'. Galand makes the interesting observation that 'on ne connaît aucun exemple de ligature [i.e. monogram] associant deux consonnes identiques, ce qui tendrait à montrer que les consonnes tendues ne sont pas senties comme des géminées' (1996). See further Galand 1997.

126 The inscription was found by the Safaitic Epigraphic Survey Programme in 2000 and will be published in the project's final report which is in preparation. For another very interesting case, this time in a Hismaic inscription from southern Jordan, see Macdonald in press c.

earliest evidence we have for this pronunciation, which is found in some early Arabic papyri and is nowadays typical of urban Arabic dialects.[127] Another example of writing 'as one speaks' can be seen in the frequent, but unsystematic, assimilation of [n] in the Safaitic inscriptions, a feature also common in texts written by English-speaking children who learn to write before they can read.[128]

In Safaitic, there is no set direction of writing and texts can run left-to-right, right-to-left, boustrophedon, up, down, round and round in circles or in a coil, etc. The same is true for the Tifinagh, though in practice there are not as many variations. The Tuareg say that the deciding factor is the comfort of the writer, and it seems likely that the same was true for those who carved the Safaitic inscriptions. There are, of course, differences. Most Safaitic inscriptions are carved on basalt rocks or boulders with irregular and twisted shapes. A text could therefore be carved in whatever direction was most convenient to the author but it tended to be continuous, either boustrophedon or meandering over one or more faces of the rock according to the whim of the writer and the space available.[129] The Tuareg most often sit or recline on the ground and write with their fingers in the sand, though they also carve on rocks.[130] Since the determining factor is the writer's comfort, the distance a text can extend from his body is limited by the reach of his arm while in the position in which he is sitting or reclining. Traditionally, texts have been written from bottom-to-top either horizontally on the ground (i.e. going away from the writer's body) or (in the past) on a vertical rock-face. Because the writing is a slow process, by the time his arm has reached its furthest extent it is tired and so boustrophedon, which would require it to remain out-

[127] In his collection of early Arabic dialect features preserved in the works of the Arab grammarians and lexicographers, Kofler notes that the evidence for /q/ > /ʾ/ in the early Arabic dialects is 'nur sehr dürftig und dazu anonym' (1940: 115–16). I cannot find any reference to this feature in Hopkins 1984 or Blau 1966–67. The only reference to /ẓ/ > /ḍ/ which I can find in Kofler's collection is the dialectal pronunciation of the word *baẓr* as *baḍr* which is mentioned in passing in *Lisān al-ʿArab* (Kofler 1940: 95). Hopkins notes that the earliest certain occurrence of this feature in the early Arabic papyri dates from 101 A.H (1984: 38–40 § 39) and Blau gives some slightly later examples from Christian texts in southern Palestine (1966–67: 113–14). For these features in the modern dialects see Holes 1995: 56–59.

[128] See note 7.

[129] Compare the effects of the shape of the surface and the space available on the lay-out of texts carved on rocks in the Tifinagh (Drouin 1998). It is interesting to note that Jewish children in mediaeval Cairo seem to have learnt to *read* Hebrew from any angle. Since 'books were expensive and not always available for elementary teaching ... several children sat around a single book, and this effectively meant that they learnt to read it also sideways and even upside-down. This practice is well attested in Geniza fragments: in a letter by the dayyan R. Yehiel ben R. Elyakim, for example, children are said to learn to read the book from its four sides' (Olszowy-Schlanger 2003: 56).

[130] Coninck and Galand report that the Tifinagh are used for 'les graffiti amoureux que l'on trouve sur les parois des rochers ou les murs de terre des maisons de Tombouctou' (1957–60: 79).

stretched, is rarely used. Instead, the author brings his arm back close to the body and begins another line parallel with the first either to its right or its left.[131] This is the traditional way of writing the Tifinagh, as used by old people and women (who are generally not in contact with other scripts). However, it can also be written horizontally, from left to right by those who have been educated in French, and from right to left by those educated in Arabic.[132] Texts in the Tifinagh are normally only written in a circle or in spirals, in games.[133]

This lack of any fixed direction is another feature of a script used primarily for carving informal texts on stone or writing them in the sand, since habitual writing in ink tends to be the impetus to unidirectional writing, as a means of saving space and to avoid smudging what has just been written.[134] Neither the Safaitic script nor the Tifinagh developed ligatures between letters, since 'joined-up' writing is only helpful to someone habitually writing in ink, while for those who only carve on stone, or write slowly with their fingers in the sand, joining letters just makes more work.

Safaitic is written continuously without spaces or dividers between words. Word-division is a feature which provides clarity for the reader.[135] But if a script is used only for self-expression rather than for communication, for passing the time by carving one's thoughts on a rock among millions of

[131] Aghali-Zakara and Drouin 1973–79: 259–60. However, for some examples of graffiti in horizontal boustrophedon see Drouin 1996: 2.

[132] Some Libyco-Berber inscriptions were also written horizontally, perhaps under the influence of Latin or Punic (see, for instance, Galand 2000a: 5).

[133] Aghali-Zakara and Drouin 1973–79: 260–61. However, see line 4 of Lettre 14(a) in Galand 1999: 176ff., which begins in the middle of the page running left-to-right, then, when it nears the edge of the page, runs downwards before turning back to run right-to-left. This lay-out is mirrored in Lettre 17.

[134] It is interesting that, of the 33 extant messages written in the Tifinagh which Père de Foucauld received from members of the Tuareg Kel-Ahaggar, twenty are set out in parallel lines from right-to-left, almost as if the act of writing with ink encouraged this arrangement. On the other hand, it is clear that this lay-out was by no means habitual with these authors, since characters occasionally spill over the ends of lines and run boustrophedon or vertically (top-to-bottom and bottom-to-top), rather than being placed at the beginning of the next line (e.g. Lettres 12/10, 13/11, 16/2, etc.), though it is possible that this was done to avoid breaking an aural or semantic unit made up of words and particles (?). Moreover, the same authors who used this lay-out also wrote whole messages in vertical or horizontal boustrophedon or other arrangements. Compare, for instance, Lettres 1(a), 2, 3(a) and 4 (all written right to left in parallel lines) by Chikat ag Mokhammed, with Lettre 6 by the same person, which is written boustrophedon. See also the messages by Akhamouk agg Ihema, of which Lettre 10b is in horizontal boustrophedon, 15 is in vertical boustrophedon, and 16 is in parallel lines from right to left (apart from the last four characters of line 2).

[135] On the origins of word division in the Hebrew and Aramaic scripts see Millard 1970 and 1982: 147. Word division was a feature of the South Arabian formal (monumental) and informal (minuscule) scripts from earliest times and of the Ancient North Arabian scripts used by settled peoples (Dadanitic and possibly Taymantic). See note 98 above.

others in the desert, with no expectation that anyone will read it, the need for clarity, and hence word-division, does not arise.[136] Traditionally, word-dividers were also not used when writing in the Tifinagh,[137] possibly for similar reasons, though *scriptio continua* is also useful in writing games where the object is to hide the meaning from the reader, rather than to clarify it. The Safaitic alphabet is also entirely consonantal and does not show strengthened or doubled consonants and for the most part this is also true of the Tifinagh. Like word division, *matres lectionis* assist the reader more than the writer and so if a script is used more or less entirely for self-expression rather than for communication, there is little impetus to develop them. After all, the writer knows what he means and without *matres lectionis* he needs to carve fewer characters.

In view of all these features, I would suggest that these are scripts and orthographies whose development has been conditioned by the limited and very particular circumstances in which they were used, and this applies equally to the Hismaic, Thamudic B, C and D and Southern Thamudic alphabets, none of which seem to have been the scripts of literate societies. In this, they are in stark contrast with Dadanitic which makes a systematic, if minimal, use of *matres lectionis*.[138]

In modern times, attempts have been made to print Christian religious texts and, in Niger, government publications, in the Tifinagh characters (Fig. 5). But it is significant that once the script began to be used for 'literate' purposes, its shortcomings were widely felt. Various schemes for showing vowels were developed,[139] the direction of writing was stabilized, letter forms were stan-

[136] Of course, in other circumstances, there are other reasons for employing *scriptio continua*, as in Classical Greek inscriptions and manuscripts. Some of the earliest Greek inscriptions employ word-dividers and punctuation, but these were later abandoned both in handwriting and in inscriptions (Thomas 1992: 87–88). Ann Hanson, discussing scribes writing Greek in Roman Egypt, gives a description of the process, which would apply to most Greek documentary papyri of the period: 'professional scribes that worked in the government bureaux produced a cursive writing that flowed swiftly and smoothly over the papyrus; individual letters seldom received full articulation, and the scribe's nubbed pen remained in contact with the surface of the papyrus, producing a chain of letters joined together in ligature .... The scribe continued to write on until a shortage of ink impelled him to lift his pen and refill' (1991: 173). Thus, the use of *scriptio continua* would not, by itself, be an argument that the Safaitic script or the Tifinagh were used more for writing than reading. However, taken with the content of the texts, with the features of the scripts already mentioned, and with what we know of the uses of the Tifinagh, it fits very well into the working hypothesis I have presented.

[137] Nowadays, young people who have learnt Arabic and/or French at school tend to import the concept of word-division from these scripts when they write the Tifinagh (Aghali-Zakara and Drouin: 1973–79: 263).

[138] See Drewes 1985 and Macdonald 2004: 495. On the possible use of *matres lectionis* in Sabaic see Robin 2001: 570–77.

[139] See, for instance, Coninck and Galand 1957–60 on the use by the Kel Antessar (an Arabized tribe in the region of Timbuktu, Mali) of the Arabic signs *fatḥah, kasrah,* and *ḍammah*

ϟ+El ⋯ +IICE ⊙ EⵔI +II⦂·C
aytedən akh təlmaad as dasən-təlaakkəm.

EꞀO +⦂·O⦂·E+ +· E+ꞀCIIO+ +I CE⦂
dəffər təkərakit̂ ta əd-təfəllist ten əmmədu

ℸCE ⦂O E⦂⦂II +CE+ I+ ⦂O Ꞁ⦂
igmə͡d, wər-d-iqqel təmidit net har fəw.

Fig. 5. A page from a brochure issued about 1970 by the Service de l'alphabétisation et education des adultes, Niger. Text in modified Tifinagh characters with a transcription into Roman letters. (Reproduced from Galand 1989: 339, by kind permission of Professor L. Galand and the publishers Helmut Buske Verlag, Hamburg).

dardized, and even a 'cursive version' was developed (see Aghali-Zakara 1993: 147).

It is important to remember that the people using the Safaitic alphabet and the Tifinagh characters, even if fully literate in these scripts (and sometimes others), lived in non-literate societies in which, as far as we can see, literacy had taken over none of the functions of memory and oral communication. In the case of Safaitic, in one or two respects, writing was used to enhance existing customs, such as the practice of burying beloved or respected individuals under large cairns to which each of the mourners brought a stone.

on the Tifinagh characters to show both long and short vowels, as well as *sukūn* and *šaddah*. compare the uses of the Vai script in urban contexts, described in note 26.

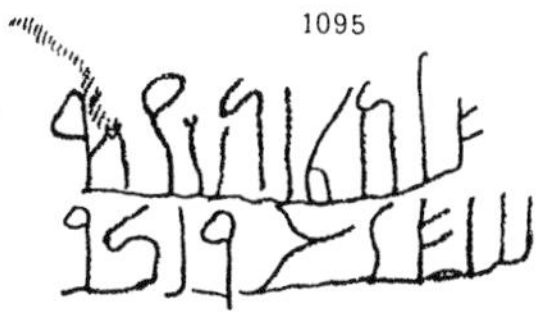

1095 **šlm ʾlmbqrw**
br nšygw b-ṭb

1108 **šlm ʾwšw br klbw w-klbw br{-h} b-ṭb**

566 **dkyr ʾṣlḥw**
br yʿly

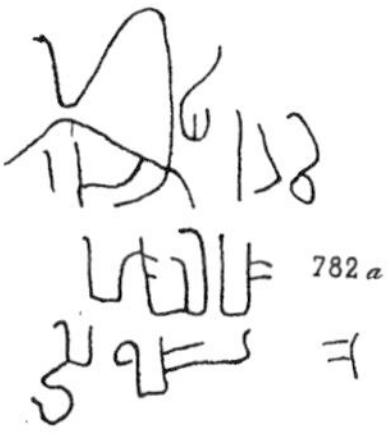

782 **ʾbnʾl{h}{y}**
šlm ḥr-
yšw b{l}y [?]

788 **dkyr ʿlm**
b-ṭb ʿmrw
ʾšbt{y} Y

952 **šl{m} šl{m} šlm {š}mr-**
{ḥ}w br ʾt-
mw bṭb

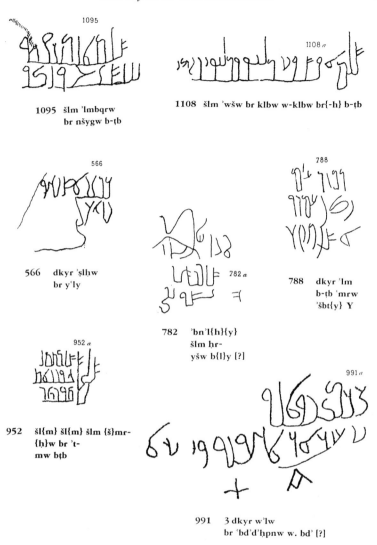

991 **3 dkyr wʾlw**
br ʿbdʾdʾḥpnw w. bdʾ [?]

Fig. 6. Examples of Nabataean graffiti from Sinai (from CIS ii). See note 142.

With the advent of literacy, some mourners inscribed the stones they placed on the cairn, giving their name and the name of the deceased and sometimes their relationship to him or her, but this is an enhancement of, not a great departure from, previous practice.[140]

[140] See Harding 1953: 8; and the discussion in Macdonald in press b. See also Lancaster W. and Lancaster F. 1993 for an interesting study of modern burials of a similar kind, though with possibly significant differences.

I would suggest that another example of writing used for play can be found in the 'Nabataean' graffiti in Sinai. These provide an interesting example of the use of an alphabet and orthography which had developed as the script of a literate society, being used predominantly by members of what was probably an oral one.[141] Nabataean is a ligatured script and, as I have said, this is more of a nuisance than an advantage to those who write only on stone. So, one might have expected that the population of Sinai would have adapted it by dropping the ligatures and writing each letter separately. Some did, but others went to the opposite extreme and, if anything, increased the number of ligatures and played with the letter-shapes and the joins between them with an extraordinary exuberance (Fig. 6).[142] This playful attitude to writing is of course an occasional feature of graffiti everywhere. There are examples of mirror-writing,[143] names made into drawings,[144] etc.[145] An interesting example can be seen in the Safaitic text from Jordan on Fig. 7 where the letter *ʿayn* (literally 'eye') has been given a pupil and the letter *yôd* (literally 'forearm', 'hand') has been given fingers.[146] This suggests that, despite there being no evidence for formal teaching of writing, this author at least was aware of the traditional names of the letters. Some letters have different names in the Phoenico-Aramaic and the Arabian alphabetic

[141] I say 'predominantly' because, while most of the Nabataean texts in Sinai seem to have been carved by local herdsmen and others, a significant number were almost certainly the work of pilgrims and travellers who are likely to have had quite different attitudes to writing.

[142] Thus, for instance, on Fig. 6 in nos 1095, 1108 and lines 2 and 3 of 952 a line has been drawn along the bases of the letters regardless of whether or not they 'should' be joined. In 1108, certain letters contrast with the rest by being joined at their tops. In 566, the *l* of the last name (*ʿly*) is joined at its top to the line linking the first four letters in the line above, and at its base to the final *y*, producing a sort of reversed 'Z' (or perhaps an enormous final *y*?). In 782 the joins are used to form bizarre patterns, whereas in 788 they have been all but eliminated. The *l* of the second *šlm* in 952 is simply an extension of the stem of the *š* and it shares its *m* with the first *šlm*, etc.

[143] See, at random, Euting 1885: 10, fig. 6 'Kufi 1' (Arabic) on which now see al-Moraekhi 2002: 123–25, and the excellent photograph in Deputy Ministry of Antiquities and Museums of Saudi Arabia 2003, vii: 115. For another such Arabic inscription, see Moraekhi 2002: 125–128. A Greek example can be seen below CIS ii 969 (CIS ii.1.3.Pl. LXXVII).

[144] At random, CIL.IV, nos 4742 and 4755 (Latin from Pompeii, on which see Franklin 1991: 94), Moritz 1908: 407, no. 4, where the *s*^{1} of the name *Bʾs*^{1} has been turned into a drawing of a man in the Thamudic B inscription *l bʾs*^{1} *h- rgl* 'the man is by Bʾs^1'.

[145] Sometimes 'playing' with letters could apparently be for serious purposes as in Greek curse tablets of the fifth and fourth centuries BC (Thomas 1992: 80).

[146] This text (Wādī Irenbeh 1) reads *l s*^{1}*kʿ bn ʾs*^{2}*ym* 'By S^{1}kʿ son of ʾs^{2}ym'. The inscription along the right edge of the stone (Wādī Irenbeh 2) reads *l ḥrkn bn s*^{2}*kr* 'By Ḥrkn son of S^{2}kr' and the third text (Wādī Irenbeh 3) reads *l yṯʿ bn rbn* 'By Ythʿ son of Rbn'. All the names are attested except the first in text 1. Cf. Arabic *sākiʿ* 'aimless wanderer, sleep-walker, intruder, stranger'.

Fig. 7. A Safaitic inscription from Wādī Irenbeh in north-eastern Jordan.

traditions, but *ʿayn* is the same in both and *y* is called *yôd* ('forearm', 'hand') in the former and *yaman* ('right hand')[147] in the latter.[148]

The Safaitic graffiti often contain considerably more information than those of other literate nomads such as the Tuareg, or those who wrote the Hismaic graffiti in southern Jordan and northern Saudi Arabia, or the Thamudic B, C and D and Southern Thamudic graffiti in various parts of the Peninsula. Although the majority of Safaitic texts consist of the author's name and part of his genealogy, a large minority of authors go on to say what they were doing or feeling and to date their texts by events of importance in the desert or in the wider world, about both of which they were generally well-informed. A large number end with prayers, mostly for security, often for rain or a change of circumstances, and very often invoking curses on those who vandalize the inscription and blessings on those who leave it alone. It is clear that this was a necessary precaution, since vandalising other people's inscriptions (often in subtle and mischievous ways) seems to have been a pastime second only in popularity to writing one's own!

It is also important to remember that these literate nomads almost certainly coexisted with other nomads and with sedentaries who either spoke

[147] If one assumes the 'hand' in the inscription is facing palm outwards, it would be a *right* hand. But, of course, there is no way of knowing this.

[148] On the letter names in the Arabian ('South Semitic') alphabetic tradition see Ryckmans J. 1988: 225–27. There appear to be no traditional names for the Tifinagh letters and in the Hoggar 'the letters have names which are formed by prefixing *yă* to the represented consonants, e.g. *yăb* "letter b"' (van den Boogert 2000: 476) whereas in other regions the names are formed with pre-fixed and suffixed vowels e.g. əmma (= m) (Aghali-Zakara and Drouin 1973–79: 249).

unwritten languages, such as Arabic,[149] or who spoke, but were illiterate in, such written languages as Aramaic, Greek or Sabaic.

Many of those who speak unwritten languages live in non-literate societies and so exist entirely without writing. But this is not always the case. Although their immediate community may remain non-literate, it may exist within a larger literate society, as is the case today in Oman and Yemen with speakers of the Modern South Arabian languages (Jibbālī, Mahrī, etc.). If a speaker of an unwritten language needs to write something down he has two choices. He can write, or commission, a text in a written language. Or, alternatively, he can try to write down what he wants to say in his spoken tongue using a script normally associated with another language. Thus, if a speaker of, say, Jibbālī in Dhofar wants to put something in writing, he would either have to write (or have something written for him) in Arabic, or—if he was able to—he could write his spoken language in Arabic letters, as has occasionally been done. Normally, it would only be worth doing the second for personal satisfaction, or to make a political point, or if he was in a society where relatively large numbers of people both understood his spoken language and could read the script. This is how Old Arabic[150] came to be written occasionally in the Sabaic, Dadanitic, Nabataean and other scripts. It was probably also how the Nabataean alphabet, as it came to be used more and more to transcribe spoken Arabic, gradually came to be thought of as the 'Arabic script'.[151]

An example of how easy it is for this to happen occurred at the site of Lachish in Palestine. When the Lachish letters were discovered during the excavations there in 1935 (see Torczyner *et al.* 1938), Gerald Lankester Harding, as a joke, taught the ancient Hebrew script of the letters to his Bedouin workmen, who were completely illiterate in Arabic. They picked it up immediately and began to write their spoken Arabic dialect in the ancient Hebrew script. Of course, they were writing only simple notes to Gerald Harding and to each other and were doing so just for fun, but this story illustrates how easy it is for someone with a well-trained memory to pick up not merely the letter-forms, but the concept of dividing units of sense (that is words) into sounds, and expressing each of these by a particular sign. Indeed, in this case the process was even more complicated since they were having to express the approximately 28 consonants of their spoken Arabic dialect by the mere 22 letters of the Hebrew alphabet. So they had to learn which sounds to omit and which letters had to do duty for more than one sound. Yet they

[149] See below.

[150] That is Arabic from the pre-Islamic period as it has been preserved independently of the Arab grammarians and lexicographers of the early Islamic period. For more details see Macdonald 2000: 36–37, 48–54, 61; and in press d.

[151] See Macdonald 2000: 57–60. See also, Kropp 1997–98: 93 on the general point of spoken languages written in 'borrowed' scripts.

had no problem in picking up both the principle and the practice, just as the ancient nomads learnt the different orthographic rules for writing Greek and Safaitic.

Could this be a clue to a famous incident in the early history of the Nabataeans, when they were still nomadic? As is well known, in 312 BC Antigonus the One-eyed sent an army to pillage the Nabataeans (Diodorus Siculus: 19.94.1–19.100.3). The latter, after giving chase, punished his army 'manfully' (as Diodorus puts it), recovered the booty and *wrote him a letter*. This in itself would be an unusual thing for nomads to do at any time, but the story is made more curious by Diodorus' description of the letter as being 'in Syrian [i.e. Aramaic] characters'.[152] There is not enough evidence to be sure what language the Nabataeans spoke at this time, but if they had written the letter in the Aramaic language, one might have expected Diodorus to have said so, rather than specifying that it was in Aramaic *letters*. It therefore seems to me possible that if the Nabataeans at this time spoke Arabic, for instance, they might have dictated the text of the letter in that language and the scribe could have written it in the Aramaic alphabet, there being, of course, no Arabic script at the time.

If the story of the letter has any historical basis, one has also to think of the practical implications. The letter would have had to be delivered to Antigonus by the most august ambassador the Nabataean nomads could find. He would almost certainly have recited the contents of the letter in his own language, say Arabic or Aramaic—or possibly using Aramaic as a vehicular language—and an interpreter would have translated it into Greek for Antigonus. In none of this would the written text of the letter have been necessary, since the ambassador would have had to have had his piece by heart. Moreover, if the letter was not in the Aramaic language but in another tongue set down in Aramaic letters, it would probably have been more or less incomprehensible to Antigonus' chancellery, even if it still contained Aramaeophone clerks. The letter, therefore, would simply have been a theatrical prop, to add dignity to the Nabataeans' embassy. If so, it would be a rather unexpected, but by no means unique, use of literacy by members of a non-literate society in contact with a literate one. Of course, we are unlikely ever to know whether the letter actually existed or whether Diodorus, or his source, simply invented the story, so this must remain pure speculation.

I would like to end by proposing hypotheses on the origins of three ancient documents, which, I would suggest, can be better understood in the light of the discussion in this paper, and each of which may illustrate a different aspect of the interplay of literate and non-literate communities. I emphasize that these are speculations—alas, the evidence is too fragmentary

[152] ἐπιστολὴν γράψαντες Συρίοις γράμμασι (Diodorus 19.96.1).

[153] See Macdonald 2000: 36–37, 48–54, and in press d, Robin 2001: 564–65, and on the Jabal Says graffito Robin and Gorea 2002.

for anything else—but, as long as this is recognized, these hypotheses may, I hope, be of some interest.

Arabic, apparently, remained a mainly spoken language until the sixth century AD, when the first documents in the 'Arabic script' appear.[153] Thus, before that time, many Arabic-speakers would have been in the position of Jibbālī or Mahrī speakers today: that is inhabiting an 'oral enclave' within a society which was literate in a different language. I have described elsewhere some of the different ways in which individuals coped with this interface between orality and literacy and the hybrid texts which resulted (Macdonald 2000: 48–60).

There is no doubt that the settled Nabataean kingdom was a literate society, in the sense of my initial definition. Yet I think it may be possible to identify an oral enclave at its very heart. In the fourth century AD, Epiphanius reports that the Nabataeans sang hymns to their deities in Arabic.[154] Since Arabic was still at that time an unwritten language, this suggests that the liturgies, possibly of great antiquity, would have been passed by word of mouth from one generation of priests to the next and that habitual worshippers may have had at least parts of them off by heart. In the Negev, within sight of the cult centre of the deified Nabataean king Obodas, lies a rock on which a six-line inscription has been carved in the Nabataean alphabet.[155] The author, a certain Garmallahi son of Taymallahi, records that he dedicated a statue to Obodas the god and he follows this statement with two lines of Arabic, written in 'Aramaic letters', which look as if they might come from the liturgy in praise of Obodas. If this is so, and it can be no more than an hypothesis, Garmallahi may have wanted to quote what was for him a particularly appropriate section of the liturgy and so transcribed this passage into Nabataean letters. Interestingly, the inscription opens with blessings on whoever reads (and therefore inevitably recites)[156] the text.

[154] 'Αραβικῇ διαλέκτῳ ἀξυμνοῦσι. Epiphanius of Eleutheropolis [Beit Jibrīn], Bishop of Salamis (AD 315–403), *Panarion* 51.22.11.

[155] See Negev, Naveh and Shaked 1986. The text has been treated by a considerable number of authors. For one of the most recent discussions and an extensive bibliography see Lacerenza 2000. Elsewhere, I have compared this text with the inscription at Qāniya in Yemen which is in the Sabaic script but apparently in the (normally unwritten) Himyaritic language (Macdonald 1998: 181). For a careful and extremely interesting assessment of current thinking on this text see Robin 2001: 516–22, and for a summary of recent work on the Himyaritic language ibid. 522–28.

[156] The verb used is *qr'*. Unfortunately, direct evidence from the ancient Near East for reading silently or aloud seems to be extremely thin, but the dual meanings in East and many Central Semitic languages of the verb *qr'* (i.e. 'to read' *and* 'to say something out loud [recite, call, shout, invoke, summon, name]') suggest that reading aloud may have been the norm. See, for instance, Koehler and Baumgartner 1994–2000, iii: 1128–31 for a convenient brief summary of the different meanings in different languages. Professor Galand has kindly informed me that in Berber, particularly in the dialects used in southern Morocco, 'le même verbe ğr ... est employé à la fois pour "appeler", "crier" et "lire". Il s'agit, me semble-t-il d'un héritage commun plutôt que

For it should be remembered that silent reading was a relatively rare accomplishment before the late Middle Ages, and thus the distinction between reading and recitation was far less clear-cut than it is today.[157] This is exemplified in the Arabic verb *qara'a* (and its Aramaic cognate used in this text) which, from pre-Islamic times to the present today has meant both 'to read' and 'to recite'. The habit of reading aloud had profound influence on the form and nature of writing in public places and was one of the principal ways in which illiterates in a literate society received information displayed in writing. It needed only one person actually to read the inscription and the crowd around him would automatically receive its content. It has been suggested that in Archaic Greece the custom of expressing tomb-inscriptions in the first person may have developed so that when a passer-by read the inscription he would speak the name of the deceased.[158] One such tomb-inscription even thanks the passer-by for 'lending his voice' in this way (Thomas 1992: 64). This is paralleled by a Hismaic inscription from central Jordan which invokes a blessing on a particular individual and 'every true friend' and extends this blessing to 'anyone who reads [i.e. recites] this our inscription', presumably because by so doing the reader will have invoked the blessing, out loud, once more.[159] Mediaeval Arabic graffiti containing prayers will also often extend the prayer to cover whoever reads the text, and so recites, the prayer.[160]

d'un emprunt au sémitique *qr'*. Toutefois une interférence avec l'arabe n'est pas exclue, surtout au sens de "lire" ....' (personal communication). Texts in the Berber language written in Arabic letters are also read aloud. Indeed, 'les manuscrits chleuhs en écriture arabe font souvent mention d'une lecture à haute voix, souhaitée explicitement, pour son propre bénéfice spirituel, par l'auteur ou le copiste ; le maître dans la zaouia lit devant ses auditeurs. Dans les témoignages que donnenent les manuscrits sur l'enseignement dans les zaouias, quand il a recours à la lecture comme base, les termes employés évoquent bien la voix, c'est-à-dire, en même temps qu'une perception visuelle pour le lecteur, une perception auditive du texte pour le lecteur comme pour les destinataires' (Galand-Pernet 1998: 29). 'La voix peut précéder, dans la création, ou suivre, dans la diffusion, la mise par écrit de l'oeuvre' (ibid. 79). Svenbro argues that the Greek verbs for 'to read' imply 'to read aloud' (1993: 35–36, note 47, and chapters 3, 6 and 9). For a slightly different explanation of the purpose of reading aloud this inscription see Kropp 1997–98: 112–13.

157 It is generally agreed, that in the Greek and Roman worlds (for which we have most evidence), most readers read most material aloud. As B.M.W. Knox puts it 'ancient books were normally read aloud, but there is nothing to show that silent reading of books was anything extraordinary' (1965: 435). Svenbro compares the approach of ancient Greek readers to the written word with our attitude to musical notation: 'not everyone can read music in silence, and the most common way to read it is by playing it on an instrument or singing it out loud to hear what it sounds like' (1993: 18; and see also 44–63, 160–68; and Thomas 1992: 13).

158 For the psychological and anthropological complexities of this, see Svenbro 1993: *passim*.

159 Milik 1958–59: 349, no. 6 *...w ḏkrt lt N w kll ʿs^2r ṣdq w kll mn yqry wqʿ-n ḏʾ* '... and may Lt be mindful of N and of every true friend and of everyone who reads/recites this our inscription'. Note that the final letter, read as *h* in the edition, is clearly *ʾ* on the photograph.

160 See, at random, LPArab nos 5, 93; Abbadi 1986: 261, no. 8 (and several more unpublished from the same site), as well as the references in Hoyland 1997: 80, n. 14. This point is also made explicitly by F. Imbert (2000: 388).

There is another type of transcription, made for a very different purpose, which neatly illustrates a member of an oral society being introduced to literacy for a specific purpose. This is a fragmentary document consisting of four sides of parchment, which was found at the end of the 19th century during clearance of Qubbat al-Khaznah in the Umayyad mosque in Damascus. It was published in 1901[161] and has apparently since disappeared. The text consists of part of the Septuagint version of Psalm 78 (LXX, 77) in a column on the left, with an Arabic translation written in Greek letters in a parallel column on the right (Fig. 8). It is important to note that the Arabic is not an idiomatic translation, but a gloss to the Greek text, that is it gives an Arabic equivalent for each Greek word, following the word order of the Greek text word by word, regardless of how this distorts the Arabic syntax.[162] In the West, such glosses were usually placed above or below the original text but here they are in parallel columns, with very short lines in which the text and the gloss are almost always on the same line. It is interesting to compare this parchment with the large number of fragments of Arabic translations of the Torah, written in Hebrew letters, which have been preserved in the Cairo Geniza. Olszowy-Schlanger concludes that 'the common structure of these manuscripts, as interlinear or parallel columns in which a Hebrew verse is followed by the Arabic one, may also indicate their use for teaching purposes'.[163] According to Violet's description, the Greek manuscript is not a tidy one and it is important to remember this, for his published transcription (Fig. 8) gives the impression of a much neater production. Thus, on the original, only the verso of the second leaf is ruled, the separation of the columns is very irregular and is sometimes only marked by a dot. He described the script of the left column (the Greek text of the psalm) as 'griechische Unciale' and that of the gloss as 'griechische Majuskel'. It is difficult to know if he intended to make a distinction or was simply describing the same type of script by two synonymous terms. While the left column (the Greek text) has accents and breathings, in the right column (the gloss) there are dots in the middle of words, as well as accents and 'Häkchen' which Violet was unable to interpret (1901: 386). This then is not a carefully copied manuscript of the psalm, and indeed may not be a fragment of a psalter, but something much humbler and possibly more personal.

161 Violet 1901. Violet announced that he hoped to publish photographs of the fragment at a later date (1901: 429, n. 1), but apparently did so only in a *Berichtigter Sonderabzug* of his article, published in the same year, which is now extremely rare. I have so far been unable to find a copy of this.

162 As noted by Violet (1901: 430) and well illustrated on cols 387–402 where he has placed his transcription of the original columns on the left page and opposite them a transliteration of the Arabic gloss into an Arabic font, with below each line the equivalent line from the traditional Arabic *translation* of the psalm.

163 Olszowy-Schlanger 2003: 68. On the use of the Hebrew script to write Arabic in mediaeval Jewish communities see above at the beginning of Section III.

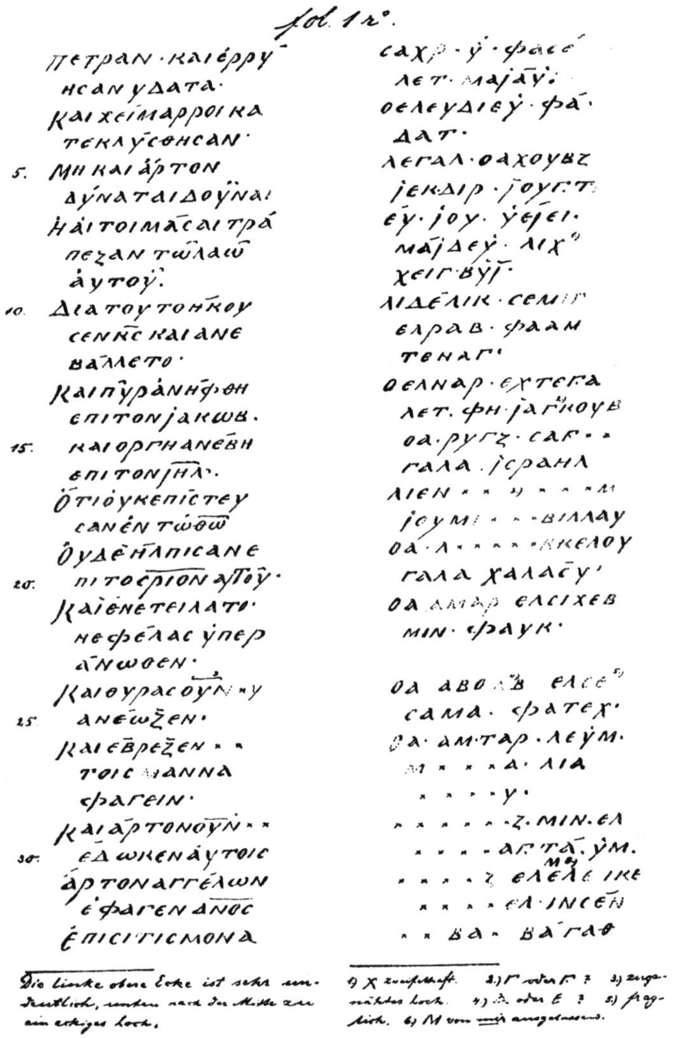

Fig. 8. B. Violet's transcription of part of the Psalmfragment, *with the Septuagint text of Psalm 78 (left) and an Arabic gloss in Greek letters (right).*

We know nothing about this text beyond the description given by its first editor and, as far as I know, it is unique.[164] Thus, any explanation of how it came to be written can be no more than an hypothesis. I would suggest that it was intended to help an Arabic speaker, with only limited Greek, to

164 The nearest comparable document is perhaps a fragment of an Arabic version of part of the *Vita eremitarum* transcribed in Coptic letters (Casanova 1901). However, this is a simple transcription, of unknown date, rather than a Coptic text with Arabic gloss.

understand the Greek text of this psalm, and in the process to improve his knowledge of the language. We know that there were Arabic-speaking Christians in Syria by at least the sixth century and their presence both in the north and the south is beautifully demonstrated by two of the earliest inscriptions in the Arabic script: those at Zebed south-east of Aleppo (AD 512) and Ḥarrān in the Lejā (AD 568), both of which were on the lintels of churches. While at Zebed the Arabic inscription simply records a prayer for a number of persons—the principle foundation texts being in Greek and Syriac—the inscription is clearly part of the original epigraphic scheme and these persons must presumably have been benefactors of the church. At Ḥarrān, the Arabic is the principal text, with a Greek translation, and records—in the first person—the foundation of the martyrion by a certain Sharaḥil son of Ẓalmu.[165] This suggests that Arabic-speakers may have formed a significant element of the Christian population of Syria, at least in these areas and it is likely that some would have come forward as candidates for the priesthood. These would have needed to learn Greek in order to study the Scriptures, perform the liturgy and understand the commands of their superiors. It seems possible that this parchment with its Septuagint text and Arabic gloss was produced as an aid to such training. Unfortunately, there is no objective evidence by which it can be dated.[166] However, it seems to me inconceivable that this Arabic gloss would not have been written in the Arabic script, had the latter been in use in Christian circles in Syria, as we know it was from at least the early sixth century onwards.[167] I would therefore suggest that it dates from

[165] See Robin in press for the most recent discussion and re-readings of these texts.

[166] Violet dates the manuscript to the end of the eighth or beginning of the ninth centuries AD on the grounds of (a) his ascription of the Greek uncial script in which it is written to this period, though he gives no reasons for dating it so late (1901: 386), and (b) his assumption that no translation into Arabic would have been necessary before the Islamic conquest in the mid-seventh century, but that, at any time much later than that, a translation would have been written in the Arabic script (1901: 429). The second assumption we now know to be invalid. Arabic was spoken in Syria centuries before the Islamic conquest and was occasionally transcribed in the Nabataean alphabet (the Namārah inscription) and from the sixth century onwards written in the Arabic script (the Zebed, Harran and Jabal Usays inscriptions). It is much more difficult to judge Violet's palaeographical argument. Nowhere does he state his reasons for dating the script to the late eighth century and one cannot help feeling that in doing so he may have been influenced by his assumption that Arabic would not have been used in Syria before the Islamic conquest. The Greek uncial is, as he admits, extremely difficult to date and was in use from the mid-fourth century AD until it was superseded by the minuscule in the course of the ninth. I am most grateful to Professor Cyril Mango for this information. Naturally, I alone am responsible for any errors in its transmission. Thus, in the absence of any evidence to the contrary, a pre-Islamic date for this manuscript must be regarded as just as likely as a post-conquest one, if not more so.

[167] The argument that after the Islamic conquest the Arabic script was too closely associated with Islam for Christians to want to use it, does not seem to me very cogent in this case. In Syria, Arabic-speaking Christians had been using the Arabic script for at least 120 years before the Islamic conquest, a situation quite different from that of say Coptic-speaking Christians in Egypt, where written Arabic appears to have been introduced with Islam. The analogy drawn

a period before Arabic was habitually written in Syria, that is some time before the sixth century AD.

Presumably, those for whom this manuscript was intended had already achieved the level of the West African children, mentioned above,[168] who were taught the approximate pronunciation of the Arabic letters in order to read the text of the Qur᾽ān, without understanding the meaning of the individual words; a translation of the whole passage being recited to them later. In Byzantine Syria, the Arabic-speaking novices, whom I envisage would already have learnt how to pronounce the Greek letters (almost certainly out loud), would now be using this 'crib' to obtain an understanding of the meaning of the Greek words which they would previously have been reading parrot-fashion, as the West African children read Arabic.

If I am correct in this analysis, this document would present not only a fascinating instance of ancient language teaching, but an interesting example of the interplay of literacy and non-literacy. For here, an unwritten language, Arabic, would have been recorded in the Greek script in order to help novices who spoke Arabic but were not literate in it (because as yet it had no script), to learn Greek, which they could read but could not yet understand! It would represent a bridge between the oral environment of the speakers of Old Arabic and the literate society of Greek. Alas, until the manuscript or a clear photograph of it can be found, all this must remain a tantalizing hypothesis.

For a final example of a use of literacy in an oral environment, I would turn to Rawwāfah, an isolated site in the desert of north-west Arabia, where, between AD 166[169] and 169, two successive governors of the Province of Arabia oversaw the building of a small temple probably for the worship of

with Karshūnī and Judaeo-Arabic is also, I would suggest, a false one. These came into use long after the Islamic conquest, when Arabic had become the everyday language of the whole population, including the Christian and Jewish communities in which, as I have explained at the beginning of Section III, reading for most people was restricted to the scriptures which were written, respectively, in the Syriac and Hebrew scripts. However, it is unlikely that the Greek alphabet would have had a similar significance for Arabic-speaking orthodox Christians in Syria, who had been using the Arabic script for religious inscriptions since the early sixth century, even if only two are known so far! On the contrary, I would suggest that these Christians (many of whom regarded the Arab conquerors as liberators) would have regarded the Arabic alphabet as *their* script, which marked them off from the (often oppressive) Greek-speaking and Greek-writing Byzantine authorities. In these circumstances, the fact that the Arabic script had also come to be used by the Muslims, would surely not have made it 'foreign'.

168 See note 29.

169 Bowersock (1975: 516–17, and 1994: 432*), followed by Sartre (1982: 84), has shown that Modestus could not have become governor of the Province of Arabia until AD 167, because he was preceded in the post by Q. Antistius Adventus Postumius Aquilinus, who was governor in AD 166–167, and who is also mentioned in the inscription.

the local god *ʾlh*.[170] The external walls were adorned with a long and beautifully carved Greek-Nabataean bilingual inscription 'for the perpetuity/safety/victory and perpetuity'[171] of the Roman emperors Marcus Aurelius and Lucius Verus. The nominal founder of the temple and 'author' of the inscription was, I have argued, an auxiliary unit (ἔθνος in the Greek text, *šrkt* in the Nabataean)[172] levied by the Roman army from the famous tribe of Thamūd.[173]

As is well known, the Thamūd first appear in the Assyrian annals of the eighth century BC, and are mentioned by several Classical writers and probably two Safaitic inscriptions. According to the Qurʾān they were finally destroyed for rejecting the word of God brought to them by the Prophet Ṣāliḥ.[174] We have no evidence at all as to whether the Thamūd at this time were nomadic or settled, wholly or in part. The position of the temple at Rawwāfah, far from any visible remains of settlement, might suggest that at least those involved in its construction were nomadic, but this is far from conclusive. Although, again, there is no evidence attributable to this period, it is probable that the members of this tribe spoke an Ancient North Arabian

[170] The reference to the deity is not in the main, bilingual, inscription, but in the Nabataean inscription from the same site to which Milik gave the siglum CIS ii no. 3642a (1971: 57–58). See the excellent photograph in Anon 1975: 92. This is a text of five surviving lines carved within a *tabula ansata* recording that 'Šʿdt the priest of ʾl[h]ʾ built the temple for ʾlh[ʾ] the god ....' The text is badly damaged but at the end of line 4 the word *hgmwnʾ* ('governor') is clear, though unfortunately Milik's reading (from Philby's copies and rubbing rather than from photographs, which only became available later) of the word at the end of line 3 as *b-ḥfyt* ('grâce au zèle de') does not seem to be possible on the photograph.

[171] In text A it is 'Ὑπὲρ αἰωνίου διαμονῆς, in text B it is *ʿl šlmʾ*, and in text C it is ʾΕπὶ νείκῃ καὶ αἰωνίῳ διαμονῇ.

[172] See Macdonald 1995b: 99, where I argue that ἔθνος is the Greek equivalent of Latin *natio*, the technical term for such a unit used in Pseudo-Hyginus (*De munitionibus castrorum* 29, 43) which, according to Speidel, can now be assigned 'unequivocally to the years A.D. 170–175' (1975: 206), and is therefore almost exactly contemporary with the Rawwāfah inscription.

[173] Macdonald 1995b: 98–100, where I point out that the word *šrkt* (an Arabic loan-word in the Nabataean inscription) has the sense of an association into which one enters *voluntarily*, not one into which one is born. Hence, the word *šarikah* is never used in Arabic of a tribe, or tribal confederation, the structures which define your *congenital* identity. Arabic *šarikah* therefore covers much of the same semantic field as English 'company' (though, it has to be admitted, not the military sense!) and it is used today as the normal Arabic word for a commercial 'company'. There is a nice comparison of which I was unaware when I wrote the 1995 paper, which is that the word *Kɔŋpiŋ* (a loan-word from English 'company', just as Nabataean *šrkt* was a loan from the Arabic word of similar meaning) 'is a term widely used for a 'voluntary' or *non-kinship association* in West Africa' (Goody, Cole and Scribner 1977: 300, n. 3 [my italics], who refer to this in the context of its use for a religious association, ibid. 290).

[174] For all references, except the Safaitic, see the excellent treatment in Beaucamp 1979: 1469–71. The Safaitic texts are WH 3792 a (*s^1nt ḥrb gs^{2}m ʾl ṯmd*) and 3792 c (*s^1nt ḥrb gs^{2}m ṯmd*) 'the year of the war between Gs^{2}m and (ʾl) Ṯmd'. There is, of course, no proof that *ṯmd* here refers to the tribe of Thamūd, though it seems likely.

tongue or a dialect of Old Arabic and it would seem unlikely that they spoke, or read, Nabataean Aramaic or Greek. To the best of my knowledge, there is not a single inscription, graffito or other document in Nabataean or Greek which could be said to be by (or even commissioned by) a member of the tribe of Thamūd, apart from the Rawwāfah inscription. Indeed, there is precious little evidence of literacy in any script, at any time, in this tribe.[175] Of course, these are all *argumenta e silentio*, but, alas, silence is all we have in this case. So the argument must remain simply an hypothesis.

So, why should two successive Roman governors have ordered this very elegant inscription for the perpetuity of their emperors' reign to be placed on this temple in the desert of north-west Arabia, in languages and scripts which the nominal dedicators, and most other passers-by, were unlikely to have been able to read? This is not the equivalent of a monumental inscription set up in a city where, even when carved in *stoichedon*, its author(s) could expect it to be read aloud and its message communicated. On a miniature scale, Rawwāfah is an Arabian Bīsutūn, an inscription whose content is important, set up in a place where no one is likely to be able to read it: a text only for the eyes of the gods and of history.

I would suggest that a Roman temple presumably to a local deity, built in the name of the Thamūd, for the well-being of the emperors, must have been intended as a symbol of the tribe's entry into the Roman military and administrative system, and as a powerful reminder of where its loyalties should now lie.[176] However, since few but the Thamūd were likely to see this temple, and they were unlikely to have been able to read the texts, it would seem that, as so often with monumental inscriptions, symbolism was more important than comprehension. The two languages and two scripts—the Nabataean sandwiched between the Greek, its swirls and curves in marked contrast to the straight lines and sharp angles of the Greek—represented the two sides to the agreement, Greek for the Romans and the only available local written language for the tribesmen. The temple and its inscriptions were

175 There are two Ancient North Arabian texts in which it seems fairly certain that the author is claiming membership of the tribe (JSTham 280 *N h-ṯmd(y)*, 300 *l N h-ṯmd*), two in which he may or may not be (Dghty 51/2 *s¹t h-ṯmd* ..., HU 172 *h ʾlh ṯmd* ...) and two others where either the reading or the interpretation is uncertain (JSTham 339, HU 453). This is not necessarily conclusive, however, since the Ancient North Arabian graffiti from the areas of Arabia which the Thamūd are thought to have inhabited are generally very brief and only rarely give the author's affiliation to a social group. Moreover, if the Thamūd were a large tribe, or even a confederation, its members would be more likely to give their affiliation to one of the smaller sub-groups within it since this would be more specific and would anyway carry the implication of being part of the larger tribe.

176 Macdonald 1995b: 98–101. Speidel quotes a Latin inscription set up by a unit of the *Mauri Mic(ienses)* in Dacia Apulensis in AD 204 (1975: 209). This, like the Rawwāfah inscription, is of course framed as a dedication for the safety of the emperors (and the imperial family), and records the restoration by the unit and its prefect of a *templum deorum patriorum*, i.e. of the ancestral gods of the Mauri.

surely intended to stand as a symbol and as a reminder to the Thamūd, as they prayed to their god, of the loyalty they now owed to the literate Roman state and that they should turn their backs on the oral society from which they came. Thus, it also symbolized the tribesmen's transition from being non-literate in their own oral culture to being *ill*iterate in literate Roman society. Some 230 years later there were auxiliary units named after the Thamūd in the Roman army,[177] but whether these had anything to do with the tribesmen of the Rawwāfah inscription is unknown, for alas the Thamūd have left us no texts of their own.

By contrast, the *literate* nomads who used the Ancient North Arabian scripts have provided our only first-hand evidence, at any period, for life in the Syro-Arabian desert. Their texts suggest that, despite their widespread literacy, their society remained entirely non-literate, and writing never usurped the functions of memory and oral communication. Ironically, thanks to their literate pastimes and the writing materials they used, we know far more about the daily life, social structure, religion and personal feelings of these nomads than we do about those of any of their contemporary neighbours, who lived in settled societies where literacy had key functions, but from which few if any personal documents have survived.

SIGLA

A2	A Safaitic alphabet published in Macdonald, Al Muʾazzin and Nehmé 1996: 439–43.
Brussels	*Inoubliable Pétra. Le royaume nabatéen aux confins du désert.* Catalogue of an exhibition at the Musées Royaux d'Art et d'Histoire, Bruxelles 1980, edited by D. Homès-Fredericq. Bruxelles: Musées Royaux d'Art et d'Histoire, 1980. [This was the same exhibition as that at Lyon, see below].
CIH	Inscriptions in *Corpus Inscriptionum Semiticarum.* Pars IV. *Inscriptiones ḥimyariticas et sabaeas continens.* Paris: Reipublicae Typographeo, 1889–1932.
CIL. IV	Latin inscriptions in *Corpus Inscriptionum Latinarum.* IV. *Inscriptiones parietariae pompeianae herculanenses stabianae ....* Berlin, 1873.
CIS ii	Aramaic inscriptions in *Corpus Inscriptionum Semiticarum.* Pars II. *Inscriptiones aramaicas continens.* Paris, 1889–1954.
Dghty 51/2	Thamudic B inscription copied by Doughty. See van den Branden 1950: 233.

[177] In the *Notitia Dignitatum*, see Seeck 1876: 59 (*Equites Saraceni Thamudeni*), and 73 (*Equites Thamudeni Illyriciani*).

HU	Thamudic B, C and D, Taymanitic and Hismaic inscriptions copied by C. Huber and republished with a new numeration in van den Branden 1950.
JSLih	Dadanitic inscriptions in Jaussen and Savignac 1909–22.
JSNab	Nabataean inscriptions in Jaussen and Savignac 1909–22.
JSTham	Taymanitic, Hismaic and Thamudic B, C and D inscriptions in Jaussen and Savignac 1909–22.
KRA	A Safaitic alphabet published in King 1990a: 62–63, Fig. 2, pl. IIb.
KSA	A Hismaic alphabet from Khirbat al-Samrāʾ, Jordan, originally published in Knauf 1985, but see Macdonald 1986: 105–12.
KJC	Hismaic inscriptions in King 1990b.
LP	Safaitic inscriptions in Littmann 1943.
LPArab	Arabic inscriptions in Littmann 1949.
LPNab	Nabataean inscriptions in Littmann 1914.
Lyon	*Un royaume aux confins du désert. Petra et la Nabatène.* Catalogue of an exhibition at the Muséum de Lyon, 18 November 1978 to 28 February 1979. Lyon: Muséum de Lyon, 1978. [This was the same exhibition as that at Brussels, see above.]
MaSA	A Safaitic alphabet published in Macdonald 1986: 101–5.
SEG XVI	*Supplementum Epigraphicum Graecum.* Volumen XVI. Lugduni Batavorum: Sijthoff, 1959.
WH	Safaitic inscriptions in Winnett and Harding 1978.
WTI 23	Dumaitic inscription in Winnett and Reed 1970.

BIBLIOGRAPHY

Abbadi, S.

1986 'An archaeological survey of Ǧabal Qurma', *Archiv für Orientforschung* 33: 259–62.

Aghali-Zakara, M.

1993 'Les lettres et les chiffres. Écrire en berbère', pages 141–55 in J. Drouin and A. Roth (eds), *À la croisée des études libyco-berbères. Mélanges offerts à Paulette Galand-Pernet et Lionel Galand.* (Comptes Rendus du Groupe Linguistique d'Études Chamito-Sémitiques. Supplément, 15; Paris: Geuthner).

1999 'L'écriture touarègue', pages 109–17 in L. Galand (ed.) 1999.

2001 'Unité et diversité des libyco-berbères', *Epigraphie Libyco-Berbère. La Lettre du RILB Répertoire des Inscriptions Libyco-Berbère* 7: 4–6.

Aghali-Zakara, M., and J. Drouin

1973–79 'Recherches sur les Tifinagh', *Comptes rendus du Groupe Linguistique d'Études Chamito-Sémitiques* 18–23: 245–72, 279–92.

Anon

1975 *'An Introduction to Saudi Arabian Antiquities',* (Riyadh: Department of Antiquities and Museums).

Arazi, A., and H. Ben-Shammay
1995 'Risāla 1', pages 532–39 in *The Encyclopaedia of Islam*. 8 (Leiden: Brill).

Beaucamp, J.
'Rawwafa (et les Thamoudéens)', cols 1467–75 in L. Pirot, A. Robert, *et al.* (eds), *Supplément au Dictionnaire de la Bible* 9 (Paris: Letouzey).

Beeston, A.F.L., M.A. al-Ghul, W.W. Müller and J. Ryckmans
1982 *Sabaic Dictionary (English-French-Arabic)*. (Publication of the University of Sanaa, YAR; Louvain-la-Neuve: Peeters/Beyrouth: Librairie du Liban).

Blau, J.
1966–67 *A Grammar of Christian Arabic Based Mainly on South-Palestinian Texts from the First Millennium*. (3 volumes). (Corpus Scriptorum Christianorum Orientalium. Subsidia, 267/27, 276/28, 279/29; Louvain: Secrétariat du Corpus SCO).

Bowersock, G.W.
1975 'The Greek-Nabataean bilingual inscription at Ruwāfa, Saudi Arabia', pages 513–22 in J. Bingen, G. Cambrier, G. Nachtergael (eds), *Hommages à Claire Préaux*. (Le Monde Grec 52; Bruxelles: Université Libre de Bruxelles faculté de Philosophie et de Lettres). [Reprinted with addenda as pp. 203*–12*, 432* in Bowersock 1994].
1994 *Studies on the Eastern Roman Empire: Social, Economic and Administrative History, Religion and Historiography*. (Bibliotheca Eruditorum, 9; Goldbach: Keip).

Carruthers, M.J.
1990 *The Book of Memory: A Study of Memory in Medieval Culture*. (Cambridge: Cambridge University Press).

Casajus, D.
1999 'La vie saharienne et les « Vies » de Charles de Foucauld', pages 47–100 in L. Galand (ed.) 1999.

Casanova, M.P.
1901 'Un texte arabe transcrit en caractères coptes', *Bulletin de l'Institut Français d'Archéologie Orientale* 1: 1–20.

Chomsky, C.
1971 'Invented spelling in the open classroom', *Word* 27: 499–518.

Clanchy, M.T.
1993 *From Memory to Written Word: England 1066–1307*. (Second edition; Oxford: Blackwell).

Clark, V.A.
1981 'Archaeological investigations at two burial cairns in the Ḥarra region of Jordan. With contributions from B. MacDonald and with a report on the skeletal remains by S.L. Rolston', *Annual of the Department of Antiquities of Jordan* 25: 235–65.

Coninck, I.P. de, and L. Galand

1957–60 'Un essai des Kel-Antessar pour améliorer l'écriture touarègue', *Comptes rendus du Groupe Linguistique d'Études Chamito-sémitiques* 8: 78–83.

Crone, P., and S. Moreh (transl.)

2000 *The Book of Strangers: Mediaeval Arabic Graffiti on the Theme of Nostalgia. Attributed to Abū ʾl-Farağ al-Iṣfahānī* (Princeton Series on the Middle East; Princeton, NJ: Wiener).

Daviau, P.M., N. Mulder-Hymans, L. Foley and C.J. Simpson

2000 'Preliminary report of excavations at Khirbat al-Mudayna on Wādī ath-Thamad (1996–1999): The Nabataean buildings', *Annual of the Department of Antiquities of Jordan* 44: 271–82.

Dentzer, J.-M., and J. Dentzer-Feydy (eds)

1991 *Le djebel al-ʿArab: histoire et patrimoine au Musée de Suweidāʾ* (Paris: ERC).

Deputy Ministry of Antiquities and Museums of Saudi Arabia

2003 *Silsilat āṯār al-mamlakat al-ʿarabīyat al-suʿūdīyat.* (13 volumes). (Riyāḍ: Wakālat al-āṯār wa-ʾl-matāḥif).

Diodorus Siculus

1954 *Library of History*. Books XIX.66–XX. Ed. and transl. R.M. Geer (Loeb Classical Library; London: Heinemann/Cambridge. MA: Harvard University Press).

Drewes, A.J.

1985 'The phonemes of Liḥyanite', pages 165–73 in C. Robin (ed.), *Mélanges linguistiques offerts à Maxime Rodinson par ses élèves, ses collègues et ses amis* (Comptes Rendus du Groupe Linguistique d'Études Chamito-Sémitiques. Supplément, 12; Paris: Geuthner).

Drouin, J.

1996 Déchiffrer n'est pas traduire. *Epigraphie Libyco-Berbère. La Lettre du RILB Répertoire des Inscriptions Libyco-Berbère* 2: 2–3.

1998 Espace et orientations graphiques. *Epigraphie Libyco-Berbère. La Lettre du RILB Répertoire des Inscriptions Libyco-Berbère* 4: 3.

2003 Les *incipit* dans les inscriptions rupestres. *Epigraphie Libyco-Berbère. La Lettre du RILB Répertoire des Inscriptions Libyco-Berbère* 9: 2–3.

Durkan, J.

2001 Schools and schooling. I. To 1696. Pages 561–63 in M. Lynch (ed.), *The Oxford Companion to Scottish History* (Oxford: Oxford University Press).

Epiphanius of Salamis (ed. K. Holl)

1980 *Epiphanius II. Panarion haer. 34–64.* (2. bearbeitete Auflage herausgegeben von J. Dummer). (Die griechischen christlichen Schriftsteller der ersten Jahrhunderte; Berlin: Akademie-Verlag).

Euting, J.
1885 *Nabatäische Inschriften aus Arabien* (Berlin: Reimer).
Foucauld, C. de, and A. de Calassanti-Motylinski
1984 *Textes touaregues en prose de Charles de Foucauld et A. de Calassanti-Motylinski*. Édition critique avec traduction par S. Chaker, H. Claudot, M. Gast (Aix-en-Provence: Edisud).
Franklin, J.L.
1991 'Literacy and the parietal inscriptions of Pompeii', pages 77–98 in Humphrey 1991.
Galand, L.
1966 'Inscriptions libyques', pages 1–79 in L. Galand, J. Février and G. Vajda, *Inscriptions antiques du Maroc* (Paris: Éditions du CNRS).
1989 'Les langues berbères', pages 330–53 in I. Fodor and C. Hagège (eds), *Language Reform: History and Future* (Hamburg: Busken).
1996 'Le piège des consonnes tendues', *Epigraphie Libyco-Berbère. La Lettre du RILB Répertoire des Inscriptions Libyco-Berbère* 2: 1.
1997 'Graphie et phonie. Les caractères à valeur biconsonantique', *Epigraphie Libyco-Berbère. La Lettre du RILB Répertoire des Inscriptions Libyco-Berbère* 3: 1–2.
1998 'L'écriture libyco-berbère', *Comptes rendus des séances de l'Académie des Inscriptions & Belles-Lettres*: 593–601.
1999 (ed.) *Lettres au Marabout: Messages touaregs au Père de Foucauld* (Paris: Belin).
2001a 'Un vieux débat: l'origine de l'écriture libyco-berbère', *Epigraphie Libyco-Berbère. La Lettre du RILB Répertoire des Inscriptions Libyco-Berbère* 7: 1–3.
2001b 'Note sur des inscriptions de Libye', *Les Cahiers de l'AARS, Bulletin de l'Association des amis de l'art rupestre saharien* 6 (mai 2001): 3–5.
2002a 'Du berbère au libyque: une remontée difficile', pages 3–28 in L. Galand, *Études de linguistique berbère* (Société de linguistique de Paris. Collection Linguistique, 83; Louvain/Paris: Peeters). [Originally published as: pages 77–98 in *LALIES, Actes des sessions de linguistiques et de littérature,* 16 (Carthage, 21 août–2 septembre 1995; Paris: Presses de l'E.N.S. 1996)].
2002b 'La notion d'écriture dans les parlers berbères', pages 409–13 in L. Galand, *Études de linguistique berbère* (Société de linguistique de Paris. Collection Linguistique, 83; Louvain/Paris: Peeters). [Originally published in *Almogaren* (Hallein) 5–6, 1974–75: 93–97].
Galand-Pernet, P.
1998 *Littératures berbères. Des voix. Des lettres* (Paris: Presses Universitaires de France).
1999 'Écrire le berbère', pages 105–8 in L. Galand (ed.) 1999.
Galand-Pernet, P., and H. Zafrani
1970 *Une version berbère de la Haggadah de Pesaḥ: Texte de Tinrhir*

du Todrha (Maroc). (2 volumes). (Supplément 1 aux *Comptes rendus du Groupe Linguistique d'Études Chamito-sémitiques*; Paris: Geuthner).

Gamble, H.Y.
1995 *Books and Readers in the Early Church: A History of Early Christian Texts* (New Haven, CT: Yale University Press).

Goody, J., M. Cole and S. Scribner
1977 'Writing and formal operations: a case study among the Vai', *Africa* 47: 289–304.

Graff, H.J.
1986 'The legacies of literacy: continuity and contradictions in western society and culture', pages 61–86 in S. De Castell, A. Luke, K. Egan (eds), *Literacy, Society, and Schooling: A Reader* (Cambridge: Cambridge University Press).

Hanson, A.E.
1991 'Ancient illiteracy', pages 159–98 in Humphrey 1991.

Harding, G. Lankester
1953 'The cairn of Haniʾ', *Annual of the Department of Antiquities of Jordan* 2: 8–56.
1978 'The cairn of Saʿd', pages 242–49 in P.R.S. Moorey and P.J. Parr (eds), *Archaeology in the Levant: Essays for Kathleen Kenyon* (Warminster: Aris and Phillips).
1971 *An Index and Concordance of Pre-Islamic Arabian Names and Inscriptions* (Near and Middle East Series, 8; Toronto: University of Toronto Press).

Harris, W.V.
1989 *Ancient Literacy* (Cambridge, MA: Harvard University Press).

Holdaway, D.
1979 *The Foundations of Literacy* (Sydney: Ashton).

Holes, C.
1995 *Modern Arabic: Structures, Functions and Varieties* (Longman Linguistics Library; London: Longman).

Hopkins, S.
1984 *Studies in the Grammar of Early Arabic: Based upon Papyri Datable to Before A.H. 300/A.D. 912* (London Oriental Series, 37; Oxford: Oxford University Press).

Horsfall, N.
1991 'Statistics or states of mind?', pages 59–76 in Humphrey 1991.

Hoyland, R.G.
1997 'The content and context of early Arabic inscriptions', *Jerusalem Studies in Arabic and Islam* 21: 77–102.

Humphrey, J.H. (ed.)
1991 *Literacy in the Roman World* (Journal of Roman Archaeology: Supplementary Series 3; Ann Arbor, MI: Journal of Roman Archaeology).

Imbert, F.
2000 'Le Coran dans les graffiti des deux premiers siècles de l'Hégire', *Arabica* 47: 381–90.

Jaussen, A., and M.R. Savignac
1909–22 *Mission archéologique en Arabie* (6 volumes). (Paris: Leroux/Geuthner). [Reprinted Cairo: Institut Français d'Archéologie Orientale, 1997].

Jeffery, L.H., and A. Morpurgo-Davies
1970 *ΠΟΙΝΙΚΑΣΤΑΣ* and *ΠΟΙΝΙΚΑΖΕΝ*: BM 1969. 4-2.1, a new archaic inscription from Crete. *Kadmos* 9: 118–54.

Johansson, E.
1977 *The History of Literacy in Sweden, in Comparison with some other Countries* (Educational reports, Umeå, 12; Umeå: Umeå University and School of Education).
1988 'Literacy campaigns in Sweden', *Interchange* [The Ontario Institute for Studies in Education] 19/3–4: 135–62.
1998 *Alphabeta Varia*: *Orality, Reading and Writing in the History of Literacy. Festschrift in Honour of Egil Johansson on the Occasion of his 65th Birthday March 24, 1998*. Edited by D. Lindmark (Album Religionum Umense, 1; Umeå: Department of Religious Studies, Umeå University).

King, G.M.H.
1990a 'The Basalt Desert Rescue Survey and some preliminary remarks on the Safaitic inscriptions and rock drawings', *Proceedings of the Seminar for Arabian Studies* 20: 55–78.
1990b *Early North Arabian Thamudic E*: *Preliminary Description Based on a New Corpus of Inscriptions from the Ḥismā Desert of Southern Jordan and Published Material*. PhD thesis, School of Oriental and African Studies, University of London. [Unpublished].

Knauf, E.A.
1985 'A South Safaitic alphabet from Khirbet es-Samrāʾ', *Levant* 17: 204–6.

Knox, B.M.W.
1965 'Silent reading in antiquity', *Greek, Roman, and Byzantine Studies* 9: 421–35.

Koehler, L., and W. Baumgartner
1994–2000 *The Hebrew and Aramaic Lexicon of the Old Testament*. Subsequently revised by W. Baumgartner and J.J. Stamm with assistance from B. Hartmann, Z. Ben-Hayyim, E.Y. Kutscher and P. Reymond. Translated and edited under the supervision of M.E.J. Richardson in collaboration with G.J. Jongeling-Vos and L.J. De Regt (5 volumes) (Leiden: Brill).

Kofler, H.
1940 Reste altarabischer Dialekte [I]. *Wiener Zeitschrift für die Kunde des Morgenlandes* 47: 61–130, 232–62.

Kropp, M.
1997–98 'Iatromagie und der Beginn der arabischen Schriftsprache: die nabatäisch-arabische Inschrift von ʿAyn ʿAbada', *Mélanges de l'Université Saint-Joseph* 55: 91–117.

Lacerenza, G.
2000 'Appunti sull'iscrizione nabateo-araba di ʿAyn ʿAvdat', *Studi Epigrafici e Linguistici sul Vicino Oriente Antico* 17: 105–14.

Lancaster, W.
1981 *The Rwala Bedouin Today* (Cambridge: Cambridge University Press).

Lancaster, W., and F. Lancaster
1993 'Graves and funerary monuments of the Ahl al-Ğabal, Jordan', *Arabian Archaeology and Epigraphy* 4: 151–69.

Lane Fox, R.
1994 'Literacy and power in early Christianity', pages 126–48 in A.K. Bowman and G. Woolf (eds), *Literacy and Power in the Ancient World* (Cambridge: Cambridge University Press).

Lewis, N., Y. Yadin and J.C. Greenfield
1989 *The Documents from the Bar Kokhba Period in the Cave of Letters: Greek Papyri*. Aramaic and Nabatean Signatures and Subscriptions edited by Y. Yadin and J.C. Greenfield. (Judaean Desert Studies, 2; Jerusalem: Israel Exploration Society).

Littmann, E.
1914 *Nabataean Inscriptions from the Southern Ḥaurân*. (Publications of the Princeton University Archaeological Expeditions to Syria in 1904–1905 and 1909. Division IV. Section A). Leyden: Brill.
1943 *Safaïtic Inscriptions*. (Syria. Publications of the Princeton University Archaeological Expeditions to Syria in 1904–1905 and 1909. Division IV. Section C; Leden: Brill).
1949 *Arabic Inscriptions*. (Syria: Publications of the Princeton University Archaeological, Expeditions to Syria in 1904–1905 and 1909; Division IV. Section D; Leden: Brill).

Macdonald, M.C.A.
1980 'Safaitic Inscriptions in the Amman Museum and Other Collections II', *Annual of the Department of Antiquities of Jordan* 24: 185–208.
1986 'ABCs and letter order in Ancient North Arabian', *Proceedings of the Seminar for Arabian Studies* 16: 101–68.
1992 'On the placing of *Ṣ* in the Maghribi *abjad* and the Khirbet Al-Samrāʾ ABC', *Journal of Semitic Studies* 37: 155–66.
1993 'Nomads and the Ḥawrān in the late Hellenistic and Roman periods: a reassessment of the epigraphic evidence', *Syria* 70: 303–413.
1995a 'Ṣafaitic', pages 760–62 in *The Encyclopaedia of Islam*. 8 (Leiden: Brill).

1995b 'Quelques réflexions sur les Saracènes, l'inscription de Rawwāfa et l'armée romaine', pages 93–101 in H. Lozachmeur (ed.), *Présence arabe dans le croissant fertile avant l'Hégire*. Actes de la Table ronde internationale organisée par l'Unité de recherche associé 1062 du CNRS, Études sémitiques, au Collège de France, le 13 novembre 1993 (Paris: Éditions Recherche sur les Civilisations).

1998 'Some reflections on epigraphy and ethnicity in the Roman Near East', pages 177–90 in G. Clarke and D. Harrison (eds), *Identities in the Eastern Mediterranean in Antiquity*. Proceedings of a Conference held at the Humanities Research Centre in Canberra 10–12 November, 1997. *Mediterranean Archaeology* 11.

2000 'Reflections on the linguistic map of pre-Islamic Arabia', *Arabian Archaeology and Epigraphy* 11: 28–79.

2003 'Languages, scripts, and the uses of writing among the Nabataeans', pages 36–56, 264–66 [notes], 274–82 [references] in G. Markoe (ed), *Petra Rediscovered: Lost City of the Nabataeans*. (New York: Abrams/Cincinnati, OH: Cincinnati Art Museum).

2004 'Ancient North Arabian', pages 488–533 in R.D. Woodard (ed), *The Cambridge Encyclopedia of the World's Ancient Languages* (Cambridge: Cambridge University Press).

in press a 'Towards a re-assessment of the Ancient North Arabian alphabets used in the oasis of al-ʿUlā', in S. Weninger (ed), *Epigraphik und Archäologie des antiken Südarabien* (Wiesbaden: Harrossowitz).

in press b 'Burial between the desert and the sown: cave-tombs and inscriptions near Dayr al-Kahf in Jordan', *Damaszener Mitteilungen* 15.

in press c 'From Dadan to Iram in four Ancient North Arabian inscriptions', in D.F. Graf and S.G. Schmid (eds), *Fawzi Zayadine Festschrift* (Annual of the Department of Antiquities, Supplement 1; Amman: Department of Antiquities of Jordan).

in press d 'Old Arabic (epigraphic)', in K. Versteegh (ed), *Encyclopedia of Arabic Language and Linguistics* (Leiden: Brill).

in prep 'The Hismaic inscriptions from the Madaba region of Jordan.'

Macdonald, M.C.A., and G.M.H. King

2000 'Thamudic', pages 436–38 in *The Encyclopaedia of Islam*. 10 (Leiden: Brill).

Macdonald, M.C.A., M. Al Muʾazzin and L. Nehmé

1996 'Les inscriptions safaïtiques de Syrie, cent quarante ans après leur découverte', *Comptes rendus des séances de l'Académie des Inscriptions & Belles-Lettres*: 435–94.

Maraqten, M.

1998 'Writing materials in Pre-Islamic Arabia', *Journal of Semitic Studies* 43: 287–310.

2003 'Some notes on Sabaic epistolography', *Proceedings of the Seminar for Arabian Studies* 33: 273–86.

Meek, D.

2001 'Religious life. 8: Highlands since the Reformation', pages 517–22 in M. Lynch (ed.), *The Oxford Companion to Scottish History* (Oxford: Oxford University Press).

Milik, J.T.

1958–59 'Nouvelles inscriptions sémitiques et grecques du pays de Moab', *Liber Annuus* 9: 330–58.

1971 'Inscriptions grecques et nabatéennes de Rawwafah', pages 54–58, pls 26–31 in P.J. Parr, G.L. Harding, J.E. Dayton, Preliminary Survey in N.W. Arabia, 1968, Part II: Epigraphy. *Bulletin of the Institute of Archaeology, University of London* 10: 36–61, pls 17, 19–31.

Millard, A.R.

1970 '*Scriptio Continua* in early Hebrew: ancient practice or modern surmise?', *Journal of Semitic Studies* 15: 2–15.

1982 'In praise of ancient scribes', *Biblical Archaeologist* 45: 143–53.

1991 'The uses of the early alphabets', pages 101–14 in C. Baurain, C. Bonnet, and V. Krings (eds), *Phoinikeia Grammata. Lire et écrire en Méditerranée.* Actes du Colloque de Liège, 15–18 novembre 1989 (Collection d'Études Classiques 6; Namur: Société des Études Classiques).

2000 *Reading and Writing in the Time of Jesus* (Sheffield: Sheffield Academic Press).

al-Moraekhi, M.

2002 'A new perspective on the phenomenon of mirror-image writing in Arabic calligraphy', pages 123–33 in J.F. Healey and V. Porter (eds), *Studies on Arabia in honour of Professor G. Rex Smith.* (Journal of Semitic Studies Supplement, 14; Oxford University Press on behalf of the University of Manchester).

Moritz, B.

1908 'Ausflüge in der Arabia Petraea', *Mélanges de la Faculté Orientale de l'Université Saint Joseph* 3: 387–436.

Mowry, L.

1953 'A Greek inscription at Jathum in Transjordan', *Bulletin of the American Schools of Oriental Research* 132: 34–41.

Müller, W.W.

1980 'Some remarks on the Safaitic inscriptions', *Proceedings of the Seminar for Arabian Studies* 10: 67–74.

Negev , A.

1981 *The Greek Inscriptions from the Negev.* (Studium Biblicum Franciscanum Collectio Minor, 25; Jerusalem: Franciscan Printing Press).

Negev, A., J. Naveh and S. Shaked

1986 'Obodas the God', *Israel Exploration Journal* 36: 56–60.

Olszowy-Schlanger, J.

2003 'Learning to read and write in medieval Egypt: children's exercise books from the Cairo Geniza', *Journal of Semitic Studies* 48: 47–69.

Piccirillo, M., and E. Alliata

1994 *Umm al-Rasas Mayfa'ah* I. *Gli scavi del complesso di Santo Stefano*. (Studium Biblicum Franciscanum Collectio Maior, 28; Jerusalem: Studium Biblicum Franciscanum).

Prasse, K.-G.

2000 'Ṭawāriḳ', pages 379–81 in *The Encyclopaedia of Islam* 10 (Leiden: Brill).

Pseudo-Hyginus (ed. and transl. M. Lenoir)

1979 *Pseudo-Hygin: des fortifications du camp*. (Collection des Universitaires de France; Paris: Société d'édition « Les Belles Lettres »).

Ray, J.

1994 'Literacy and language in Egypt in the Late and Persian Periods', pages 51–66 in A.K. Bowman and G. Woolf (eds), *Literacy and Power in the Ancient World* (Cambridge: Cambridge University Press).

Reygasse, M.

1932 'Contribution à l'étude des gravures rupestres et inscriptions Tifinar' du Sahara central', pages 437–534 in *Cinquantenaire de la Faculté des Lettres d'Alger (1881–1931): Articles publiés par les professeurs de la faculté par les soins de la Société Historique Algérienne* (Alger: Société Historique Algérienne).

Robin, C.J.

1996 'Sheba. 2. Dans les inscriptions d'Arabie du Sud. Col. 1047–1254', in J. Brend, E. Cothenet, H. Cazelles, A. Feuillet (eds), *Supplément au Dictionnaire de la Bible*. 12 (fasc. 70) (Paris: Letouzey).

2001 'Les inscriptions de l'Arabie antique et les études arabes', *Arabica* 48: 509–77.

in press 'La réforme de l'écriture arabe, à l'époque du califat médinois', in F. Déroche (ed), *Proceedings of the International Conference on Manuscripts of the Qur'ān. Università di Bologna, Centro Interdipartimentale di Scienze del'Islam, 28–29 September 2002. Mélanges de l'Universitié St Joseph.*

Robin, C.J., and M. Gorea

2002 'Un réexamen de l'inscription arabe préislamique du Ǧabal Usays (528–529 è. chr.)', *Arabica* 49: 505–10.

Ryckmans, G.

1951 'Inscriptions ṣafaïtiques au British Museum et au Musée de Damas', *Le Muséon* 64: 83–91.

Ryckmans, J
1988 'Données nouvelles sur l'histoire ancienne de l'alphabet', *Bulletin des séances de l'Académie Royale des Sciences d'Outre-Mer* 34: 219–31.
1992 'Récentes découvertes épigraphiques et archéologiques en Arabie du Sud antique', *Acta Orientalia Belgica* 7: 315–23.
1993 'Pétioles de palmes et bâtonnets inscrits: un type nouveau de documents du Yémen antique', *Bulletin de la classe des lettres et des sciences morales et politiques de l'Académie Royale de Belgique* 4: 15–32.

Ryckmans, J., W.W. Müller and Y.M. Abdallah
1994 *Textes du Yémen antique inscrits sur bois*. (With an English summary). Avant-Propos de J.-F. Breton. (Publications de l'Institut Orientaliste de Louvain, 43; Louvain-La-Neuve: Institut Orientaliste).

Sartre, M.
1982 *Trois études sur l'Arabie romaine et byzantine*. (Collection Latomus, 178; Bruxelles: Latomus).

Schürer, E.
1973–87 *The History of the Jewish People in the Age of Jesus Christ (175 B.C.–A.D. 135)*. A new English version revised and edited by G. Vermes, F. Millar, M. Black and M. Goodman (4 volumes) (Edinburgh: Clark).

Schwabe, M.
1954 'Note on the Jathum Inscription', *Bulletin of the American Schools of Oriental Research* 135: 38.

Scribner, S., and M. Cole
1978 'Literacy without schooling: testing for intellectual effects', *Harvard Educational Review* 48: 448–61.
1999 *The Psychology of Literacy* (Cambridge, MA: Harvard University Press).

Seeck, O.
1876 *Notitia Dignitatum accedunt Notitia Urbis Constantinopolitanae et Laterculi Prouinciarum* (Berlin: Weidmann).

Skeat, T.C.
1995 'Was papyrus regarded as "cheap" or "expensive" in the ancient world?', *Aegyptus* 75: 75–93.

Smout, T.C.
1982 Born again at Cambuslang: new evidence on popular religion and literacy in eighteenth century Scotland. *Past and Present* 97: 114–27.

Speidel, M.P.
1975 'The rise of ethnic units in the Roman imperial army', pages 202–31 in H. Temporini (ed.), *Aufstieg und Niedergang der Römischen Welt*. 3 Principat, 2/3 (Berlin: De Gruyter).

Stark, J.K.
1971 *Personal Names in the Palmyrene Inscriptions* (Oxford: Clarendon).

Svenbro, J.
1993 *Phrasikleia: An Anthropology of Reading in Ancient Greece.* Translated by J. Lloyd (Ithaca, NY/London: Cornell University Press).

Thomas, R.
1992 *Literacy and Orality in Ancient Greece.* (Key Themes in Ancient History; Cambridge: Cambridge University Press).

Torczyner, H., G. Lankester Harding, A. Lewis and J.L. Starkey
1938 *Lachish I (Tell ed Duweir): The Lachish Letters.* (The Wellcome Archaeological Research Expedition to the Near East; London: Oxford University Press).

van den Boogert, N.
2000 'Tifinagh', pages 476–78 in *The Encyclopaedia of Islam.* 10 (Leiden: Brill).

van den Branden, A.
1950 *Les inscriptions thamoudéennes.* (Bibliothèque du Muséon, 25 Louvain: Institut Orientaliste de l'Université de Louvain).

Violet, B.
1901 'Ein zweisprachiges Psalmfragment aus Damascus', *Orientalistische LiteraturZeitung* 4: col. 384–403, 425–41, 475–88.

Winnett, F.V., and G. Lankester Harding
1978 *Inscriptions from Fifty Safaitic Cairns.* (Near and Middle East Series, 9; Toronto: University of Toronto Press).

Winnett, F.V., and W.L. Reed
1970 *Ancient Records from North Arabia.* With contributions by J.T. Milik and J. Starcky. (Near and Middle East Series, 6; Toronto: University of Toronto Press).

Youtie, H.C.
1966 'Pétaus, fils de Pétaus, ou le scribe qui ne savait pas écrire', *Chronique d'Égypte* 41: 127–43.

Zeinaddin, H.
2000 'Safaitische Inschriften aus dem Ǧabal al-ʿArab', *Damaszener Mitteilungen* 12: 265–89.

KEILSCHRIFT VERSUS ALPHABETSCHRIFT
ÜBERLEGUNGEN ZU DEN *EPIGRAPHS* AUF KEILSCHRIFTTAFELN

Wolfgang Röllig

Vor 20 Jahren hat A.R. Millard seinen Aufsatz 'Assyrians and Arameans' veröffentlicht (Millard 1983), der in der ihm eigenen nüchternen und präzisen Sprache und unter Einbeziehung der damals bekannten Texte das gegenseitige Verhältnis der beiden Bevölkerungsgruppen Mesopotamien-Syriens analysierte. Einige der dort geäußerten Gedanken möchte ich hier mit Dank an den verehrten Kollegen ein wenig weiter verfolgen.

Seit 1978 werden in Tall Šēḫ Ḥamad, dem assyrischen Dūr-Katlimmu, am syrischen Ḫābūr Ausgrabungen durchgeführt, die in vieler Hinsicht ungewöhnliche Funde und Befunde liefern. Besonders erfreulich ist es, dass auch zahlreiche Textzeugnisse aus mittelassyrischer und neuassyrischer Zeit ans Licht gekommen sind.[1] Die zuletzt genannten Texte sind eben von Karen Radner publiziert worden (Radner 2002). Auf den 205 Texten und größeren Fragmenten finden sich 61 z.T. längere Aufschriften (*epigraphs*)[2] in altaramäischer Schrift und Sprache,[3] darunter z.B. auch auf den ins 2. Jahr Nebukadnezars II. datierten Texten BATSH 6,37 und 39.[4] Ferner treten diesen 205 neuassyrischen Urkunden noch rd. 135 aramäische Texte (*dockets*) gegenüber, die z.T. im gleichen archäologischen Kontext gefunden worden sind, d.h. ursprünglich wohl zu den beiden Archiven des Šulmu-šarri und des Raḫimi-il gehörten. Zwar sind diese *dockets* oft schlecht erhalten, häufig nur Bruchstücke, und inhaltlich nicht übermäßig abwechslungsreich, da es fast nur die bekannten Obligationsurkunden zu sein scheinen.[5] Dennoch sind sie schon

[1] Drei neubabylonische Texte, die sich im Gebäude W in der Nordost-Ecke der Unterstadt fanden, werden demnächst von E. Cancik-Kirschbaum im Archiv für Orientforschung publiziert.

[2] Anders als A.R. Millard, der in Millard 1983 stets von 'dockets' spricht und F.M. Fales, der bereits im Titel seines Buches 'Aramaic Epigraphs on Cuneiform Tablets' (Fales 1986) generell den Terminus 'epigraphs' verwendet, ziehe ich es vor, diese Bezeichnung für die Beischriften auf Tontafeln (bei A.T. Clay noch 'indorsements' genannt) einzuschränken und nur die dreieckigen bzw. herzfömigen Tafeln mit aramäischer Beschriftung als 'dockets' dagegen abzugrenzen.

[3] In Radner 2002 bearbeitet von W. Röllig.

[4] Hier sollte noch darauf verwiesen werden, dass es umgekehrt auch babylonische Texte gibt, die in assyrischer Manier noch nach Eponymen datieren, s. Brinkman and Kennedy 1983: 61f.

[5] Vgl. schon Röllig 1997, ferner die Dockets der Sammlungen Schøyen und Moussaieff, die A. Lemaire kürzlich (Lemaire 2001) publiziert hat.

allein durch ihrer große Masse bemerkenswert, da bisher aus dem assyrischen Kernland verhältnismäßig wenige dieser Urkunden bekannt waren, hauptsächlich aus Assur,[6] ferner aus Ninive und Nimrud,[7] mehr allerdings aus den Provinzen, z.B. vom Tall Halaf und Maʾallanāte aus der Gegend von Harran.[8] Das überrascht nicht, sind doch diese Regionen altes aramäisches Stammesgebiet: Bīt Baḫiani bzw. Azallu um Tall Halaf und Harran,[9] Bīt Ḫalupe um Dūr-Katlimmu. Auch das Onomastikon des 1. Jt.v.Chr. aus dieser Region macht das deutlich. Das Problem der Zweisprachigkeit stellt sich hier also anders als in Assyrien: Ist es dort die assyrische Sprache in ihrer neuassyrischen Ausformung,[10] die zu dominieren scheint, so dürfte in den westlichen Provinzen das Aramäische vorherrschend gewesen und das Assyrische nur als 'Amtssprache' verwendet worden sein. Hier stellt sich dann auch die Frage nach dem Verhältnis von Keilschrifttext (= assyrisch) und Alphabetschrifttext (*epigraph* = aramäisch) in besonderem Masse.

Zunächst: Zweisprachigkeit ist in der altorientalischen Welt nichts Ungewöhnliches, sondern ein sehr häufiges Phänomen. Es ist allerdings selten an zwei unterschiedliche Schriftsysteme gekoppelt: Zweisprachige sumerisch-akkadische Texte werden natürlich in der beiden gemeinsamen Keilschrift geschrieben. Auch das Hethitische geht hier noch keinen eigenen Weg. Denn sowohl diese Sprache als auch Hattisch und Hurritisch werden in Boğazköy in Keilschrift niedergeschrieben. Das Luwische verwendet zwar zwei verschiedene Schriftsysteme, die Keilschrift einerseits, die sog. 'Hieroglyphen' andererseits, letztere treten aber lediglich bei Siegelinschriften neben der Keilschrift in Erscheinung. Das Ägyptische kann hier ganz vernachlässigt werden, denn die wenigen farbigen Punkte auf einigen literarischen Amarna-Tafeln sind allem Anschein nach Verständnishilfen für die Schreiber-Schüler, die die Texte benutzten, keine Glossierungen o.ä.,[11] und der hieratische Vermerk auf einem Brief diente offenbar der internen Palastadministration.[12]

Das ändert sich offenbar mit dem Aufkommen der Alphabetschrift. In Ugarit–und es ist wohl unbestritten, dass dort bereits das System der kanaanäischen Konsonantenschrift bekannt war–wird zwar formal weiterhin Keilschrift geschrieben, meist auch zwischen den Sprachen getrennt: Ugaritische Schrift für ugaritische Sprache, babylonische Schrift für baby-

[6] Lidzbarski 1921.

[7] Zusammengestellt z.B. von Hug 1993.

[8] Die leider noch immer nicht publizierten Texte aus Maʾallanāte befinden sich in den Musées royaux d'Art et d'Histoire in Brüssel, s. dazu vorläufig Lemaire 2001: 132ff. Nr. 10*–*32 ünd zületzt E. Lipiński 2003: 185–90, bes. Anm.2.

[9] S. zuletzt Dion 1997: 44–48; Lipiński 2000: 119–33.

[10] Vgl. dazu vorläufig Hämeen-Anttila 2000.

[11] So schon Knudtzon 1915: 25.

[12] EA 23, vgl. P. Artzi 1986.

lonische Sprache. Dennoch gibt es einige Texte–auch außerhalb der Vokabulare–die babylonische Sprache in ugaritischer Schrift festgehalten haben.[13] Im 1. Jt.v.Chr. verstärkt sich diese Tendenz. Jetzt werden Bilinguen auch in dem jeweiligen nationalen Schriftsystem abgefasst: In Kilikien auf dem Karatepe, in Cineköy und in Ivriz wird neben luwischen Hieroglyphen für den luwischen Text auch die phönizische Schrift für die phönizische Version des Textes verwendet. In Arslan Tash haben wir sogar den Fall, dass neben der assyrischen Keilschrift auch luwische Hieroglyphen und aramäische Alphabetschrift geschrieben wurde. Allerdings handelt es sich hier nicht in strengem Sinne um Bilinguen, sondern um in der jeweiligen Formulierung leicht abweichende Texte. 'Offizielle' Inschriften, d.h. solche von regierenden Königen, in beiden Sprachen und Schriftsystemen scheinen von den Assyrern nicht zugelassen worden zu sein. Vielmehr waren für königliche Verlautbarungen assyrische Sprache und Keilschrift offenbar obligatorisch.

Das ist ein wichtiges Faktum. Zeigt sich daran doch, dass die auf der Keilschrift basierende Tradition der königlichen Verlautbarungen nicht durchbrochen werden sollte. Ihre Terminologie und Phraseologie war festgelegt und hatte wahrscheinlich im Bereich der Keilschriftkulturen einen Symbolcharakter. Dieser reicht bis in die Achaimenidenzeit, in der durch Darius II. für solche Verlautbarungen, und wohl nur für diese, eine eigene, formal noch der Keilschrift verhaftete Schrift eingeführt wird. Trotzdem wird der inzwischen gründlich veränderten historischen Situation und auch dem Selbstverständnis des Weltreiches entsprechend für die Verbreitung der Inschriften dadurch gesorgt, dass eine aramäische Version auf Papyrus geschrieben und wahrscheinlich in die einzelnen Satrapien des Reiches verschickt wird.[14]

Da hatten es die aramäischen Stammesfürsten leichter. Sie waren keiner solchen Tradition verhaftet, konnten–das beste Beispiel dafür ist Zincirli/Samʾal–allein aramäische Sprache und Schrift verwenden und damit ein neues historisches Selbstbewusstsein demonstrieren. Allerdings ist an einigen Orten, besonders in Sikani und dem benachbarten Guzana, die Übermacht der Tradition des Assyrerreiches doch stärker: Zunächst wird ein Statuensockel noch in einer archaisch anmutenden aramäischen Schrift beschrieben,[15] aber schon Hadad-yisʿi, Statthalter bzw. König von Sikani und Guzana, lässt in der Mitte des 9. Jh. v.Chr. die berühmte Bilingue aus Tall Fecherīye zwar in Aramäisch und Assyrisch abfassen. Aber damit, dass er die

13 Die insgesamt vier fragmentarischen Texte (KTU 1.67; 1.69; 1.70; 1.73,1–8) sind von Huehnergard 1989 in Appendix 9 (p. 338) zusammengestellt.

14 So stammt die überlieferte aramäische Version aus Elephantine an der äußersten südlichen Grenze des Reiches. Vgl. jetzt Greenfield and Porten 1982.

15 KAI I^5 231, s. Dankwarth and Müller 1988; Lipiński 1994: 15–18.

Keilschrift-Version auf der Vorderseite, d.h. der Schauseite anbringen lässt, macht er deutlich, dass er sich der assyrischen Tradition verpflichtet weiß. Kapara, der Sohn Ḫadianus, schreibt wenig später nur noch Keilschrift und ein Schreiber namens Kammaki macht es ihm in der 1. Hälfte des 8. Jh. nach (s. Röllig 2003). Auch die assyrischen Statthalter in Suḫu und Mari am Euphrat Šamaš-rēš-uṣur und Ninurta-kudurri-uṣur schreiben in der ersten Hälfte des 8. Jh. v. Chr. selbstverständlich noch Keilschrift, denn sie stehen klar in assyrischer–wenn nicht gar babylonischer–Tradition (Cavigneaux/ Ismail 1990).

Die Situation ändert sich offenbar im 7. Jahrhundert grundsätzlich. Zwar gibt es nach wie vor im assyrischen Reichsgebiet keine 'offiziellen' Inschriften in aramäischer Schrift und Sprache, wohl aber eine stark anwachsende Zahl von Texten und *epigraphs*, und das nicht nur in den peripheren Regionen des Reiches, sondern nun auch in den Residenzen: in Ninive allein sieben *dockets* und 36 *epigraphs*.

Trotzdem ist es auffällig, dass nur ganz bestimmte Urkundentypen durch aramäische Texte ersetzt bzw. durch *epigraphs* erläutert werden. So steht den außerordentlich zahlreichen Briefen in assyrischer Sprache und Schrift nur ein einziger aramäischer Brief gegenüber, ein Ostrakon, das zwar in Assur gefunden wurde, das aber letztlich aus Babylonien stammt.[16] Man wird dagegen kaum einwenden können, dass Ostraka vielleicht in früheren Grabungen keine Beachtung gefunden haben und weggeworfen wurden. Da müsste sich das Bild in den letzten Jahrzehnten gründlich geändert haben, in denen sorgfältig auf derlei Dokumente geachtet wurde. Aber in all den Jahren hat sich kein weiterer aramäischer Brief gefunden.

Aramäisch abgefasst sind—mit ganz wenigen Ausnahmen—vor allem Schuldurkunden, Obligationen,[17] aber keine Gerichtsurkunden, keine Erbteilungen, keine Eheverträge usw.[18] Doch werden sicher die Vertragspartner bzw. die Kontrahenten in vielen Fällen in aramäischer Zunge gesprochen haben. Warum also diese Einschränkung?

Zunächst: *epigraphs* sind kurze Hinweise auf den Tatbestand, der auf der Tafel beurkundet ist. Das müssen keineswegs nur Obligationen sein, sondern als Keilschrifttexte erscheinen auch Urkunden über Grundstücks- oder Sklavenkauf. Die *epigraphs* geben aber, und das ist ihr eigentliches Charakteristikum, den Inhalt der Transaktion nur jeweils mit einem Stichwort wieder, etwa *ʾgrtʾ zy ʾmt*... 'Urkunde betreffend die Sklavin ...' oder *dnt zy* PN

[16] KAI 233 = TSSI 2,20. Vgl. dazu Fales 1987: 451–69; Hug 1993: 19–21 (Sigle: AssB).

[17] Dazu zuletzt Lipiński 2000: 580–93.

[18] Auch hierfür gibt es natürlich Ausnahmen. Z.B. wurde 1998 in Tall Šēḫ Ḥamad ein Tonklumpen (SH 98/6949 I 95) mit Eindruck eines Kinderfußes und einer sehr schwer lesbaren, eingeritzten aramäischen Inschrift gefunden, die wahrscheinlich die Annahme eines Findelkindes beurkundet.

'Dokument des PN',[19] bedienen sich also keiner juristischen Fachterminologie. Diese Vermerke haben ja offensichtlich auch nur den Charakter eines Ordnungsvermerks: Der Besitzer der Tafel, von dem wir annehmen, dass er des Aramäischen in Wort und Schrift mächtig war, konnte aufgrund des *epigraphs* feststellen, um welche Rechtssache es sich handelte, ohne dass er den Keilschrifttext mit seiner Fachterminologie lesen musste. Das modifiziert die Feststellung von A.R. Millard (Millard 1983: 101) 'at Nineveh ... were scribes at work there who could not read cuneiform, yet who would need to distinguish one document from another'. Wahrscheinlich konnte er ihn auch gar nicht lesen, sondern dafür gab es speziell ausgebildete Schreiber. Denn–und das scheint mir wichtig–es gibt nirgends Keilschrifttafeln, die eine Kurzfassung in Form eines '*epigraphs* in Keilschrift' auf dem Rand tragen. Diese hätten den Eigentümern der Tontafeln nichts genützt, weil sie sie wohl nicht lesen konnten.

Mit Recht unterscheidet A.R. Millard die Tintenaufschriften, die jederzeit mit der Binse oder der Rohrfeder[20] auf den harten Ton aufgetragen werden konnten, von den geritzten *epigraphs*, die den noch weichen Ton voraussetzen. Allerdings lässt sich gelegentlich durch das Ausreißen des Tons feststellen, dass diese Beischriften erst nach dem Keilschrifttext angebracht wurden. Auf den neuassyrischen Tafeln aus Tall Šēḫ Ḥamad sind 31 von 61 *epigraphs* in Tinte ausgeführt, davon allein 6 neben geritzten Beischriften, die sie z.T. duplizieren. Für diese doppelte Beschriftung habe ich keine Erklärung, es sei denn, man wollte die leicht vergängliche Tintenaufschrift durch eine geritzte Inschrift ersetzen.

Gerne wüssten wir, wer die *epigraphs* auf den Tontafeln anbrachte. Drei Möglichkeiten bieten sich an: Erstens könnte der Besitzer der Tontafel, wenn er selbst die Keilschrift nicht lesen konnte, doch den aramäischen Text, den er verstand, auch nachgetragen haben. Das müsste dann ziemlich rasch nach Fertigstellung des Textes geschehen sein, jedenfalls ehe er völlig getrocknet war. Zweitens könnte es ein speziell für das Aramäische ausgebildeter Schreiber geschrieben haben. Die Existenz eines *ṭupšarru aramāyu* ist mehrfach–wenn auch nicht in Dūr-Katlimmu–bezeugt (Radner 1997: 83 mit Anm. 434), und die neuassyrischen Reliefs mit Schreiberdarstellungen machen ja auch den Unterschied im Beschreibstoff, in der Handhaltung und sogar in der Haartracht deutlich. Ob man allerdings außerhalb der assyrischen

[19] Radner 2002: 51 a/b. Es ist auffällig, dass die Formulierungen mit *dnt* entspr. akkadisch *dannutu*, von mir ebd. im Gegensatz zu *'grt* 'Urkunde' als 'Dokument' übersetzt, in der Mehrzahl der Fälle (Fales 1986: Nr. 4; 5; 14; 16?; 23; 27; 31?; Radner 2002: Nr. 7; 43; 44; 45; 53; 54; 60?; 74; 104; 105; 119; 134; 142?; 143) nach diesem Terminus lediglich einen Eigennamen nennt.

[20] Dass Rohrfedern benutzt wurden ist daran ersichtlich, dass diese gelegentlich abgenützt und dann gespalten waren, was man auf den originalen Aufschriften gelegentlich erkennen kann.—Aus welchen Ingredienzien die Tinte bestand und welches Wort dafür verwendet wurde, weiß ich nicht.

Hauptstadt eine so starke Spezialisierung der Schreiber kannte, ist zumindest recht zweifelhaft. Allein für das Anbringen von *epigraphs* wird man sie sicher nicht beschäftigt haben. Drittens könnte natürlich der Schreiber für assyrische Keilschrift auch die Fähigkeit gehabt haben, aramäische Alphabetschrift zu schreiben. Da z.B. für Dūr-Katlimmu mehr als 15 Schreiber bekannt sind (Radner 2002: 22), ist das sehr wahrscheinlich und erklärt auch die unterschiedlichen 'Handschriften', die sich zumindest bei den *dockets* aus dieser Stadt ausmachen lassen. Dennoch: Einen konkreten Hinweis auf den jeweiligen Schreiber besitzen wir bisher noch nicht.

Die Deutung der Epigraphs als 'Ordnungsmittel für Nicht-Keilschriftkundige' erklärt auch das Phänomen, dass solche Beischriften auf Tontafeln mit literarischen Texten, die ja häufig einen langen Kolophon tragen, nie zu finden sind, auch wenn es sich angeboten hätte, hier ebenfalls Inhaltsangaben in aramäischer Sprache und Schrift zu machen. Die Schreiber, die solche Texte verwendeten, waren selbstverständlich noch voll und ganz mit der Keilschrift vertraut und brauchten keine 'modernen' Hilfsmittel.[21]

Es scheint so, als ob die *epigraphs* zunächst ein rein assyrisches Phänomen waren. Sie sind es aber nicht geblieben. Vielmehr sind auch aus Babylonien, wo ja die Aramaisierung schon viel früher als in Assyrien nachweisbar ist (Lipiński 2000: 409ff.), zahlreiche *epigraphs* bekannt.[22] Auffällig ist aber, dass diese alle erst aus der Zeit nach dem Zusammenbruch des assyrischen Reiches stammen. Auffällig ist ferner, dass sehr viele der Texte, die aramäische *epigraphs* tragen, aus Nippur stammen, das bekanntlich ein Zentrum der assyrischen Verwaltung Babyloniens war. Sollte sich also hier eine von den Assyrern eingeführte Praxis weiter erhalten haben? Dem steht entgegen, dass die meisten dieser Texte erst in die Zeit der Achaimeniden und Seleukiden datieren, wobei Herrscher wir Artaxerxes I. (464–424) und Darius II. (423–405) besonders häufig vertreten sind. Ein einziger Text scheint älter zu sein (BRM 1,22: Nabû-mukīn-zēri, 731–729),[23] doch ist er so kurz und zweifelhaft, dass er hier nicht ins Gewicht fällt.[24] Die Formulierungen sind meist so, dass sie ebenfalls den Sachverhalt des Textes kurz resümieren. Lediglich das Einleitungswort ist verschieden: *šṭr* 'Schriftstück' anstelle des assyrischen *dnt* bzw. *ʾgrt*. Allerdings scheint die Sitte zeitlich und räumlich sehr beschränkt gewesen zu sein, denn schon in hellenistischer Zeit fehlen solche *epigraphs* auf Keilschrifttafeln fast völlig

[21] Der einzige nicht-juristische Keilschrifttext mit einer aramäischen Beischrift, Knudtzon 1893: Nr. 120 = Starr 1990: Nr. 162, vgl. Fales 1986: Nr. 9, wurde zwar in Kujundjik gefunden, doch scheinen seine Verfasser Nabû-ušallim (*nbwšlm*) und Aqaraja (*ʾq*[*ryʾ*?]) Babylonier gewesen zu sein. Beachte die Schreibung *šlm* statt assyr. *slm* und s. I. Starr zur Stelle.

[22] Gesammelt zunächst bei A.T. Clay 1908 bzw. L. Delaporte 1912. Dem Vernehmen nach bereitet F. Joannès eine neue Gesamtbearbeitung der *epigraphs* auf babylonischen Tontafeln vor.

[23] Vgl. dazu Lipiński 2000: 421 Anm.63.

[24] Ins Jahr 41 Nebukadnezars datiert die Urkunde Nr. 2 in McEwan 1982.

(Oelsner 1986: 245–48). Das mag seinen Grund aber auch darin haben, dass in dieser Zeit privatrechtliche Urkunden immer seltener, d.h. wohl durch Papyrusurkunden ersetzt werden. Mit den *epigraphs* auf assyrischen Rechtsurkunden des 8./7. Jh. v. Chr. tritt uns also eine ganz spezifische, den Bedürfnissen einer bilinguen Gesellschaft angepasste Art von Dokumenten entgegen, der kein langes Leben und keine große Verbreitung vergönnt war.

Bibliography

Artzi, P.
1986 'Observations on the "Library" of the Amarna Archives', in K. R. Veenhof (ed.), *Cuneiform Archives and Libraries* (Leiden): 210–12.

Brinkman, J.A., and D.A. Kennedy
1983 'Documentary evidence for the economic base of early Neo-Babylonian society', *JCS* 35: 1–90.

Cavigneaux, A., and B. Khalil Ismail
1990 'Die Statthalter von Suḫu und Mari im 8. Jh. v. Chr.', *BagM* 21: 321–456.

Clay, A.T.
1908 *Aramaic Indorsements on the Documents of the Murašû Sons* (Philadelphia).

Dankwarth, G., and C. Müller
1988 'Zur altaramäischen "Altar"-Inschrift vom Tell Ḥalaf', *AfO* 35: 73–78.

Delaporte, L.
1912 *Épigraphes araméens* (Paris).

Dion, P.-E.
1997 *Les Araméens à l'Âge du Fer: Histoire politique et structures sociales* (Paris).

Fales, F.M.
1986 'Aramaic epigraphs on cuneiform tablets', *StudSemNS* 2 (Rome).
1987 'Aramaic letters and Neo-Assyrian letters: philological and methodological notes', *JAOS* 107: 451–69.

Greenfield, J.C., and B. Porten
1982 *The Bisutun Inscription of Darius the Great: Aramaic Version.* Corpus Inscriptionum Iranicarum Part I, vol. V, Texts I (London).

Hämeen-Anttila, J.
2000 'A sketch of Neo-Assyrian grammar', *SAAS* 13 (Helsinki).

Huehnergard, J.
1989 'The Akkadian of Ugarit', *HSS* 34 (Atlanta).

Hug, V.
1993 'Altaramäische Grammatik der Texte des 7. und 6. Jh.s v. Chr.', *HSAO* 4 (Heidelberg).

Knudtzon, J.A.
1893 *Assyrische Gebete an den Sonnengott* (Leipzig).
1915 'Die El-Amarna-Tafeln', *Vorderasiatische Bibliothek* Bd. 2 (Leipzig).
Lemaire, A.
2001 *Nouvelles Tablettes Araméennes* (Genf).
Lidzbarski, M.
1921 *Altaramäische Urkunden aus Assur* (Berlin).
Lipiński, E.
1994 'Studies in Aramaic inscriptions and onomastics II', OLA 57 (Leuven).
2000 'The Aramaeans: their ancient history, culture, religion', OLA 100 (Leuven).
2003 'Ḥaddiy's wine or donkeys', in R. Deutsch (ed.), *Sholmo: Studies ... in Honour of Sholomo Moussaieff* (Tel Aviv, Jaffa).
McEwan, G.J.P.
1982 *The Late Babylonian Tablets in the Royal Ontario Museum* (Toronto).
Millard, A.R.
1983 'Assyrians and Arameans', *Iraq* 45: 101–8.
Oelsner, J.
1986 *Materialien zur babylonischen Gesellschaft und Kultur in hellenistischer Zeit* (Budapest).
Radner, K.
1997 'Die neuassyrischen Privatrechtsurkunden als Quelle für Mensch und Umwelt', *SAAS* 6 (Helsinki).
2002 *Die neuassyrischen Texte aus Tall Šēḫ Ḥamad. Berichte der Ausgrabung Tall Šēḫ Ḥamad/Dūr-Katlimmu* Bd.6 (Berlin).
Röllig, W.
1997 'Aramaica Haburensia 2. Zwei datierte aramäische Urkunden aus Tall Šēḫ Ḥamad, FS H. Klengel', *AoF* 24: 366–74.
2003 'Das Sitzbild des Kammaki ...', in R. Dittmann, Chr. Eder, B. Jacobs (eds), *Altertumswissenschaften im Dialog, FS W. Nagel, AOAT* 306 (Münster): 421–32.
Starr, I.
1990 *Queries to the Sungod. State Archives of Assyria IV* (Helsinki).

The Writing on the Wall: Law in Aramaic Epigraphy

John F. Healey

This paper is concerned solely with Middle Aramaic inscriptions of approximately 100 BC to AD 300, and this restriction focuses attention on the Greek and Roman periods in the Middle East. The inscriptions come from Petra (the capital of the Nabataeans in Jordan), Palmyra (in the Syrian desert), Edessa (modern Urfa in southern Turkey) and Hatra (in northern Iraq). I will also refer to Jewish Aramaic materials of the same period, though these have not been neglected as much as the others and are not here my prime concern.

In a famous article published in 1982, Ramsay MacMullen drew attention to the fact that what he called 'the epigraphic habit' among the Romans can be shown through statistics to have flourished in the early Roman Empire period and reached a peak around AD 150. While he did not say much about why this habit developed in this period, answers have been supplied by other scholars who have followed this line of enquiry, such as E.A. Meyer (1990), who wrote specifically about epitaphs and saw the habit of writing inscriptions of this kind as an expression of Romanization in an expanding empire. However, this proves to be rather complicated. Thus G. Woolf (1998: 103) drew attention to the fact that very large numbers of the new writers of inscriptions, especially in the West, had non-Roman names: imitation of an élite rather than change of identity may have been a major motive. Almost all earlier comments on this phenomenon concentrate on Greek and Latin within the boundaries of the Empire. However, it can be shown that the epigraphic habit was also taken up by the independent and semi-independent states on the fringe of the Roman East, and not only in Greek (there is very little Latin in the Roman Near East), but also in the main language of the populations of Palestine, Syria, southern Anatolia and northern Mesopotamia, i.e. Aramaic.

In recent books Alan Millard (2000) and Catherine Hezser (2001) have dealt in great detail with the situation in Palestine in the context of discussion of Jewish literacy around the time of Jesus. However, this discussion looks beyond Palestine, which cannot, I would claim, be taken to be typical of the East, since the Jewish culture of that area may have had a special role in the development of literacy and the epigraphic habit (though the recent book by Nicole Belayche (2001) is a salutary reminder that there were lots of pagans in Palestine as well as Jews). But another factor that makes Judaea different is the fact that it was mostly under direct Roman rule when the inscriptions were written, unlike Petra, Edessa and Hatra.

We have to come clean immediately over one weakness in what we have to say about the epigraphic habit in Nabataea, Palmyra (which *was* Roman), Edessa and Hatra, and that is that the surviving evidence is very unevenly distributed. Also in sheer numerical terms it does not compare at all with the vast amounts of epigraphic and documentary material from the Empire itself. Bodel (2001: 4, 8) gives a figure for all Greek and Latin inscriptions from antiquity of 600,000, of which 60,000 are Latin inscriptions from North Africa and 100,000 are Latin inscriptions from Rome alone. As we will see, the Aramaic inscriptions of the Semitic East pale into insignificance by comparison. However, before providing some rough figures I would note two contradictory but obvious consequences of the paucity of material:

(i) Inscriptions and documentary materials (legal texts and letters), especially the highly formulaic ones, are best studied in quantity, like archaeologically recovered pottery. A single Mycenaean sherd from a Near Eastern site cannot form the basis of any conclusion in the realm of narrative history. But hundreds of Mycenaean sherds scattered over a site and, perhaps, concentrated in certain buildings but not others, might give a glimmer of narrative light and can certainly lead to typological analysis and comparison with non-ceramic evidence. So also an isolated tomb inscription tells us little—it might be a one-off written by an eccentric—but *series* of such inscriptions can be significantly informative about the society in which they were produced. The first of what I have called obvious consequences, therefore, is that the sparser the evidence, the less useful it is.

(ii) But this is contradicted by another obvious consequence of paucity of evidence. Where only a few inscriptions survive they are individually of even more importance than in situations in which there are hundreds of examples, since we can only deal with what survives and in many ancient Near Eastern contexts every scrap has to be exploited to the full. Both the Millard and the Hezser books demonstrate this in action. The skill and challenge for the epigraphist and historian is to avoid overinterpreting what *does* survive. In some of the epigraphic 'provinces' I will describe shortly, everything which is concluded, whether about religion or social structures, is concluded provisionally, pending the discovery of further material. There are many potential dangers in the use of epigraphic evidence (as discussed recently by Macdonald (1998)), but somehow we have to struggle through with the evidence as we have it: it is no use sitting in silence waiting for more evidence to turn up, since, as Macdonald notes, there will never be *enough* evidence.

So what survives? Here I am addressing myself to *Aramaic* materials and the Greek and Roman periods, and it should not be forgotten that there are vast earlier survivals of writing from Mesopotamia and Egypt, and there are other non-Aramaic materials of the Roman period from the Near and Middle East, including 20,000 plus 'Safaitic' inscriptions, to mention only those which are most closely connected with the Aramaic-using areas. These are, as noted by Harris (1989: 189), an intense manifestation of literacy which demands some explanation—perhaps they can be explained in terms of having been produced over a very long period (like the 13,000 plus inscriptions under the title 'Thamudic').

The really big block of material in Aramaic is the Nabataean. There is no systematic corpus and it is hard to estimate the numbers even of texts which have been published, but we are dealing with well over 5,000 items. It must immediately be noted that we are referring here to the Nabataean *script* used for writing Aramaic, not implying a connection with the Nabataean kingdom. The script continued in use well beyond the date of the annexation of Nabataea by the Romans in AD 106 and it was used over a vast territory from nothern Egypt, especially Sinai, to northern Arabia and southern Syria, as well as in the Nabataean heartland around Petra. But we do appear to be dealing here with a quantity of written material which is comparable, at least, with that of, for example, Roman North Africa (60,000 Latin inscriptions according to Bodel).

Unfortunately a very large proportion of the surviving texts consists of little more than names and short genealogies. But even so, there is a substantial body of material relating to religion (dedications of temples, references to deities, etc.) and to funerary matters (since many of the longest and best preserved inscriptions are funerary in character and a good deal more informative on social and legal affairs than one might have expected). But the study of this epigraphic material is not 'supported', so to speak, by the survival of any contemporary or later *literature* in Nabataean: there is nothing of the kind surviving. This is an interesting and significant point of contrast with Greek, Latin and Hebrew epigraphy. It means that the interpretation of the inscriptions can only be based on material drawn from within the epigraphic corpus and through the use of comparison with other languages or dialects. The task of the epigraphist thereby becomes much more difficult.

However, a major advance over the last few years has been the publication of the first and early second centuries AD Nabataean legal papyri from the Cave of Letters (most importantly in Yadin *et al.* 2002). The result of these publications and of other lesser documentary finds is that there are now around 20 items in the list of Nabataean documents, about half of which are substantial (e.g. legal papyri with over 40 lines of text). This is still meagre compared with the thousands of published papyrus documents from Egypt: Harris in the late 1980s (1989: 10, 121–24) gives an estimate of 1,500 published papyri from Egypt, reflecting an expansion in bureaucracy. But something is better than nothing!

The Palmyrene epigraphic harvest is also substantial. Quite apart from the inscriptions written in Greek at Palmyra, there are in the latest (more or less complete) corpus 2,832 Palmyrene Aramaic inscriptions (Hillers and Cussini 1996). The Palmyrenes certainly shared the epigraphic habit which had spread with the Roman Empire and many of these inscriptions are dedications of statues and tombs, as well as foundation documents related to temples and building work associated with temples. A particular benefit comes with the fact that many of these inscriptions are bilingual, in Greek and Aramaic (see recently Taylor 2002; Kaizer 2002: 27–34), but unfortunately for Palmyrene Aramaic we have no literature and only minute fragments of documentary material from Dura Europos (a probable line of Palmyrene in a Greek papyrus dated *c*. AD 225–40 (Dura 27 d) and a fragment of a parchment lease, also of the third century (Dura 152): Welles *et al*. 1959). The only really big text preserved in Palmyrene Aramaic is the famous bilingual Tariff of AD 137. This has about 160 lines of Aramaic (not all well preserved). Given that Palmyra, even at its height, was really rather small, with few outposts outside the city itself, the amount of surviving material is quite good.

Edessa, by contrast, is deeply disappointing epigraphically, though with it we are linguistically in a much more satisfactory position since its Aramaic dialect, by convention called Syriac, survived as a literary language, so that there is a vast literature in Syriac from later times. Unfortunately, though, this later literature is almost entirely Christian and it is not very informative on pagan Edessa during the first few centuries AD. For *that* period we have to turn to the meagre harvest of 107 inscriptions (including very small fragments) in a recent corpus (Drijvers and Healey 1999). Few of these are more than a line or two in length, though they do provide some dates and some information on religious and funerary culture. A significant number of the dated texts come from mosaics. Somewhat redeeming this general situation of paucity is the fact that there are three long legal documents on parchment of around 40 lines each and dating to the 240s AD. These were found in Dura Europos and elsewhere in northern Mesopotamia, but were clearly written in or near Edessa.

And finally in this survey we have the Hatran Aramaic inscriptions (no documents on papyrus or parchment, and no related literature) which number 416 in Beyer's useful compendium (1998; see also Vattioni 1981 and 1994; Aggoula 1991), to which should be added about 55 additional related items and 44 inscriptions from Assur which belong to the same tradition (Aggoula 1985). A total, therefore, of just over 500. There are other Aramaic inscriptions from Mesopotamia/Iraq in this period, but they are scattered and few in number.

There is much that is in common between these corpora, despite the fact that the scripts differ considerably from place to place and each, of course, had its own religious and cultural particularities. A result of this common background culture is that even where there is little material (for example from Edessa) it can often be interpreted in the light of what is known better from Nabataean or Palmyrene. This is true of certain religious epigraphic formulae, but it is also true of the legal tradition which was evidently common, and shared also to a large extent with the Jewish community in Palestine.

Of religious formulae I will mention briefly two which have had systematic treatment elsewhere. In both cases it is worth emphasizing that they have to be interpreted according to a defined social context and *Sitz im Leben*. The question we have to answer ultimately concerning any particular genre of inscription is 'how did this kind of inscription actually work or how was it imagined to work or, if it is *purely* formulaic, how did it originally work?' How did the writing on the wall relate to real life?

(i) In all four Aramaic provinces in question the most common epigraphic formula is the *dkīr* formula (Healey 1996). This word means 'remembered be' and it usually begins the inscription and is followed by one or more personal names. So far as we can tell it is not normally a question of remembering the dead, but of remembering the person concerned by naming him in the presence of a deity, who is himself or herself also often named. The remembering is usually specified as being 'remembering for good' and the full formula, where it occurs, is 'Remembered be so-and-so before the god so-and-so for good'. We know that mentioning the name before the god is a key part of the real world to which the inscription refers because in a few cases we have reference to a curse on anyone who sees the inscription and fails to mention the name of the person before the god. So there is much more to the formula than at first appears and the fact that there are dozens of examples of this type of inscription makes it susceptible to detailed analysis.

(ii) Another very common and widespread formula of Aramaic epigraphy is the *ʿal ḥayy* ('for the life of') inscription. Essentially this type of inscription says that something has been dedicated to the god so-and-so 'for the life of' a particular person. In a very high proportion of cases the person making the dedication is a subordinate of someone in high office, frequently a king, and he makes the offering of a statue or an altar or building 'for the life of my lord the king'. This kind of inscription is essentially connected with social and political loyalty and expresses that loyalty in a public way. This type of inscription has been extensively studied by Dijkstra (1995), who brings out its socio-political implications. Again there is much more to it than at first meets the eye.

I now want to move on to discuss another type of inscription, not defined on a formal basis as specifically as these two, but in which the common element is the public display of cultic rules and regulations, carved on stone, visible in temples and embodying religious laws. I will then at the end say a little about some non-obvious aspects of tomb-inscriptions.

There is one extremely well known instance of a religious regulation inscribed visibly in a temple, and this is the case of the injunction in the Jerusalem temple written in Greek and Latin against gentiles entering the courtyard restricted to Jews. The existence of such inscriptions in Herod's temple is indicated in several places by Josephus, who also tells us that this restriction had the sanction of the civil authorities (*War* V, 194; VI, 124–28; *Ant.* XV, 417; VIII, 95; XII, 145–56). Amazingly, Clermont-Ganneau discovered the Greek text of one of these inscriptions in Jerusalem in the late nineteenth century and his discovery, which was supplemented by the discovery of a further fragment in 1935 (Iliffe 1936), generated a large literature bringing all the evidence and considerations together (Clermont-Ganneau 1872; Dittenberger 1905: no. 598; Bickerman 1946–47; Rabello 2000 (original 1970)). The text reads:

> Μηθένα ἀλλογενῆ εἰσπορεύεσθαι ἐντὸς τοῦ περὶ τὸ ἱερὸν τρυφάκτου καὶ περιβόλου. Ὃς δ'ἂν ληφθῇ, ἑαυτῷ αἴτιος ἔσται διὰ τὸ ἐξακολουθεῖν θάνατον.
>
> 'No alien may enter within the balustrade around the sanctuary and the enclosure. Whoever is caught, on himself shall be put blame for the death which will ensue' (Bickerman).

In this context commentators frequently mentioned the presence of similar inscriptions at other temples in the Graeco-Roman world such as one at Samothrace *c*. AD 200, where the inscription, bilingual in Greek and Latin, indicated that the uninitiated were forbidden to enter (Lehmann-Hartleben 1939). There was also, from nearer Jerusalem, a Greek inscription from the temple at Mount Hermon, which said:

> 'By the order of the greatest and holy god. From here (inwards) only the convenanters/those who have taken the oath' (Clermont-Ganneau 1903; Cumont 1913).

Here we have a very clear case of a ban written up precisely in the place where the rule came into effect, just as in the Jerusalem case, where the inscriptions were on the balustrade of the forbidden area.

It is worthy of note that it was the habit also in Hatra to set up similar injunctions within the precinct of temples (see in brief Degen 1977 and Segal

1982). Some of these are different in spirit from those mentioned already, but one is an undated inscription commanding that shoes should not be worn beyond a certain point in the temple complex (Hatra inscription no. 29):

1. *bgn mrn*
2. *wmrtn wbrm[ryn]*
3. *wšḥrw wb‘šm[yn]*
4. *w’tr‘t’ ‘l [mn]*
5. *dl‘wl lhk’*
6. *bmšn<yn>*

‘Invocation of Māran and Mārtan and Barmārēn [the Hatran triad] and Šaḥru and Ba‘alšamin and Atargatis against whoever enters here in footwear.’

This falls into the pattern of the inscriptions already mentioned in which the inscription marks the spot at which the regulation comes into force. It is not difficult or fanciful to imagine the *Sitz im Leben* here: no doubt there would have been plenty of temple police or busy-bodies ready to point to the sign. In this particular case no sanction is mentioned other than the curse of the gods. In the Jerusalem case the sanction was death and apparently could be applied forthwith (cf. discussion of Rabello 2000).

There is, however, another group of Hatra temple inscriptions containing rules governing the conduct of temple employees in which the death penalty is explicitly indicated. The first is Hatra inscription no. 281 (which is replete with difficulties of vocabulary and syntax):

1. *bgn mrn wmrtn*
2. *wbrmryn ‘l mn dy*
3. *lnsb mškn’ ’w*
4. *ḥṭm’ ’w mr’*
5. *wnrg’ wksyd’*
6. *wgblyt’ wmkl’*
7. *wḥṣn’ mn ‘bd’*
8. *dy brmryn wmn dy*
9. *lnsb ḥd mn grb’*
10. *hlyn mn dy brmryn*
11. *ḥwy ḥlm’ dy*
12. *’rgmyt mrgym*

‘Invocation of Māran and Mārtan and Barmārēn against anyone who takes a tent or hammer (?) or spade or axe or chisel (?) or mould (?) or bolt or adze from the work of Barmārēn. And whoever takes one of these pieces of equipment (?) from those of Barmārēn, the dream(-priest?) has revealed: I have indeed ordered his stoning to death.’

There are several other instances of the death penalty and stoning for theft. This was evidently a well-known feature of Hatra legal tradition since it is picked out by the Syriac philosopher Bardaisan (AD 154–222) as a typical practice of the people of Hatra.

We have a second inscription of this type in Hatra no. 344:

1. *[b]mlt [š]mšḥdyt [rbytʾ]*
2. *wḥpyzy qšš wḥṭr[yʾ]*
3. *klhwn hkyn psqw*
4. *šlhy ʾnš dlzbyn lk[pʾ]*
5. *wlkṣrʾ wlgṣʾ mn ḥd*
6. *ʿglʾ dy byt ʾlhʾ*
7. *mnṭlt dy nsybw ʾgr*
8. *bdyhwn mn byt ʾlhʾ*
9. *wʾyn lzby[n] mnhwn kpʾ*
10. *ʾw kṣrʾ ʾw gṣʾ*
11. *ʾw gṣʾ ʾ[w] lb(!)r mnhwn*
12. *ʿgltʾ lmwt mwtʾ*
13. *ʾlhʾ*

'By the order of Šamašḥadet the administrator and Ḥapīzay the elder and all the Hatrans, thus they decided: it is forbidden (?) that anyone should buy stone or straw or lime from any of the carters (?) belonging to the house of the gods, since they have taken payment in their hands from the house of the gods. And if he sells any of them, stone or straw or lime (or lime), or, apart from them, the cart itself, he will die the death of the gods.'

The death of the gods is a particular punishment, possibly open-ended and left for the temple authorities to decide. We find it again in inscription no. 342, from the mid second century AD:

1. *hkyn psqw nrgl dḥ*
2. *špṭʾ wsnṭrwq mlkʾ*
3. *wrʾyt rbytʾ wʾstnq*
4. *qšyšʾ dy kwl zmrtʾ*
5. *wqyntʾ dy mrn wmrtn*
6. *[w]brmryn dy tšbw[q] mqmh*
7. *wtʾzy[l..]ṣrkʾ bmwtʾ*
8. *dy ʾlhʾ [tmwt w]dy lnpq*
9. *zmrt[ʾ...] lh gbʾ*
10. *bmwtʾ dy ʾ[l]hʾ lmwt hw*
11. *[g]brʾ š[t]r [m]n snṭrwq*
12. *mlkʾ dʿb[...b]r ʿmh*
13. *ʾmty d[...] lšndrh*
14. *lbym[...] ʿbyd wdkyr*

'Thus have decided Nergal, chief of the guards, and king Sanaṭrūq and Raʾīt the administrator and Astanaq the elder, that any female musician or singer of Māran and Mārtan and Barmārēn who leaves her place and departs in disgrace (?) will die by the death of the gods and whoever enables the (said) female musician to go out ... for her a hiding-place (?), by the death of the gods that man will die. Decree from king Sanaṭrūq, who ... his people, when ... he will send it to the tribunal (?) ... Let it be done and remembered.'

Finally, there are gateway inscriptions dated to AD 151/2. No. 343 was found in the east gate of the city, while no. 336, almost identical, was found just inside the north gate of the city. The text contrasts two different forms of the death penalty:

1. *byrḥ knwn d463 bmlkʾ dy*
2. *ʾlhʾ ʾṣṭbw šmšbrk rbytʾ*
3. *wḥṭryʾ qšyšʾ wdrdqʾ wʿrbyʾ*
4. *klhwn* wkwl dy ʿmr bḥṭrʾ whkyn psq<w>*
5. *dy kwl dlgnwb lgw mn mlʾ hdyn*
6. *wlgw mn šwrʾ bryʾ ʾyn gbrʾ*
7. *hw gwyʾ lqṭyl bmwtʾ dy*
8. *ʾlhʾ wʾyn gbrʾ hw bryʾ*
9. *lrgym*
*336 adds: *wkl dy ʿl wnpyq lḥṭrʾ*

'In the month of Kānūn of 463, on the advice of the gods, Šamašbarak the administrator and the Hatrans old and young and the inhabitants of ʿArab, all of them, (*and all who enter and leave Hatra) and all who live in Hatra agreed and thus decided, that anyone who steals within (the area of) this ramp and inside the outer wall (of the city), if he is a native he will be killed by the death of the gods and if he is an outsider he will be stoned.'

In this last example we again have very specific topographical references, including 'within the ramp' and 'inside the wall'. The word translated 'ramp', *mlʾ* (only here and in no. 336, but cf. Hebrew *millōʾ* in 2 Sam. 5:9 etc.), has been interpreted very satisfactorily by Steiner (1989). Both inscriptions were found in gateways and the starting-point for the explanation is the fact that the thing being referred to must have been visible from the place where the inscription was erected. Steiner argues well that the *mlʾ* must have been part of the gateway structure where the inscription was displayed. It probably refers to an artificial infill or ramp. Thus the inscription covers theft inside the adjoining gate area as well as inside the city-wall itself.

Apart from these Hatra inscriptions there is little that is comparable in other contemporary forms of Aramaic, but attention may be drawn to a fragmentary inscription dated AD 26/27 and originally displayed in the so-called 'Temple of the Winged Lions' at Petra (Hammond *et al.* 1986; Jones 1989). It refers to regulations governing the conduct of priests attached to the temple:

1. *mh dy yʾtʾ lh mn ksp wdhb wqrbwn wzwn klh wmn kspʾ wnḥ[šʾ]///*
2. *wlkmryʾ plgʾ ʾḥrnʾ ʿm ʾkltʾ kryz hww qdm dnh pytḥlqwn ///*
3. *ʿlwhy dy ʿbd kʿyr kl dy ʿlʾ ktyb pyprʿ mh dy yštkḥ ʿ[lwhy] ///*
4. *bywm ʾrbʿh bʾb šnt tltyn wšbʿ lḥrtt mlk nbṭw rḥm ʿmh wtw ///*

'Whatever he receives of silver or gold or offerings or any provisions, or of silver coin or bronze coin ... and to the priests the other half with the foodstuffs: they have been subject to a proclamation before this time, so that they will be divided ... against him that he has done other than all that is written above, he will pay whatever will be found against him ... On the fourth day of Ab in the year thirty-seven of Ḥaretat, king of the Nabataeans, lover of his people. And ...'

This is hard to disentangle in its present state. It appears to deal with rules governing offerings received by priests in the temple.

Another example of a series of ritual regulations is the first century AD Palmyrene inscription giving the regulations governing the *thiasos* of the gods Bolʿastor and Baʿalshamīn (Teixidor 1981; Hillers and Cussini 1996: PAT 0091). This is another clear case of a regulation appearing as writing on the wall. I use the term 'regulation' because in none of these cases are we dealing with laws as in the Greek city law-codes put up in public places. The only Aramaic law remotely resembling those inscriptions is the Palmyrene tax tariff.

Finally, we may add something very briefly about some non-temple inscriptions which function in the same way by proclaiming a legal situation, the tomb inscriptions of the Nabataeans and Palmyrenes. It is worth pointing out that these tomb texts are not epitaphs in the conventional sense of Greek and Roman epitaphs (Lattimore 1942). They do not comment on the qualities of the deceased or express religious pieties about life after death or even simply say 'Here lies so-and-so'. Rather they are *legal* declarations. Typical is the following, dated AD 31/32, and from a tomb-façade at the Nabataean city of Ḥegra in northern Saudi Arabia (Healey 1993: no. 36):

'This is the tomb which Ḥalafu son of Qōsnatan made for himself and for Suʿaydu, his son, and his brothers, whatever male children may be born to this Ḥalafu, and for their sons and their descendants by hereditary title for ever. And his children (?) may be buried in this tomb: this Suʿaydu and Manūʿat and Ṣanaku and Rībamat and Umayyat and Salīmat, daughters of this Ḥalafu. And none at all of Suʿaydu and his brothers, males, and their sons and their

> descendants has the right to sell this tomb or write a deed of gift or anything else for anyone at all, except if one of them writes for his wife or for his daughters or for a father-in-law or for a son-in-law a document for burial only. And anyone who does other than this will be liable for a fine to Dushara the god of our lord [the king] in the sum of five hundred Haretite drachmas and to our lord similarly, according to the copy of this deposited in the temple of Qaysha. In the month of Nisan, the fortieth year of Ḥaretat, King of the Nabataeans, lover of his people. Rūma and ʿAbdʿobodat, the masons.'

Another, dated AD 16/17 and on another façade reads (Healey 1993: no. 27):

> 'This is the tomb which Taymallāhi son of Ḥamilat made for himself. And he gave this tomb to Amah, his wife, daughter of Gulhumu, from the date of the deed of gift which is in her hand, that she might do with it whatever she wishes. From the 26th of Ab, the 25th year of Ḥaretat, King of the Nabataeans, lover of his people.'

This is a document of legal cession, similar to the cession documents inscribed on a number of Palmyrene tombs (Hillers and Cussini 1996: PAT 0058 of AD 265; 0095 of 239; 0042 of 237; 0555 of 193, etc.; cf. Cussini 1995). A very short example is PAT 0047 dated AD 213:

1. *byrḥ ṭbt šnt 524*
2. *ʿgʾ rḥqt lʿttn šʾr*
3. *ʾksdrʾ šḥymʾ*

> 'In the month of Ṭebet of the year 524, I, ʿOggā, have ceded to ʿAtētan the rest of the unconsecrated exedra (arcade).'

The reasons for treating texts like these as legal are very precise:

(i) The texts are formal statements of ownership and cession, sometimes indicating restrictions regarding usage and disposal. They often refer to fines arising from the disregarding of these restrictions and they are almost always dated.

(ii) The texts are full of legalistic formulae and terminology. To give a single example, the most important element in the sale documents among the Nabataean, Syriac and Jewish Aramaic papyri and parchments, is the so-called *kyrieia* clause (κυριεία), the clause empowering the purchaser to do what he or she likes with the property (see Greenfield 1974: 69–70). Thus in papyrus Yadin 2:9 the key wording passes on:

> 'the right to buy and to sell and to pledge and to bequeath and to grant as a gift and to do with these purchased items *kl dy yṣbh* = whatever he wishes.'

The wording may vary slightly but the formula is a well established one which appears everywhere from Neo-Assyrian law and down to the Middle Ages (Rabinowitz 1956: 124–41). In the second of the Nabataean tomb inscriptions cited above (no. 27) we find:

> '... he gave this tomb to Amah, his wife ... that she might do with it whatever she wishes = *kl dy tṣbʾ*.'

(iii) Perhaps most significant of all is the fact that in the first of the inscriptions cited earlier (no. 36) we are explicitly told that a version of the legal document on papyrus—it must mean papyrus—is lodged in a particular archive. This practice of lodging copies of texts in archives is known from Syriac legal texts from Edessa: the lodged document in a legal registry would allow ultimate recourse in case of dispute to the 'superintendent of sacred and civic archives', mentioned in one of the Syriac texts (Drijvers and Healey 1999: P1, lines 27–28 in Greek).

These tomb inscriptions, therefore, illustrate further the social significance of the writing on the wall. Again we are pointed in the direction of seeking out the *Sitz im Leben*, the real life situation. In the case of legal texts we ask ourselves what the legal wording is trying to achieve and this, in my view, makes even these unpromising tomb-inscriptions a worthwhile subject of study.

BIBLIOGRAPHY

Aggoula, B.
1985 *Inscriptions et graffites araméens d'Assour*, AION supplement 43 (Naples: Istituto Orientale).
1991 *Inventaire des inscriptions hatréennes*, Bibliothèque Archéologique et Historique 139 (Paris: P. Geuthner).

Belayche, N.
2001 *Iudaea-Palaestina: The Pagan Cults in Roman Palestine (Second to Fourth Century)*, Religion der Römischen Provinzen 1 (Tübingen: Mohr Siebeck).

Beyer, K.
1998 *Die aramäischen Inschriften aus Assur, Hatra und dem übrigen Ostmesopotamien* (Göttingen: Vandenhoeck and Ruprecht).

Bickerman, E.J.
1946–47 'The warning inscriptions of Herod's temple', *JQR* 37: 387–405.

Bodel, J.
2001 'Epigraphy and the ancient historian', in J. Bodel (ed.), *Epigraphic Evidence: Ancient History from Inscriptions* (London/New York: Routledge): 1–56.

Clermont-Ganneau, C.
1872 'Une stèle du Temple de Jerusalem', *Revue Archéologique* 23: 214–34, 290–96 and pl.
1903 'Le Mont Hermon et son dieu d'après une inscription inédite', in C. Clermont-Ganneau, *Recueil d'Archéologie Orientale* V (Paris: Ernest Leroux): 346–65.

Cumont, F.
1913 '3) Hermon', in *Pauly-Wissowa* VIII (Stuttgart: J. B. Metzler): 893.

Cussini, E.
1995 'Transfer of property at Palmyra', *Aram* 7: 233–50.

Degen, R.
1977 'A note on the law of Hatra', *AION* n.s.27: 486–90.

Dijkstra, K.
1995 *Life and Loyalty: A Study in the Socio-Religious Culture of Syria and Mesopotamia in the Graeco-Roman Period Based on Epigraphical Evidence* (Leiden: E. J. Brill).

Dittenberger, W.
1905 *Orientis Graeci Inscriptiones Selectae: Supplementum Sylloges Inscriptionum Graecarum* II (Leipzig: S. Hirzel).

Drijvers, H.J.W., and J.F. Healey
1999 *The Old Syriac Inscriptions of Edessa and Osrhoene*, Handbuch der Orientalistik I/42 (Leiden: E. J. Brill).

Greenfield, J.C. [Ḥ.Y.]
1974 'Studies in the legal terminology in Nabataean funerary inscriptions' [Hebrew], in E.Y. Kutscher *et al.* (eds), *Henokh Yalon Memorial Volume* (Jerusalem: Kiryat Sefer): 64–83.

Hammond, P.C., D.J. Johnson and R.N. Jones
1986 'A religio-legal Nabataean Inscription from the Atargatis/Al-ʿUzza temple at Petra', *BASOR* 263: 77–80.

Harris, W.V.
1989 *Ancient Literacy* (Cambridge, MA/London: Harvard U.P.).

Healey, J.F.
1993 *The Nabataean Tomb Inscriptions of Madaʾin Salih*, Journal of Semitic Studies Supplement 1 (Oxford: Oxford University Press).
1996 '"May he be remembered for good": an Aramaic formula', in K.J. Cathcart and M. Maher (eds), *Targumic and Cognate Studies: Essays in Honour of Martin McNamara*, JSOT Supplement 230 (Sheffield: JSOT): 177–86.

Hezser, C.
2001 *Jewish Literacy in Roman Palestine*, Texts and Studies in Ancient Judaism 81 (Tübingen: Mohr Siebeck).

Hillers, D.R., and E. Cussini
1996 *Palmyrene Aramaic Texts* (Baltimore: Johns Hopkins UP).

Iliffe, J.H.
1936 'The ΘΑΝΑΤΟΣ inscription from Herod's temple: fragment of a second copy', *QDAP* 6: 1–3 and pls I–II.

Jones, R.N.
1989 'A new reading of the Petra temple inscription', *BASOR* 275: 41–46.

Kaizer, T.
2002 *The Religious Life of Palmyra*, Oriens et Occidens 4 (Stuttgart: Franz Steiner).

Lattimore, R.
1942 *Themes in Greek and Latin Epitaphs* (Urbana: University of Illinois Press).

Lehmann-Hartleben, K.
1939 'Excavations at Samothrace', *AJA* 43: 133–45.

Macdonald, M.C.A.
1998 'Some reflections on epigraphy and ethnicity in the Roman Near East', *Mediterranean Archaeology* 11: 177–90 and pl.

MacMullen, R.
1982 'The epigraphic habit in the Roman Empire', *American Journal of Philology* 103: 233–46.

Meyer, E.A.
1990 'Explaining the epigraphic habit in the Roman Empire: the evidence of epitaphs', *JRS* 80: 74–98.

Millard, A.R.
2000 *Reading and Writing in the Time of Jesus*, The Biblical Seminar 69 (Sheffield: Sheffield Academic Press).

Rabello, A.M.
2000 'The "Lex de Templo Hierosolymitano", prohibiting Gentiles from entering Jerusalem's sanctuary', IIIa and IIIb in A.M. Rabello, *The Jews in the Roman Empire: Legal Problems from Herod to Justinian* (Aldershot/Burlington VT: Ashgate/Variorum [original 1970]).

Rabinowitz, J.J.
1956 *Jewish Law: Its Influence on the Development of Legal Institutions* (New York: Bloch Publishing Company).

Segal, J.B.
1982 'Aramaic legal texts from Hatra', *JJS* 33 [Yadin Volume]: 109–15.

Steiner, R.C.
1989 'New light on the Biblical *Millo* from Hatran inscriptions', *BASOR* 276: 15–23.

Taylor, D.G.K.
2002 'Bilingualism and diglossia in late antique Syria and Mesopotamia', in J.N. Adams, M. Janse and S. Swain (eds), *Bilingualism in Ancient Society: Language Contact and the Written Word* (Oxford: O.U.P.): 298–331.

Teixidor, J.
1981 'Le Thiase de Bêlastor et de Beelshamên d'après une inscription récemment découverte à Palmyre', CRAIBL: 306–314.

Vattioni, F.

1981 *Le Iscrizioni di Ḥatra*, AION supplement 28 (Naples: Istituto Orientale).

1994 *Hatra*, AION supplement 81 (Naples: Istituto Orientale).

Welles, C.B., R.O. Fink and J.F. Gilliam

1959 *The Excavations at Dura-Europos: Final Report V, Part I. The Parchments and Papyri* (New Haven: Yale UP).

Woolf, G.

1998 *Becoming Roman: The Origins of Provincial Civilization in Gaul* (Cambridge: CUP).

Yadin, Y., J.C. Greenfield, A. Yardeni and B.A. Levine

2002 *The Documents from the Bar Kokhba Period in the Cave of Letters: Hebrew, Aramaic and Nabatean-Aramaic Papyri* (*Judean Desert Studies*), 2 vols (Jerusalem: Israel Exploration Society/Hebrew University/Shrine of the Book).

'MISSPELLINGS' IN CUNEIFORM ALPHABETIC TEXTS FROM UGARIT: SOME CASES OF LOSS OR ADDITION OF SIGNS

David Toshio Tsumura

Introduction

In a recent article, Edward Lipiński warns against 'qualifying non-standard spellings as erroneous or anomalous too quickly, i.e. before pursuing all other possibilities of explaining them'. He especially directs our attention to 'first-hand texts', such as graffiti, ostraca, letters, contracts on papyrus or clay tablets, as well as proper names which 'rarely contain errors not caused by a phonetic phenomenon or a linguistic substratum' (Lipiński 2003: 168).

Lipiński's warning against too quickly taking abnormal spellings as mistakes can be applied also to literary texts in the ancient Near East. I have examined so-called 'scribal errors' in the Masoretic Text of the Books of Samuel, which it has been claimed is extremely corrupt because of its peculiar and 'impossible' spellings, and have suggested that many of them are simply 'phonetic spellings' (Tsumura 1999: 390–411). In the present article, dedicated to the distinguished scholar Professor Alan Millard, I would like to take up the same problem by dealing with some obscure spellings in the texts of some Ugaritic myths and epics written in the cuneiform alphabet.

Usually, spellings represent normal linguistic forms in a language. However, it should be remembered that scripts were often borrowed to write down languages for which those scripts were not invented (e.g. the cuneiform scripts for Hittite). Even the alphabetic system is not completely adequate in representing the sounds of particular languages, as in the case of Hebrew, where the letter ש serves 'polyphonously' as both ś and š (Gordon 1965: §5.12 (p. 29)). Also, sometimes the writing system is not native to a particular scribe, as in the case where a non-Ugaritic (Hurrian?) scribe wrote Ugaritic using the cuneiform alphabet.[1] There are often variant spellings for the same linguistic phenomenon even in the same language (see Tsumura 2003: 36–50).

Therefore, abnormal forms as reflected in obscure spellings of a certain language can significantly illuminate spoken or phonetic aspects of the

[1] KTU 4.277; see Gordon 1965: §5.1 (p. 26).

language, especially in narrative and poetic texts, which are essentially 'aural' (Tsumura 1999: 410–11) by nature. In other words, abnormal spellings often reflect the phonetic reality of the narrators or poets in ancient society, although it is true that some misspellings are due to copyists' errors.

Vowel sandhi

Textual critics naturally focus their attention on how something *is* written, rather than how it *was* pronounced, when they deal with various manuscripts. However, in order to deal with any linguistic phenomenon realistically, it is important to get behind the written forms. One can deal with the relationship between scripts and sounds by paying attention to phenomena such as sandhi.[2]

It was C.H. Gordon's *Ugaritic Textbook* (1965) that first drew my attention to this particular phonological phenomenon (1965: §5.38 (p. 34)). He lists *ʿbdk* (UT 3 Aqht obv.:22 [= KTU 1.18:IV:22]) 'I shall set thee' and *wank . ʿny* (UT 137:28 [= KTU 1.2:I:28]) 'and I shall answer' as examples of the loss of the first singular preformative before ʿ in sandhi. However, as explained elsewhere,[3] the loss of the <a> sign does not indicate the loss of the morpheme /ʾa/ in these examples. Rather, it involves vowel sandhi, the fusion of two contiguous vowels, which resulted from the loss of the intervocalic *aleph* in Ugaritic language.

Vowel sandhi refers to the phonological adjustment between two vowels at word or morpheme boundaries resulting in the absorption of one vowel by another ($V_1 + V_2 \rightarrow V_1$ or V_2), which is different from the contraction of two vowels ($V_1 + V_2 \rightarrow V_3$) (Tsumura 1997: 577).

Phonetic spellings which resulted from sandhi[4] are often attested in historical narratives such as the Books of Samuel. This is all the more clear when 2 Samuel 22 is compared with the almost identical poem in Psalm 18.

For example (Tsumura 1992: 57–64), וַתְּאַזְּרֵנִי (Ps. 18:40) is linguistically more regular than its counterpart, וַתַּזְּרֵנִי (2 Sam. 22:40), which has been explained as the 'contracted (spoken) form' (Cross and Freedman 1975: 154). More specifically, however, the shorter form can be explained as the result of three stages of phonological change, including vowel sandhi.

(1) intervocalic *aleph* (ʾ) dropped:

/wattĕʾazzĕrēnî/ → /wattĕazzĕrēnî/

(2) *vowel sandhi* occurred:

/wattĕ+azzĕrēnî/ → /wattazzĕrēnî/

[2] See Matthews 1974: 97–115 on 'sandhi'.

[3] Tsumura 1982: 111–26. An expanded version in English appears in Tsumura 1991: 427–35.

[4] Phonetic spellings also result from metathesis, assimilation, etc. See, for example, Tsumura 1995: 122–23.

(3) the spelling was shortened:

/wattazzĕrēnî/ → /wattazrēnî/

Thus, the *aleph*-less form וַתַּזְרֵנִי in 2 Sam. 22:40 was not caused by a scribe's carelessly dropping the *aleph* letter from the 'correct' spelling וַתְּאַזְּרֵנִי which we find in Ps. 18:40.

This phenomenon of loss of an intervocalic *aleph* followed by vowel sandhi can also be identified in the following cases:

וַאעְשִׁר (Zech. 11:5)[5]

/wĕʾaʿšîr/ → /wĕaʿšîr/ → /waʿšîr/ : *waʾʿšī(y)r*

כַּאבִּיר (Isa. 10:13)[6]

/kĕʾabbîr/ → /kĕabbîr/ → /kabbîr/ : *kaʾbbîr*

לֶחָי (1 Sam. 25:6)[7]

/ləʾeḥāy/ → /ləeḥāy/ → /leḥāy/ 'to my brother' (cf. Vulg.)

In the first two examples, the *aleph* sign is written as a historical spelling like חֹטאים (ḥōṭiʾym) *ḥōtîm* [← *ḥōṭəʾîm*] in 1 Sam. 14:33, while in the third, the word is spelled phonetically, without *aleph*, like כָּלוּ *kālû* [← *kāləʾû*] in 1 Sam. 6:10. It should be noted that vowel sandhi occurs regardless of the *aleph* sign. In fact, the loss of the *aleph* sign for לֶחָי does not correspond to the loss of the syllable which begins with *aleph*, i.e. /ʾe/. For the first two examples, even with the *aleph* sign, the vowel of the original /ʾa/ remains as the vowel of the first syllable. In other words, the loss of the sign *aleph*, <ʾ>, does not mean that the syllable /ʾa/ disappeared in Hebrew.

Thus, a loss of a sign may represent an important linguistic feature; it may not be simply the result of careless writing by a copyist. In the following, first I should like to deal with various abnormal spellings in Ugaritic texts which lack or add one or more signs and find out what phonetic elements are involved in these linguistic forms. Next, I should like to concentrate on a particular text, KTU 1.10, which is usually labelled as a 'scribal exercise' text, in order to find whether there are any phonetic reasons for several abnormal spellings.

Loss and addition of signs

A. Loss of <ʾ>[8]

Some examples in Ugaritic of loss of intervocalic *aleph* followed by vowel sandhi are:

[5] Gordon 1965: §5.38 (p. 34, n. 2). Cf. Kautszch and Cowley 1910: §19k takes this as an example of 'syncope of א with šewâ'.

[6] Bergsträsser 1962: 91 note: 'Text unsicher'.

[7] Driver 1913: 196: 'most perplexing and uncertain word'. See also 1 Sam. 1:17, 6:10, 15:5, 31:10, 2 Sam. 2:2, 19:14, etc.

[8] Sivan 1997: 32–33 treats this as 'elision' of the consonantal aleph.

i) *Loss of intervocalic aleph before /ʿ/*[9]

ʿl aqht. ʿdbk (1.18:IV:22): /ʿal ʾaqhata̲ʿdubka/ ← /ʿal ʾaqhata̲+̲a̲ʿdubka/
← /ʿal ʾaqhata̲ ̲ʾ̲a̲ʿdubka/

wank ʿny (1.2:I:28):[10] /wa-ʾanāka̲ʿniyu/ ← /wa-ʾanāku̲+̲a̲ʿniyu/
← /wa-ʾanāku̲ ̲ʾ̲a̲ʿniyu/

wʿnnh (1.2:I:35):[11] /wa̲ʿannen(na)-hu/ ← /wa̲+̲a̲ʿannen(na)-hu/
← /wa̲-̲ʾ̲a̲ʿannen(na)-hu/

pʿbd. an. ʿnn (1.4:IV:59): ← /...ʾana̲ʿunan(na)/ ← /...ʾani̲+̲a̲ʿunan(na)/
← /...ʾani̲ ̲ʾ̲a̲ʿunan(na)/

ii) *Loss of intervocalic aleph*[12]

ap. ab. k mtm tmtn (1.16:I:17f.): /ʾappu ʾabī̲ka . . ./ ← /ʾappu ʾabī̲+̲ī̲ka . . ./
← /ʾappu ʾabī̲ ̲ʾ̲ī̲ka . . ./

yḥd. bth. sgr (1.14:II:43): /yaḥdu betaha̲sgur/ ← /yaḥdu betahu̲+̲a̲sgur/
← /yaḥdu betahu̲ ̲ʾ̲a̲sgur/

bd:[13] /ba̲d/ ← /bi̲+̲a̲d/ ← /bi̲-̲ʾ̲a̲d/

bhlm (1.19:IV:52): /ba̲hlīma/ ← /bi̲+̲a̲hlīma/ ← /bi̲-̲ʾ̲a̲hlīma/

šbʿd : /šabʿa̲d/ ← /šabʿa̲+̲i̲d/ ← /šabʿa̲ ̲ʾ̲i̲d/ : šbʿid

aylt mt (1.133:8–9):[14] /ʾayalati̲mitta/ ← /Åayalati̲+̲i̲mitta/
← /Åayalati̲ ̲Å̲i̲mitta/

wm (3.9:6):[15] /wa̲m/[16] ← /wa̲+̲i̲m/ ← /wa̲-̲ʾ̲i̲m/ : w im[17]

ksh (1.161):[18] /kussi̲hu/ ← /kussi̲+̲i̲-hu/ ← /kussi̲ʾ̲i̲-hu/ : ksih

w.ṯth (4.339:4): /wa̲ṯ̲ṯatuhu/ ← /wa̲+̲a̲ṯ̲ṯatuhu/
← /wa̲ʾ̲a̲ṯ̲ṯatuhu/ : w.aṯth

In the light of the above, we can see that the loss of the sign <Å> represents a phonetic feature of those linguistic forms rather than a careless scribal mistake.

[9] See Tsumura 1982: 111–26; 1991: 430–31; 1997: 580.

[10] Adopted by Smith 1994: 267, n. 88, and 291–92. Also see Sivan 1997: 33.

[11] Adopted by Smith 1994: 266, n. 82, and 291–92. Also see Sivan 1997: 33.

[12] See Tsumura, 1991: 432–35; 1997: 581.

[13] See Smith 1994: 322, n. 182.

[14] Tsumura 1997: 581.

[15] Tsumura 1991: 432. Note that Sivan 1997: 34, takes this as an example of 'elision of h', i.e. whm → wm; also Tropper 1989: 421–23. Cunchillos (1996) reads w m (hm); cf. km in Dietrich *et al.* 1995: 203.

[16] Segert 1984: 140 and 179: /w(a)-(ʾ)im/. Formerly I followed Segert's vocalization /wim/ but now I read /wam/, believing that in Ugaritic the dominance, rather than a position, of a vowel takes the determining role in vowel sandhi. In other words, /a/ absorbed /i/ because of its higher dominance. See Tsumura 1997: 579.

[17] This is a variant form of *hm* 'if': e.g. 1.6:V:21, 2.15:8.

[18] Tsumura 1993: 51–52.

B. Loss of <r>, <l>, <n>, and <m>

Signs drop from normal spellings for more than one phonetic reason. When resonants (i.e. /r/, /l/, /n/ and /m/) are assimilated totally[19] to the preceding or following consonant, the signs for them are usually not written. Also, the signs for resonants are not written when they are absorbed by a neighboring vowel.

i) Loss of <r>

The resonant /r/ seems to have assimilated to the following consonant in Ugaritic similarly to the case of Akkadian *kakkaru* or Hebrew *kikkār* 'round disk, talent' (< *krkr*).[20]

ygb (1.102:15):← /yag̱g̱ub-/ ← /yarg̱ub-/ : *yrgb*

On the other hand, the sign <r> is sometimes dropped at the word final position (Gordon 1965: §5.27 (p. 33, n. 1). For example,

DN[21] *kṯ* (1.3:VI:18) ← *kṯr*

ʿqš (1.100:33-34) ← *ʿqšr*

verbal form: *yṯb* (1.19:III:2, 17) ← *yṯbr* /yaṯbur/ (jussive)

The same phenomenon is recognizable in Phoenician אש (cf. Heb. אשר) as well as in the Egyptian name צָפְנַת פַּעְנֵחַ *ṣāpənat paʿnēaḥ* (Gen. 41:45) 'My provision is god, the living one' in which the Egyptian term for 'god' *nṯr* loses the *r* in the final position:

nṯr → *nṯ(r)* : נַת

Also, see צִחָא ṣiḥāʾ (Neh. 7:46) 'Face speaks' ← Eg. *ḏ(d)-ḥ(r)*[22]

This loss of <r> at the word- or syllable-final position might be caused by the vowel's absorption (or swallowing up) of the following resonant /r/. In other words, this is a phonetic fusion or 'crasis':[23]

V + r → V

rather than a simple mistake of dropping the sign <r>. Here too Ugaritic scribes wrote phonetically, spelling out words as they heard. What they heard was probably similar to British English *car* [ka:] where /r/ is not realized in post-vocalic position.

The spelling *šʿt* (4.705:6) could also be the result of the fusion of a vowel and a resonant /r/. It is certain that the normal spelling for this term is *šʿrt,* as

19 E. Lipiński notes that 'Assimilation between consonants takes most often place between a liquid *l*, *r* or the nasal *n* and another consonant'. See Lipiński 1997: §27.3.

20 'The assimilation of *r* to the following consonant is well attested in various West Gurage dialects . . . It occurs in North and West Semitic . . .' (Lipiński 1997: 188).

21 For the divine names (DN), *ʿAṯta*(*r*) (ESA) and *Issa*(*r*) (Neo-Assyrian), see Lipiński 2003: 168.

22 Muchiki 1999: 224 and 259.

23 When this fusion occurs at word or morpheme boundaries, it is called sandhi. See Tsumura 1991: 427 and n. 3. For the term 'crasis', see Lipiński 1997: §22.15 (p. 171); Huehnergard 1987: 248, n. 154. Huehnergard (1987: 249, n. 156) however, explains 'crasis' as *sandhi*-spelling (e.g. *Mi-il-ki-lu* for /milkī-ʾilu/) over a morpheme boundary.

it appears in line 1. The term was originally a monosyllable: /šáʿr-/, which was suffixed by the feminine ending /-at/. However, in the light of the syllabic transcription, *šá-ḫar-tu*, the term /šáʿrat-/ seems to have developed to /šáʿart-/. Huehnergard explains that 'the unstressed sequence *ra* apparently developed into a vocalic *r̥* when post-consonantal' (1987: 284). Thus:

(1) /šáʿrat-/ → /šáʿr̥t-/ = /šáʿart-/

For the spelling *šʿt,* one can propose that the word experienced a further phonetic change, namely fusion of V + r → V as noted above.

(2) /šáʿa̠+r̠t-/ → /šáʿa̠t-/

Thus, the loss of the word- or syllable-final sign <r>, which has been called 'apocopy' (Lipiński 2003: 167f.), is explained phonetically as a fusion or 'crasis', in which one sound absorbs another.

ii) Loss of <l>

Lipiński notes that 'vowelless *l* assimilates to various consonants, most prominently in the case of Arabic article *ʾal-* (e.g. *ʾal-šams* > [*aššams*]), but also in Assyro-Babylonian, in Hebrew, in Aramaic, in colloquial Arabic, in Tigre' (1997: 187–88). This phenomenon might be also attested in Ugaritic in the following example:

yak (1.4:V:41)

where the syllable final /l/ is possibly assimilated to the following /ʾ/:

/yiʾʾak-/ ← /yilʾak-/ : *ylak*

On the other hand, this spelling *yak* could also be explained as an example of the absorption of resonant /l/ by a preceding vowel:

V + l → V

thus,

yak : /yi̠ʾak-/ ← /yi̠+l̠ʾak-/ : *ylak*

Whichever explanation is the right one, *yak* does not need to be corrected to the normal spelling *ylak*. The same might be true of the following examples:

ap (1.10:III:16; cf. apl in 4.212:1):

/ʾa̠pu/ ← /ʾa̠+l̠pu/ : *alp*

b-akt (1.19:II:20): 'in the stubble'[24]

/bi-ʾakū̠ti/ ← /bi-ʾakū̠+a̠ti/ ← /bi-ʾakū̠+l̠ati/[25] : *b-aklt*

iii) Loss of <n>

In Ugaritic, the consonant /n/ when not followed by a vowel is usually assimilated to the following consonant within a word (Sivan 1997: 30). The following cases might be explained as such rather than as scribal mis-spellings.

mdym (2.62:4):[26]

/ma̠d̠d̠ayīma/ ← /ma̠n̠d̠ayīma/ : *mndym*

---

[24] Or 'waste land'; see Olmo Lete and Sanmartín 2003: 45; cf. ak<l>t.

[25] G. passive participle, fem. sing. Cf. Akk. *akkullātu* refers to 'clods or similar undesirable formations on a field'; see *CAD*, A/1 (1964), 275.

[26] Olmo Lete and Sanmartín 2003: 562 explains this as 'a mistake'.

bš (4.338:16)[27] :

/bušš-/ ← /bunš-/ ← /bunuš-/ : *bnš*

Sometimes, the consonant /n/ is assimilated to the following consonant even over a word boundary. Such 'sandhi-spelling', as Lipiński notes, is attested in some Old Phoenician inscriptions (1997: §27.20). The same is true of the following Ugaritic examples:

b ǵlmt (1.4:VII:54, 4.754:18):

/biǵ+ǵalmati/ ← /bin ǵalmati/ : *bn ǵlmt*

aph . ǵzr (1.17:I:1):[28]

/ʾaphVǵ+ǵazru/ ← /ʾaphVn ǵazru/ : *aphn . ǵzr*

y ʿd (1.114:3):

/yēʿ+ʿad/ ← /yēnʿad/ ← /yēna ʿad/ : *yn ʿd*

iv) Loss of <m>

In the following Ugaritic example, the second consonant /m/ is no longer spelled out independently and, hence, the <m> of *ilmt* stands for /mmô/.

bn ilmt (1.6:VI:30):

/ bin ʾilīm+môt/ ← /bin ʾilīma môt/ : *bn ilm mt*

C. Addition of <q>

Signs are not only lost but sometimes also added. The most common addition is that of prosthetic *aleph* (Sivan 1997: 33). However, there is a case when a <q> was added directly before <k>, probably in order to indicate a middle stop, as Gordon notes (1965: §5.42 (p. 35)):

ḥqkpt (1.3:VI:13):

/ḥa-qka-patu/ ← /ḥa-ka-patu/ : *ḥkpt*

KTU 1.10

The text KTU 1.10 has been called a 'scribal exercise?' (Dietrich *et al.* 1995: 31) due to the fact that there are seemingly many orthographic mistakes, i.e. misspellings. There are not only several possible cases of loss of a sign but also superimpositions of one sign on another as well as an insertion of a sign. We should investigate these cases one by one to see if any phonetic reason could be involved.

[27] So, Cunchillos [date]: TU4.338:16, Dietrich and Loretz 1990: 95; cf. lbé (Dietrich et al. 1995: 340).

[28] Olmo Lete and Sanmartín 2003: 90 explains this as a 'mistake'.

Loss of <*b*>
kkbm (1.10:I:4) is an unusual spelling in Ugaritic, but it can be explained as assimilation of /b/ to the following /k/:

kkbm : /kakkabūma/ ← /kabkabūma/ : *kbkbm*

Loss of <*l*>
As discussed above, *ap* (III:16) can be explained thus:

ap : /ʾapu/ ← /ʾa+lpu/ : *alp*

Here, the resonant /l/ is absorbed by the preceding vowel.

In two places, III:12 and 26, one sign is superimposed on another. In III:12, *w* is superimposed on *b*. There is no possibility of miscopying, for these two signs are not similar formally: 𐎆 (w) and 𐎁 (b). One can explain it by saying that the word was first phonetically written as the assimilated form *bbn* [bubun] and then corrected to the normal spelling *wbn* [wubun]. In III:26, *t* is superimposed on *ṣ*. Here, too, there is no way of mistaking the two signs: 𐎚 (t) and 𐎕 (ṣ). The phrase, which means 'the colostrum of his infancy',[29] was probably written phonetically with *ṣ* as:

šḫp ṣǵrth : /šaḫapā ṣaǵirti-hu/

resulting from the following changes:

/šaḫapā ṣaǵirti-hu/ ← /šaḫapaʾ ṣaǵirti-hu/[30]
← /šaḫapat ṣaǵirti-hu/ : *šḫpt ṣǵrth*

In this example, glottalization (/t/ → /ʾ/) was probably the cause of the loss of the sign <t>. Then, *t* was superimposed on *ṣ* to correct it to the normal spelling.

Loss of <*t*>
Glottalization caused the loss of <t> in two other places also. In III:9, the scribe first wrote a word phonetically as *blt,* and then he inserted the sign *t* into the middle of the sign *l*. The first, shorter form could be explained phonetically thus:

blt : /bālatu/ ← /baʾlatu/ ← /batlatu/ : *btlt*

In other words, the first /t/ of the word *btlt* was glottalized and the scribe wrote it phonetically. The same glottalization of /t/ can be recognized again in this text (II:9):

mla : /malʾā/ ← /malʾaʾ/ ← /malʾat/ : *mlat*

Loss of <*r*>
As noted above, the loss of <r> at the word- or syllable-final position was probably caused by the fusion of a vowel and a resonant /r/. The form *drd* in

[29] Olmo Lete and Sanmartín 2003: 813: 'colostrum, first milk'.

[30] We assume here a phonetic change: aʾ → ā, like Heb. /māṣaʾ/ → /māṣā/.

III:6 might be explained as this kind of phonetic change.

drd : /darda/ ← /dardar/ : *drdr*

Hence, there is no need to correct *drd* to *dr* or *drdr*.[31]

Conclusions

Various examples of the loss and the addition of signs in Ugaritic texts exhibit the phonetic reality of the language used by scribes rather than careless mistakes in orthographic practices. Especially the text KTU 1.10 reflects phonetic reality in these abnormal spellings. It may be that the scribe wrote down according to what he heard and then later he corrected some spellings according to the normal rules. Hence, such 'errors' must have occurred often in 'literary works when the scribe wrote down from dictation' (Lipiński 2003: 158). In such cases one should not dismiss those anomalous spellings as erroneous too quickly.

BIBLIOGRAPHY

Bergsträsser, G.
1962 *Hebräische Grammatik* I/II (Hildesheim: Georg Olms [orig. 1918]).

Cunchillos, J.-L.
1996 *Banco de Datos Filológicos Semíticos Noroccidentales* (Madrid: GSRC).

Cross, F.M., and D.N. Freedman
1975 *Studies in Ancient Yahwistic Poetry* (Missoula: Scholars Press).

Dietrich, M., and O. Loretz
1990 'Schiffshandel und Schiffsmiete zwischen Byblos und Ugarit (KTU 4.338:10–18)', *UF* 22.

Dietrich, M., O. Loretz and J. Sanmartín
1995 *The Cuneiform Alphabetic Texts from Ugarit, Ras Ibn Hani and Other Places* (*KTU: second, enlarged edition*) (Münster: Ugarit-Verlag).

Driver, S.R.
1913 *Notes on the Hebrew Text and the Topography of the Books of Samuel*. Second edition (Oxford: Clarendon).

Gordon, C.H.
1965 *Ugaritic Textbook* (Rome: Pontifical Biblical Institute).

[31] Wyatt 1998: 158, n. 16. Olmo Lete and Sanmartín 2003: 280: *dr*.

Huehnergard, J.
1987 *Ugaritic Vocabulary in Syllabic Transcription* (HSS 32; Atlanta: Scholars Press).

Kautszch, E., and A.E. Cowley
1910 *Gesenius' Hebrew Grammar*. Second English edition (Oxford: Clarendon).

Lipiński, E.
1997 *Semitic Languages: Outline of a Comparative Grammar* (Orientalia Lovaniensia Analecta 80; Leuven: Peeters).
2003 '"Spelling mistakes" and related matters', *Dutch Studies,* vol. 5, nr. 1–2 (Leiden: Near Eastern Languages and Literatures).

Matthews, P.H.
1974 *Morphology* (Cambridge: Cambridge University Press).

Muchiki, Y.
1999 *Egyptian Proper Names and Loanwords in North-West Semitic* (SBLDS 173; Atlanta: Society of Biblical Literature).

Olmo Lete, G. del, and J. Sanmartín
2003 *A Dictionary of the Ugaritic Language in the Alphabetic Tradition* (Leiden: Brill).

Segert, S.
1984 *A Basic Grammar of the Ugaritic Language* (Berkeley: University of California Press).

Sivan, D.
1997 *A Grammar of the Ugaritic Language* (Leiden: Brill).

Smith, M.S.
1994 *The Ugaritic Baal Cycle,* Vol. 1: *Introduction with Text, Translation & Commentary of KTU 1.1–1.2* (SVT 55; Leiden: Brill).

Tropper, J.
1989 'Ugaritisch *wm* (KTU 3.9:6) und der Schwund von anlautendem *h* im Semitschen', *UF* 21.

Tsumura, D.T.
1982 'Sandhi in the Ugaritic language', *Studies in Language and Literature* (Language volume; Institute of Literature and Linguistics, the University of Tsukuba), vol. 7 [Japanese; see English summary in *Old Testament Abstracts* 6 (1983)].
1991 'Vowel sandhi in Ugaritic', *Near Eastern Studies Dedicated to H. I. H. Prince Takahito Mikasa on the Occasion of His Seventy-Fifth Birthday* (BMECCJ 5; Wiesbaden: Otto Harrasowitz).
1992 'Some problems regarding Psalm 18', *Exegetica* 3 [Japanese with English summary: see *Old Testament Abstracts* 16 (1993)].
1993 'The interpretation of the Ugaritic funerary text KTU 1.161', in E. Matsushima (ed), *Official Cult and Popular Religion in the Ancient Near East* (Heidelberg: C. Winter).
1995 'Bedan, a copyist's error?', *VT* 45.
1997 'Vowel sandhi in Biblical Hebrew', *ZAW* 109.

1999 'Scribal errors or phonetic spellings? Samuel as an aural text', *VT* 49.

2003 'Some examples of linguistic variants in 1–2 Samuel', *Orient: Report of the Society for Near Eastern Studies in Japan* 38.

Wyatt, N.

1998 *Religious Texts from Ugarit: The World of Ilimilku and his Colleagues* (Sheffield: Sheffield Academic Press).

Some Uses of Writing in Ancient Israel in the Light of Recently Published Inscriptions

Graham Davies

Although excavations have yet to uncover large display inscriptions in Hebrew of the kind that are known from Egypt and Mesopotamia, and even from ancient Israel's closer neighbours, an impressive quantity of epigraphic material is now known from the Old Testament period. Around 2,000 items have been published and a growing number of aids to their study, in the form of editions, dictionaries, survey articles and concordances, is helping to make them better known and understood. This textual material has a good deal to tell us about the uses of writing in ancient Israel, though it of course needs to be emphasized at the outset, as with all archaeological discovery, that some of what I shall say is based on inference and interpretation rather than 'brute facts' and that the selectivity of preservation and discovery inevitably skews any account that we may give.

In an essay that eventually appeared in 2002, which was based mainly on items published up to 1990, I ended with the following summary:

> The inscriptions also shed light on many aspects of everyday life in ancient Israel and Judah... They give a glimpse of agricultural life, royal bureaucracy, the training of scribes, military affairs and a variety of religious practices (Davies 2002: 285).

Of course that means '*the uses of writing in relation to* agricultural life, royal bureaucracy...' Here I am going to use, almost entirely, items published more recently, between 1990 and 2000, to provide what can inevitably only be a partial account of the uses of writing in ancient Israel. In the first part I shall simply present some texts in translation, with brief introduction and comment, to illustrate what some people wrote and why they wrote it; in the second part there will be a more thorough discussion and analysis of some other examples, which may prove more interesting to some and less so to others!

Ostraca and a fragment of a monumental inscription

Excavations directed by I. Beit-Arieh at what is now called Horvat Uza (formerly Khirbet Ghazzeh) between 1982 and 1996 uncovered the remains of an Israelite fort of the seventh and early sixth centuries. It has been reported that over thirty ostraca (inscribed potsherds) were found there (Beit-Arieh and Cresson 1991: 133; Beit-Arieh 1999: 30). The site is located in the Eastern Negev about 5 m. south-east of Tel Arad, and one of the inscriptions is in the Edomite language, possibly reflecting the fall of the site to Edomite invaders at the time of the Babylonian invasions (Beit-Arieh 1985, 1989; but see Bienkowski and van der Steen 2001: 39 for an alternative view). Of the Hebrew ostraca only five have been published to my knowledge, four since 1990 (for the fifth see Beit-Arieh 1986–87 = Davies 1991: 37.001). Two of the latter are very similar lists inscribed on the same jar: they include not only names, but numerals and references to commanders:[1]

1. (Beit-Arieh 1993a = Davies 2004: 37.004; cf. Lemaire 1995: 223)

rʾšn	A 'first'(-rank soldier??)
ʿl ydy ntn. nḥmy[hw]	under the command of Nathan: Nehemi[ah]
qṣyn. lmṭh. gdly {*or* gʿly} [ ]	Commander below: Gedali…
šny lnḥmyhw ʾl[ ]	A 'second' for Nehemiah: El[ ]
šny ltḥtnh. ml[š]	A 'second' for Tachtenah (*or* 'down below'): Mala[sh]
šlšy. ʿl y[dy]	A 'third' under the comm[and of …]
šlš[y]	A 'thir[d]'…
rbʿ[y]	A 'four[th]'…
hw[ ]	Ho[shaiah (son of) Naweh?]…

2. (Beit-Arieh 1993a = Davies 2004: 37.005; cf. Lemaire 1995: 223)[2]

[ ]	[ ]
[q]ṣyn ʾlntn	[C]ommander: Elnathan
[q]ṣyn lmṭh. gdly {*or* gʿly} [ ]	Commander below: Gedali…
šny ldṭd {*or* lḥpr.} mlš	A 'second' for Dṭd(?): Malash

[1] The texts throughout this essay are given as they are presented in Davies 1991 and 2004, except for nos 4 and 12 (in the latter case I have given the reading of the official publication, with one addition by F.M. Cross). A dot above a letter indicates that the reading is uncertain. Where an alternative reading is provided for the Hebrew text, it is not generally included in the translation, for the sake of simplicity.

[2] It is not certain that there was any text before the reference to the first 'commander' in this case.

šny lgʿly {*or* lgdly} ʾbyhw	A ‘second’ for Gedali: Abijah
šlšy. lmlš yʾznyhw bn ṣ[ ]	A ‘third’ for Malash: Jaazaniah son of Z[ ]
šlšy lʾbyhw ʾlyšb	A ‘third’ for Abijah: Eliashib
rbʿy lyʾznyhw yʾznyhw bn [ ]	A ‘fourth’ for Jaazaniah: Jaazaniah son of [ ]
hwšʿyhw nwh. mplqṁ {*or* ḃplqm}	Hoshaiah (son of) Naweh divides/allocates them(?)

These lists seem to be concerned with the allocation of soldiers, according to their seniority, to different detachments based at the fort. Another list may have a related purpose. It began with the word ‘Tenth’ (not ‘Ten’, as others have translated it, in view of the final ‘t’).

3. (Beit-Arieh 1999 = Davies 2004: 37.008)

ʿšrt	Tenth (month? year? unit?)
[m]nḥ̇m bn ḥ[ ]	[Me]nahem son of Kh[ ]
ṅryhw bn smk[yhw]	Neriah son of Semach[iah]
nryhw bn mšk[n]y[hw]	Neriah son of Mishka[n]i[ah]
ntnyhw bn ḥ̇ṭḃ	Nethaniah son of Khatab
ʾwryhw bn šlṁ[yhw]	Uriah son of Shelem[iah]
gdlyhw bn ʾwryh[w]	Gedaliah son of Uriah
ydnyhw bn špṭ[yhw]	Jedoniah son of Shefat[iah]
hwdwyhw bn ʿ[ ]	Hoduiah son of A[ ]

The fourth inscription is of an entirely different character: despite the considerable difficulties with the reading of the text and its translation, it is at least clear that it is not a list. The translation offered is necessarily tentative, and some words in the Hebrew original are read differently by F.M. Cross.

4. (Beit-Arieh 1993b = Davies 2004: 37.006–007; cf. Cross 2000)[3]

ʾm bšlẇ bmšr	If in calm (and) uprightness
lšntnh ʾl gdlyh [ ]	you reviled him/her to Gedaliah,
hnḣ lšnth [ ]	behold you reviled him/her…(justly?)
wʾm lʾ {*or* wʾml)} ẏḋk [ ]	But if not, your hand…
[ ]hm yšqlk	…he shall weigh you
[ ]ly[ ]h[ ]	……………………

[3] The text presented here draws on the readings proposed by both Beit-Arieh and Cross, and at one point (in line 7) I have ventured to make a new suggestion: see the comments in the main text.

ʾl mṫyk wrqʿ bšʿt šbtk	to your menfolk and he will stamp his foot(?) at the hour when you sit down,
wʿllk̇ ysʿ[ ]	and your child he will remove…
ʿl pn[ykh] whtʿrʿrth	before you and you shall be stripped naked
bḋnḣ	in judgment(s),
ẏmḥṣ żrʿtykh [ ] bpls-	he will shatter your arms… with shuddering(?),
ʾṣr ymt whyh q[wr]ʿṣ	what has been stored up over days (will come) and (your…?) [will be shat]tered
wqbrkh ḥrb	and your grave will be desolate.

Although very little of the detail is certain, the structure of the text can be made out. It begins with two alternatives: either the person addressed ('you') has reviled someone in words spoken to Gedaliah justifiably or (s)he has not: I take the verbs in ll. 2–3 as perfect (Piel?) forms of *lšn*, 'slander, revile' (cf. Ps. 101:5; Prov. 30:10). The (energic) suffix in l.2 may as well be feminine as masculine. If the reviling is unjustified, someone ('he') will bring down terrible judgment on the addressee. In l. 7 I read, tentatively, *wrqʿ*, in the sense found in 2 Sam. 22:43 and Ezek. 6:11, 25:6. The contents of the threat are similar in general terms and in some details to prophetic threats of judgment. It is possible in fact that this is the text of a prophetic oracle against an individual, though in the absence of any specific reference to God as the subject of the verbs in the second half one might also understand it as a threat of vengeance or punishment by a human being, perhaps the Gedaliah named in l. 2. Professor B.S. Jackson has suggested to me that the text might be about a divorce case, and this deserves serious consideration. Another possibility is that it relates to the kind of impropriety cited in Exod. 21:7, Num. 5:11–31 and Deut. 22:13–21. Beit-Arieh and Cross have called this a 'literary' text, the latter suggesting that it is part of a larger document. One is reminded of some parts of the dialogue in the book of Job. Alternatively it might, as suggested above, be regarded as a prophetic diatribe, or even as some kind of legal or quasi-legal text. It is, in any case, by the normal standards of Hebrew epigraphy, justifiably described by Beit-Arieh as 'an unconventional document'.

A larger number of ostraca have been published recently without their exact provenance being known. According to A. Lemaire some twenty items are in the possession of one private collector alone (1997: 456; cf. Bordreuil *et al.* 1996: 49 n.1). Three of these are again lists of names, like others previously known from e.g. Lachish (Davies 1991: 1.001, 1.011, 1.019, 1.022) and especially Arad (Davies 1991: 2.022–23, 2.027, 2.031, 2.035–36,

2.038–39, 2.049, 2.058–59, 2.072).[4] Of the new lists of names two are interesting for the abbreviations and other signs which they include:

5. (Deutsch and Heltzer 1995: 83–88, no. 77 = Davies 2004: 99.004; cf. Lemaire 1999: 173)

ʿšyhw bn ʾlnr n 1 ṣ 2	Asaiah son of Elinur n 1 ṣ 2
ḥgy {*or* ḥby} bn yšmʿʾl n 3	Haggai son of Ishmael n 3
yʾznyhw bn ʿżr n 3 ṣ 2	Jaazaniah son of Ezer n 3 ṣ 2
brkyhw bn ḥlqyhw n 2 ṣ 2	Berechiah son of Hilkiah n 2 ṣ 2
ʾḥyqm bn ʿzr n 2	Ahiqam son of Ezer n 2
mšlmt bt ʾlkn n 3 ṣ 2	Meshullemet daughter of Elkan n 3 ṣ 2

6. (Deutsch and Heltzer 1995: 89–92, no. 78 = Davies 2004: 99.005; cf. Lemaire 1997: 458, and Hurowitz 1998: 132–35)

lywʾlẏhw	(Belonging?) to Yoaliah:
smkyhw	Semachiah
ʾlntn {*or* ʾlkn} bn ʾlkn	Elnathan son of Elkan
ʿšyhw hgzh	Asaiah the stone-cutter
yrm bn šqṣ	Yoram son of Sheqez
pdyhw bn ʿrs	Pedaiah son of Eres
btr	Bether

7. (Deutsch and Heltzer 1995: 93–102, no. 79 = Davies 2004: 99.006; cf. Lehmann 1998; Lemaire 1999: 173; Renz 1999)

mkyḣẇ [bn] {*or* mky ḃṅ [ ]}	Micaiah [son of…]
+ slʾ bn zkr[ ]	+ Sela son of Zechar[ ]
+ yqmyhw bn mḥṡ[ ]	+ Jeqemiah son of Mahse[iah]
+ ʾḥmlkh bn yhwṭr {*or* yhwʾr} k 5	+ Ahimalkah son of Jehotar k 5
myʾmn bn ṣdqyhw k 4	Miamen son of Zedekiah k 4
– lmnḥm bn nmš[r] k 4	– For Menahem son of Nimshar k 4
nʿr ʾšyhw bn nms]r k 4	The ‘squire’ of Eshaiah son of Nimshar k 4
bn šḥr lʾḥqm k 4	The son of Shachar, for Ahiqam k 4
ywʿlyhw bn ʿbdẏḣẇ {*or* ʿbdḥẏ} k 3	Yoaliah son of Obadiah k 3

[4] See the classification in Renz and Röllig 1995: II/1, 19–22, where further examples are added.

mṣry bn šknyhw k 8̇	Mizri son of Shechaniah k 8
– nḥmyhw bn ʿkbr k 7	Nehemiah son of Achbor k 7
+ qwh {*or* tqwḣ} bn ʾḥb k 8	+ Qawah son of Ahab k 8
[y]ṙmyhw {*or* ṙmyhẇ} k 3	[Je?]remiah k 3
(verso)	*(reverse)*
lbḥr	For Bahar
– mnġl[ ] k 4–	– Mngl[ ] k 4
– ywʿl[y]ḣw k 4	– Yoal[i]ah k 4
– gmryhw [ ] 5	– Gemariah [ ] 5
– hṣlyhw ḃṅ bnyhw k 3	– Hizziliah son of Benaiah k 3

'n' in the first list has been thought to stand for *nbl*, 'wine-skin' or 'wine-jar', which occurs as a quantity in the Samaria ostraca; 'ṣ' might then stand for another (smaller?) container (*ṣpḥt* = 'flask'?). There are three interesting features in the third text. The 'k' might represent *ksp*, 'silver'. The 'minus sign' in lines 6, 11, 15–18 also occurs on an ostracon from Jerusalem (Davies 2004: 4.129), where it has been compared to 'check-marks' in later Aramaic inscriptions from Egypt (Naveh 2000: 4). The 'plus sign' may be a variant of that. The original publication of the third text observed differences in the letter forms from one line to the next and suggested that each person wrote his own name to acknowledge receipt of the amount stated (as wages?). If true, this would have important implications for the extent of literacy at the time (probably the second half of the seventh century BC). Lemaire has questioned the observation (1999: 173), but the more detailed study of Renz (1999: 127–31 and 147) confirms it, at least for the obverse, and so does Lehmann (1998: 399).

Next, two items connected with temple worship. The first is a decanter with a capacity of *c*. 1.27 litres:

8. (Deutsch and Heltzer 1994: 23–26, no. 6 = Davies 2004: 99.002)

lmtnyhw. yyn. nsk. rbʿt.	Belonging to Mattaniah. Wine, for pouring/libation, a quarter.

The term *nsk* is a cultic one and it means 'drink-offering, libation' (Gen. 35:14 etc.). According to the sacrificial laws 'a quarter of a hin' of wine was the appropriate amount for the offering of a lamb (Exod. 29:40, Lev. 23:13, Num. 15:5–7, 28:7 etc.). The capacity of this vessel fits in very well with the estimate for a hin at 6 litres given by M.A. Powell (1992: 904–5). The inscription would have helped to ensure that the right measure was used:

perhaps Mattaniah was a temple official who had his personal decanter marked with his name to prevent it from being ‘borrowed’.

The other cultic item, an ostracon, records a payment made to the temple by royal command. Like the next one, there is some debate about the authenticity of this inscription.[5]

9. (Bordreuil *et al.* 1996: 49–61; 1998: 2–13 = Davies 2004: 99.007; cf. Ephal and Naveh 1998)

kʾšr ṣwk. ʾšy	As you were ordered by Eshai-
hw. hmlk. ltt. byd	ah the king, to give into the hand of
[z]kryhw. ksp tr	[Z]echariah, silver of Tar-
šš. lbyt yhwḣ.	shish for the house of Yahweh,
š 3	3 shekels.

Presumably it is a receipt kept by the ‘donor’. The king’s name could be a variant form of the name of either Joash or Josiah, both of whom are said in 2 Kgs. (12:4–8; 22:3–7) to have collected money for temple repairs. ‘Silver of Tarshish’ is mentioned in Jer. 10:9.

The next ostracon is certainly from the legal world: it records an appeal to an official (*śr*) on the part of a widow who is seeking to secure a share of her husband’s inheritance. In its form and situation it is exactly similar to the now well known inscription from Yavneh-Yam (Metsad Hashavyahu) (Davies 1991: 7.001; see also Renz and Röllig 1995: I, 315–29, IIA, 17).[6]

10. (Bordreuil *et al.* 1996: 49–61; 1998: 2–13 = Davies 2004: 99.008; cf. Ephal and Naveh 1998, Berlejung and Schüle 1998)

ybṙkk̇. yhwh bšlṁ. wʿt. yšm	May Yahweh bless you with prosperity!
ʿ. ʾdny. hš̈r ʾt ʾmtk̇ mt	And now, may / my lord the official listen
ʾyšy. lʾ bnm. whyh. ydk.	to your maidservant. / My husband has
ʿmy. wntth. byd. ʾmtk .ʾt. h	died, without children. This is how it
nḥlh ʾšr. dbrth. lʿms	should be: your support / should be with
yhw. wʾt. šdh. hḥtm. ʾš	me and you should give into the hand of

[5] Scientific tests reported by C.A. Rollston appear to confirm the inscription’s antiquity (Bordreuil *et al.* 1998: 8–9), but objections on the grounds of palaeography and the possible copying of phrases from texts already known were raised by Ephal and Naveh (1998: 269–73).

[6] Similar scientific tests to those referred to in the previous note were carried out on this inscription, with the same results.

r bnʿmh. ntth. lʾḥyw.	your maidservant the / inheritance about which you spoke to Amas/iah, seeing that the field of wheat which / is at Naamah you have given to his brother.

It is interesting to see that legal claims could be put into writing, and were not simply made orally in court. In this case the widow was seeking something not provided for in Old Testament law, which awarded the whole inheritance in such a situation to the husband's family, in contrast to Mesopotamian law and later Jewish practice (see de Vaux 1965: 53–55). The authenticity of this inscription has been disputed on the grounds, among others, that *lʾ bnm* is not good classical Hebrew grammar—one would expect *ʾyn* (Joüon and Muraoka 1991: §160g: cf. Berlejung and Schüle 1998: 69). But 1 Chr. 2:30 and 32 provide examples of this precise phrase in Late Biblical Hebrew at least, and Ps. 74:9 offers an older parallel (see also Joüon and Muraoka 1991: §160c; Ephal and Naveh 1998: 272, n.12).

A final ostracon, said to have come from the Judaean hills, is apparently a list of provisions:

11. (Lemaire 1997: 460 = Davies 2004: 99.012)

lḥm 50 *lethech seah*	Bread 50 'lethech' 1 seah
grgrm {*or* gḥgḥm} 10 1 *seah*	Berries/dried olives 11 seah
ḥlt 10 5 *lethech seah*	Holy cakes 15 'lethech' 1 seah
yrq 10 2 *seah*	Vegetables 12 seah
ʾšprm 10 5 [ ]	Raisin cakes 15 …
[ ] yyn [ ]	… wine
b 3	3 baths
šbt [ ]	Sabbath(?)
šbt [ ]	Sabbath(?)

Some of the terms used recur in 2 Sam. 6:19. The quantities are quite substantial, more than a family would need. For example, a bath was a measure of volume in excess of 20 litres (Powell 1992: 902; Renz and Röllig 1995: IIA, 36–38) and the lethech and seah have been estimated at respectively 60 and 12 litres (Powell 1992: 902). The amounts are broadly comparable to those supplied to the Kittim in the Arad ostraca and it is quite possible that this document too has some connection with the supply of a military unit. The interpretation of the word *šbt* in the final lines remains entirely uncertain in the broken context.

The final item in this part of the paper is something very different, one that may well be part of precisely the kind of large public inscription in Hebrew whose lack I commented on at the beginning. It was found in Roman-period debris during Yigal Shiloh's excavations on the Ophel ridge in Jerusalem, and was first referred to in an article published in 1979. It has recently been more fully published in the Inscriptions volume of the final excavation report, with minor variations in the readings, and F.M. Cross has added some further suggestions. It appears to contain parts of the first four lines of the inscription:

12. (Shiloh 1979: 170 = Davies 1991: 4.120; cf. Naveh 2000: 1–2, no. IN1; Cross 2001)

[ ]ṣbr. hṁ[ ]	...the collection of the ...
[ ] ḃšbʿ. ʿšṙ[ ]	...in the seventeenth [year?]...
[ ]rbʿy w[ ]	...the fourth [day/month/generation etc.) and ...
[ ]ḃ[ ]	

The script is similar to that of the Siloam Tunnel Inscription, so that an attribution to the reign of Hezekiah in the late eighth century is possible (so Cross 2001), though Naveh prefers a date in the seventh century. Although the contents of the inscription cannot be determined, the style of writing and the use of well-prepared stone points to some kind of official monument. Another similar fragment was found in Jerusalem in debris a little to the north of Shiloh's excavations in 1982 (Naveh 1982 = Davies 1991: 4.125), and a further one in the excavations at Samaria (Sukenik 1936: 156 = Davies 1991: 3.312).

Seals and seal-impressions

Seals and seal-impressions constitute more than half the known inscriptions in Hebrew, and in the past ten years there have been some important developments in the study of them. Comprehensive publications by P. Bordreuil (1996 [1992]), N. Avigad and B. Sass (1997) and W. Röllig (Renz and Röllig 2003: 81–445) based on older material have appeared, in the first two cases now supplemented by previously unknown examples, mainly from private collections (see especially Overbeck and Meshorer 1993; Deutsch 1997; Avigad, Heltzer and Lemaire 2000; Deutsch and Lemaire 2000). The cache of bullae from (for once!) a controlled excavation, in the City of David in Jerusalem, has also been definitively published in a posthumous publication of Y. Shoham (2000; for earlier versions see Shoham 1994, 1999). The contributions which seals can make to the study of ancient Israelite society were described by N. Avigad on the basis of what was known in 1986 in an essay that has recently been reprinted (in Avigad and Sass 1997: 21–31). Before turning specifically to some of the more recently published items I would like to underline a point made by Avigad in another of his publications (1986: 113–20; cf. Avigad and Sass 1997: 31–46). This concerns the significance of bullae for the extent of writing. The term ‘bulla’ refers to a piece of clay, impressed with a seal-impression, normally for the purpose of sealing a document. From biblical references we can learn that this might be a letter (1 Kgs. 21:8), a legal document for the sale of land (Jer. 32:10), a public declaration (Neh. 9:38, 10:1) and even a prophecy (Isa. 8:16; cf. 29:11). Many of the Hebrew bullae that are known have on their back side the impression of the cord which tied up the document and the papyrus fibres themselves. What this means is that almost every bulla is evidence of a written document that no longer survives. How many does that mean? Avigad and Sass (1997: 170–241) have 262 entries for bullae, from which perhaps half a dozen should be deducted because they were clearly not attached to documents. On the other hand many of these entries represent multiple examples of the same impression, and this raises the total number of bullae to 314. To these must be added those which have come to light since the cut-off point of the Avigad/Sass volume, which is in effect Avigad’s death in 1992. There are over 100 of these in R. Deutsch’s catalogue (1997) and around 50 more in other recent publications. There are a further 65 from a Persian-period archive which Avigad and Sass deliberately omitted from their corpus because of their date (Avigad 1976). The total of known Hebrew bullae is therefore upwards of 500. This points to a massive number of written documents of the kinds mentioned, and perhaps others. It is possible (we do not know either way) that some documents had more than one bulla on them, as happened in later times, but on the other hand no one would imagine that we possess anything like the full total of bullae that were made in the Old Testament period. It is worth adding that examples of bullae, where they have a secure archaeological provenance, are by no means limited to Jerusalem: examples are known from Lachish (Davies 1991: 100.253–58, 779), Beth-zur (Davies 1991: 100.110), Beersheba (Davies 1991: 100.281), Tell en-Nasbeh (Davies 1991: 100.769) and Tell el-Hesi (Davies 1991: 100.778).[7] As far as dates are concerned, the securely dated groups are from *c.* 600 BC and they account for more than half of the items known. Just a few can be dated, either by their references to kings (Davies 2004: 101.020, 025, 182–84: additional examples in Deutsch 2002 and 2003a) or archaeologically (Davies 1991: 100.281) to the eighth century. All but a few of the bullae

[7] However, the distribution of bullae seems to be far less widespread than that of inscribed jar stamps, on the evidence available.

with royal names are from the reign of Hezekiah at the very end of the century, but one names Hoshea, the last king of the Northern Kingdom and several more are from the reign of Ahaz, Hezekiah's predecessor, whose reign began *c*. 740 BC. An impression of the (or a) royal seal of Ahaz can serve as an example:

13. (Deutsch 1997: 49–51, no. 1 = Davies 2004: 101.025)

lʾḥz. y	Belonging to Ahaz (son of) Je-
hwtm. mlk.	hotam, king of
yhdh	Judah

The clear evidence is therefore of a plethora of written documents from the late Judaean monarchy, and so far there is a lot less evidence of this kind from the eighth century and only one piece, perhaps surprisingly, from the northern kingdom of Israel. Of course there are seals from the north (including the famous one of 'Shema servant of Jeroboam') and from earlier in the eighth century in the south (Davies 1991: 065, 067–068). But we do not know how, or how often, they were used.[8] It may perhaps be significant that the bullae so far identified from the eighth century are predominantly royal, while the later ones are, with a few exceptions, not obviously connected with the royal court. This would be compatible with a situation in which, comparatively speaking, the kind of written documents to which bullae were attached were in the eighth century rather limited in number and mainly products of the royal bureaucracy, whereas by the end of the seventh century such documents were being produced by or on behalf of a much wider spectrum of the population. But new discoveries, or the dating of the rather large number of undated bullae, could of course change that picture.

The newly published seals and impressions are particularly interesting for the light which they shed on the administrative bureaucracy of the kingdom of Judah. Two important sets of seal-impressions, the *lmlk* stamps and the so-called private jar-handle stamps, both widely distributed in the kingdom of Judah of the late eighth century, have already provided material on this topic (see Lemaire 1981; Garfinkel 1984 and 1985), which has been turned to good use for the study of Israelite society and prophecy (Kessler 1992: 178–86). Now a new group of seven seal-impressions, from four different seals, has gradually come to light over the past decade or so and, while further similar

[8] There is in fact a group of *c*. 50 uninscribed bullae found in the excavations at Samaria, with the characteristic impressions on the back that indicate their use to seal written documents (Crowfoot *et al*. 1957: 2, 88). The archaeological context is disturbed, but some of these items have been dated typologically to the Israelite monarchy period, while others are clearly of a later date.

discoveries may well be made in the future, it is possible to reach a considered view of them and their role in the developing royal bureaucracy (see already Deutsch and Heltzer 1999: 65–66; Avishur and Heltzer 2000: 132–34).

14. (Avigad 1990: 262–65 = Davies 2004: 100.901)

b 20 6	In the 26th
šnh	year.
ʾltld	Eltolad.
lmlk	For the king.

15. (two copies: Avigad and Sass 1997: 178, no. 422 (cf. Lemaire 1999: 175) = Davies 2004: 101.122; Deutsch 1997: 137–39, no. 97B = Davies 2004: 101.278)

b 10 4	In the 14th
šnh	year.
ṙʾšnh {*or* ṙʾšny}	First consignment.
lkš l	Lachish. For
mlk	the king.

16. (Deutsch 1997: 139–40 = Davies 2004: 101.279)

b 20 šnh	In the 20th year.
nṣb	Nezib.
lmlk	For the king.

17. (three copies: Deutsch and Heltzer 1999: 66–68, no. 150 = Davies 2004: 101.350)

b 10 9 šnh	In the 19th year.
[h]ġbm.	Ha-Gevim.
lmlk.	For the king.

In between three and five short lines of text these impressions all contain the following elements: 1) a date-formula, ‘in the x-th year’ (*b* [numeral] *šnh*); 2) a place-name; 3) the phrase ‘to/for the king’ (*lmlk*), as on the well-known *lmlk* stamps, where it is accompanied just by one of four place-names. Of the four places named, three (Eltolad, Nezib and Hagevim) are all of minor importance, though mentioned at least once in the Old Testament, but the fourth is the very important city of Lachish, the second city of the kingdom of Judah after Jerusalem.[9] The other places are so insignificant that one must assume that there were many more such bullae, from other towns, which have so far not turned up.[10] This seems to have been a much more local system of attribution than that to which the more numerous *lmlk* stamps belonged, which have only one of four place-names on them. Geographically the places named on the new impressions are spread widely in the territory of Judah: one was a little to the north of Jerusalem, two were to the south-west, and the fourth was in the far south, near Beersheba. The physical character and therefore the precise use of these bullae divides them into two groups: nos 14 and 15 are conical lumps of clay, presumably attached to containers of some kind, but the others like most bullae have the impressions of papyrus fibres and a cord on the back, indicating that they were for sealing documents. What were they for? One might perhaps suppose that they were the ancient equivalent of postage stamps, from the 'royal mail' of ancient Judah. More plausibly, we should begin from the similarity of the text on these bullae to elements of the recurring formulae on the Samaria ostraca, the hundred or so inscribed potsherds found in the ruins of the eighth-century royal palace of the northern kingdom of Israel (Davies 1991: 3.001–107; for a brief description see Davies 2002: 277–78).

18. (Davies 1991: 3.004)

[b]št hts]ʿṫ. mq	[In] the ninth year. From Qu-
[ṣh.] lgdyw. nbl.	[zeh]. For Gaddiyaw. A skin (*or* jar)
[yn. yšn.]	[of old wine].

As this example (Ostracon 4) shows, the Samaria ostraca typically included a date and a place-name, and also the names of one or more individuals and the quantity of a commodity such as oil or wine. Often the same dates, places and names recur on more than one ostracon. They are normally seen as records of deliveries to the palace of taxes in kind from various localities or royal estates in the surrounding region. It is very likely that the bullae being considered here played a part in a similar system in the southern kingdom of Judah, from which in fact two unconnected but similar ostraca are also known:

9 The addition of *rʾšnh* in this case may be related to the size and significance of Lachish ('first delivery'?).

10 Since this paper was delivered, a new publication has included a further bulla with a place-name (Maon) and the word *lmlk* but no date, and reference is also made there to four more examples of the 'standard' pattern, with two more new names (Arab and Keilah), which are to be published later in 2003 (Deutsch 2003b: 58–60).

19. (Diringer 1953: 339, no. 20 = Davies 1991: 1.020)

btšʿyt byt [ ]yhw	In the ninth (year). Beth-[ ]iah.
ḥklẏ[hw]żṅ[ ]1̇	Haqali[ah] [ ]zn[ ] 1

20. (Deutsch and Heltzer 1995: 81–83, no. 76 (cf. Lemaire 1997: 458) = Davies 2004: 99.003)

bšnh hš	In the sixth year,
št. bšbʿy	in the seventh (month).
mwdh {*or* mqdh} slt	Makkedah. Fine flour,
ḥq3t 5	50 heqats.

The bullae seem to represent an interesting technological development in the use of writing. On the one hand the key elements of the delivery formula are no longer written out by hand, but stamped in a single act, thereby saving time—a small step in the automation of bureaucracy. On the other hand, one group of the bullae were attached to papyrus documents, and the question arises as to what was written on these documents. It is not very adventurous to suggest that they included those elements of the formulae on the Samaria ostraca which are not represented on the bullae, i.e. the names of individuals, the commodities supplied and perhaps the quantities of each. The system seems not to have been completely uniform, or perhaps it developed over time. In addition to the two 'old-fashioned' ostraca already mentioned and the main group of bullae, there are two further bullae which lack one or two of the key elements of the main group, but include something that is missing from them, namely a name or names of individuals. One has a date and a place-name, but no *lmlk*, as far as we can see (but it might have been in the lost final line):

21. (Deutsch 1997: 141–42, no. 100 = Davies 2004: 101.281)

† {*or* ṫ} bʿšrt	(?) In the tenth (year).
ḣʾrbt	Ha—Arubbot.
[yš]ṁʿʾl	[Ish]mael.
[ ]	[ ]

Arubbot is mentioned in the list of Solomon's administrative districts (1 Kgs. 4:10), which places it in the territory of the (former?) northern kingdom. Y. Aharoni located it in the central coastal plain (1979: 313), but more recently A. Zertal has argued for an identification with Khirbet el-Hammam, in the hills between Samaria and Megiddo (see Zertal 1992). Either way, the location of Arubbot outside the boundaries of Judah raises important questions which cannot be discussed in detail here. Is this bulla a remnant of a similar administrative development in the northern kingdom before its fall in the late eighth century? Or is it an indication of a time when Judaean rule extended into the territory of the former northern kingdom, as is often conjectured for the later part of the reign of Josiah?

Another bulla has only the date from the common formula:

22. (Deutsch and Heltzer 1999: 64–66, no. 149 = Davies 2004: 101.349)

20 1 šnh	Twenty-first year.
lyšmʿl	For Ishmael.
ʿšyhw	Asaiah.

In this case one personal name is preceded by the preposition *l* and the other is not, which prompts similar questions to those raised by the Samaria ostraca about the different roles of the persons named. It is also tempting to suggest that the same Ishmael might be meant as in the preceding bulla (so Renz and Röllig 2003: 421), but given the frequency of the name in Hebrew inscriptions (less so in biblical passages referring to the monarchy period) it would be hazardous to assume this.

One final bulla, again with a date, seems likely to be related to the administration of the temple in Jerusalem:

23. (Deutsch 1997: 141, no. 99 = Davies 2004: 101.280)

bšlšt	In the 3rd (year).
lmks	For a contribution.

The word for 'contribution', *mks*, is known from other Semitic languages as well as post-biblical Hebrew in the general sense of 'tax' (von Soden 1965–81: 652; Hoftijzer and Jongeling 1995: 625). Its five occurrences in Biblical Hebrew are all in one short passage (Num. 31:37–41) and refer to a portion of the spoils of war (0.1%) which is dedicated to Yahweh. It is attractive, though not compelling, to connect the bulla with the practice of collecting contributions for repairs to the temple that is mentioned in 2 Kgs. 12:4–15 and 22:3–7 (and compare the comments above on text no. 9). This bulla also has the imprints of papyrus on the back, so that it must have been used, like other impressions from the same seal, to authenticate documents which listed, presumably, the names of contributors and the amounts which they had given.

To sum up, we have in this limited selection of texts evidence of military administration, a literary, prophetic or legal text, evidence of temple practices and contributions to their cost, a legal plea, a list of provisions, and indirect evidence of papyrus documents of various kinds and developments in the tax system(s) of ancient Israel. That is rather an 'official' slant to the uses of writing in ancient Israel; but it would take another paper to deal with the more everyday uses of writing in a wider range of situations.[11]

Bibliography

Aharoni, Y.
1979 *The Land of the Bible*, 2nd ed. (Burns and Oates: London).

Avigad, N.
1976 *Bullae and Seals from a Post-Exilic Judean Archive* (Qedem 4: Jerusalem).
1986 *Hebrew Bullae from the Time of Jeremiah: Remnants of a Burnt Archive* (Israel Exploration Society: Jerusalem).
1990 'Two Hebrew "fiscal" bullae', *IEJ* 40: 262–65.

Avigad, N., M. Heltzer and A. Lemaire
2000 *West Semitic Seals, Eighth–Sixth Centuries* BCE (Reuben and Edith Hecht Museum: Haifa).

Avigad, N., and B. Sass
1997 *Corpus of West Semitic Stamp Seals* (Israel Academy of Sciences and Humanities; Israel Exploration Society; Institute of Archaeology, The Hebrew University: Jerusalem).

Avishur, Y., and M. Heltzer
2000 *Studies on the Royal Administration in Ancient Israel in the Light of Epigraphic Sources* (revised and enlarged edition of the original Heb. version of 1996; Archaeological Center Pubs.: Tel Aviv).

Beit-Arieh, I.
1985 'An Edomite ostracon from Ḥorvat ʿUza', *TA* 12: 96–101.
1986–87 'The ostracon of Ahiqam from Ḥorvat ʿUza', *TA* 13–14: 32–38.
1989 'New data on the relationship between Judah and Edom toward the end of the Iron Age', *AASOR* 49: 125–31.
1993a 'An inscribed jar from Ḥorvat ʿUza', *EI* 24: 34–40 (Heb.).
1993b 'A literary ostracon from Ḥorvat ʿUza', *TA* 20: 55–65 (with a contribution from F.M. Cross).
1999 'The "Ten" ostracon from Ḥorvat ʿUza', *EI* 26: 30–34 (Heb.).

[11] Just such a study of some inscriptions with a very different background to those examined here has recently appeared (Parker 2003). It deals with some graffiti discovered in caves, which are seen as the work of fugitives. Parker's work could be enriched by some inscriptions published by J. Naveh which probably have a similar origin (Naveh 2001).

Beit-Arieh, I., and B.C. Cresson
1991 'Ḥorvat ʿUza: a fortified outpost on the eastern Negev border', *BA* 54: 126–35.

Berlejung, A., and A. Schüle
1998 'Erwägungen zu den neuen Ostraka aus der Sammlung Moussaïeff', *ZAH* 11: 68–73.

Bienkowski, P., and E. van der Steen
2001 'Tribes, trade and towns: a new framework for the Late Iron Age in Southern Jordan and the Negev', *Bulletin of the American Schools of Oriental Research* 323: 21–47.

Bordreuil, P.
1996 [1992] 'Sceaux inscrits des pays du Levant', in L. Pirot *et al.* (eds), *Supplément au Dictionnaire de la Bible* (Letouzey and Ané: Paris): 12, cols 86–212.

Bordreuil, P., F. Israel and D. Pardee
1996 'Deux ostraca de la collection Sh. Moussaïeff: I) Contribution financière pour le temple de YHWH; II) Réclamation d'une veuve auprès d'un fonctionnaire', *Semitica* 46: 49–76.
1998 'King's command and widow's plea: two new Hebrew ostraca of the Biblical period', *Near Eastern Archaeology* 61: 2–13.

Cross, F.M.
2000 'An ostracon in literary Hebrew from Ḥorvat ʿUza', in L.E. Stager, J.A. Greene and M.D. Coogan (eds), *The Archaeology of Jordan and Beyond: Essays in Honor of James A. Sauer* (Eisenbrauns: Winona Lake): 111–13.
2001 'A fragment of a monumental inscription from the City of David', *IEJ* 51: 44–47.

Crowfoot, J.W., G.M. Crowfoot and K.M. Kenyon
1957 *Samaria-Sebaste III: The Objects* (Palestine Exploration Fund: London).

Davies, G.I.
1991 *Ancient Hebrew Inscriptions: Corpus and Concordance* (Cambridge University Press; Cambridge).
2002 'Hebrew inscriptions', in J. Barton (ed.), *The Biblical World* (Routledge: London and New York): 1, 270–86.
2004 *Ancient Hebrew Inscriptions: Corpus and Concordance. Part 2* (Cambridge University Press: Cambridge).

Deutsch, R.
1997 *Messages from the Past: Hebrew Bullae from the Time of Isaiah Through the Destruction of the First Temple. Shlomo Moussaieff Collection and an Up to Date Corpus* (Heb.) (Archaeological Center Pubs.: Tel Aviv).
2002 'Lasting impressions: new bullae reveal Egyptian-style emblems on Judah's royal seals', *BAR* 28/4: 42–51, 60–61.
2003a 'New Hebrew bullae of officials in the court of Hezekiah', paper read at the SBL International Meeting, Cambridge, July 2003.

2003b 'A hoard of fifty Hebrew clay bullae from the time of Hezekiah', in R. Deutsch (ed.), *Shlomo: Studies in Epigraphy, Iconography, History and Archaeology in Honor of Shlomo Mousaieff* (Archaeological Center Pubs.: Tel Aviv): 45–98.

Deutsch, R., and M. Heltzer

1994 *Forty New Ancient West Semitic Inscriptions* (Archaeological Center Pubs.: Tel Aviv).

1995 *New Epigraphic Evidence from the Biblical Period* (Archaeological Center Pubs.: Tel Aviv).

1997 *Windows to the Past* (Archaeological Center Pubs.: Tel Aviv).

1999 *West Semitic Epigraphic News of the 1st Millennium* BCE (Archaeological Center Pubs.: Tel Aviv).

Deutsch, R., and A. Lemaire

2000 *Biblical Period Personal Seals in the Shlomo Mousaieff Collection* (Archaeological Center Pubs.: Tel Aviv).

Diringer, D.

1953 'Early Hebrew inscriptions', in O. Tufnell (ed.), *Lachish III: The Iron Age* (Oxford University Press: London): 331–59.

Ephal, I., and J. Naveh

1998 'Remarks on the recently published Moussaieff ostraca', *IEJ* 48: 269–73.

Garfinkel, Y.

1984 'The distribution of identical seal-impressions', *Cathedra* 32: 35–52 (Heb.).

1985 'A hierarchic pattern in the private seal impressions on the "LMLK" jar-handles', *EI* 18: 108–15 (Heb.).

Hoftijzer, J., and K. Jongeling

1995 *Dictionary of the North-West Semitic Inscriptions* (E.J. Brill: Leiden).

Hurowitz, V.

1998 'Notes on a recently published administrative document', *IEJ* 48: 132–35.

Joüon, P., and T. Muraoka

1991 *A Grammar of Biblical Hebrew* (Subsidia Biblica 14; Pontifical Biblical Institute: Rome).

Kessler, R.

1992 *Staat und Gesellschaft im vorexilischen Juda* (SVT 47: Leiden).

Lehmann, R.G.

1998 'Typologie und Signatur: Studien zu einem Listenostrakon aus der Sammlung Moussaieff', *UF* 30: 397–459.

Lemaire, A.

1981 'Classification des estampilles royales Judéennes', *EI* 15: 54–60.

1995 'Épigraphie Palestinienne: nouveaux documents II—Décennie 1985–1995', *Henoch* 17: 209–42.

1997 'Nouvelles données épigraphiques sur l'époque royale Israélite', *REJ* 156: 445–61.

1999 Reviews of Deutsch and Heltzer 1995 and 1997, and Deutsch 1997, *BO* 56: 172–77.

Naveh, J.
1982 'A fragment of an Ancient Hebrew inscription from the Ophel', *IEJ* 32: 195–98.
2000 'Hebrew and Aramaic inscriptions', in D. T. Ariel (ed.), *Excavations at the City of David, 1978-1985, Directed by Yigal Shiloh, VI: Inscriptions* (Qedem 41: Jerusalem): 1–14.
2001 'Hebrew graffiti from the First Temple period', *IEJ* 51: 194–207.

Overbeck, B., and Y. Meshorer
1993 *Das heilige Land: Antike Münzen und Siegel aus einem Jahrtausend jüdischer Geschichte* (Staatliche Münzsammlung: München).

Parker, S.B.
2003 'Graves, caves and refugees: a study in microhistory', *JSOT* 27: 259–88.

Powell, M.A.
1992 'Weights and measures', in D.N. Freedman (ed.), *The Anchor Bible Dictionary*, 6: 897–908.

Renz, J.
1999 'Schrifttypologie und Handschrift. Eine synchrone Studie der Inschrift DEUTSCH/HELTZER 1995, Ostrakon Nr.4 im Kontext gleichzeitiger Inschriften', *ZDPV* 115: 127–62.

Renz, J., and W. Röllig
1995 *Handbuch der althebräischen Epigraphik. I. Text und Kommentar. II/1. Zusammenfassende Erörterungen, Paläographie und Glossar. III. Texte und Tafeln* (Wissenschaftliche Buchgesellschaft: Darmstadt).
2003 *Handbuch der althebräischen Epigraphik. II/2. Materialien zur Althebräischen Morphologie. Siegel und Gewichte* (Wissenschaftliche Buchgesellschaft: Darmstadt).

Shiloh, Y.
1979 'City of David excavation 1978', *BA* 42: 165–71.

Shoham, Y.
1994 'A group of Hebrew bullae from Yigal Shiloh's excavations in the City of David', in H. Geva (ed.), *Ancient Jerusalem Revealed* (Israel Exploration Society: Jerusalem), 55–61.
1999 'Hebrew bullae from the City of David', *EI* 26: 151–75 (Heb.).
2000 'Hebrew bullae', in D. T. Ariel (ed.), *Excavations at the City of David 1978-1985, Directed by Yigal Shiloh, VI. Inscriptions* (Qedem 41: Jerusalem): 29–57.

von Soden, W.
1965–81 *Akkadisches Handwörterbuch* (Harrassowitz: Wiesbaden).

Sukenik, E.L.
1936 'Note on a fragment of an Israelite stele found at Samaria', *PEFQS* 156.

de Vaux, R.
1965 *Ancient Israel: Its Life and Institutions*, 2nd ed. (Darton, Longman and Todd: London).

Zertal, A.
1992 'Arubboth', in D.N. Freedman (ed.), *The Anchor Bible Dictionary*, 1: 465–67.

Now You See It, Now You Don't! The Monumental Use and Non-use of Writing in the Ancient Near East

K.A. Kitchen

Introduction

It is a quite special pleasure to add here a very modest, surface-skimming contribution—a *survol*, our French colleagues might say!—on a topic involving one of my esteemed friend and colleague's major interests (like me, he has many!) in a broad context of which most of us are conscious but never usually have the time or inclination to investigate in any depth. This study may not be much different, but at least the matter is worth a look; let us see what little does emerge—maybe a mole-hill from a mountain!

A. Definitions and circumstances

(a) Definitions

1. Human-scale, held-in-the-hand writings—ostraca, most papyri, clay tablets, wooden writing-boards and tablets (waxed or not), etc.,—are NOT 'monumental', but simply everyday, practical supports for scripts recording language and texts. These are not our subject.
2. At the opposite extreme, extending around often large temples and palaces, stone (or stone-clad) walls up to (say) 30 or 50 feet high and tens or hundreds of feet long can be found bearing acres of large-scale inscriptions, often with accompanying scenes of ritual or war. These are genuinely 'monumental' witnesses to the piety and/or power of the authorities or rulers responsible.
3. There is an *intermediate* zone. Stelae and rows of stones cladding walls ('orthostats') equally may bear texts and/or scenes. These can be of monumental scale (and so, qualify under 2 above), or else may be quite modest, and not truly qualify as major witnesses to the persons and ideas of their originators. Large rock texts and/or scenes do qualify as 'monumental'; mere graffiti do not.

(b) Circumstances

1. Very large and showy 'monumental' texts (and scenes) were normally intended to have an audience upon whom to impress their message; they are a form of public display. The publics may be 'eternal' (for the delectation of deities) or 'temporal' (for human observers to take in), or both.
2. Especially where human observers are concerned, the range of display may occur on either the *exterior* of buildings and also on rock faces for anyone to see, or on the *interior* of buildings and thus be aimed at the specific publics having access thereto.
3. The media of support are often different, for exterior and interior displays. For major buildings, *exterior* walls were stone-built, or at least stone-clad, on which texts (and scenes) may be placed. Such texts, etc., were engraved into the stone, and possibly painted also. Likewise for rock-texts/scenes. For *interiors*, things are different. From early times, with most buildings brick-built, texts and scenes on interior walls would be painted on plaster on such walls. But stone cladding could be used within brick buildings (cf. Neo-Assyrian palaces), or the whole building might be of stone anyway (cf. major Egyptian temples). In these cases (as with exteriors), sculptured and painted texts/scenes feature.
4. Decorum and economics. While many of the cultures and civilizations in the ancient Near East have much in common, they in each case had their own distinctive and distinguishing features and attitudes. So, widely inscribed and decorated walls might be natural in some cultures, but avoided in others; or, modes and moods changed through the centuries in any given culture. Furthermore, there are questions of practical cost. The petty chief of some very minor city-state a few score miles square, and away from lucrative trade-routes or saleable resources, was normally in no position to need, or pay for, the execution of monumental texts in (necessarily) expensive, monumental contexts, unlike the emperor of far-flung domains enjoying rich revenues, and able to indulge in conspicuous display.

B. Who preferred what, when and where?

Tastes in the use of monumental texts (and scenes) did vary considerably in both time and place throughout the greater Near East. We now take a whirlwind tour, through 3,000 years of time and space!

(a) Egypt

1. Monumental building began with the pharaohs themselves (monumental tomb-complexes, some exterior painted décor, 1st Dynasty and onwards).

The oldest public-display monumental texts come from the 3rd Dynasty onwards (*c*. 2700 BC), as labelling for large-scale victory-scenes of kings in marginal areas, to claim rule there and impress the locals—so, in Sinai (references, Porter and Moss 1952: 339–42), and (from 6th Dynasty *c*. 2300) at Aswan, gateway to Nubia (references, Porter and Moss 1937: 246 near end). Public buildings—we know mainly of pyramid-temples at present—had entirely blank walls, inside and out, until the 5th Dynasty (*c*. 2500). Then, while exterior walls remained firmly plain, the walls of interior courts and halls received major texts and scenes with texts; for the main court (interior) of the pyramid-temple of Sahure, see Borchardt (1910: pl. VI (reconstruction)), or Vandier (1954: 107, fig. 72 (in reduction)). And, surprisingly, that is how things stayed generally for the next thousand years, from the heart of the Old Kingdom Pyramid Age, though the Middle Kingdom and into the early Empire (New Kingdom), into the 18th Dynasty, when Tuthmosis III (*c*. 1479–1425) began to add the lengthy texts of calendars of temple-festivals on the south exterior walls of his temples at Karnak (in eastern Thebes), further north in Abydos, and further south at Aswan (Elephantiné). On these calendars (with reconstructions), see El-Sabban (2000: especially pp. 13 (with pls 7–8), 22–31 (with pl. 11) and 31–37 (with pl. 12)).

2. The major 'sea-change' came with the Ramesside kings (19th–20th Dynasties, *c*. 1295–1070 BC)—new men with new ideas, and the need to bolster their position with maximum publicity for their new regime. In contrast to minor, tentative efforts from Tuthmosis III down to Haremhab, Sethos I and Ramesses II henceforth began to cover the exterior walls of major temples with war and ritual scenes on the grand scale, accompanied not only by 'labels' but also by major monumental texts of some length, a trend taken still further by Ramesses III (*c*. 1184–1153). This grandiose use of texts and scenes on outer walls of temples (not palaces!) remained in force all the way down into Graeco-Roman times, and is visible to all visitors today. During the Middle and New Kingdoms, large rock-inscriptions and scenes continued to be carved, not least abroad, again to claim rule and impress locals.

As for interiors, throughout Egyptian history, when traces survive, brick-built edifices (palaces, houses, minor chapels) are known to have had painted scenes and label-texts on plaster, but this is not monumental in scale except in the major halls of palaces. Along the Nile Valley, of course, the Egyptians had easy access to good stone—limestone, sandstone, hard stones (granite, basalt) and decorative stones (alabaster, schists, etc.).

(b) Mesopotamia

1. The sanctuary of the Late Uruk temple at Tell ʿUqair (*c*. 3000 BC) did have painted walls with a dado of animal and human figures (cf. Lloyd 1978:

52, fig. 23 and n. 33). However, in the 3rd millennium BC, no buildings are yet known to show monumental-scale pictographic or cuneiform inscriptions, externally or internally (or scenes), a situation which continued through almost all of the 2nd millennium also. But the use of monumental stelae bearing both inscriptions and scenes is known, whatever their physical setting was originally. These run from the famous 'Stela of the Vultures' of Eannatum (*c*. 2500 BC; e.g., in Strommenger 1964: pls 66–68) down to the splendid Laws-Stela of Hammurabi of Babylon (e.g., in Strommenger 1964: pls 158–60), of (probably) the 18th century BC. Brick-built palaces in his time had painted decoration on plaster, as vividly shown at Mari (Parrot 1950: coloured frontispiece; other parts, Strommenger 1964: pls 164–65 and XXVIII–XXIX)—but these do not (yet) offer us suitably monumental texts to match. Likewise Karaindash and Kurigalzu I of Kassite Babylon (both before *c*. 1400) adorned temples with façades having moulded figures, but no significant texts—a practice followed by Shilhak-Inshushinak of Elam at Susa (*c*. 1130 BC; all three, cf. Clayden 2000). In the late 13th century, Tukulti-Ninurta I (*c*. 1230) may have adorned his palace in Assur with scenes and texts on coloured, glazed bricks and orthostats (Frankfort 1954: 67 and pl. 74; but Grayson 1991: 180:7 and 184–85:15, appears to attribute all such work to Tukulti-Ninurta II). This technique was still later utilized by Tukulti-Ninurta II (*c*. 890), again with scenes of war, etc., having cuneiform label-texts (Andrae ed. Hrouda 1977: 193, 195, abb. 170). Between these kings, Tiglath-pileser I (*c*. 1100) had set up orthostats and large figures of mythical creatures at the entry of the 'Old Palace' in Assur (cf. Andrae ed. Hrouda 1977: 192 and 299–300 n. 20, with references; cf. Weidner 1958), and rock-texts of his are reported abroad. But overall, temples were not adorned with major texts and scenes (such as Egypt now preferred), but retained plain, architecturally-panelled walls.

2. Then, with the 9th century BC, from Assurnasirpal II (*c*. 890) onwards, the Neo-Assyrian Empire moved forward in our sphere also. From now on, the major kings who achieved progressively wider conquests also used monumental art and texts to proclaim their power to the state élite at court and to visiting vassals alike. Assurnasirpal II, Shalmaneser III and (at an interval) Tiglath-pileser III lined the great courts and halls in the interior of their major palaces with long runs of stone slabs, carrying both scenes (war, rites) and texts to these ends, as did the mighty quartet that followed them—Sargon II and Sennacherib, and Esarhaddon and Assurbanipal (much of it in the British Museum, see Budge 1914; Smith 1938; Barnett and Falkner 1962; and Barnett 1976; since 1976, see running references in Caplice *et al*. 1976 to the present). But neither palaces nor temples had equivalent runs of monumental art all around their outside wall-surfaces.

Only at, and flanking, entrances and façades do we find lines of sculptured slabs, running outwards from the heraldic—and inscribed—winged bulls that marked the major portals. Whence this impulse originated is not clear; Egypt had been doing this kind of triumphal art in previous centuries, and it may be that (as with the Hittites?) Assyrian envoys to Egypt in the 14th/13th-century whirl of international diplomacy reported back on Egypt's triumphalist art-usage.

And, as with the Hittites (again, earlier), the Assyrians may have thence adopted the concept of using monumental, pictorial signs for limited decorative purposes. Of late, the huge 'decorative motifs' spread across Neo-Assyrian palace-façades (and found on lesser stone monuments) have been deciphered as in fact 'Assyrian hieroglyphs'—known as 'Astroglyphs'—that spell out the names and style of Assyrian kings and deities; on these, see Roaf and Zgoll (2001), with earlier literature. But clearly, this was a limited system, almost certainly known to, and understood by, a rather select scribal élite (even more so than for cuneiform itself?). Its closest parallel, functionally, is the so-called 'cryptographic' hieroglyphic writing sometimes used monumentally in Egyptian temples, from at least the 19th Dynasty onwards (*c*. 1300 on) So, late on, the Assyrians had two forms of monumental display of writing: the use of cuneiform (often annalistic) texts along with scenes of wars and triumphs in their palaces, and the almost esoteric 'Astroglyphs' that expressed their names and style across the bases of palace-façades. The Neo-Babylonian Empire that followed them in power had its seat in the alluvial south; no stone, no runs of texts and reliefs. Even the resumption of coloured glazed-brick façades was without textual counterpart. But both empires had kept up the age-old habit (shared with Egypt and others) of blazoning text and scenes writ large on rock-surfaces in the wider reaches of their domains (like those of Sennacherib, cf. Curtis and Reade 1995: 2 fig. 10 and 37 fig. 17).

3. Not Mesopotamia, but closely linked with it, we have also the civilizations of neighbouring Iran. Here too, from an early date, we find Elamite and neighbouring kings boldly imposing their names and images on rock faces, the mysterious Annubanini and others (for whom, see Debevoise 1942). Perhaps two thousand years later, this tradition was kept up with a vengeance, with the vast rock-scene of Darius I at Behistun (*c*. 520 BC), with its long inscriptions in Elamite, Old-Persian and Akkadian (Babylonian). Otherwise, large monumental public inscriptions find little employment in this sector; the Old-Persian inscriptions at, for example, Persepolis occur on palace walls and column-bases, but are not particularly prominent. All the main Old Persian texts can be found transliterated and translated in the work of Kent 1953.

(c) The Hittite realm: Anatolia and North Syria

1. Only from the early 2nd millennium BC do we have a brief record of an Early Anatolian ruler, Anum-khirbi (on whom, cf. Balkan 1957: 34–38), who invaded North Syria, and left an inscribed rock-inscription at Mt Atalur in that area, to be seen almost 1,000 years later by the powerful Assyrian king Shalmaneser III (in Grayson 1996: 17, 25, 29, 103). Monumentality in and from Anatolia only resumed about 500 years after Anum-khirbi with the rise of the Hittite Empire from *c.* 1360 BC, under Suppiluliuma I. However, even in the capital Hattusas (Bo azköy), never mind beyond, no use was immediately made of monumental display. But in the 13th century BC, things began to change. Kings such as Hattusil III and, especially, Tudkhalia IV and Suppiluliuma II adopted a hieroglyphic, i.e. pictorial, script for monumental and formal purposes (alongside rock-reliefs, and a rock-temple with sets of labelled scenes). These are the modestly famous 'Hittite hieroglyphs'. Culturally, and by royal patronage, they are 'Hittite', but the language which they were used to express was Luvian, sister-tongue to Hittite proper (Nesite). It was probably Tudkhalia IV whose craftsmen executed the long series of deities in scenes, in the open-air rock-cut temple at Yazılıkaya (close to Bo azköy), with Hittite Hieroglyphic label-texts carved next to the figures of the main deities, and to his own figure. Use of such inscriptions was extended by Tudkhalia IV and Suppiluliuma II to historical inscriptions on rock-surfaces (the Ni anta text), to large stone altars, and to a curious spring-sanctuary at Bo azköy (for which, see Hawkins 1995). This was full monumental usage, as in Egypt—and perhaps inspired by the sight of Egyptian monumental stelae in the Levant, or from Egypt itself, if Tudkhalia IV (before accession) had been the prince Hishmi-Sharruma who visited the highly monumental Egypt of Ramesses II.
2. After the fall of the Hittite Empire, *c.* 1190/1180 BC, two major successor-states very quickly established themselves as its moral successors. The most visible and senior was the Kingdom of Carchemish, which exerted a supremacy over North Syria as in imperial times, and over other adjoining areas to east and west—a 'mini-empire', and so its rulers appropriately termed themselves 'Great Kings', until their domain broke up by *c.* 1000 BC, just under 200 years later. The other, to their north-west across the Taurus mountains, was a similar domain, Tarhuntassa, in south-east Anatolia, which likewise became a 'mini-empire' under 'Great Kings', and ultimately lasted to become the kingdom of Tabal, down to the 7th century. Both of these states developed the use of Hieroglyphic Luvian inscriptions on a monumental scale, worthy of their rank. For Tarhuntassa/Tabal, this is at present limited to large rock-reliefs, like those of king Hartapus (for which see Hawkins 2000: I/2, 433–42 and I/3,

pls 236–43); but at Carchemish, its rulers moved on (early 1st millennium) from stelae to whole runs of large orthostats along the outer walls of important buildings, these slabs bearing not only series of pictorial reliefs but also some considerable hieroglyphic inscriptions, dealing in part with local history (cf. Hawkins 2000: I/1, 72–223, I/3, pls 1–90). We have such texts also from other Neo-Hittite centres in the early 1st millennium BC—Hamath, Bit-Adini, Karatepe, etc. (Hawkins 2000: I/1, 224–48 with I/3, pls 91–105; I/2, 398–423 with pls 213–35, etc.). This was the nearest thing to major monumental inscriptions (as in Egypt or Assyria) in the Levant at any time.

(d) The West Semitic world, in the Levant

Elsewhere in the Levant, we find a striking contrast with the Egyptian, Assyrian and Hittite traditions of monumental writing (with or without pictorial matter). The Neo-Hittites' close neighbours, the Arameans, did ape their neighbours in part by use of orthostats and monumental sculpture—but not with corresponding monumental texts; their texts only occur on stelae and statues of relatively modest size (no giant colossi here). The rest of the Levant's local rulers restricted themselves very largely to modest-size stelae, not always inscribed either. One thinks of such stelae for deities in Late Bronze Ugarit (13th century BC); but also for texts—Iron Age stelae and texts such as Phoenician examples from Byblos, or the Moabite Stone (*c*. 830 BC), and minor texts and scattered fragments from Philistia (Ekron), Israel (Samaria), and Judah (Jerusalem). Runs of wall-reliefs and texts might adorn Egyptian temples or Assyrian palaces, but the long stone walls of the palace at wealthy Late Bronze Ugarit had no texts (or scenes) either inside or out, nor did its temples so far as preserved. The same goes for Byblos, and other Levant sites of note, where no such phenomenon is traceable among the admittedly fragmentary finds. This ubiquitous non-use of monumental wall-inscriptions and scenes in the West Semitic Levant may be indicative of attitudes different to those in Egypt, Assyria or the Hittite realm. Does it bear any relation to the rise of aniconism in the Near East (avoidance of use of animate representations of deity; cf. review-paper by Lewis 1998)? A point worth investigation, perhaps.

(e) Ancient Arabia

1. In this realm, most of our data come from the south-west kingdoms of ancient Yemen, namely Saba (biblical Sheba), Main, Qataban and Hadramaut (bibliography of texts, see Kitchen 2000). The Old South Arabian alphabet seems to have been deliberately invented in about the 12th century BC (11th, only at very latest), based on the Late Canaanite alphabet of the Late Bronze Age (15th–11th centuries BC), see Kitchen 1994: 132–36 and references on data and views. Between the 10th

century BC and the 6th century AD, we have some 6,000 inscriptions from this region (plus some more in north-west Arabia), not counting the increasing number of everyday (non-monumental) writings on palm-sticks. Many of our 6,000 are simply graffiti (like the north Arabian Safaitic and other such texts) and thus do not concern us.

2. But with major texts from at least the 8th century BC onwards, it is a very different matter. Once the kings of Saba, Main and elsewhere began to build monumental architecture—mainly stone temples—they soon began to adorn these with suitably monumental texts, often in quite large Old South Arabian lettering. But (unlike Egypt and Assyria), interestingly, scenes and reliefs played very little part, and seem to disappear after the early 8th century BC, leaving only texts. For the latter, one may instance the superb inscriptions of early Sabean rulers such as Yada'il Dharih II at both the capital Marib (Awwam temple); and Sirwah (temple, outer wall), and by officers of the kings of the 4th–3rd centuries BC (Marib, Awwam temple); and in some measure by Minean kings and their merchants around the footings of the walls and bastions of ancient Yathill (now Baraqish), and so on. These are deliberately 'monumental' texts, that 'he who runs may read'. Major inscriptions were cut for display at the south gate of Tamna, capital of Qataban, and in Hadramaut, some rulers (Il-azz Yalit III; Yada'il Bayyin IV) equally advertised themselves and their deeds out at the lodge at Al-Uqla in the early/mid 3rd century AD. So, here, we have a practical aniconism in terms of reliefs after the 8th century, but definite use of major texts—be it temple dedications/building texts, notes of royal decrees and court acts, or whatever.

(f) East is East, West is West, end of tale!

1. Going out extreme east, beyond Iran, we reach the Indus civilization. This in its heyday certainly used inscribed personal seals in a distinctive pictorial script—but its major building-complexes offer us neither series of scenes nor habitual use of long texts on a monumental scale (or even otherwise); one large-scale epigraph (from Dholavira, found by Bisht; only about seven signs!) I owe mention of, to Michael Macdonald.
2. Going out extreme west, into the Aegean/East Mediterranean, the Minoan and Mycenean civilizations offer us some splendid palatial art, in terms of wall-paintings on interiors of palaces (Knossos, Crete) and major mansions (Santorini/Thera settlement) in the Bronze Age—but no monumental texts to go with them, still less separately. The Linear A and B texts seem restricted to everyday matters. Conspicuous monumentality in text or scenes was not part of Aegean culture any more than with the Indus at the opposite extreme, it would seem.

(g) Summing-up so far

What is the state of evidence, so far surveyed? We have the following physical results:

1. There were no large-scale monumental texts (or even major exterior scenes) in use on/in buildings before the later 2nd millennium BC. Internal scenes (but not texts) occurred in Mesopotamia *c.* 3000 BC (ʿUqair).
2. From the 3rd millennium BC down through the 2nd and 1st, we find in several cultures the use of large rock-scenes with label (or longer) texts, and large rock-texts from Egypt to Elam/Iran, from Anatolia to South Arabia. Especially in areas subdued by external rulers who left such memorials, these were public markers of claim-to-rule and of royal might.
3. From the mid/later 2nd millennium, Egypt's rulers first used exterior walls extensively, for major texts and scenes. Assyria began to use texts/scenes in palace-contexts. The later kings of the Hittite Empire had an open-air rock-temple with runs of reliefs with hieroglyphic label-texts, and began to use hieroglyphic texts in open areas.
4. In the early 1st millennium, Neo-Hittite successor-states (headed by Carchemish) continued and developed the use of monumental hieroglyphic inscriptions and reliefs on series of orthostats, a not too distant parallel with Egyptian usage in principle. A little later, Neo-Assyria wholeheartedly adopted the concept of long series of monumental reliefs and texts within the public areas of their palaces, and on façades used also 'Astroglyphs'. Except for the latter on occasional façades, their temples had few wall-decoration/texts (inside or out).
5. By contrast, West Semitic kingdoms in the Levant made almost no use of either large monumental inscriptions or sets of scenes; only the northern Arameans adopted the use of scenes on orthostats from their Neo-Hittite neighbours—but not large monumental texts! Modest-size stelae (and occasionally inscribed statues, about life-size) were the norm in this area.
6. An interesting partial contrast is Old South Arabia. After the 8th century BC, there was no use of sets of scenes, but certainly there was of major monumental text-dedications, etc., on temples, including especially exterior surfaces.
7. In the extreme east, there is almost nothing of this kind for the Indus. In the extreme west, there are paintings within palatial residences but no monumental texts in the Minoan/Mycenean world.

C. Why is what, what it is? Why do some do, and some don't?

Here, given the splendidly varied patchwork of cultures and civilizations, no one single answer can be expected to suffice. Even the changes within just one culture may have multiple causes. A real overall multiplex answer is not possible here and now, and most likely never will be. But, we can content ourselves with humbly picking up a few crumbs and hints from amidst the wrecks of Time.

(a) Why Yes? The positive cultures—Egypt and South Arabia in the south-west and south, and the Hittites and Assyrians in the north-east and north—face each other across a transverse east-west belt of cultures not using monumental texts in conspicuous architectural contexts (Minoan/Mycenean; West Semitic in Levant; Sumer/Babylonia; Iran other than rock-texts; Indus). In all the north and south positive cases, there was ready access to good, reasonably easy-use stone (such as limestone, sandstone) for indulging in monumental stone architecture and monumental texts on these. It is also the case that the considerable size and resources of Egypt at most periods, of Hatti and Neo-Assyria in imperial mode (plus Carchemish in a position of wealth) and of Old South Arabian kingdoms having wealth by agriculture and trade in their high periods—in these cases, there was economic power and manpower to satisfy the ambitions of rulers, for themselves and their bosses (i.e. their deities); and often ambitions to match, and people to impress.

(b) Why Not? Across our middle belt, there are several seemingly obvious reasons for some abstentions. First, the political organizations in the Aegean and Indus alike were probably not oriented to the ruler being regarded as the kingpin between the peoples concerned and deity in the often quasi-absolutist way visible in such polities as Egypt, Hatti and Assyria (plus the stronger of the Old South Arabian regimes).

Second, the natural resources and context of some lands did not favour the kind of stone architecture that most lends itself to monumental texts and scenes. Everything in Sumer and Babylonia was of brick; and even coloured, glazed brick was too complex a medium for casual indulgence in major texts; stone supplies were too distant (Iraq/Iran hills) to be economically exploited on a large scale (unlike in Assyria).

Third, the smaller states of the Levant (especially on its margins and in the southern part) at most times simply did not have the need (or the economic clout) to go in for large stone complexes, or matching display texts. Nor did they have imperial triumphs to boast of very often, nor often the scale of buildings that merited major building-texts. Practicality, economics, and more limited horizons played their part.

Fourth, there is the question of cultural norms and beliefs, especially religious and cultic. Some lands (especially the politically dominant ones) developed elaborate cults and elaborate 'theological' imagery to match their wealth and the burgeoning thought-world of their leisure-times of religious (=philosophical) reflection. But others at times preferred to exemplify the mystery and hiddenness of deity by resort to aniconism, limited or non-use of pictorial imagery, or banned such imagery on purpose (e.g., the Hebrews).

Most cults in the Levant (even wealthy Ugarit) preferred to invest their devotions in the apparatus of cult, not in decorating or inscribing the buildings in which the cults were conducted. As for palaces, again, even wealthy Ugarit did not ostentatiously inscribe its ample palace-walls, inside or out, nor did most of the rest of the Levantine kingdoms. However, in many (be it Mari, Alalakh, Tell Kabri, etc.), bright wall-paintings on plaster are attested—but so far without any texts (ostentatious or otherwise).

Finis

This deliberately wide-ranging survey may not have advanced the cause of scholarly understanding of the ancient Near East very visibly, or (alas!) even at all; and I may have erred little or much, and have overlooked things, too. But at least I hope that it may provide, if not a gargantuan feast, at least the academic equivalent of a thin biscuit and half a cup of tea, and encourage us to look around for better fare in either case!

Bibliography

Andrae, W., ed. B. Hrouda
1977 *Das wiedererstandene Assur*, 2nd ed. (Munich: C.H. Beck).

Balkan, K.
1957 *Letter of Anum-hirbi of Mama to King Warshama of Kanish* (Ankara: TTKB).

Barnett, R.D.
1976 *Sculptures from the North Palace of Ashurbanipal at Nineveh* (London: British Museum).

Barnett, R.D., and M. Falkner
1962 *The Sculptures of Tiglath-pileser III* (London: British Museum).

Borchardt, L.
1910 *Das Grabdenkmal des Königs Sa3hure,* I (Leipzig: Hinrichs).

Budge, E.A.W.
1914 *Assyrian Sculptures in the British Museum: Reign of Ashur-nasir-pal* (London: British Museum).

Caplice, R., *et al.* (and successors)
1976ff. *Keilschriftbibliographie*, 37ff. to the present, in *Orientalia NS* 45ff. to the present.

Clayden, T.
2000 'Moulded mud-brick at Dur Kurigalzu', *Al-Rafidan* 21: 71–82, pl. 1.

Curtis, J.E., and J.E. Reade
1995 *Art and Empire: Treasures from Assyria in the British Museum* (New York: Metropolitan Museum of Art).

Debevoise, N.
1942 'The rock reliefs of ancient Iran', *JNES* 1: 76–83.

El-Sabban, S.
2000 *Temple Festival Calendars of Ancient Egypt* (Liverpool: Liverpool University Press).

Frankfort, H.
1954 *The Art and Architecture of the Ancient Orient* (Harmondsworth: Penguin Books).

Grayson, A.K.
1991 *Assyrian Rulers of the Early First Millenium* BC, *I (1114–859* BC*)*, Royal Inscriptions of Mesopotamia, Assyrian Periods, Volume 2 (Toronto: University of Toronto Press).
1996 *Assyrian Rulers of the Early First Millenium* BC, *II (858–745* BC*)*, Royal Inscriptions of Mesopotamia, Assyrian Periods, Volume 3 (Toronto: University Press).

Hawkins, J.D.
1995 *The Hieroglyphic Inscription of the Sacred Pool Complex at Hattusa (Südburg)* (Wiesbaden: Harrassowitz).
2000 *Corpus of Hieroglyphic Luvian Inscriptions,* I/1–3 (Berlin: de Gruyter).

Kent, R.G.
1953 *Old Persian—Grammar, Texts, Lexicon,* American Oriental Series, 33, 2nd ed. (New Haven).

Kitchen, K.A.
1994 *Documentation for Ancient Arabia*, I (Liverpool: University Press).
2000 *Documentation for Ancient Arabia*, II (Liverpool: University Press).

Lewis, T.J.
1998 'Divine images and aniconism in ancient Israel', *Journal of the American Oriental Society* 118: 36–53.

Lloyd, S.
1978 *The Archaeology of Mesopotamia* (London: Thames and Hudson).

Parrot, A. (ed.)
1950 *Studia Mariana* (Leiden: Brill).

Porter, B., and R.L.B. Moss
1937 *Topographical Bibliography of Ancient Egyptian Hieroglyphic Texts, Reliefs and Paintings,* VI (Oxford: Griffith Institute).
1952 *Topographical Bibliography of Ancient Egyptian Hieroglyphic Texts, Reliefs and Paintings,* VII (Oxford: Griffith Institute).

Roaf, M., and A. Zgoll
2001 'Assyrian astroglyphs: Lord Aberdeen's black stone and the prisms of Esarhaddon', *Zeitschrift für Assyriologie* 91: 264–95.

Smith, S.
1938 *Assyrian Sculptures in the British Museum from Shalmaneser III to Sennacherib* (London: British Museum).

Strommenger, E.
1964 *The Art of Mesopotamia* (London: Thames & Hudson).

Vandier, J.
1954 *Manuel d'archéologie égyptienne*, II/1 (Paris: Picard).

Weidner, E.
1958 'Die Feldzüge und Bauten Tiglathpilesers I.', *Archiv für Orientforschung* 18: 342–360.

What has Delphi to do with Samaria? Ambiguity and Delusion in Israelite Prophecy

Daniel I. Block

Introduction

Among Professor Alan Millard's many lasting contributions to biblical scholarship will be his rigorous demand that the biblical writings, both Old and New Testament, be read within the literary and cultural contexts from which they emerge and which they address. It is a privilege to present this study in his honour. Although this essay touches Professor Millard's specific interest in writing in the ancient Near East only tangentially, it will seek to apply his broader concern to a specific biblical text, viz., 1 Kgs. 22:1–40.

The account of Micaiah ben Imlah's confrontation with Ahab and the latter's subsequent demise has attracted the attention of scholars for a variety of reasons and elicited responses from a wide range of perspectives. Source- and redaction-critical approaches have focused on isolating the primary account from secondary and tertiary editorial layers.[1] The boundaries

[1] The following represent the most important discussions in chronological order. Ernst Würthwein (1967: 245–54; 1984: 253–62) identifies a battle report with fairy tale features (*märchenhafte Zügen*) in vv. 2b–4, 29–37; and a multi-layered prophetic story in vv. 5–28a (stratum 1, vv. 5–9. 13–18, 26–28a; stratum 2, vv. 10–12, 24–25; stratum 3, vv. 19–22, 23). Simon J. De Vries has provided the most thorough analysis (1978: 1–51, cf. his summary [1985: 265–66]). De Vries isolates two primary narratives, A (a battle report, vv. 2*b*–4*a*, 4*bb*–9, 15–18, 26–28) and B (a prophetic story, vv. 10–12*a*, 14, 19, 20*aa*, 20*b*–25), plus minor additions. Helga Weippert (1988: 457–79) proposes a complex literary process consisting of five stages: (1) The original core involved an account of the heroic death of a king of Israel (vv. 3a–c, 11a–d, 29a*, 34a–35c). (2) This core was integrated into the narrative cycle concerning the wars between Israel and Aram (vv. 1a,b, 2a, 36a–37c). (3) This material was then incorporated in the Ahab-history (vv. 35d–38a, 40b). (4) A Jehoshaphat recension added a theological *Lehrstück* consisting of a Prologue (vv. 2b, 4a–f), body (vv. 5a–10b, 12a–28c), and an epilogue (vv. 30a–33c), inserting 'Jehoshaphat' in v. 29a. (5) The late gloss in 28d,e identifies the Micaiah of this account with the prophet Micah (cf. Mic. 1:2a). Hedwige Rouillard (1993: 100) finds an original kernel concerning some king of Israel other than Ahab in vv. 2b–4 and 29–38, which has been overlaid by the account of his death in battle with the Aramaeans (vv. 5–28). Nadav Na'aman (1997: 153–73) argues for a pre-Dtr 'battle report' of Ahab's death (vv. 1–18, 29–37), to which Dtr added vv. 19–28, which reflected the conflicts

between redaction criticism and form criticism often blur, but the latter tend to view the text more holistically. In this chapter some form critics have identified two forms, both with a readily identifiable structure: a 'battle report' (vv. 1–18)[2] and a 'prophetic vision report' (vv. 19–22), recognizing that visions commonly arise in response to a request for an oracle.[3] Alexander Rofé (1976: 233–44) prefers to treat the entire text as a didactic example story, deriving from the heyday of classical prophecy and offering an excellent source for the theology of classical prophecy.[4]

This observation provides a convenient transition to a third approach that finds in this text a helpful source for tracing the history of the prophetic tradition in ancient Israel, noting especially the nature and dynamics of the prophetic institution,[5] the access that prophets appear to have had to the heavenly court,[6] and the conflict that seems to have arisen regularly between true and false prophets.[7]

Scholars who approach this text as historians are concerned with the nature of the events described and the location of those events within the history of Israel and Aram. The results proposed by many are not encouraging, inasmuch as the contents of 1 Kgs. 22 are often deemed not to fit the context of Ahab's reign.[8]

Through 'close readings' of 1 Kgs. 22 recent scholarship has been especially concerned to understand how the chapter functions as narrative

involving true and false prophecy in his time. Relying on much of the work of H.-J. Stipp (1987: 152–229), Bernhard Lehnart (2003: 454–59) recognizes three editorial strata in the chapter: the *Grundschicht* involving the exchange between Micaiah and 400 prophets of Ahab (vv. 3,6,9,15–17,29*,30*,34,36–38); the Zedekiah stratum (vv. 1–2*,11–12,13–14,24–28a,31); and the Jehoshaphat stratum (vv. 2b,4,5,7–8,10,18,29*,30a,32–33). Remarkably in a volume on prophecy Lehnart leaves vv. 19–23 unaccounted for.

[2] Operating as a form critic Na'aman (1997: 165) recognizes the following structure in the 'battle report': (1) Situation and agreement to wage war (vv. 1–4); (2) Consultation with prophets (vv. 5–18); (3) The battle and its outcome (vv. 29–37). Cf. De Vries (1986: 21–22), who classifies this chapter as a whole as a 'prophetic battle story'.

[3] De Vries (1986: 22–24) classifies vv. 12–20 as a 'report of an oracular inquiry'. For fuller discussion see Long (1976: 353–65, esp. 359, 365). Long identifies the present text more specifically as a 'dramatic word-vision'. Elsewhere (1984: 230–40) he identifies the chapter as a whole as a 'prophetic story', that incorporates elements of conventional 'battle reports' and 'reports of symbolic actions' (v. 11) and 'vision reports' (vv. 17, 19–22).

[4] 'For a helpful review of Rofé see Roth (1982: 127–31).

[5] On the relationship between Israelite prophecy and divination see Overholt (1989: 117–47) and Barstad (1993: 47–49). On the relationship between prophecy and ecstasy see the still helpful study by Haller (1960: 5–39).

[6] Cf. Isaiah 6:1 and Job 1–2. For a recent helpful discussion of the relationship of vv. 19–23 to these texts see Dafni (2000: 375–85).

[7] Note especially De Vries' (1978) discussion. See also Hossfeld and Meyer (1973: 27–36).

[8] See Whitely (1952: 137–52); Miller (1966: 441–54; 1967: 307–24; 1968: 337–42; 1976: 20–39). For a survey of historians' efforts prior to 1991 see McKenzie (1991: 88–93). For more positive assessments see Provan, *et al.* (2003: 263–66); and apparently Cogan (2001: 489–98).

literature: how the plot develops and the participants in the reported events are characterized.[9] Even though Elijah is not mentioned in this chapter, some explore how this passage contributes to the characterization of this prophet in the broader context of 1 Kgs. 17–2 Kgs. 2 (Firth 2000: 174–85).

Finally, to biblical and dogmatic theologians 1 Kgs. 22 poses special challenges. How can Yahweh authorize a member of his heavenly court to deceive a person? And how is it that Yahweh does not appear to have full control of the course and outcome of historical events? We delay a discussion of this matter until later, but for the moment we note that the answers to this question vary greatly from those who argue that the 'lying spirit' involved was a demon,[10] if not actually Satan (Mayhue 1993: 135–63), to Yahweh himself being totally truthful but sovereignly controlling a 'spirit of deceit' (Williams 2002: 58–66; cf. Seow 1999: 166–67), to God lies and God does not really control nor even know the course or the outcome of future events (Roberts 1988: 211–20; Hamilton 1994: 649–63; Fretheim 1999:126–28).

Despite the extraordinary scholarly energies that have been expended in trying to understand 1 Kgs. 22, consensus on many issues eludes the scholarly guild. The wide variety of approaches to and interpretations of this chapter both encourage and discourage renewed efforts. On the one hand, the lack of consensus challenges us to experiment with new approaches. On the other hand, it forces us to speak both modestly and tentatively when we propose possible solutions. The purpose of this paper is to take another look especially at the oracle uttered by the prophets of Ahab in 1 Kgs. 22:6, interpreting it not only within its present literary context but also in the broader light of oracular narratives in the Old Testament and against the backdrop of extra-biblical oracular prophecy. Our hypothesis is that the ambiguity of the oracle represents the key to the understanding of this text.

The context of the oracle

According to 1 Kgs. 22:1–2, two significant historical developments set the stage for the events described in this chapter. First, they transpire at the end of a three-year truce in hostilities between the northern kingdom of Israel and the Aramaean kingdom centered in Damascus. The statement in v. 1 alludes to chapter 20, which describes Ahab's resounding defeat of Ben-Hadad at Aphek in fulfillment of a series of prophetic oracles (20:13–14, 22, 28).

9 See Brenneman (2000: 89–107); Longman (1987: 101–11). This is essentially the approach taken in the recent commentary by Walsh (1996: 342–60).

10 Cf. Crenshaw (1971: 81). For a response Saggs (1978: 107–10). Carroll (1979: 199) finds in the account of Micaiah ben Imlah the classical expression of the deity deceiving people.

However, apparently contrary to another oracle (v. 42), instead of killing Ben-Hadad as Yahweh had commanded, Ahab entered into a covenant relationship with him.[11] Presumably as an act of gratitude for the clemency Ahab had shown him, Ben-Hadad promised to restore to Ahab control over Ramoth-gilead, which the Aramaeans had wrested from the Omrides some time earlier, and give Israelite merchants free access to the markets of Damascus (Cogan 2001: 469). However, it appears that with the retreat of the Assyrian menace after the Battle of Qarqar in 853 BC,[12] the fraternal relationship between Ahab and Ben-Hadad disintegrated, and the hostilities resumed (Provan, *et al.* 2003: 264).

Second, the events described in this chapter occur during a visit to Samaria by Jehoshaphat, king of Judah (22:2). Although the narrator of Kings does not declare the purpose of the visit, based upon the Chronicler's report (2 Chr. 18:1–2), this may have been a follow-up visit to the alliance Ahab and Jehoshaphat had struck and sealed with the marriage of the former's daughter Athaliah to the latter's son Jehoram (2 Kgs. 8:18, 26).[13] While Jehoshaphat was in Samaria, Ahab raised the contentious issue of Ramoth-gilead with his courtiers: despite Ben-Hadad II's promises, he had failed to hand over the territory to the Israelite king and the latter's officials had taken no initiative to ensure that this happened. Capitalizing on the visit of Jehoshaphat, Ahab invited his political ally *pro tempore* to join him in a military campaign to seize Ramoth-gilead from the Aramaeans. Though cast in epigrammatic form, Jehoshaphat's initial response appears affirmative, as he commits his own energy and his military resources to the adventure (v. 4). However, he requests that before they enter the fray Ahab should make oracular inquiry concerning the wisdom of the campaign (v. 5).

[11] Whereas Ben-Hadad apparently would have been grateful to become Ahab's vassal (*'ebed*, v. 32), the Israelite king accepts him as a peer (*'āḥ*, literally 'brother'). On vassaldom understood as 'sonship' see 2 Kgs. 16:6 (Ahaz vis à vis Tiglath-Pileser). Cf. Weinfeld (1970: 190–94). On political parity understood as 'brotherhood' see 1 Kgs. 9:13 (Solomon and Hiram). Cf. Weinfeld (1970: 194); Fishbane (1970: 313–18).

[12] At this point the narrator of 1 Kings says nothing about the threat of the Assyrians under Shalmaneser III. Although the Aramaeans interpret Ahab's earlier sparing of Ben-Hadad's life as an act of mercy (20:31), he may have been driven by expediency, viz., the need for allies to face the growing Assyrian menace. According to the 'Monolith Inscription', in 853 BC, 'Ahab the Israelite' along with 'Adad-idri' and a half dozen other allies engaged Shalmaneser III of Assyria in battle at Qarqar. If Adad-'idri is to be identified with Ben-Hadad II, as seems most likely (cf. K.A. Kitchen, 'Ben-Hadad', *IBD* [1980] 1.184), then these two kings appear to have taken advantage of their truce to present a common front against the Assyrians.

[13] Although most of the material in 2 Chr. 18 is borrowed verbatim from 1 Kgs. 20, a few significant additions and deviations from the latter shift the focus from Ahab to Jehoshaphat. So also Japhet (1993: 756).

The form and style of the oracle

In requesting a divine oracle before entering into a military campaign Jehoshaphat appealed to a common practice not only in ancient Israel,[14] but also in the international context beyond Israel (Weippert 1972: 472–76; van der Spek 1993: 265–67; Nissinen 1998: 1164–65). Although the report of the oracle in 1 Kgs. 22:5–6 consists of only 31 words[15] it provides the only account of an oracular inquiry in the Old Testament containing all the essential elements (Jeffers 1996: 237). These elements may be highlighted as follows:

The Request for an Oracle	וַיֹּאמֶר יְהוֹשָׁפָט אֶל־מֶלֶךְ יִשְׂרָאֵל דְּרָשׁ־נָא כַיּוֹם אֶת־דְּבַר יְהוָה׃	And Jehoshaphat said to the king of Israel, 'Inquire first for the word of Yahweh'.
The Preparation for the Oracle	וַיִּקְבֹּץ מֶלֶךְ־יִשְׂרָאֵל אֶת־הַנְּבִיאִים כְּאַרְבַּע מֵאוֹת אִישׁ	Then the king of Israel gathered the prophets, about four hundred men,
The Question for the Oracle	וַיֹּאמֶר אֲלֵהֶם הַאֵלֵךְ עַל־רָמֹת גִּלְעָד לַמִּלְחָמָה אִם־אֶחְדָּל	and he said to them, 'Shall I go against Ramoth-gilead, to battle? or shall I desist?'
The Response of the Oracle	וַיֹּאמְרוּ עֲלֵה וְיִתֵּן אֲדֹנָי בְּיַד הַמֶּלֶךְ׃	And they said, 'Go up, and the Lord will give into the hand of the king'.

Whereas the conventional formula for inquiry regarding the divine will before battle involved *šāʾal bĕYHWH*, 'to ask of Yahweh' (Num. 27:21; Judg. 1:1; 1 Sam. 23:2; 30:8), presumably because the inquiry is to be made through a prophet (Cogan 2001: 489), Jehoshaphat employs the phrase, *dāraš ʾet dĕbar YHWH*, 'to seek a word of Yahweh' (cf. 1 Kgs. 14:5). His

[14] Such oracles were received before the Ark of the Covenant (Judg. 20:27–28; cf. 1 Sam. 14:18[Heb]), before the priest dressed in the ephod and equipped with Urim and Thummim (1 Sam. 28:6; 30:7; cf. 14:18[LXX]), through dreams (Judg. 7:13), or mediums (*ʾōbōt,* 1 Sam 28:7), or prophets (1 Kgs. 22:5–6,17). Judg. 18:5 provides an example of an oracular inquiry concerning a reconnaissance (and ultimately military) adventure before an illegitimate priest.

[15] The parallel text in 2 Chr. 18:4–5 is identical to the Kings text with the following exceptions: (1) the approximation in the number of prophets, *kĕʾarbaʿ mēʾôt* ('about four hundred') is removed and the number made precise, *ʾarbaʿ mēʾôt* ('four hundred'); (2) the singular *hāʾēlēk* ('Shall I go?') is rendered plural, *hănēlēk* ('Shall we go?'; (3) the preposition *ʿal* ('against') is replaced by the preposition *ʾel*; (4) the titular reference to the deity as *ʾădōnāy* ('Lord') is replaced by the generic designation, *hāʾĕlōhîm* ('God').

specification of Yahweh as the deity to be addressed accords with his own spiritual allegiance as king of Judah. After all, the temple that Solomon had built for Yahweh stood next to his own palace in Jerusalem. Despite Ahab's longstanding promotion of the cult of Baal, especially his having constructed a temple compound for Baal in Samaria (1 Kgs. 16:31–32), Jehoshaphat apparently assumed that Ahab would consult the patron deity of all Israel.

Ahab seems to have acceded willingly to Jehoshaphat's request, though the nature of his response is interesting on several counts. First, rather than going to the temple to consult with priests, he seeks an oracle from the prophets. We do not know what kind of oracular options were open to Ahab. According to Num. 27:21, in the days of Moses and Joshua Yahweh had established the pattern that should be followed in events like this: the leader is to appear before the priest (presumably at the Tabernacle/Temple), who would make inquiry on his behalf by manipulating Urim before Yahweh.[16] However, in view of the religious situation instituted by Jeroboam almost a century earlier (1 Kgs. 12:25–33), Ahab could not go to Jerusalem for the inquiry for obvious reasons. Nor could he have brought the priest from there up to Samaria, without compromising the Northern Kingdom's religious (and political) independence and undermining his own Baalistic religious establishment in Samaria. Furthermore, the latter would have been precluded by Jehoshaphat's specific request to 'seek a word from Yahweh'. By inquiring of the prophets he may have hoped to avoid objections from the king of Judah.[17]

However, the narrator creates a certain ambiguity by refusing to identify these prophets. If they were true prophets of Yahweh then we wonder how they survived Jezebel's pogrom (1 Kgs. 18:4,13; cf. 19:10, 14). If they were prophets of Baal (cf. 18:19), then we wonder how they had escaped Elijah's massacre (18:40), and conclude that the Baalistic establishment was more deeply entrenched than the narrative had suggested. The fact that Ahab assembled 400 prophets provides a numerical link with 18:19, according to

[16] The idiom used is *šāʾal bĕmišpaṭ hāʾûrîm*, 'to inquire by the judgment of the Urim'. For a thorough analysis of the use of the Urim and Thummim for oracular purposes see Van Dam (1997: 177–93).

[17] According to Cogan (2001: 490) this is the earliest reference to the consultation of prophets prior to a battle. Technically this is correct, but this is not the first time prophets have been involved in military situations. According to Judg. 4:5, in the face of the crisis created by Jabin's military control over northern Israel the people came to the prophet Deborah for oracular consultation. As the prophetic agent of Yahweh Deborah called Barak to lead Israel's army (vv. 6–8), predicted the successful outcome of the battle (v. 9), and announced the time for attack (v. 14). For a more detailed discussion of Deborah's primarily prophetic role see Block (1994: 229–54; 2001: 34–40,49–52.

[18] The link is strengthened by the use of the verb *qābaṣ*, 'to assemble', in both contexts.

which Elijah had challenged Ahab to gather not only 450 prophets of Baal, but also 400 prophets of Asherah, who ate at Jezebel's table.[18] The absence of any reference to these prophets or to Asherah in the account of the contest on Mount Carmel (18:20–40) suggests that they may have survived Elijah's purge. Although some interpret the number typologically or hyperbolically,[19] it is preferable to take it seriously and either to associate these with Jezebel's prophetic entourage or to view them as a nationalistic cadre perhaps based in Bethel (cf. 12:28–29). In view of Zedekiah's explicitly Yahwistic performance in vv. 11–12 the latter seems more likely (Wiseman 1993: 185). Apparently two forms of Yahweh worship existed simultaneously in the Northern Kingdom: the syncretistic form represented by the calf cult and designed to prop up the monarchy, and the orthodox version represented by Elijah, Elisha, and Micaiah ben Imlah in this chapter (Burney 1903: 252). Evidently Jehoshaphat's response to the oracle (v. 7) indicates that he questioned not only the validity of the oracle they pronounced, but also their status as legitimate prophets of Yahweh. Later both the 'spirit of delusion' and Micaiah will refer to these as Ahab's prophets (vv. 22, 23).[20]

The question Ahab poses for the prophets is simple, calling for an up or down answer: 'Shall I go to battle against Ramoth-gilead, or shall I desist?'[21] Although the narrator does not indicate how the prophets received their message,[22] they responded unanimously. The response is a simple statement, beginning with the verb *ʿălēh*, 'Go up',[23] followed by a promissory version of the committal formula, *wayyittēn ʾădōnāy bĕyad hammelek*, 'and the Lord will give into the hands of the king'.[24] Although variations of this oracle will occur twice more in this chapter (vv. 12, 15), it bears a striking resemblance to several found elsewhere in the Old Testament, as illustrated by the following synopsis:

[19] For the former see Cogan (2001: 490); for the latter, Jones (1984: 364).

[20] Targum Jonathan explicitly and repeatedly refers to them as 'prophets of falsehood' (*nbyy šqrʾ*): vv. 6–10,12, 13. Josephus notes similarly that Jehoshaphat recognized 'by their words that they were false prophets (*pseudoprofētai*)'.

[21] Similar questions are posed elsewhere: by Saul, with reference to the Philistines (1 Sam. 14:37); by David, with reference to the Philistines (1 Sam. 23:2; 5:19; 1 Chr. 14:10), and with reference to one of the cities of Judah (2 Sam. 2:1). Because the last example began vaguely ('Shall I go up into any of the cities of Judah?'), a positive response from Yahweh called for a follow-up inquiry, 'To which [city] shall I go up?' To this query Yahweh answered, 'To Hebron', which he then established as his capital.

[22] In the ancient Near East the will of the gods was sought through sheep-omens and/or astrological phenomena, but also received spontaneously through dreams or prophetic revelations. Cf. Weippert (1972: 470–71). For full length studies see Jeffers (1996) and Cryer (1994).

[23] The verb is idiomatic, based on the common practice of establishing fortifications on hilltops or mounds.

[24] German *Übergabeformel,* which Long (1984: 264) renders 'conveyance formula'.

Judg. 20:28	וַיֹּאמֶר יְהוָה עֲלוּ כִּי מָחָר אֶתְּנֶנּוּ בְיָדֶךָ׃	And Yahweh said, 'Go up, for tomorrow I will give them into your hand'.
2 Sam. 5:19; cf. 1 Chr. 14:10	וַיֹּאמֶר יְהוָה אֶל־דָּוִד עֲלֵה כִּי־נָתֹן אֶתֵּן אֶת־הַפְּלִשְׁתִּים בְּיָדֶךָ׃	And Yahweh said to David, 'Go up, for I will certainly give the Philistines into your hand'.

War oracles lacking the committal formula are also attested:

Judg. 20:23	וַיֹּאמֶר יְהוָה עֲלוּ אֵלָיו׃	And Yahweh said, 'Go up against them'.
2 Kgs. 18:25; cf. Isa. 36:10	יְהוָה אָמַר אֵלַי עֲלֵה עַל־הָאָרֶץ הַזֹּאת וְהַשְׁחִיתָהּ׃	Yahweh said to me, 'Go up against this land, and destroy it'.
Jer. 50:21	עַל־הָאָרֶץ מְרָתַיִם עֲלֵה עָלֶיהָ וְאֶל־יוֹשְׁבֵי פְּקוֹד חֲרֹב וְהַחֲרֵם אַחֲרֵיהֶם נְאֻם־יְהוָה וַעֲשֵׂה כְּכֹל אֲשֶׁר צִוִּיתִיךָ׃	'Against the land of Merathaim go up against it, and against the inhabitants of Pekod. Kill, and devote them utterly to destruction', the declaration of Yahweh, 'and do all that I have commanded you'.

War oracles of this type may also be adduced from extra-biblical sources. An oracle reported in a letter of Mukannišum to Zimri-Lim concerning the threat of Hammurabi of Babylon (*ARM* 26 209 = *ARM* 13 23) dated a millennium earlier than the present pronouncement contains all the critical elements of war oracles:

Command to Announce the Oracle	[*a*]*na bēlīya qibīma*	Speak to my lord:
Citation formula	*Umma Mukannišum* *waradkāma*	Thus Mukannišum, your servant:
Report of the Preparation for the Oracle	*nīqam* *ana Dagan* *ana balāṭ bēlīya*	I have made the offerings for Dagan for the sake of the life of my lord.
Introduction to the Oracle	*aplûm* *ša Dagan ša Tutt*[*ul*] *itbēma* *kīam ummāmi*	A prophet of Dagan of Tutt[ul] arose and spoke as follows:

The Content of the Oracle	The Challenge	*Bābilu* *mīnam tettenēpeš*	'Babylon, what are you constantly doing?
	The Committal Formula	*ana pûgim u ša-ka-ri-im* *upaḫḫarka* *bītāt* *sebet awīlī atḫî u* *makkuršunu* *a[n]a [q]āt Z[i]mrī-L[im]* *lumallêm*	I will gather you into a net and . . . . The dwellings of the seven accomplices and all their wealth I give in the hand of Zimri-L[im]'.[25]

Although the oracle itself is addressed in the second person to Hammurabi, it is obviously intended for Zimri-Lim, having been declared in response to a sacrifice at the oracle site. However, history teaches us that while this oracle must have encouraged Zimri-Lim, it proved false, for Hammurabi put a final end to his kingdom at Mari (cf. Ellermeier 1968: 137).

In this context we might also cite a series of prophetic texts concerning the affairs of Esarhaddon and Ashurbanipal, kings of Assyria deriving from a time closer to the historical context of 1 Kgs. 22.[26] Especially instructive for the present discussion is a letter written by the Babylonian scholar and diviner Bel-ušezib to encourage Esarhaddon in his war with the Manneans.[27] In this letter Bel-ušezib makes it clear that Marduk (Bēl) has willed the destruction of the Manneans (rev. 4–5), and that Esarhaddon enjoys his favour (rev. 19–22), but he is hesitant to offer strategic advice. In a remarkable move at the end of the letter, Bel-ušezib appeals to a prophetic oracle from four centuries earlier[28] that contains the basic features of the kind of war oracle represented by our text:

[25] Text and translation as given by Nissinen (2003: 44). For commentary on the oracle see Ellermeier (1968: 136–37).

[26] These are conveniently produced in text and translation by Nissinen (2003: 78). See also the series of queries by Esarhaddon to the sun-god Šamaš concerning his political and military affairs gathered in transliteration and translation by Starr (1990: 111–35).

[27] *ABL* 1237 = SAA 10). For transliteration and translation of the entire text see Parpola (1993: 89–90) and Nissinen (2003: 155–57). For commentary on the text see Nissinen (1998: 96–101). This citation of an earlier prophecy is reminiscent of Jeremiah's reference to Micah in Jer. 26:18.

[28] Marduk-šapik-zeri was king of Babylonia from 1081–1069 BC. According to Nissinen (2003: 133) the quotation derives 'from written sources, that is, from archival copies of prophetic oracles accessible to them'. If Nissinen is correct, these documents give credence to Alan R. Millard's long-standing contention that prophetic oracles were sometimes written down on the day they were uttered, and then brought together and stored as collections. See Millard 1985: 125–45; 1999: 237–41.

Citation Formula	*Bēl iqtabi*	Bel has said,
The Divine Blessing	*Umma akī Marduk-šapik-zēri* *Aššūr-aḫu-iddina* *šar māt Ašš[ū]r* *ina kussîsu lū ašib*	'Like Marduk-šapik-zeri may Esarhaddon, king of Assyria, be seated on his throne!
The Committal Formula	*u māt[āti] gabbi* *ana qātēšu* *ammani*	And I will deliver all the countries into his hands!'

In light of this comparative biblical and extra-biblical evidence, on the surface the oracle delivered by Ahab's 400 prophets appears quite conventional. However, upon closer inspection it turns out to be rather anomalous in several important respects. Whereas all the other oracles are explicitly presented as the utterance of a deity (always Yahweh in the biblical texts) and precise in their intent, the present oracle is both vague and ambiguous in every respect.[29] First, the prophets refer to the deity guaranteeing victory not by name ('Yahweh') but by title, *ʾădōnāy*, 'Lord'.[30] Although the Massoretes vocalized the expression as the common title for Yahweh,[31] the epithet 'lord' for deities can be found in most religions.[32] So from the outset it is not clear that Yahweh is the deity involved. Second, the prophets do not specify whom the deity will deliver. Contrary to virtually all English translations,[33] in the Hebrew the verb lacks a direct object. Accordingly, it is not clear whom the Lord will deliver into the king's hands. Third, the prophets do not identify the 'king' into whose hands whatever/whomever the Lord will deliver. *bĕyad hammelek* could refer either to Ahab or some other king. The only detail that is clear is the charge to Ahab, *ʿălēh*, 'Go up'.

[29] The ambiguities are also noted by Walsh 1996: 345.

[30] Contrary to the ben Asher family of texts represented by the *Leningrad Codex*, numerous Hebrew manuscripts read *yhwh* for *ʾădōnāy* in v. 6, no doubt a harmonistic reading based on vv. 12 and 15. This distinction is obscured in LXX, which renders both the tetragrammaton and *ʾădōnāy* as *kurios,* a practice carried over into almost all English translations, which render the former as 'LORD' and *ʾādôn/ʾădōnāy* as 'Lord'. Many lay leaders miss the significance of the changes in font. 2 Chr. 18:5 reads *hāʾĕlōhîm*, 'God', but this is equally ambiguous.

[31] Originally the title will have been written without vowels and probably without final *mater lectionis* (vowel letter).

[32] *ʾādôn* and derivatives occur only in the Canaanite languages; the Aramaic semantic equivalent is *mārēʾ*; the Akkadian is *bēl* (cognate to Hebrew *baʿal*). For further discussion see K. Spronk (1999: 531–33).

[33] The following supply the object 'it': *NAS, NIV, AV, ESV, NRSV, REB, NAB, NJB*; so also the *Revised Luther Bible*. The German *Einheitsübersetzung* is even more explicit in specifying 'die Stadt'. To the credit of *AV* and *NAS* the object 'it' is italicized, indicating for those who have read the preface that the word is supplied. *NLT* omits an object but removes the ambiguity by paraphrasing, 'for the Lord will give you a glorious victory!'

From the ensuing events it is evident that Ahab interpreted the oracle as favourable to him: he was the king into whose hands the Lord would deliver Ramoth-gilead. But Jehoshaphat immediately expressed doubts, inquiring of Ahab whether or not a true prophet of Yahweh was available for consultation. The narrator does not explain why the oracle failed to convince the king of Judah. Was it the unanimity of 400 prophets?[34] Was it their failure to specify the oracle as the words of Yahweh (cf. his request in v. 5)? Was there something in their tone or demeanour that betrayed insincerity? Whatever the reason, the ambiguity of the oracle represents the key not only to the chapter in general, but also to the veracity of Macaiah ben Imlah and Yahweh himself.

Despite the specificity of the biblical parallels cited above, this is not the first ambiguous oracle in the Old Testament. Judg. 18:6 recounts another classic example, also involving persons with syncretistic religious bent. There the narrator sets the stage by reporting that, having failed to claim the territory allotted to them, the Danite tribe sent out five of their men as scouts to find land that they could occupy (vv. 1–2a). In their trek across the highlands of Ephraim they stumbled upon a Levitical priest in the house of Micah whom they knew from a previous encounter (vv. 2b–4). Upon learning that Micah had engaged this Levite officially as his priest, they seized the opportunity to seek a divine oracle concerning the prospects for their venture.[35] The form in which the narrator describes the oracular exchange is strikingly similar to the present oracle, as the following synopses of the original and the translated texts demonstrate:

Formal Element	Judges 18:5–6	1 Kings 22:5–6
The Request for an Oracle	וַיֹּאמְרוּ לוֹ שְׁאַל־נָא בֵאלֹהִים וְנֵדְעָה	וַיֹּאמֶר יְהוֹשָׁפָט אֶל־מֶלֶךְ יִשְׂרָאֵל דְּרָשׁ־נָא כַיּוֹם אֶת־דְּבַר יְהוָה׃
The Preparation for the Oracle		וַיִּקְבֹּץ מֶלֶךְ־יִשְׂרָאֵל אֶת־הַנְּבִיאִים כְּאַרְבַּע מֵאוֹת אִישׁ וַיֹּאמֶר אֲלֵהֶם
The Question for the Oracle	הֲתַצְלִיחַ דַּרְכֵּנוּ אֲשֶׁר אֲנַחְנוּ הֹלְכִים עָלֶיהָ׃	הַאֵלֵךְ עַל־רָמֹת גִּלְעָד לַמִּלְחָמָה אִם־אֶחְדָּל
The Response of the Oracle	וַיֹּאמֶר לָהֶם הַכֹּהֵן לְכוּ לְשָׁלוֹם יְהוָה דַּרְכְּכֶם אֲשֶׁר תֵּלְכוּ־בָהּ׃	וַיֹּאמְרוּ עֲלֵה וְיִתֵּן אֲדֹנָי בְּיַד הַמֶּלֶךְ׃

34 Thus the rabbis, who maintained that Jehoshaphat called for an outsider's opinion precisely because the 400 spoke with one voice (*Sanhedrin* 89a).

35 For a discussion of the oracular exchange see Block 1999 (497–98).

Formal Element	Judges 18:5–6	1 Kings 22:5–6
The Request for an Oracle	And they said to him, 'Inquire of God, please, so we may know,	And Jehoshaphat said to the king of Israel, 'Inquire first for the word of Yahweh'.
The Preparation for the Oracle		Then the king of Israel gathered the prophets, about four hundred men, and he said to them,
The Question for the Oracle	'Will the mission on which we are going succeed?'	'Shall I go to battle against Ramoth-gilead, or shall I desist?'
The Response of the Oracle	And the priest said to them, 'Go in peace. Your mission on which you are going is before Yahweh'.	And they said, 'Go up, and the Lord will give into the hand of the king'.

The report of the priest's response exhibits two significant features that set this oracle apart from the normal pattern of oracular utterance.[36] First, like Ahab's prophets, the priest made no claim to divine inspiration. He seemed to know the answer to the Danites' query instinctively. Second, as was the case with the oracle of Ahab's prophets, the priest's utterance was utterly vague and ambiguous. Contrary to many English translations, which render the oracle as an outright assurance of Yahweh's favour,[37] the Hebrew is best translated as something like, 'Go in peace; your mission on which you are going is before Yahweh'.[38] This could mean that it has the approval of Yahweh's watchful eye, but it could also mean the opposite.[39]

The ambiguity of the utterance of Ahab's prophets finds a remarkable parallel in the Delphic oracle in response to Croesus' inquiry regarding the outcome of his possible conflict with Cyrus and the Persians.[40] Although

[36] The link between these two oracles is strengthened by the use of the verb *hiṣlîaḥ*, 'to succeed', which appears in both the prophets' later version of the oracle (v. 12) and in Micaiah's parroting of the same (v. 15).

[37] The rendering of *NIV* is typical of many: 'Your journey has the LORD's approval'. Cf. *NAS, REB, NAB.*

[38] *NRSV* captures the ambiguity better: 'The mission you are on is under the eye of the LORD'. *NJB*'s 'Yahweh is watching over your journey', is technically correct, though in English the idiom 'to watch over', is generally interpreted positively. Similarly *NLT*'s, 'The LORD will go ahead of you on your journey'.

[39] As in Amos 9:4. 'To be before Yahweh' may function as the obverse of 'Yahweh has set his face against', as in Lev. 17:10; 20:3,5; Jer. 21:10; 44:11.

[40] For a helpful investigation into the Delphic oracle see Hoyle (1968). For a discussion of Croesus and the oracle see especially pp. 148–52.

Adam Clarke recognized the link between these two oracles almost two centuries ago (Clarke 1930: 475 [reprint]), to my knowledge no modern commentators take this connection seriously.[41] But the similarities between Herodotus' report of the Greek oracle and the Hebrew historian's report of the utterance of Ahab's prophets are striking. Determined to learn the will of the gods concerning the coming conflict with the Persians, the Lydian King Croesus first established that the most reliable oracles were to be found at Delphi. After lavish offerings to the Temple at Delphi to secure the favour of the gods, he sent his agents to the oracles with the question: 'Shall Croesus send an army against the Persians, and shall he strengthen himself with a military alliance?' Both oracles responded with the same message: if Croesus would attack the Persians he would destroy a great empire. The oracles also counselled him to determine which was the strongest of the Greek states and to make them his friends (*Histories* 1.53). Delighted with the answer and convinced that he would destroy the Persians, Croesus followed the first inquiry with a second, seeking to know whether his reign would endure for a long time. The priestess of Delphi answered this request with the following oracular pronouncement:

> When comes the day that a mule shall sit on the Median throne,
> Then, tender-footed Lydian, by pebbly Hermus
> Run and abide not, nor think it shame to be a coward (*Histories* 1.55).

Since a mule would never become king of the Medes the Lydian king concluded that he and his descendants would remain in power forever. Interpreting the ambiguous oracles[42] as favourable to himself, Croesus began the war. When the outcome proved to be a total disaster, Croesus sent a delegation back to Delphi charging the Greek gods with thanklessness and the oracle with deceit for telling him that he would destroy Cyrus' power (1.90). Herodotus explains the oracle's response to the latter charge as follows:

> As to the oracle, Croesus had no right to find fault with it: the god had declared that if he attacked the Persians he would bring down a mighty empire. After an answer like that, the wise thing would have been to send again to inquire which empire was meant, Cyrus' or his own. But as he misinterpreted what was said and made no second inquiry, he must admit the fault to have been his own. Moreover, the last time he consulted the oracle he failed also to understand what Apollo said about the mule. The mule was Cyrus, who was the child of parents of different races—a nobler mother and a baser father. His mother was a Mede and daughter of Astyages, king of Media; but his father was a Persian, subject to the Medes, and had married his queen to whom he was in every way inferior. (*Histories* 1.91)

41 Williams (2002: 63) makes only a passing reference to Clarke's interpretation in a footnote.

42 Χρησμοῦ κιβδήλου, *Histories* 1.75.

This is precisely the way Ahab should have responded to his prophets' utterance. He should have made a second inquiry to determine *which God* would deliver *what* into *whose* hands. Like virtually all modern translations and most commentators, Ahab assumed that the object to be delivered was Ramoth-gilead, and that the king into whose hands God would deliver the town was himself. In the end he would discover that he was the object being handed over and the victorious king would be the Aramaean.

The origin of the oracle

The narrator does not identify the source of the oracle declared by the 400 prophets of Ahab. Was it the god who was worshiped at Bethel in the form of the calf? Was it a pagan deity associated with the temple of Baal or Asherah in Samaria? Was it a uniquely Samarian manifestation of the national God of Israel?[43] Was it Yahweh whose residence was in Jerusalem? Whatever the 400 prophets' perception of their own inspiration, according to the vision that Micaiah describes in vv. 19–23, their utterance originated with a member of the heavenly court who was authorized by Yahweh to be a *rûaḥ šeqer* in the mouths of the prophets of Ahab. As already noted, interpretations of this phrase have ranged widely from the 'lying spirit' actually being Satan, to Yahweh sovereignly controlling a 'spirit of delusion', to God actually lying. However, with our interpretation of the oracle we may have stumbled upon a solution that not only overcomes the weaknesses of each of these suggestions, but may also satisfy the needs of the context better than these proposals. To explore the issue further we need to answer two questions: What was the status and role of the 'spirit' (*rûaḥ*) who volunteered to be a *rûaḥ šeqer* in the mouths of Ahab's prophets? What does the expression *rûaḥ šeqer* mean?

With respect to genre and form, 1 Kgs. 22:19–23 has been rightly classified as a 'prophetic vision report' (Long 1984: 238; De Vries 1978: 43; Dafni 2000: 375–76) that has been embedded in the surrounding narrative. Micaiah tells Ahab he has witnessed a scene in heaven that transpired prior to Ahab's decision to engage the Aramaeans in battle, and that attributed the present oracle to a 'spirit' authorized by Yahweh to give the prophets a message for Ahab.[44] In exploring the status and role of this 'spirit' we notice three significant details.

[43] The perception of such a deity is reflected in the Kuntillet ʿAjrud Pithos A inscription dated to the early eighth century BC: *ʾmr . ʾ* [. . . .]*h*[. .] *k . ʾmr . lyhl*[. .] *wlyw ʿšh . w . . . brkt . ʾtkm lyhwh . šmrn . wlʾšrth*, 'Thus says ʾ[. . .] (PN 1) . . . : Say to Yehalle[lel?] (PN 2), Yoʿasa (PN 3) and . . . (PN 4): I bless you (herewith—or: have blessed you) to/before Yahweh of Samaria and his *asherah*'. As translated by Keel and Uehlinger (1998: 225–26; cf. p. 28). For further discussions of this text see Dijkstra (2001: 26–31) and Hadley (2000: 121–25).

[44] On prophetic access to the council (*sôd*) of Yahweh see Lindblom (1962: 112–13).

First, this 'spirit' is a member of Yahweh's heavenly court. The scene that Micaiah describes is based upon the model of an earthly court, with Yahweh the king on his throne surrounded by his courtiers. The description is reminiscent of Isaiah's vision in Isaiah 6, but it displays even closer structural and thematic affinities with the heavenly scene described in Job 1:6–8,[45] as the synopsis on the following page illustrates.

The present text identifies the heavenly courtiers as *kol ṣĕbāʾ haššāmayim,* 'all the host of heaven' (v. 19), which is equivalent to the *bĕnê hāʾĕlōhîm*, 'sons of God', in Job 1:6. Their posture/status is described as *ʿōmēd ʾālāyw mîmînû ûmiśśĕmōʾlô*, 'standing by him to the right and to the left', an idiom for being on official duty,[46] equivalent to *wayyābōʾû lĕhityaṣṣēb ʿal YHWH*, 'and they came and stationed themselves by Yahweh', in Job 1:6. The member of the heavenly host who is singled out for a special role in the account is identified as *hārûaḥ*, 'the spirit'.[47] His status parallels that of *haśśāṭān,* 'the adversary', in the prologue to the book of Job: he is a member of the heavenly court standing before Yahweh.[48]

45 Analogues to this scene are attested in several extra-biblical texts. From second millennium BC Mari, in *ARM* 10.9 (*ANET,* 632; Nissinen 2003: #18, pp. 42–43) the *āpilum* Shibtu apparently witnesses and overhears members of the heavenly council discuss the fate of Mari. The Deir ʿAllah Plaster Inscription from the Transjordan (dated *c.* 800 BC) reports in considerable detail the conversation concerning issues of heaven and earth by the heavenly council consisting of El, who presides, and the *šdyn* ('Shaddai-gods') who surround him. For the text in transliteration and translation see Nissinen (2003: #138, pp. 207–12); in translation with commentary see Levine (2000: 140–45).

46 According to the Rabbis those standing on God's left and on his right represent members of the court who pleaded for Ahab's life and death respectively (*Tan. B.* I.96; II, 8,84; *Tan. Shemot* 18; *Mishpatim* 15). Cf. Ginsburg 1968: 312.

47 On the use of *rûaḥ/rûḥôt* as designations for Yahweh's heavenly envoys (*malʾākîm*) see Ps. 104:4. Cf. Heb. 1:7.

48 It is beyond the scope of this paper to resolve the questions concerning the identity and role of *haśśāṭān* in Job 1–2. Traditionally this figure has been interpreted as Satan, that is an outsider in this assembly and the adversary of God and human beings, but several contextual considerations render this interpretation less secure than is often supposed. (1) The word occurs with the article, as it does everywhere else except in 1 Chr. 21:1, suggesting it was understood as a common noun, rather than a name. (2) According to Job 1–2, *haśśāṭān* appears in the midst of (*bĕtôk*) the *bĕnê ʾĕlōhîm*, 'the sons of God', who comprise the heavenly court and are found in the presence of Yahweh. It is difficult to conceive of Satan gaining access here. (3) When Yahweh asks *haśśāṭān* from where he has come, he answers, *miššûṭ bāʾāreṣ ûmithallēk bāh*, 'from going back and forth on the earth and patrolling it'. Nothing in the context suggests that he is about sinister business, let alone looking for prey (cf. 1 Pet. 5:8). On the contrary, the conversation between the *śāṭān* and Yahweh seems cordial throughout. (4) In the present context Yahweh is the initiator of the conversation, drawing Job to the *śāṭān*'s attention. Indeed through *haśśāṭān*'s response, viz., that Job fears God because it pays (Job 1:9–10), the author announces a (if not the) major theme of the book: the basis of religious faith. Thereupon Yahweh authorizes *haśśāṭān* to test whether or not Job's righteousness and his fear of Yahweh were

Feature	1 Kings 22:19–23	Job 1:6–8
The Heavenly Court Scene	I saw Yahweh sitting on his throne, and all the host of heaven standing beside him on his right hand and on his left;	Now there was a day when the sons of God came to present themselves before Yahweh, and the Adversary also came among them.
Yahweh's First Question	and Yahweh said, 'Who will entice Ahab, that he may go up and fall at Ramoth-gilead?'	Yahweh said to the Adversary, 'From where have you come?'
The Courtier's Answer	And one said one thing, and another said another. Then the spirit came forward and stood before Yahweh, saying, 'I will entice him'.	The Adversary answered Yahweh and said, 'From going to and fro on the earth, and from walking up and down on it'.
Yahweh's Second Question	And Yahweh said to him, 'By what means?'	And Yahweh said to the Adversary, 'Have you considered my servant Job, that there is none like him on the earth, a blameless and upright man, who fears God and turns away from evil?'
The Courtier's Proposal	And he said, 'I will go out, and will be a spirit of delusion in the mouth of all his prophets'.	Then the Adversary answered Yahweh and said, 'Does Job fear God for no reason? Have you not put a hedge around him and his house and all that he has, on every side? You have blessed the work of his hands, and his possessions have increased in the land. But stretch out your hand and touch all that he has, and he will curse you to your face.'

Yahweh's Authorization	And he said, 'You are to entice him, and you shall succeed; go out and do so.'	And Yahweh said to the Adversary, 'Look, all that he has is in your hand. Only against him do not stretch out your hand.'
Conclusion	Now therefore look, Yahweh has put a spirit of delusion in the mouth of all these your prophets; Yahweh has declared disaster for you.[49]	So the Adversary went out from the presence of Yahweh.

Second, the 'spirit' is sent on a mission by Yahweh. According to v. 20, in response to Yahweh's challenge he volunteers to 'try to persuade Ahab to go up and fall at Ramoth-gilead'.[50] The scene is quite extraordinary: whereas elsewhere we read of the heavenly hosts mustering to fight the enemies of Yahweh on Israel's behalf (Isa. 13:1–13; Joel 4:9–12 [Eng. 3:9–12]; 2 Kgs. 6:15–19; 7:6), here they are called into session by Yahweh to plot the defeat of Israel and more particularly the death of Israel's king. Interpreted within the broader literary context this decision represents the implementation of the threat that Elijah had announced to Ahab in 21:21–24 in the wake of his confiscation of Naboth's field and the murder of the man (Firth 2000: 183–84). Having volunteered for the mission (v. 21), the spirit explains how he would achieve this goal (vv. 22a). In the end Yahweh not

based on his experience of positive divine providence. (5) In the conclusion to the book the narrator expressly attributes Job's calamities to Yahweh ('all the calamity [*hārāʿâ*] that Yahweh had brought on him'). In Job he seems to function as the celestial agent through whom God tests the faith of this man. Analogues to his role in Job may be found in Num. 22:22, where *haśśāṭān*, 'the adversary', is used interchangeably with *malʾak* YHWH, 'the messenger/angel of Yahweh', and 1 Chr. 21:1 where *śāṭān*, 'an adversary' (without the article), apparently incites David to number the people on Yahweh's behalf (cf. 2 Sam 24:1). For further discussion of the role of the *śāṭān* in Job see Clines (1989: 17–30); of the *śāṭān* in the Old Testament as a whole see Day (1999: 726–30).

49 The links between the accounts are strengthened by the attribution of the initiative in both to Yahweh, and the identification of the effects of the respective agents' actions as *rāʿâ*, 'disaster', here and in Job 42:11, where Job's calamities are described as 'all the disaster that Yahweh had brought on him'.

50 Hebrew *yĕpatteh* is traditionally rendered 'entice' (*NRSV, REB, NAB, NJB, ESV, NAS, NIV, NLT*). However, as in Jer. 20:7 (cf. *NLT*, *NIV*, footnote), here the piel form is best interpreted as 'to [try to] persuade'. For a discussion of the verb see Clines and Gunn (1978: 20–27).

only authorizes him to go, but also announces in advance the success of the mission (v. 23).[51]

Third, the 'spirit' declares that he will try to persuade Ahab by being a *rûaḥ šeqer* in the mouth of all his prophets. This phrase is a crux.[52] The Old Greek's πνεῦμα ψευδὲς, 'false spirit', renders the second word according to the common meaning of *šeqer*, 'deceit, falsehood', and follows this version's pattern of renderings involving other attributive expressions.[53] However, Yahweh's question, 'How [will you try to persuade him]?' suggests that *šeqer* should not be interpreted as an attribute of this spirit, but as descriptive of the effect his actions will have upon Ahab. This calls for a translation something like 'spirit of delusion'.[54] Accordingly this *rûaḥ šeqer* functions similarly to the *rûaḥ rāʿâ*, 'spirit of disaster', that Yahweh commissions *(šālaḥ)* to break up the alliance between Abimelech and the men of Shechem (Judg. 9:23), and the *rûaḥ ʾĕlōhîm*. *rāʿâ*, 'bad spirit of God', that is, 'from Yahweh', that torments Saul with some sort of mental derangement in 1 Sam. 16:14–23 and 18–12.[55]

Although the text does not identify the *rûaḥ* as either a *rûaḥ rāʿâ* or a *rûaḥ ʾĕlōhîm,* the operation of the spirit in 2 Kgs. 19:7 presents a remarkable analogue to the present picture. Speaking for Yahweh, Isaiah declares with reference to the king of Assyria, 'Look, I will put (*nātan*) a *rûaḥ* in him, so that he shall hear a rumour and return to his own land, and I will make him fall by the sword in his own land'. The contrasts in these two accounts are obvious. Whereas the *rûaḥ šeqer* operates in the *mouth* of Ahab's prophets, this spirit operates in the *ears* of the Assyrian. Whereas Ahab leaves the security of his capital to go out to battle, the Assyrian leaves the scene of battle and heads for home. But their fates are the same: the work of the spirit sent/put by Yahweh ends in the death of the principal character in the narrative. In the present context the spirit proposes to be a *rûaḥ šeqer* in the mouth of Ahab's prophets.[56] This statement recalls the utterance of Yahweh

51 *tĕpatteh wĕgam tĭkāl ṣēʾ waʿăśēh kēn*, 'You shall try to persuade [him] and you shall succeed; go and act accordingly'.

52 The Hebrew of 1 Kgs. 22:20 reads *wĕhāyîtî rĭaḥ šeqer bĕpî kol nĕbîʾāyw*, 'And I will be a spirit of deception in the mouth of all his prophets'. The parallel text in 1 Chr. 18:20 reads *wĕhāyîtî lĕrĭaḥ šeqer*, 'And I will *become* a spirit of deception', suggesting a change in function.

53 LXX reads πνεῦμα πονηρὸν for *rûaḥ rāʿâ* in Judg. 9:23 and 1 Sam. 16:14, and πνεῦμα ἀκάθαρτον for *rĭaḥ haṭṭumʾâ* in Zech. 13:2. Cf. Dafni (2000: 378–79).

54 *HALOT* (p. 1201) correctly associates *rûaḥ šeqer* with *rûaḥ tardēmâ*, 'spirit of deep sleep' (Isa. 29:10); *rûaḥ ʿiwʿîm*, 'spirit of confusion' (Isa. 19:14); *rûaḥ qinʾâ*, 'spirit of jealousy' (Num. 5:14,30); *rûaḥ zĕnûnîm*, 'spirit of harlotry' (Hos. 4:12); etc. This interpretation is preferable to that of Larry Herr (1997: 29–31), who heightens the insulting tone of Micaiah's reference to the *rûaḥ šeqer* by translating the phrase, 'lying wind'.

55 For further discussion of these texts see Block (1999: 323–24; 1997a: 50–52).

56 The singular 'mouth' (*pî*) highlights the unanimity of the 400 prophets in their oracular pronouncement: they speak with one mouth.

in Exod. 4:12, 'I will be with your mouth and instruct you what you are to speak'. However, whereas in this context the utterances will lead to the rescue of Israel, in the present context the spirit will place words in the prophets' mouth in order to drive Ahab to his death (Dafni 2000: 379).

But this raises the theological question of how a spirit from the heavenly court of Yahweh can function as a 'spirit of delusion'. The answer lies in part in the meaning of *šeqer*. In the Old Testament the word is used with a broad range of meanings from 'breach of faith', to 'unreliability', to 'hypocrisy', to 'deception', and even 'nothingness'.[57] The link between 'deception' and 'nothingness' is reflected in the propensity of the prophets to characterize false prophesy as *šeqer*. It is *šeqer* because it is untrue,[58] because it is inauthentic,[59] and because it is worthless.[60]

But how can a prophecy authorized by Yahweh have these characteristics? The answer lies in the ambiguity of the utterance that comes from the mouths of the 400 prophets of Ahab. Whatever the prophets' perception of the origin of their declaration in v. 6, it is clear that Micaiah viewed this prophecy to have been inspired in a perverse sort of way by Yahweh. He put the 'spirit of delusion' in the mouth of the prophets, and thereby pronounced disaster (*rāʿâ*) against Ahab (v. 23). Just as the *rûaḥ rāʿâ* elsewhere functions as a 'spirit that causes disaster', so here this 'spirit' causes 'delusion'. He achieves this result by inspiring an utterance from the prophets that is capable of more than one interpretation, and then having Ahab opt for the wrong one.[61] The reader may find it hard to believe that Yahweh would come to the

[57] Cf. Martin A. Klopfenstein, 'שקר *šqr* to deceive', *TLOT* 3.1399–1405 (=*THAT* 2.1010–19); cf. Klopfenstein's more detailed study (1964). The last named sense is reflected in the substitution of *šāwʾ*, 'worthless, empty, vain', for *šeqer* in the Deuteronomic version of the Decalogic command:

Exod. 20:16 לֹא־תַעֲנֶה בְרֵעֲךָ עֵד שָׁקֶר You shall not give a false testimony against your neighbour.

Deut. 5:20 וְלֹא־תַעֲנֶה בְרֵעֲךָ עֵד שָׁוְא You shall not give an empty/worthless testimony against your neighbour.

For discussion see Klopfenstein (1964: 315–20).

[58] Accordingly, in the present context *šeqer* functions as the polar opposite to *ʾĕmet*, 'true' (v. 16).

[59] The claim to divine inspiration and authorization (i.e., in the name of Yahweh), is a lie. Cf. Jer. 14:13–15; 23:25–32; 29:21

[60] On the utterances of false prophets as *šeqer* see Klopfenstein, 1964: 99–120).

[61] Thus interpreted *šeqer* covers roughly the same semantic range as the Greek term κίβδηλος, which denotes fundamentally 'base, adulterated', but in a metaphorical sense means 'fraudulent, deceitful'. Cf. Liddell and Scott (1996: 950). Herodotus uses to word to refer to ambiguous oracles, as in *Histories* 1.66, οἱ Λακεδαιμόνιοι . . . ρησμῷ κιβδήλῳ πίσυνοι, 'The Lacedaemonians . . . trusted in the ambiguous oracle'; and 1.75, καὶ δὴ καὶ ἀπικομένου χρησμοῦ κιβδήλου, ἐλπίσας πρὸς ἑωτοῦ τὸν χρησμὸν εἶναι, ἐστραρεύετο ἐς τὴν Περσέων μοῖραν, 'And when the ambiguous answer arrived, he [Croesus] interpreted it as favourable to himself and led his army to the Persian territory' (cf. the translation of Sélincourt, pp. 38 and 42 respectively). These comments describe precisely how Ahab interpreted the oracle of his prophets.

aid of the one who had murdered Naboth (cf. 21:20–24) and who had brought on himself the divine death sentence by sparing the enemy in a previous campaign (cf. 20:42), but Ahab is deluded into thinking that with Yahweh's help he will regain Ramoth-gilead. As already observed, strictly speaking the prophets' word is not a lie. Ahab will indeed experience its literal fulfillment: *some* Lord will give *someone/something* into the hands of *some* king. The delusion occurs when he interprets this ambiguous prophecy in his favour—and well he might have under normal circumstances, since the prophets who uttered it were his lackeys.[62]

The evolution of the oracle in vv. 7–18

Variations of the oracle pronounced by Ahab's 400 prophets in v. 6 are heard twice more in this chapter, once from the lips of these same prophets (v. 12), and once from the mouth of Micaiah ben Imlah, the prophet of Yahweh whom Jehoshaphat had requested (v. 15). Although the repetition impresses even the casual reader, the deviations from the original form (v. 6) are telling, as the following synopsis illustrates:

V. 6 עֲלֵה וְיִתֵּן אֲדֹנָי בְּיַד הַמֶּלֶךְ:
V. 12 עֲלֵה רָמֹת גִּלְעָד וְהַצְלַח וְנָתַן יְהוָה בְּיַד הַמֶּלֶךְ:
V. 15 עֲלֵה וְהַצְלַח וְנָתַן יְהוָה בְּיַד הַמֶּלֶךְ:
V. 6 Go up, and the Lord will give into the hand of the king,
V. 12 Go up to Ramoth-gilead and succeed, and Yahweh will give into the hand of the king.
V. 15 Go up, and succeed and Yahweh will give into the hand of the king.

Common to all three versions of the oracle are the command to 'Go up', and the promissory form of the committal formula, 'And *DN* will give into the hand of the king'. The modifications in the prophets' second version are in the direction of removing ambiguities from the original utterance: the destination is specified as Ramoth-gilead; the promise of success is added, and the divine title *ʾădōnāy* is replaced by the tetragrammaton, *YHWH,*

[62] In this text 'false prophets' turn out to be the opposite of what obtained in Mesopotamian courts. According to Nissinen (1998: 166–67), because kings were deemed to be tools in the hands of the gods prophetic declarations against the king's interests were by definition false, regardless of the source of the inspiration. As Ahab recognized in v. 16 (ironically perhaps), in this instance he considered Micaiah's first utterance to be false because it apparently predicted his success.

'Yahweh'.[63] When Micaiah repeats the oracle he drops the reference to Ramoth-gilead; otherwise his version is identical.[64] Nevertheless, although the deity and the destination of Ahab's venture are specified, some ambiguity remains; it is still unclear who will be given into the hands of whom. Ahab apparently interpreted the addition of *wĕhaṣlaḥ*, 'and succeed', as reinforcement of the promise that his efforts to reclaim Ramoth-gilead would be successful. However, the verb could also apply to the divine mission: Ahab will go up and fall in accordance with the plan declared in v. 20.

However, in the event Ahab apparently does not even consider this option. Despite the fact that he requested Micaiah to confirm the oracle with a pronouncement that would also be favourable (*ṭôb*) to him (v. 13), Ahab finds it disconcerting that Micaiah's utterance agrees with those of his own prophets. Just as something about the unanimous utterance of Ahab's 400 prophets had raised the suspicions of Jehoshaphat (vv. 7–8), so now something about Micaiah's parroting of the prophecy raised the suspicion of Ahab. It was obviously out of character, for Micaiah had a history of consistently prophesying evil concerning Ahab (*raʿ*, v. 13). But there seems to have been more to this communicative event than the words spoken. Whether it was the sarcasm in his voice, or a non-verbal gesture accompanying the verbal declaration, something about Micaiah's utterance communicated an insincerity that not even his strong affirmation, 'As Yahweh lives, what Yahweh says to me, that I will speak' (v. 14),[65] had convinced him.[66] Though Ahab seems not to have been interested in the truth, when he demanded it Micaiah obliged, delivering an oracle that was not only unequivocal. According to Ahab's interpretation of his previous utterance, it was also totally contradictory. Micaiah's second oracular pronouncement sealed Ahab's doom:

> I saw all Israel scattered on the mountains,
> as sheep that have no shepherd.

[63] Zedekiah's use of the citation formula explicitly attributing his utterance to Yahweh, his performance of the sign-act, and his verbal interpretation of the action (v. 11) leave no room for any other interpretation.

[64] The moves to eliminate the ambiguity are even stronger in 1 Chr. 18:

V. 5	בְּיַד הַמֶּלֶךְ׃	וְיִתֵּן הָאֱלֹהִים		עֲלֵה
V. 11	בְּיַד הַמֶּלֶךְ׃	וְנָתַן יְהוָה	רָמֹת גִּלְעָד וְהַצְלַח	עֲלֵה
V. 14	בְּיֶדְכֶם׃	וְיִנָּתְנוּ	וְהַצְלִיחוּ	עֲלוּ

[65] Readers who are familiar with the Balaam story will recognize here an echo of Balaam's response to Balak's envoys (Num. 22:18,20,35; cf. 23:12,26; 24:13), though now the issues are reversed. Though Yahweh had called for the death of Ahab, Micaiah apparently pronounced success in this mission.

[66] Cf. Sternberg (1985: 407). According to Bodner (2003: 537), 'Micaiah deploys his sarcastic comment as a rhetorical instrument to provoke a response from the king and to involve Ahab personally in this contest surrounding the veracity of the prophetic word'.

> And Yahweh said, 'These have no master;
> let each return to his home in peace' (v. 17).

Ironically, when his own prophets delivered an ambiguous pronouncement, Ahab trusted in the meaning favourable to him, but when Micaiah issued an oracle unfavourable to him he rejected it, and rushed headlong into the fate that Yahweh had decreed for him.[67]

Conclusion

This is not the last time we read about Yahweh toying with faithless human beings, acceding to their inquiries but responding with oracles that delude. Speaking for Yahweh, in Ezek. 14:9 the exiled prophet declares:

> If a prophet is deluded (*yĕputteh*) and makes a pronouncement, I, Yahweh, am the one who has deluded that prophet. I will stretch out my hand against him and destroy him from the midst of my people Israel.

As in our text, here Yahweh answers insincerity with insincerity.[68] Unrepentant kings and unrepentant people who seek affirmation for their perverse ways, and who clamour for reassurances of well-being, do not deserve a straight answer. An ambiguous message of victory in critical circumstances not only challenges the recipient to request clarification of the true meaning of the prophecy, but also sets him up for the impending disaster. By giving Ahab a message that he may interpret exactly according to what he wants to hear, Yahweh ensures his judgment.

J.J.M. Roberts (1988: 220) reminds us that this is not only an Old Testament phenomenon. According the 2 Thess. 2:9–12:

> The coming of the lawless one is by the activity of Satan with all power and false signs and wonders, and with all wicked deception for those who are perishing, because they refused to love the truth (ἀληθείας) and so be saved. Therefore God sends them a strong delusion (πλάνης), so that they may believe what is false (ψεύδει), in order that all may be condemned who did not believe the truth but had pleasure in unrighteousness.

67 Grabbe (1995: 72) rightly notes that kings normally took bad omens seriously. He comments, 'For Ahab to be so blind to a contra-indication is unusual; even more surprising is that Jehoshaphat does not react but tamely follows Ahab into battle'.

68 For an explicit declaration of this kind of poetic justice see 2 Sam. 22:26–27 (= Ps. 18:26–27[25–26]): 'With the faithful (*ḥāsîd*) you show yourself faithful (*titḥassād*), and with the blameless (*tāmîm*) you show yourself blameless (*tottammām*); with the pure (*nābār*) you show yourself pure (*tittābār*), but with the crooked (*ʿiqqēš*) you show yourself perverse (*tittappāl*)'. For further discussion of the Ezekiel text see Block (1997b: 431–35).

This describes precisely what happened to Ahab. To the king's prophets Yahweh sent a 'spirit of delusion' so that he might believe what is false and so rush to his death. The delusion is not the result of a divine lie, but the effect of the work of Yahweh on his ear and his mind so that when he hears his prophets pronounce an ambiguous oracle (from Yahweh) he puts his confidence in a mistaken interpretation. In the end his interpretation proves to be not merely irrelevant but wrong. Tragically for Ahab, the course of events was determined not by the recipient of the oracle but by the one who inspired it.

BIBLIOGRAPHY

Barstad, H.M.
1993 'No prophets? recent developments in Biblical prophetic research and Ancient Near Eastern prophecy', *JSOT* 57.

Block, I.D.
1994 'Deborah among the judges: the perspective of the Hebrew historian', in A.R. Millard, J. Hoffmeier and D. Baker (eds), *Faith, Tradition and History: Old Testament Historiography in Its Near Eastern Context* (Winona Lake, IN: Eisenbrauns).
1997a 'Empowered by the spirit of God: the work of the Holy Spirit in the historiographic writings of the Old Testament', *SBJT* 1.
1997b *Ezekiel 1–24*, NICOT (Grand Rapids: Eerdmans).
1999 *Judges, Ruth*, New American Commentary (Nashville: Broadman & Holman).
2001 'Why Deborah's different', *Bible Review* 17/3 (June).

Bodner, K.
2003 'The locutions of 1 Kings 22:28: a new proposal', *JBL* 122.

Brenneman, J.E.
2000 'Debating Ahab: characterization in Biblical theology', in W. Kim, D. Ellens, M. Floyd and M.A. Sweeney (eds), *Reading the Hebrew Bible for a New Millennium: Form, Concept, and Theological Perspective*, vol. 1, *Theological and Hermeneutical Studies* (Harrisburg, PA: Trinity Press International).

Burney, C.F.
1903 *Notes on the Hebrew Text of the Book of Kings* (Oxford: Clarendon).

Carroll, R.P.
1979 *When Prophecy Failed: Cognitive Dissonance in the Prophetic Traditions of the Old Testament* (New York: Seabury).

Clarke, A.
1930 *Clarke's Commentary*, six vols, vol. 2, *Joshua to Esther* (New York: Methodist Book Concern). Reprint of 1830 edition.

Clines, D.J.A.
1989 *Job 1–20*, *WBC* 17 (Dallas: Word).

Clines, D.J.A., and D.M. Gunn
1978 ‘“You tried to persuade me” and “Violence! Outrage!” in Jeremiah xx 7–8’, *VT* 28.

Cogan, M.
2001 *1 Kings: A New Translation with Introduction and Commentary*, *AB* 10 (New York: Doubleday).

Crenshaw, J.L.
1971 *Prophetic Conflict: Its Effect upon Israelite Religion*, *BZAW* 124 (Berlin: de Gruyter).

Cryer, F.H.
1994 *Divination in Ancient Israel and its Near Eastern Environment: A Socio-historical Investigation*, JSOTSup 142 (Sheffield: Sheffield Academic Press).

Dafni, E.G.
2000 ‘רוח שקר und falsche Propheten in 1 Reg 22’, *ZAW* 112.

Day, P.L.
1999 ‘Satan’, in K. van der Toorn and P.W. van der Horst (eds), *Dictionary of Deities and Demons in the Bible*, 2nd edn (Leiden: Brill/Grand Rapids: Eerdmans).

De Vries, S.J.
1978 *Prophet Against Prophet: The Role of the Micaiah Narrative (I Kings 22) in the Development of Early Prophetic Tradition* (Grand Rapids: Eerdmans).
1985 *1 Kings*, *WBC* 12 (Waco, TX: Word).
1986 ‘The forms of prophetic address in Chronicles’, *HAR* 10.

Dijkstra, M.
2001 ‘“I have Blessed you by YHWH of Samaria and his Asherah”: Texts with religious elements from the soil archive of Ancient Israel’, in B. Becking, *et al.* (ed.), *Only One God?: Monotheism in Ancient Israel and the Veneration of the Goddess Asherah* (London/New York: Sheffield Academic Press).

Ellermeier, F.
1968 *Prophetie in Mari und Israel*, Theologische und Orientalische Arbeiten 1 (Herzberg: Erwin Jungfer).

Firth, D.G.
2000 ‘Backward masking: implicit characterisation of Elijah in the Micaiah narrative’, *Old Testament Essays* 13.

Fishbane, M.
1970 ‘The treaty background of Amos 1:11 and related matters’, *JBL* 89.

Fretheim, T.E.
1999 *First and Second Kings*, Westminster Bible Companion (Louisville: Westminster John Knox).

Ginsburg, L.
1968 *The Legends of the Jews*, vol. 6 (Philadelphia: Jewish Publication Society).

Grabbe, L.L.
1995 *Priests, Prophets, Diviners, Sages: A Socio-Historical Study of Religious Specialists in Ancient Israel* (Valley Forge: PA: Trinity Press International).

Hadley, J.
2000 *The Cult of Asherah in Ancient Israel and Judah: Evidence for a Hebrew Goddess* (New York: Cambridge University Press).

Haller, E.
1960 *Charisma und Ekstasis: Die Erzählung von dem Propheten Micha ben Imlah 1. Kön. 22,1–28a*, Theologische Existenz Heute 82 (Munich: Chr. Kaiser).

Hamilton, J.M.
1994 'Caught in the nets of prophecy? The death of king Ahab and the character of God', *CBQ* 56.

Herr, L.
1997 'Polysemy of *Rûaḥ* in 1 Kings 22:19–25', in D. Merling (ed.), *To Understand the Scriptures: Essays in Honor of William H. Shea* (Berrien Springs: Andrews University).

Histories,
1954 *Herodotus: The Histories*, trans. Aubrey de Sélincourt (Penguin Classics; Baltimore: Penguin Books).

Hossfeld, F.L., and I. Meyer
1973 *Prophet gegen Prophet: Eine Analyse der alttestamentlichen Texte zum Thema: Wahre und falsche Propheten* (Fribourg: Schweizerisches Katholisches Bibelwerk).

Hoyle, P.
1968 *Delphi und sein Orakel: Wesen und Bedeutung des antiken Heiligtums* (Wiesbaden: F. A. Brockhaus).

Japhet, S.
1993 *I & II Chronicles*, OTL (Louisville: Westminster/John Knox).

Jeffers, A.
1996 *Magic and Divination in Ancient Palestine and Syria*, Studies in the History and Culture of the Ancient Near East 8 (Leiden: Brill).

Jones, G.H.
1984 *1 and 2 Kings*, NCB (Grand Rapids: Eerdmans).

Keel, O., and C. Uehlinger
1998 *Gods, Goddesses, and Images of God in Ancient Israel*, trans. T.H. Trapp (Minneapolis: Fortress).

Klopfenstein, M.A.
1964 *Die Lüge nach dem Alten Testament: Ihr Begriff, ihre Bedeutung und ihre Beurteilung* (Zurich/Frankfurt a. M: Gotthelf Verlag).

Lehnart, B.
2003 *Prophet und König im Nordreich Israel: Studien zur sogenannten vorklassischen Prophetie im Nordreich Israel anhand der Samuel-, Elia- und Elischa-Überlieferung*, VTSup 96 (Leiden: Brill).

Levine, B.A.
2000 'The Deir 'Alla Plaster inscription', in W.W. Hallo (ed.), *The Context of Scripture*, vol. 2: *Monumental Inscriptions from the Biblical World* (Leiden: Brill).

Liddell, H.G., and Robert Scott (eds)
1996 *A Greek-English Lexicon* (Oxford: Clarendon).

Lindblom, J.
1962 *Prophecy in Ancient Israel* (Philadelphia: Fortress).

Long, B.O.
1976 'Reports of visions among the Prophets', *JBL* 95.
1984 *1 Kings with an Introduction to Historical Literature*, FOTL 9 (Grand Rapids: Eerdmans).

Longman, III, T.
1987 *Literary Approaches to Biblical Interpretation*, Foundations of Contemporary Interpretation 3 (Grand Rapids: Zondervan).

Mayhue, R.L.
1993 'False prophets and the deceiving spirit', *The Masters Seminary Journal* 4.

McKenzie, S.L.
1991 *The Trouble with Kings: The Composition of the Book of Kings in the Deuteronomistic History*, VTSup 42 (Leiden: Brill).

Millard, A.R.
1985 'La prophétie et l'écriture: Israël, Aram, Assyrie', *Revue de l'Histoire des Religions* 202.
1999 'Oral proclamation and written record: spreading and preserving information in Ancient Israel', in Y. Avishur and R. Deutsch (eds), *Michael: Historical, Epigraphical and Biblical Studies in Honor of Prof. Michael Heltzer* (Tel Aviv/Jaffa: Archaeological Center Publications).

Miller, J.M.
1966 'The Elisha Cycle and the accounts of the Omride War', *JBL* 85.
1967 'The fall of the House of Ahab', *VT* 17.
1968 'The rest of the Acts of Jehoahaz (I Kings 20. 22, 1–38)', *ZAW* 80.
1976 *The Old Testament and the Historian* (Philadelphia: Fortress).

Na'aman, N.
1997 'Prophetic stories as sources for the histories of Jehoshaphat and the Omrides', *Biblica* 78.

Nissinen, M.
1998 *References to Prophecy in Neo-Assyrian Sources*, SAA 7 (Helsinki: Neo-Assyrian Text Corpus Project).
2003 *Prophets and Prophecy in the Ancient Near East*, Writings from the Ancient World 12 (Atlanta: SBL).

Overholt, T.W.
1989 *Channels of Prophecy: The Social Dynamics of Prophetic Activity* (Minneapolis: Fortress).

Parpola, S.
1993 *Letters from Assyrian and Babylonian Scholars*, SAA 10 (Helsinki: Helsinki University Press),

Provan, I., V.P. Long and T. Longman, III
2003 *A Biblical History of Israel* (Louisville: Westminster John Knox).

Roberts, J.J.M.
1988 'Does God lie? Divine deceit as a theological problem in Israelite literature', in J.A. Emerton (ed.), *Congress Volume: Jerusalem 1986*, VTSup 40 (Leiden: Brill).

Rofé, A.
1976 'The story of Micaiah ben Imlah and the question of the genres of the prophetical stories', in *Reflections on the Bible* (Jerusalem: Magnes).

Roth, W.
1982 'The story of the Prophet Micaiah (1 Kings 22) in Historical-Critical Interpretation 1876–1976', in R. Polzin and E. Rothman (eds), *The Biblical Mosaic: Changing Perspectives*, Semeia Studies (Philadelphia: Fortress).

Rouillard, H.
1993 'Royauté céleste et royauté terrestre en 1 R 22', in M. Philonenko (ed.), *Le Trône de Dieu* (Tübingen: J.C.B. Mohr [Paul Siebeck]).

Saggs, H.W.F.
1978 *The Encounter with the Divine in Mesopotamia and Israel* (London: Athlone Press).

Seow, C.-L.
1999 '1 and 2 Kings', in L. Keck (ed.), *The New Interpreter's Bible*, 12 vols (Nashville: Abingdon).

Starr, I.
1990 *Queries to the Sungod: Divination and Politics in Sargonid Assyria*, SAA 4 (Helsinki: University of Helsinki Press).

Sternberg, M.
1985 *The Poetics of Biblical Narrative: Ideological Literature and the Drama of Reading* (Bloomington: Indiana University Press).

Stipp, H.-J.
1987 *Elischa—Propheten—Gottesmänner:Die Kompositionsgeschichte des Elischazyklus und verwandter Texte, rekonstruiert auf der Basis von Text- und Literaturkritik zu 1 Kön. 20.22 und 2 Kön. 2–7*, ATSAT 24 (St. Ottilien: Eos Verlag).

Van Dam, C.
1997 *The Urim and Thummim: A Means of Revelation in Israel* (Winona Lake: Eisenbrauns).

van der Spek, R.J.
1993 'Assyriology and history: a comparative study of war and empire in Assyria, Athens, and Rome', in M.E. Cohen and D.B. Weisberg (eds), *The Tablet and the Scroll: Near Eastern Studies in Honor of William W. Hallo* (Bethesda, MD: CDL).

Walsh, J.T.
1996 *1 Kings*, *Berit Olam*, Studies in Hebrew Narrative and Poetry (Collegeville, MN: Liturgical Press).

Weinfeld, M.
1970 'The covenant of grant in the Old Testament and in the ancient Near East', *JAOS* 70.

Weippert, H.
1988 'Ahab el campeador? Redaktionsgeschichtliche Untersuchungen zu 1 Kön 22', *Biblica* 69.

Weippert, M.
1972 '"Heiliger Krieg" in Israel und Assyrien: Kritische Anmerkungen zu Gerhard von Rads Konzept des "Heiligen Krieges im alten Israel"', *ZAW* 84.

Whitely, C.F.
1952 'The Deuteronomic presentation of the House of Omri', *VT* 2.

Williams, P.J.
2002 'Lying spirits sent by God? The case of Micaiah's prophecy', in P. Helm and C.R. Trueman (eds), *The Trustworthiness of God: Perspectives on the Nature of Scripture* (Grand Rapids: Eerdmans).

Wiseman, D.J.
1993 *1 & 2 Kings*, TOTC (Downers Grove: InterVarsity).

Würthwein, E.
1967 'Zur Komposition von I Reg 22, 1–38', in F. Maass (ed.), *Das ferne und nahe Wort*, Festschrift L. Rost, BZAW 105 (Berlin: A. Töpelmann).

1984 *Die Bücher der Könige: 1. Kon 17–2. Kön. 25*, ATD 11/2 (Göttingen: Vandenhoeck & Ruprecht).

Darius' Accession in (the) Media

Christopher Tuplin

My topic is a monument and associated inscriptions relating to the accession of Darius—an event sealed with the death of Gaumata (*alias* King Bardiya, son of Cyrus) at a fortress in Media. Hence my frivolous title. Both monument and inscriptions come in multiple forms. The Behistun monument has versions of the inscriptions in three languages (one, Elamite, inscribed in two different places). There was also a stela in Babylon with an abbreviated icon but a full version of the Akkadian text (albeit one differing in detail from that at Behistun); and there is an Aramaic version preserved about 100 years later on a papyrus at Elephantine.[1] There may also have been other monumental sites: Ecbatana, Susa and Persepolis are possible (though only in the first is total absence of any such object in the archaeological record unremarkable because of lack of appropriate excavation),[2] and Seidl (1999: 114) has suggested a site was prepared at Van but never used. But the fact that Behistun was created in stages (and the relationship—whole to part—between it and the Babylon stela) does guarantee that Behistun is the primary site. The choice must reflect *inter alia* its location on the Mesopotamia-Ecbatana high-road and the fact that Gaumata died in Nisaya, close—some have thought very close—at hand.

[1] Old Persian: Kent 1953, Schmitt 1991. Elamite: Grillot-Susini *et al.* 1993. Akkadian: Voigtlander 1978, Malbran-Labat 1994. For reconstruction of the Babylon stela cf. Seidl 1999. Aramaic: Greenfield and Porten 1982. Lecoq 1997 provides an annotated French translation recording variations between versions. I refer to the versions as DB-OP, DB-Akkadian (distinguishing Akkadian [Behistun] and Akkadian [Babylon] as necessary), DB-Elamite (distinguishing the successive versions as Elamite[1] and Elamite[2]), DB-Aramaic. The *siglum* DB by itself refers to the full text, irrespective of language. I refer to particular passages using the paragraph numbers in DB-OP, irrespective of language (the paragraphing is different in DB-Elamite and DB-Akkadian, and different again in DB-Aramaic). For a photograph and schematic drawing see Lecoq 1997: pls 79. Similar schematic drawings can be found in Brosius 2000: figs 5a–b. There is an unusually good photograph of the icon and part of the OP text in Boardman 2000: fig. 3.27a. The Behistun monument has provoked an immense amount of scholarship over the years, so it is worth stressing that the bibliographic annotation in what follows is in no way comprehensive.

[2] Putative remains of a Susa monument (Louvre Sb 14 233: Canby 1979) have been questioned (Jacobs 1997).

My paper touches on three themes—the creation of the monument and the status of its texts; the historiographical character of the record common to all versions; and the reception of Darius' text—but what I have to say on the last is little more than a brief *envoi* to the first two, which is where the main focus of my attention lies. My concern is the history of an inscription and the inscription of history—literally of a story, metaphorically of an attitude to historical events as ideological material.

I

Thirty-six years ago Trümpelmann (1967) worked out a history of the monument's creation which has largely stood the test of time.[3] A new version produced by Huyse (1999) incorporates two slight variations suggested by Hinz (1968) and seeks to clarify the precise order of certain additions in the light of a thesis about DB 70, but none of this is seriously out of kilter with the Trümpelmann scheme.[4]

The first stage is purely pictorial. At Stage 2 we have an icon plus either a single Elamite inscription giving Darius' titulature, genealogy and contentious claim about his family's royal status (Trümpelmann) or both that inscription and a number of Elamite labels attached to other figures in the icon (Hinz, Huyse). Whichever view one takes, therefore, words already carry something important not visible in the picture, but narrative and a major written component for the monument are still to come.

[3] 1. The icon (minus the figure of Skunkha) created.
2. DBa (Elam.) = DB 1–4 added.
3. DBb-j (Elam.) and DB-Elamite(1) 1–69 added.
4. DBb-j (Akk.) and DB-Akkadian 1–69 added.
5. DBb-j (OP), DB-OP 1–70 and DBl(70: Elam.) added.
6. Skunkha added; DB-Elamite(1) erased.
DBk (El., OP), DB-Elamite(2), DB-OP 71–76 added.
7. DBa (OP) = DB 1–4 added.

[4] 1. The icon (minus the figure of Skunkha) is created.
2. DBa (Elam.) = DB 1–4 and DBb-j (Elam.) are added.
3. DB-Elamite(1) 1–69 added.
4. DBb-j (Akk.) and DB-Akkadian 1–69 added.
5. DBl(70: Elam), DBa-j (OP) and DB-OP 1–70 added.
6. Skunkha added; DB-Elamite(1) erased.
DBk (El., OP), DB-Elamite(2), DB-OP 71–76 added.

The differences from Trümpelmann are: (1) The addition of DBa (Elam.) is not distinguished from that of DBb-j (Elam.). (Hinz 1968 took the same view.) (2) The addition of DBa (OP) already at stage 5. (Again this matches Hinz 1968.) (3) The particular order of additions within stage 5, which flows from Huyse's understanding of 70 and the process by which the OP writing system was invented.

Once it arrives it happens in Akkadian and Elamite before Old Persian. On the monument Elamite has preferential position,[5] but this does not preclude DB-Elamite(1) and DB-Akkadian being added in the same overall stage—Elamite taking precedence as the written language of the Anshanite kingdom of Cyrus—and since Assyro-Babylonians were the writers of complex 'historical' narratives (there are none in Elamite), it makes sense to wonder if DB was drafted first in a semitic language, not Elamite—an idea already mooted by Borger, Bivar and Sancisi-Weerdenburg.[6]

As all who have studied the four versions for any length of time will be conscious, there is a broad tendency for them to fall into two groups: (a) DB-Akkadian and (where extant) DB-Aramaic, and (b) DB-Elamite and DB-OP. It is true that almost every other possible permutation of similarity or dissimilarity between three or four versions can be found (and there might be more if DB-Aramaic were less fragmentarily preserved), but the weight to be attached to the individual *differentiae* involved (they are very often formal rather than substantive) is probably variable and can certainly be hard to assess. Three- or four-way divergence is not particularly common, and most of the cases are ones where the normal tendency for DB-Elamite and DB-OP to differ from DB-Akkadian and DB-Aramaic is complicated by further divergence between the two Semitic-language versions.[7] The situation can be captured symbolically by a quasi-stemma with a common source drawn on separately (but not in hermetically sealed fashion) by DB-Old Persian, DB-Elamite and DB-Akkadian (Behistun) and a lost fourth version from which DB-Akkadian (Babylon) and DB-Aramaic derive.

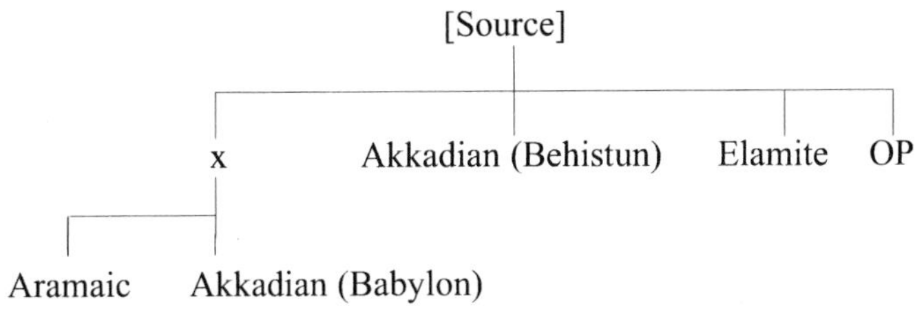

[5] It is the language used for DBa in Stage 2, it takes precedence in the labelling of the nine rebels on the icon, and it is put to the right of the icon on a more commodious space than the balancing one later assigned to Akkadian.

[6] Borger 1982: 130; Bivar 1998: 192 (his evidence strictly only suggests priority of Aramaic to Akkadian); Sancisi-Weerdenburg 1999: 103, 108, who detects the world of (Aramaic) letter-reports in the 'Thus says King Darius' paragraphing. Trümpelmann, Hinz and Huyse all make DB-Elamite(1) and DB-Akkadian into separate numbered stages, but I do not see how one can be sure of a substantive gap.

[7] Fully documenting the assertions in this paragraph would strain the space available here to breaking point, and in any case I would not claim that the analysis on which they are based is more than provisional. (No thorough four-way comparison of the versions has yet been published, so far as I am aware.)

When DB-OP does not match DB-Elamite it matches DB-Akkadian slightly more often than not. Assuming that at the head of the process was input from Darius (whose language was Persian), this global observation may (marginally) favour the notion that a Semitic version is primary. In line with this I note that another distinctive feature of DB-Akkadian is that it characteristically differs from the others by including extra or alternative material, not omitting things, and the substantive additions can be reliable and interesting.

- Both Akkadian and Aramaic versions include a type of information lacking elsewhere, viz. casualty figures.[8]
- Gaumata is explicitly a Mede, not just a magus—a substantive *datum* there is no ground to question.[9]
- Gobryas is called a Patischorian, a label which recurs on Darius' tomb-inscription and may refer to a clan-affiliation.[10]
- The location of Gandutava in Sattagydia (not the less precise Arachosia of DB-OP and DB-Elamite) is another piece of exactitude (46).
- Bivar's explanation of a wrong reference to the Babylon palace in 40 implies an earlier Aramaic text which contained a (now corrupt) toponym that disappeared in DB-OP and DB-Elamite.[11]
- Nidintu-Bel (Nebuchadnezar III) is described as a *zazakku*. This striking *datum* has not received much attention. Modern discussions of the post of *zazakku* (which is attested in a number of neo-Babylonian sources) agree on its high status, and the most recent treatment sees its holder as a royal secretary—someone, therefore, closely associated with the King. There are gaps in the record for Nabonidus' reign into which Nidintu-Bel could fit; alternatively the post continued in early Achaemenid times (a supposition normally rejected). Either way it is important information that the future 'Nebuchadnezzar III' had held such an office.[12]

The casualty figures are particularly striking because of their consistent presence in Semitic and absence in other texts. Either Semitic versions are

[8] Mostly these relate to the dead and wounded of full-scale battles; but the reports of the execution of captured 'kings' in 20, 32, 36, 38, 43 supply the numbers of high-ranking associates executed at the same time (and in 20, 36, 38 the fact that there were such other victims is something not recorded in the other versions).

[9] 11. Compare the provision of ethnics for Açina and Vahyazdata at their first appearance (16; 40), where they are lacking in DB-OP and DB-Elamite.

[10] 68. DNc (Patišuvariš). The Patischorians are a *phulon* in Strab. 15.3.1, alongside, and as if parallel to, Achaemenids, Magi, Mardians and Kyrtes (a real categorical mish-mash). Briant 1984: 108 reckons the Patischorians an Achaemenid-like clan.

[11] 40, with Bivar 1998.

[12] 16. On the office of *zazakku* cf. Beaulieu 1991, Dandamaev 1994, Joannès 1994.

primary, and this information was omitted deliberately in DB-OP and DB-Elamite—just as one battle-date was omitted accidentally[13]—or Semitic versions are secondary and add information neglected or unavailable when the others were written. But in terms of the monument DB-Akkadian is not secondary to DB-OP and is arguably co-incident with DB-Elamite(1).

There are, of course, problem cases. Use of *mar bane* for two different pairs of words or phrases might be called banalization.[14] Location of Nebuchadnezzar IV's revolt at Ur contrasts with the naming of Dubala in other texts, a site in the ambit of Sippar which fits better with the early evidence for his rule being from northern Babylonia.[15] The unique statement that troops awaited Darius in Kampanda and then joined him at Ecbatana is odd, as Kampanda was arguably on Darius' route to Ecbatana.[16] But I doubt there is anything here that precludes the priority of a Semitic text: the whole problem is that priority does not preclude error. (Nor, as we shall see in reference to 14, does it preclude over-specification.)

One further point: when Cyrus conquered Babylon he had an Akkadian proclamation composed in decently traditional manner.[17] But DB-Akkadian is not an exemplar of Assyro-Babylonian literary tradition. The general conception and content of Darius' text is novel (and the 'Proclaims Darius the King' formula is Urartian), and its Akkadian expression is done for the most part in ordinary, non-literary language (Malbran-Labat 1994; Streck 1996: 284; Malbran-Labat 1998: 64). If writers in Aramaic or Akkadian were first (even equal first) to put in writing the new King's message it was a privilege which acknowledged their cultural status on a limited front (experience in writing long 'historical' texts) but allowed little room for manoeuvre. The inclusion of odd extra bits of information (as well as the putting of a Babylonian cast on things)[18] were small exploitations of that room.

[13] Taxmaspada' defeat of the Sagartians in 33 is dated in DB-Akkadian (5 Tashritu) but not DB-Elamite or DB-OP. The third battle against Vahyazdata (47) is, by contrast, undated in all versions.

[14] (a) OP *âmâtâ* ('excellent, noble'), Elamite *šalut* ('gentleman'): 3. (b) OP *fratama anušiya* ('foremost followers'), Elam. *hatarrimanu damihupape* ('hommes en condition d'alliance qui l'avaient fidèlement suivi'): 13, 32, 42, 43, 47, 50.

[15] 49: cf. Zawadzki 1994, 1995.

[16] 25. In Isidore 781 F2(5) Kampanda (Gambadene) is the area containing Bagistana and lies west of Kangavar, Bazigraba, and Ecbatana. (See Calmeyer 1996.) Darius was coming from Babylon (DB 31).

[17] The so-called 'Cyrus Cylinder': Berger 1975; English translation: Brosius 2000: 10ff (no.12).

[18] There is a tendency to add Babylonia (so 'Persia, Media and other lands' becomes, 'Persian, Media, Babylonia and other lands': cf. 10, 12, 13, 14); compare the addition of 'King of Babylonia' to references to Nabonidus in 16, 52. The treatment of the second Babylonian rebel in 50, though not substantively different from the other versions, is more prolix. Geographical names are given 'classic' Akkadian form (so Armenia becomes Urartu, Saka Cimmerians). Calendar dates use Babylonian month-names. The Assyro-Babylonian literary convention of campaign-enumeration has been detected in DB-Akkadian's distinctive phrasing in 25, 27, 28, 30 (Malbran-

The initial monument and two texts produce a triptych—a novel conception, but executed with some epigraphic untidiness. The Akkadian text has two oddities. First, 36 lines into the 112-line text the inscription starts to stretch onto an adjacent rock-face in a different plane and the lines become very much longer: someone had apparently realized belatedly that the text would not fit otherwise. Secondly, eight different engraver-scribes have been detected—distinct in both epigraphic and scribal features.[19] Either there was a remarkable number of literate engravers in the work-force (and no orderly supervision) or the one engraver was startlingly inconsistent. Less well-known (indeed unobserved) is an oddity of DB-Elamite(1). This text is problematic because it was subsequently 'lightly erased'; but my calculations suggest Cameron's estimate of its inscribed area exceeds requirements by over 10% (14 lines of text).[20] One explanation might be that DB-Elamite(1) too did not fill the space allocated for it and the blank space at the end was also later 'erased' in the interests of neatness. (The idea would be that the masons continued to roughen the surface down to a point level with the end of column III, because that area had all been originally dressed for text-reception.)

The next stage brings something new—texts in Old Persian. Unlike DB-Elamite(1) and DB-Akkadian, DB-OP is inscribed rather tidily and in a

Labat 1998: 66). There is a tendency for Iranian names to be rendered in 'Median' rather than 'Persian' form (e.g. Barziya rather than Bardiya), which recurs in Babylonian texts in general (Schmitt 1980: 119, Zadok 1977: 111f).

[19] Voigtlander 1978: 5–6, 73. There are variations both in, for example, spacing and line-height and in ways of writing particular words. Similar phenomena have been observed in DB-OP: Schmitt 1991: 20, and in more detail Schmitt 1990: 23ff, 26ff (e.g. three different 'hands' within Column III). But no fully systematic investigation has been done (Schmitt 1990: 28).

[20] DB-Elamite(1) had four columns with 76, 63, 79 and 105? lines. DB-Elamite(2) has three columns (containing the text of DB 1–69) with 81, 85 and 94 lines. (The figure for Elamite(1) IV *is* said by Cameron 1960: 61 to be problematic, but he does not indicate the margins of error, and there is no reason to suppose they are very large.) On the basis of Cameron 1960: 61 one gets this picture of the distribution of putatively identical text in the two versions:

Elamite(1)		*Elamite(2)*
I 76	<>	I 65 (OP §17 = Elamite §16)
II 63	<>	II 37 (end of OP §28 = Elamite § 23)
III 79	<>	???
IV 105	<>	???

This seems to mean that the contents of Elamite(1) III–IV (184 lines) correspond to Elamite(2) II 38–III 94, i.e. 48 + 94 = 142 lines. But the 139 lines of Elamite(1) I–II correspond to the 118 lines of Elamite(2) I 1–II 37. At that rate 184 lines of Elamite(1) should correpond to 156 lines of Elamite(2). This is 10% more than the actual figure. (Looked at the other way round: you only need 167 lines in Elamite(1) to contain the 142 lines of Elamite(2), but we allegedly have 184 lines.) Column IV is wider than the others (2.01 m as against 1.62, 1.63 and 1.32). If the lines were longer (which Cameron does *not* actually say) this exacerbates the problem, as the putative 184 lines of Elamite(1) would contain even more text than is required to match the contents of Elamite(2) II 38–III 94. (Of course, if there was variable line length the narrower dimensions of column III might compensate and leave us more or less back where we started.)

neatly calculated space, producing four complete and nearly equal columns. A step in the right direction—but note that the columns are not disposed symmetrically beneath the icon: standards of neatness are still imperfect. The Old Persian text is one paragraph longer than DB-Akkadian and DB-Elamite(1), and the content of this paragraph is a source of heart-ache for students of the Behistun monument and its textual message(s). But let me first continue and complete the outline history of the monument.

An Elamite version of the new paragraph was included in the top left part of the icon (DBl). It was not included in DB-Elamite(2), and we cannot know whether it was added to DB-Elamite(1) (where there would have been room). If it was, the engraver of DB-Elamite(2) worked from an unemended copy of DB-Elamite(1) and failed to allow for it in his calculations (which here made his text fit perfectly into the space): so it was put on the icon. Alternatively, as an important piece of text, it was put on the icon straightaway and so not included in DB-Elamite(2). One thing *is* certain: the new paragraph was neither added to DB-Akkadian (although there was space) nor inscribed in Akkadian anywhere else. Perhaps this is *Schlamperei*, perhaps it hints that the monument-makers no longer thought Akkadian so important. Certainly the next time something new was added Akkadian was missing.

This beings us to Trümpelmann's stage 6. Once successful campaigns had been fought against the Elamite Athamaita and Scythian Skunkha 'in my second and third year', Darius ordered the addition of Skunkha (but not Athamaita!) to the line of Lie-Kings. This was done (and labelled—but *not* in Akkadian) but the result encroached on the first column of DB-Elamite(1). So DB-Elamite(1) was erased and the text re-inscribed to the left of DB-OP. At the same stage a fifth column was added to DB-OP about Athamaita and Skunkha. This was reproduced neither in Akkadian nor Elamite. There was no room at the end of DB-Elamite(2), but at least one other version could theoretically have been slipped in below the Old Persian text. Perhaps there was a feeling that, in the long inscriptions, each language should stick to a discrete space; or perhaps the monument-makers now thought Elamite did not matter so much either. The final inscription (on Trümpelmann's scheme) was purely Old Persian: the reproduction of DBa above the King, providing an Old Persian statement in the iconographic field of the titulature and claim to legitimacy which was the first written element. It may not be too fanciful to see this as a symbolic act of closure, but since Hinz and Huyse reckoned that the Old Persian version of DBa was already added at Stage 5 one can hardly insist upon the point.

Cuneiform trilingualism continues through Darius' reign and beyond. But within the time-frame covered by the creation of Behistun, introduction of a third language did not promote it. This raises the question of the relationship of the inscribed monument to later manifestations of royal discourse—and the question is raised within the text of DB-OP: for the contents of column V suggest other changes are afoot. We shall return to this. But, first, back to 70.

The crucial issue is whether its statements about what Elamite calls *tuppi* and Old Persian designates with an uncertain term (but based on the Elamite calque *dipi*) allude to the invention of Old Persian script.

(1) The place-determinative attached to Elamite *tuppi* and the general usage of the word in other contexts favours understanding it to mean 'text' rather than 'script'. Schmitt claims his Old Persian reading, *dipiciçam*, means 'form of writing'. But if *tuppi* (and *dipi*) should (or can) mean text, then—granted that *ciça* means 'type, shape, form, lineage'—the compound *dipiciçam* could designate the common content of various language forms of the text, now rendered into Aryan; and a comparable force can readily be assigned to the suffix *-me* which is attached to both of the occurrences of *tuppi* in paragraph 70.[21]

(2) *Tuppi* is used at the start and end of the paragraph; and the thing at the end which is sent to all lands should be a text not a script-type: the idea that a sign-list and user's instructions were sent around the empire seems far-fetched and inconsistent with the fact that generalized use of Old Persian never developed. We can only sustain the equation *tuppi* = script if we acknowledge that Darius had a plan for the widespread (public) use of written Old Persian which was subsequently abandoned.

(3) In DB-Elamite the statement about the *tuppi* and Aryan is annotated with the words 'another' or 'otherwise' and 'which was not before'. In DB-OP this is missing. This seems odd if what was being either said (if *tuppi* = script) or implied (if 'which was not before' means DB-OP was a *type* of text impossible previously) was precisely that Darius had (caused to be) invented a way of writing Old Persian: this ought to have been something to boast about in the new script of all places. The silence is less odd if the annotation simply indicates that a new piece of text (written, it happens, in Aryan) did not exist before it was written: the Elamite author chose to draw attention to the fact that there was now an Old Persian version whereas previously there had not been; the Old Persian author did not feel the need to make the (frankly) gratuitous point that the text of which 70 is an integral part did not exist before it was written.[22]

(4) Something is said to have been written on both clay and parchment; this must refer to versions in more than one language, Aramaic as well as

[21] ^{h}*Tuppi* as 'text' rather than 'writing-system': Huyse 1999: 46, 60 n.20 (citing earlier discussions). *Dipiciçam*: Schmitt 1990: 56–60, 1991: 73 n.89. Suffix *-me*: Huyse 1999: 46–47.

[22] Herrenschmidt 1989: 204–5 and Lecoq 1997: 213 claim that the annotation really means 'which was before', in which case this line of argument is irrelevant—and the paragraph may become evidence for the pre-existence of OP writing. Herrenschmidt held that the OP text should also be understood to say that an Aryan version already existed (Lecoq does not agree about this) and identified the OP 'document de base' as an entry in the Royal Annals—an entity attested only by Ctesias and the Bible. But the linguistic basis of all of this has not found favour.

cuneiform languages.[23] The text either says two parallel things about the *tuppi*—it was translated into Aryan; and it was put on clay and parchment—and then speaks of making a name and lineage, or it says that the *tuppi* was made in Aryan and that Darius put his name and lineage on clay and parchment. In the latter reading *tuppi* could refer to a script but does not have to; in the former it can only designate the content of the text.

We can tolerate the conclusion that 70 does not refer to invention of Old Persian writing, while believing the script was in fact new, provided that we envisage Darius as insufficiently proud of his achievement to demand its mention in the first text composed in the new system or unwilling eventually to insist on effective dissemination of the system across the empire. Can we envisage such insouciance or loss of enthusiasm? We may have to try if other arguments favour a belief that no Old Persian writing system existed before Behistun; and one such argument is the fact that DB-Elamite and DB-Akkadian were already being engraved before anyone thought of including an Old Persian version.[24] This shows one of two things: either (a) there was no Old Persian script, and it did not readily occur to anyone that there should be; or (b) there *was* a script but its use was so dissociated from the sort of context represented by Behistun that the idea of applying it there did not occur to anyone until late in the day. Since the novelty implicit in (b) would have to be very great to make it credible, the implications of the two views are pretty much the same—and both stand in stark contrast to our conclusions about 70.

Darius and his advisers had either forgotten a script which already existed or were slow to see that inventing one would be a good idea. For the former scenario, the only real possibility is that of a Median invention, used for writing things on clay-tablets not yet recovered from Ecbatana. We would have to postulate that, although Darius knew Ecbatana (certainly during the year of rebellions and probably in Cambyses' reign too) and was alive to the existence and power of the writing systems of Mesopotamia, Elam/Anshan and Egypt, he was not conscious of the Median equivalent. This sounds odd but, if the project of an *inscribed* monument was inspired by royal advisers representing the Mesopotamian/Elamite *Kulturraum* who knew nothing of a local Median script, it is just imaginable. On this scenario, when someone did eventually remember that the story could be written in Aryan, Darius commanded that this should happen and the fact be noted in the resulting text,

[23] Any translation which makes the text say specifically that the Aryan version was written on tablet *and parchment* should be rejected.

[24] Another line of argument, that involving the Pasargadae material, need not detain us long here. If (any) OP inscriptions there genuinely predate 530, Darius did not invent OP script and there is no problem. But if all of OP inscriptions there were produced after 521 (as it is very tempting to suppose: Stronach 1990, 1997a, 1997b, 2000) this still does not *prove* Darius invented the system: there may still be no problem.

but did not attach great importance to what was not his invention and indeed derived from a region with which as a Persian king he had ambiguous relations.

If, alternatively, we accept that Darius *was* responsible for creating Old Persian script, we can see the things like this: his advisers found in Darius someone receptive to the general idea of an inscription but—not being literate—detached from the details. Eventually it struck someone—not Darius but one of the court-'scholars'—that there was paradox (even impropriety) in a King of Darius' power being unwritten in his own language. He agreed—but (as a non-literate) viewed it as a technicality, something for the professionals. One thinks of the attitude some of us have to the outer reaches of Information Technology, but the situation is more extreme: what is at stake is the state of mind of a monarch for whom the output of writing technology was, after all, pretty patterns. We take it for granted that written expression of verbalized thought processes is a great good and a necessary cultural trophy. Perhaps Darius (who only included the label 'Aryan' in his protocol *after* Behistun)[25] did not see it that way.

At the same time, this extension of technology was not perhaps without effect. Despite increasing neglect of Akkadian and Elamite at Behistun, 70 announces multilingual despatch of DB around the empire. Was this not happening already? Nothing about the text's contents requires such an assumption;[26] and it begs the question to assume that its unreadibility *in situ* even by literate visitors proves an intention for it to be readable somewhere else. Moreover, one might distinguish between public display of a text with an iconographic component (something which arguably did happen rapidly at Babylon) and the more extravagant scenario of 70 in which the text alone will be sent 'to the lands' (i.e. throughout the empire). Perhaps, then, writing an Old Persian version which would 'speak' to a hitherto unaddressed audience stimulated the idea of speaking to all the lands of the empire, though not only in that language—a process as new as the necessarily new one of reading the Old Persian text back to the King (as opposed to orally translating an Elamite or Akkadian one for him), to which 70 also alludes. If so, it is psychologically significant that the paragraph notes Darius' 'making' of name and lineage. This recalls the privileged presence of this element on the icon at the outset.

25 And then only twice (DNa, DSe).

26 There is certainly concern in DB 55–69 about audience-response. Future kings are invited to beware the Lie (55), punish the Liar (64) and protect the families of Darius' fellow-conspirators (69). An unspecified future reader (56, 58) or viewer (65–67) is to believe that the contents are true (56; cf. 58), promote knowledge of the proclamation (60–61), and protect the inscription and reliefs from destruction (65–67). The last requirement relates explicitly to the Behistun monument, the others technically do not, but the question is: if the text is a single integral whole, does the monument-specific nature of 65–67 and 69 apply to other parts of 55–69? The answer is that, in default of other indications, that is what one would assume—and hence that broadcast dissemination elsewhere was not explicitly an issue.

When Darius engaged with the issue of disseminating a message, assertion of Achaemenid legitimacy is top of the agenda. I do not presume to say whether this suggests the assertion was false, just insist that to Darius it was of capital importance.

The incremental creation of the Behistun monument thus reveals a developing idea of how (recent) history might be presented. First a largely iconographic approach (lightly inscribed), which summarizes the situation *via* a representation of royal triumph indebted both to the ancient Sar-i Pol monument further along the Ecbatana-Babylon highway (Root 1979: 198–201; Potts 1999: 318f) and to neo-Assyrian congeners. Then narrative, composed in the languages (though only partially the manner) appropriate to Assyro-Babylonian tradition, and deployed in triptych arrangement to produce an unprecedented monument. Cyrus had had scholars who could show him to a Mesopotamian audience in traditional style (and with neo-Assyrian overtones); Darius and his scholars were more innovative—and the untidy results on the cliff-face suggest that the masons found it a challenge to keep up. Introducing Old Persian was the next step, one which prompted more talk about increased out-reach than technical innovation. The prospect of broadcast narrative as a means of imperial control and even of a uniquely privileged position for written Old Persian might seem about to open up. But putative evidence for the latter (incomplete trilinguality) may reflect gradual abandonment of the Behistun monument and aspects of its verbal presentation of ideologically charged material; and the former development was never carried through. Behistun inscribes several stages in the rendering of historical propaganda but does not complete the process. I turn now to another aspect of this proposition.

II

Prima facie the narrative of DB is notable for circumstantial exactitude: battles have named locations, dates and (in one strand) casualty figures; Gaumata's death is dated and located; the mutilation of some rebels is carefully delineated. But there are limits too.

(1) The text is very formulaic (not least in the battles).

(2) The material is episodic. The narrative skeleton represented by Gaumata and the nine rebels is given in three ways—the icon, the summary at 52 and the narrative—and none is chronological. The nearest thing to an organizational principle is a relation to Darius' movements.[27] We shall return to this.

[27] A Elam/Babylonia: 16–22
'... while I was in Babylonia': 21
'... I was near Elam': 23
B.1 Media + Armenia + Parthia-Margiana-Bactria: 24–39
B.2 Persia + Arachosia 40–48

(3) 21 lists two rebel lands (Egypt and Scythia) which do not reappear—an odd loose-end, not defensible by reference to the 'there is more I could have put in but I did not want to seem incredible' line (58) (a gambit which depends on either saying clearly what you are omitting—the classic *praeteritio*—or saying nothing), and liable to make the reader suspicious. Darius is more concerned to stress the extent of the challenge than to conceal some failure to meet it: nine kings in 19 battles in one year is good enough for one not to have entirely to suppress the fact that two threats were not dealt with in that time. An odd mixture of exactitude and its reverse.

(4) Dates are not always there, and the absence of one in 11 for Cambyses' death does seem odd, especially as it comes hard upon precise dates for Gaumata's rebellion (11/3/522) and 'seizure of the kingdom' (1/7/522).[28] Briant (2002: 102) speculates that Cambyses died before 1/7/522 and Darius falsely postdated the event in order to present Gaumata as a dyed-in-the-wool usurper; and his suspicion is inspired precisely by Darius' failure to provide a date. Since the distinction between uprising and becoming king appears with five other Lie-Kings,[29] and what is unusual about Gaumata is only that dates are provided for the two stages, suspicion might seem appropriate: Darius exceeds the standard formula by providing two dates but not a third. But the 'standard formula' does not include an element corresponding to Cambyses' death and treats its components as an indivisible narrative unit. The text of 11 without dates would not have proved Cambyses died after Gaumata definitively became king; it would simply be a case of the narrative-unit of uprising/kingdom-seizure being succeeded by a narrative-unit (Cambyses' death) which, at best, could be inferred to overlap with the previous one. To this model Darius attached dates for Gaumata's progress to kingship because his importance justified the trouble of identifying them (an exercise only possible because there was some specific formal event which could be taken as acquisition of the kingdom), and it did so because Gaumata was the king whom Darius displaced. That special quality is possessed neither by other rebel-kings (none of their kingships is the object of calendrical exactitude—so we have dates for their defeat in battle but not for execution, even when that is as public and stressed as those of Fravarti and Vahyazdata)[30] nor by Cambyses: the important thing about him is that he was the object of Gaumata's uprising, and no new date was needed to affirm that. The case illustrates not mendacity but the limits of the rhetoric of exactitude.

Darius goes from Babylon to Media: 31; cf. 25, 30

C Babylonia: 49–51

'... while I was in Persia and Media': 49

[28] Others are elimination of the Elamite pretenders Acina and Martiya (17, 23), and the third Arachosian defeat of Vahyazdata's forces (47).

[29] Acina, Nidintu-Bel: 16. Fravarti: 24. Vahyazdata: 40. Araxa: 49.

[30] Fravarti: 32. Vahyazdata: 43.

(5) The nature of Cambyses' death has also seemed problematic. 'Died his own death' (11) is not a standard cliché in Elamite or Akkadian. Later parallels suggest that it means 'died a natural death' (one involving no direct violent cause);[31] perhaps it was already an established Persian cliché and this detail reflects Darius' personal idiolect. But, even if so, the description is vague and uncircumstantial where, at first sight, one might have expected more was needed if it was a question of dispelling suspicions of foul play (which have certainly been entertained). Whatever the truth about Cambyses' death, its treatment certainly discloses an ingrained taste for the non-specific.

(6) More worrying is Darius' claim that there had been eight kings in his Achaemenid family (3–4). Darius links 'Achaemenid' with descent from Achaemenes. But Herodotus identifies the Achaemenids as a 'phratry' of the Pasargadaean tribe, which should mean they were a group of families not (necessarily) claiming descent from a single progenitor.[32] Some take Herodotus' description seriously, and it is certainly distinctive and unexpected, given that every individual Achaemenid in *Histories* can be located inside what DB calls Darius' 'family' (*tauma*). But there is no way to validate it. Certainly Briant's equation of phratry with Old Persian *vith* does not match usage in DB or elsewhere.[33] Darius speaks of his *tauma* and *vith*: *tauma* is a descent group (a rather wide one, potentially, if one looks back from oneself and then forward again from one's ancestors down different direct lines), *vith* either another way of describing the same thing or a designation for something narrower and more personal.[34] (Briant would say

[31] Schmitt 1991: 51 n.43, noting that the turn of phrase is found in many languages and periods. For some Greek parallels cf. Ptolem. *Tetr.*199, Ramsay 1895–97: 328 (133), 329 (187), Parker 2002. Lack of direct violence does not preclude malign human manipulation. In Joseph. *AJ* 10.121 people attempt to kill Jeremiah by lowering him into a pit full of filth so he will 'choke and die his own death' (ὅπως ἰδίῳ θανάτῳ πνιγεὶς ἀποθάνῃ): to achieve this he is left standing up to his neck in the filth to await the moment when—naturally (!)—weakness causes him to collapse and suffocate. (In the event, he was rescued.)

[32] Hdt.1.125; Lambert 1993: 3–20, 144, 220f, 267f, primarily discussing Athenian evidence—but this ought to be an adequately valid guide to Herodotus' assumptions. (The word *phretre* does not recur in Herodotus.)

[33] Briant 1990: 79. Herrenschmidt 1976 also associated *vith* and 'Achaemenid' in her reading of the categories implicit in Darius' self-description in DNa 1 as son of Hystaspes (*tauma*), Achaemenid (*vith*), Persian, son of a Persian (*dahyu*), Aryan, son of an Aryan (*ciça*). Lecoq 1997: 170 reads the same passage as revealing *vith* (family), *zana* (clan), *dahyu* (tribe) and *xšaça* (people).

[34] *Tauma*: 3, 4, 10, 12, 14 refer to the descent group from Achaemenes to Darius (including Cyrus and Cambyses); in 24, 33, 52 we have the descent group from Cyaxares (membership of which is a claim to kingship); 60, 61, 66, 67 invoke blessings or curses (including the presence or absence of descendants) on a *tauma*; 13, 63 allude unspecifically to Darius' family. *Vith*: apart from references to a physical house, this word appears in various prayer formulae in later texts; in DB we have Darius' *vith* in 14 and 63, passages where *tauma* also appears. In 63 (neither Darius nor any *tauma*-member was a Lie-follower; there are rewards for those co-operating with Darius' *vith*) the contrast between *tauma* and *vith* might be between the view from inside

that this is because Darius is lying, but that is a *petitio principii.*) In any event, I suspect *tauma* and *vith* of being deliberately generic words, not ones an Old Persian speaker would use to distinguish clearly between nuclear family, extended family, clan or wider groups. Darius is speaking in symbolic terms, perhaps because he is lying, perhaps because he thinks in such terms. In the same way he fails to identify the eight preceding Achaemenid kings: the five named ascendants plus Cyrus and Cambyses are insufficient. This is especially odd given the importance of this part of the text. Perhaps he is lying. Or perhaps he does not see that a symbolic statement—'there have been eight kings of my family and I am the ninth'—might provoke pedantic questions when put next to a list of ancestors.

(7) *Tauma* and *vith* figure in the description of Darius' restoration of the *status quo* disturbed by Gaumata (14). The elements are:

- restoration of kingship to Darius' family (*tauma*)
- religious restoration
- return of property to the 'people'
- restoration of the 'people' to its place
- general restoration of what was taken away in respect of Persia, Media and other lands
- return of 'our house' (*vith*) to its place

and all except the second and third are obviously generic or symbolic. On religion DB-Elamite and DB-Akkadian certainly refer to restoration of 'temples', while DB-OP has been claimed to speak of 'rites';[35] but in either case nothing specific is said. On property things are more complicated. The group to which property is restored is described with DB's generic word for people/army; the only handle on their identity is through Akkadian *uqu* (a distinctively Achaemenid-period word, perhaps derived from *emuqu* / *ewuqu* but also oddly homophonous with Elamite *uk-ku* = head or person). Here *uqu* is (treated as) grammatically plural and when that happens in DB it designates 'army' rather than people.[36] As for what is returned, first of all we have fields and animals, after which come in Akkadian 'day-labourers (and)

outwards (*tauma*) and that from outside in (*vith*). But this looks over-subtle in 14 (Darius restored 'our *vith*' and made it so Gaumata did not remove 'our *vith*'; he restored the kingdom which Gaumata took from 'our *tauma*').

35 Akkadian *É.MEŠ šá DINGIR.MEŠ* and Elamite ^{d}*zi-ia-an* ^{d}*na-ap-pan-na* seem unambiguous. Lecoq 1997 renders the Elamite as 'cultes des dieux'; but contrast Hinz-Koch 1987: 1095 (s.v. *si-ya-an*), 1308 (s.v. *zi-ya-an*), and note an instance of ^{h}*zi-ya-an*, with locative determinative, in an unpublished Persepolis Fortification text. OP: *ayadana* = 'rites' according to Lecoq, but Schmitt 1991: 53 opts for 'places of worship'.

36 Whereas 'army' is only a necessary translation in one case where *uqu* is singular (§ 42: *itti uqu isi*). For the grammatical doctrine cf. Voigtlander 1978: 17 (on l. 26); Stolper 1985: 57; Streck 1996: 278.

bow-estates', in Elamite '*kurtaš* [the generic worker-word in the Persepolis archives] and house/estate-artisans', in Old Persian 'house-workers, estates'. Akkadian is again the most specific: but is this reliable? Or is it an interpretation in terms of Babylonian military estates (developed by Achaemenid occupation) of a simple 'workers and estates' intended (with 'fields and animals') to summarize productive property in generic fashion and reproduced with less aggressive specificity, though not consistently, in Elamite and Old Persian? Since everything else in 14 is quite general the latter seems the preferable option.

(8) The misguided desire to find authentic exactitude in DB 14 reflects a wish to discern Gaumata's political or religious platform. Darius actually sees such things in a different light, by reference to 'The Lie'. In 10–13 the narrative successively tells us that:

(a) Bardiya was killed and nobody knew about it
(b) Gaumata claimed the kingdom on the basis of acceptance by the entire *kara*
(c) He continued in power through people's fear: Gaumata would have killed much of the *kara* that had known Bardiya to prevent the *kara* knowing that he was not Bardiya.

A natural reaction to this *non sequitur* is probably that initial ignorance of Bardiya's murder was replaced by suspicion (perhaps engendered by actual killings) mixed with fear: 'if this man is not Bardiya, then he would certainly be hard on anyone who dared to *say* that he was not'. This explains what we see as the ellipse of thought, and locates the change between stages 2 and 3. But for Darius the train of thought is different: after Bardiya's murder 'The Lie' grows in power as an independent evil force. This results in Gaumata lying about his identity and the entire *kara* following him. 'The Lie' works not by eradicating truth but by fostering a tendency to behave as if particular lies were true, so the fact that the entire *kara* accepted Gaumata as king is compatible with lots of them knowing the real truth. The ellipse is between stages 1 and 2—except there is no ellipse, because 'The Lie' fills the gap. Darius' special claim is not that he is cleverer than others in realizing Gaumata was a fraud, but that he is braver in taking action. Overcoming 'The Lie' involves acting on the basis that particular lies are just that, lies, and is extremely difficult because of the disabling power of 'The Lie'. In the pseudo-historiography of DB this symbolic account is the only sort of explanation required or provided: expecting the text to provide sound evidence for any other sort is optimistic.

In this context another point is worth mention. Gaumata's *magus*-status is clearly integral to his identity: every time he is mentioned he is 'Gaumata the *magus*', and only DB Akkadian provides the extra note that he was a

Mede.[37] But no explanation of its importance is advanced. I make just two observations. First, the uprising of Gaumata the *magus* is the first manifestation of the systematic evil of 'The Lie'. Being a *magus* is not a necessary qualification for trouble-making (other rebels also manifest 'The Lie') but Darius might have thought it appropriate in the context of a cosmic force-for-evil that things be set rolling by a religious technician. (Archive evidence shows, incidentally, that Gaumata could perfectly well also have been involved in secular administration.)[38] Secondly, a recent contention that magi were precisely *not* associated with the cult of Ahuramazda (Handley-Schachler 1998) interacts interestingly with Darius' obsession with that deity. (I say this without prejudice to the issue of Zoroastrianism.) For the other side of the cosmic explanation coin to 'The Lie' is the beneficent power of Ahuramazda.

(9) Finally, chronology again, and other ways in which it is not a problem-free zone.

A. The order of events is not chronological, but there is at first sight a quasi-chronological structure (in terms of Darius' whereabouts: see above. But when dated events are put in chronological order one sees this is misleading. Nebuchadnezzar III was King in Babylonia too early for him to have rebelled 'after I'd killed Gaumata' (16). Vahyazdata's Arachosian associates were already at war on 29 December, so he may not have rebelled 'while I was in Babylonia' (21), i.e. some unfixed date after 29 September, or against Darius at all. So the opening phrases of 16 and 21 are problematic. There are two possibilities.

A(1). Darius misrepresents by claiming to be the original object of rebellion actually initially directed against Gaumata. Why? Perhaps because his conviction that the kingdom was properly his is such that his kingship is imagined as starting when Gaumata falsely claimed it. All troublemakers are then rebels, not rivals. But Gaumata is *said* to rebel against Cambyses.

A(2). The phrases signify passage from one episode to another, not one chronological space to another. 'After I'd killed Gaumata, so-and-so happened' means 'the next thing I come to after my narrative of killing Gaumata is so-and-so'; 'when I was in Babylon, so-and-so happened' means 'the next thing I come to after my narrative of my actions in Babylon is so-and-so'. The same can apply to 49: 'when I was in Media and Persia'. Nebuchadnezzar IV was active by 17 May, so the phrase really means 'overlapping with events in the Median and Persian episodes I have just reported'.

[37] Other rebels are each given an ethnic designation, but it is not repeated each time they are named. Gaumata's repeated *magus*-designation is unusual—while his single designation as 'Mede' actually matches the pattern in other cases.

[38] Babylonia: VS 3.138/139; YOS 3.66; BIN I 40. Persepolis: Handley-Schachler 1998.

B. A slightly different case is the phrase 'this is what I did after I became King' in 10 and 15. In 10 it is followed by narrative of how Darius became king, starting with Cambyses' murder of Bardiya. In 15 it follows statements about restoration of order after Gaumata's death and precedes events introduced with 'after I had killed Gaumata' (already seen to be problematic if taken as a genuine chronological statement), and could theoretically be read both retrospectively (closing the accession narrative) or prospectively (opening a new stage in 'what I did after I became king').[39] Either way it reinforces the phrase's first appearance in 10, where it appears to embrace events happening before Darius became king. (It is at the end of 13 that Darius explicitly says he killed Gaumata and took the kingship from him.) There are three ways of looking at this.

B(1). Most of 10–14 is flash-back, and the introductory phrase implicitly downgrades Gaumata's killing compared with the restoration of order (Darius' actual first action as king). Restoration is important, so this is possible, but it does not feel quite right as a reading of the text or situation.

B(2). We re-evoke the idea that Darius imagined his kingship as starting with Gaumata's false claim. Only a little of 10 would then be flashback, and this view coheres with the way the icon and his inclusion in 52 among the nine rebels 'after I became king' assimilates his killing to other uncontroversial actions by Darius as king.[40]

B(3). We revert to the idea that apparent chronological markers actually represent narrative-transition markers. Thus, 10 is preceded by a statement about Darius being king—titulature, lineage, the extent and nature of his rule—interspersed and ending with the idea that Ahuramazda is responsible for his kingship. So the start of 10 means 'these are the next things I come to after my report on being-becoming king'. The opening nine paragraphs establish that Darius is king, and everything else 'follows'. This resembles (2) in backdating the start of Darius' kingship, but differs in articulation of the point and perhaps in the imagined moment of accession—but blunt chronological categorization of that sort is arguably not appropriate. Later royal inscriptions sometimes included the making of Darius king in a formula about Ahuramazda's creation of the world; we are not so far from 'reality', but have taken a step in that direction. One may add that the pattern in DB 1–9, 10f has some resemblance to Assyrian texts which pass straight from introductory generic statements about the King to the events of the 'start of his reign' or his 'first campaign':[41] once the King is introduced the next thing

39 The divergent Babylonian version here is more obviously retrospective, because it refers (again, as in 14) to making things as they were before.

40 Note, too, that 40 (in DB-OP and DB-Elamite) sees Vahyazdata's as the second revolt in Persia, a view which makes Gaumata a parallel manifestation.

41 cf. Tadmor 1981.

that should happen (in the text) is what happened at the beginning of his reign, even (especially?) when that was attended by some irregularity.

C. Under most of the options just surveyed the chronological markers are illusory. Either, though they technically retain the character of chronological reference points, Darius simply lies about the relationship of events to them (A[1])—and does so in the interests of a symbolic misrepresentation of the moment of his accession (an idea that recurs in B[2])—or they cease to be chronological markers in any ordinary primary sense at all (A[2], B[3])—a position which (so far as the location of the start of Darius' reign goes) has a similar, though differently achieved, effect. Only B(1) finds a way of reading one of the marker-phrases ('after I became king') literally. But it does so at the expense of turning the killing of Gaumata into a sort of prelude, and it is a solution which does not apply to the other markers under discussion so far.

D. There is a last case (another famous *crux*) to be considered: the statements in 52–53, 56–57 and 59 about what Darius did 'in a single year after I became king'. This allegedly involved defeating nine kings in 19 battles. The narrative does include nine defeated rebels and 19 battles, but three of the former were not the object of defeat in any of the 19 battles. This is neither error nor deception, merely association of two accurate figures driven by ideological re-classification—real data apprehended in symbolic fashion. The problem about the one year lies not here but in the fact that the dated events only fit in a single (intercalary) calendar year if Gaumata's death is excluded.[42] We have seen that the timing of Darius' accession can be problematized, but only in ways which back-date it or turn it into a textual moment; and anyway 52f locates Gaumata's death explicitly within the 'one year'. We are forced to the conclusion that the one year is symbolic. The distance from Gaumata's death to the last of the battles *was* only 13-and-a-half months in the Persian calendar,[43] but the mind-set of the text's composer was in the end not chronological, and the profusion of specific dates is a feature of symbolic rhetoric—dated events paradoxically (but only to our mind-set) in service of a greater and timeless truth: 'previous kings have not done as much (sc. ever) as I, with Ahuramazda's help, have done in a single year'. The Assyrian notion of the 'first year' or Urartian parallels may be relevant,[44] but I think that the result is partly reached differently: kingship is measured in years, so the year (first or otherwise) is the unit for comparison of achievement; and a liberal scatter of

[42] A widely supported view. The dates are 10/12/522–27/11/521 or 13/12/522–28/12/521, depending on whether the suppression of Frada on 28 December (38) occurred in 522 or 521.

[43] 29/9/522 to 27/11/521. (This assumes the suppression of Frada on 28 December occurred in 522. If it was 521, as some think, the overall span is 14-and-a-half months.) Vogelsang 1986 accepts this reading of the 'single year'.

[44] Assyria: see above n. 41. Urartu: Ahn 1992: 144. Westenholz 2000: 107 notes Naram-Sin's leitmotif of 'victor in nine battles in one year', and (122) apparently envisages an essential link between the Behistun icon and Naram-Sin's victory-stela of which the resemblance to the Sar-i Pol relief (cf. above) is some sort of epiphenomenon.

calendar-dates (giving just month and day) is a perfect way to reinforce the idea: for, in default of contrary indications, however many such calendar dates you name, they will all inevitably fit within a single year.

In various ways, then, DB is a historiographically odd-ball text. The rest of the corpus of Persian Royal Inscriptions is well known to privilege the generic and timeless in a fashion which those who want *histoire événementielle* find very vexing. Persian royal iconography discloses a similar mind-set. Sancisi-Weerdenburg (1999) has discerned a move in that direction in DB-OP Column V; it is certainly true that it deals with opposition differently from the rest of DB and its use of non-worship of Ahuramazda as a metaphor for political resistance resembles Xerxes' *Daeva* inscription (XPh). But her point can be extended. On the one hand, although the account of what happened 'in my second and third year' looks as though annalistic record is about to set in (another aspect of the false start in the history of Persian royal discourse already noted: see above), the narrative has no place for named places or (because there is no rhetoric of the virtual single year) precise dates. On the other hand, what precedes in the bulk of DB is, in its own way, scarcely less reflective of the attitude that informs later royal inscriptions, just as the iconographic language of the monument works in the same basic way as the visual decoration of Persepolis. I note too that DB's putatively non-Ahuramazda-worshipping *magus* implicitly prefigures the analytical framework of DB column V and of the *Daeva* text. Darius did not buy into historiography and then buy out of it again, as is sometimes thought: he never really bought into it in the first place and, as time passed, ceased even to appear to compromise with the idea of narrative self-projection.

III

Fixing a monumental text never, perhaps, guarantees that what people say about the pertinent events will not be variable and selective. The fate of the Darius version is a case in point

1. Aeschylus' informants (*Persae* 774–777) were apparently unaware of—or completely unimpressed by—Darius' version: Mardos is a 'disgrace', but not (said to be) an imposter; there is an extra ruler between Mardos and Darius whose name, Maraphis, is not readily identifiable in DB; and Artaphernes (whom one might naturally identify as Darius' brother of that name) has a prominent role unknown to DB, either as yet another ruler before Darius (!) or as a close associate in Darius' acquisition of power.[45]

[45] Apart from the commentaries of Broadhead and Hall, see West and West 1991: 182–88 (M.L.West), di Benedetto 1993. West suggests that 'Artaphernes' is really Intaphernes. The latter's fate as reported in Herodotus *could* be spin about a one-time equal partner in Darius' conspiracy—making Aeschylus' version closer to the reality of 522/521, but just as distant from DB.

2. Herodotus knew Smerdis ruled for seven months and has five of the conspirators' names right, but contradicts DB on the timing of Bardiya's murder, and supplies plentiful narrative detail quite unrelated to the spare treatment in DB.[46] Moreover, his informants were disinclined to talk about the revolts as a systematic set of events; instead we have a single-line reference to Median rebellion elsewhere in Herodotus' text and (in the accession narrative) separate traditions about a troublesome satrap in Lydia (Oroetes) and a revolt in Babylon, the second of which may have a slender distant link with the data (but hardly with the actual text) of DB.[47] No later Greek version displays even this much awareness of the Lie-Kings; of course, in the absence of circumstantial stories, they were less interesting than tales of impersonation and court-intrigue. On the other hand, Herodotus' informants *did* picture a celebratory sculpture—but of a man on horseback with an inscription which reported that Darius won his throne thanks to his horse and the groom Oebares (*Vahyabara = 'besseres bringend'). This refers to the story of Oebares fixing a hippomantic test and thus faking divine approval of the new King.[48] The fact that the Behistun monument (both image and text) is insistent on Ahuramazda as the source of Darius' power (the 'other gods' do also get in once in 62) makes the thrust of this alternative monument almost satirically appropriate. But is the story a *reaction* to Behistun or just a happy coincidence?

3. DB was still being disseminated in Aramaic a hundred years after Darius (Greenfield and Porten 1982: 3); but only a generation later Ctesias (whose own version of the accession narrative agrees with Darius on the timing of Bardiya's murder but also mixes quasi-Herodotean material with stuff that is neither Herodotean nor Darian) was capable of believing the Behistun monument was created by Semiramis (a view still reflected in Isidore's *Parthian Stations*); and when Alexander visited the region θέας ἕνεκεν, the surviving record mentions only that it was θεοπρεπέστατη χώρα, full of the wherewithal for enjoyment.[49] If Ctesias was really a royal doctor he must have passed Behistun on more than one occasion. His non-

[46] Seven months: 3.67. Conspirators' names: 3.70. Narrative detail: *passim*.

[47] Median rebellion: 1.130. Oroetes: 3.120–28; cf. Vargyas 2000. Babylon: 3.150–60, with Tuplin 1997: 353f: the length of Herodotus' Babylonian revolt matches the time from Babylonian recognition of Bardiya in 522 to the end of the second Babylonian rebellion recorded in DB. For another example of a significant coincidence of material which, however, proves nothing about access to DB compare Hdt.5.23 ('now the locals have found a leader [Histiaeus at Myrcinus] they will do what he says night and day') with DB 7 ('what has been said to them by me either by night or by day that they used to bring about'). Herodotus' version of Megabyzus' warning may draw on a genuinely royal *cliché* (Megabyzus is virtually suggesting that the Greco-Thracian population is going to turn Histiaeus into an *ersatz* Great King), but this does not mean that he had been reading DB.

[48] Hdt.3.84–88, Ctesias 688 F13(17), Just.1.10.

[49] Semiramis: Ctes.688 F1 (= Diod.2.13); Isidore 781 F2(5). Alexander: Diod.17.110.

cuneiform reader's report of the inscription (it allegedly said that Semiramis piled up panniers in order to climb the mountain) recalls Herodotus (2.125) on the diet of the pyramid-builders; his talk of the icon showing Semiramis and 100 *doruphoroi* has less excuse, but perhaps in his memory Behistun was amalgamated with the decorations of Persepolis and Susa (curiously a late 18th-century drawing by Olivier represents Darius at Behistun seated on a throne with a footstool in Persepolitan manner): the capacity of even less excitable observers to mis-remember the scale of things is well-attested (Lloyd 1995). (Ctesias says the mountain is 17 stades—3000 m—above the surrounding plain! The true figure is *c.* 500 m (Schmitt 1991: 17).) But were his questions about the monument really answered with evasion ('some old monarch'), thus enabling him to appropriate it as part of the developing Semiramis myth? However much Darius lost interest in the kind of text inscribed at Behistun, can we really imagine that the monument's identity had simply been forgotten 125 years later? Yet it is not easy to think of a *Realpolitik* reason for the artificial suppression of Darius: Cyrus' rebellion against Artaxerxes might have made stories involving rival brothers contentious—but Ctesias came up with his own version of the events of 522–1, so the events were not wholly taboo. Were they more taboo in the presence of Darius' monument than in quiet back-corridors of the royal palaces? Perhaps the only informants he could find were not Persian or simply (but unusually) ill-informed and retreated into evasive invention. But since we struggle to imagine the company Ctesias kept we cannot readily evaluate this putative evidence for ignorance about Darius. The oddity is compounded by the fact that Ctesias *does* have a story about another rock-cut monument, viz. Darius' tomb (688 F13[19]) and that (in Photius' epitome at least) this is the next item after completion of the accession narrative.

4. Over the next couple of generations Plato peddled a (very abbreviated) version which is largely un-Darian, but Deinon (perhaps) set down a version which, in a strongly Herodotean setting, suddenly reveals knowledge of the name Gaumata.[50] But this distinctively Darian feature is attached to the wrong figure—and the narrative contradicts both Darius and Herodotus on the timing of Bardiya's murder.

5. Finally, two very much later sources which perform the same trick of belatedly producing something apparently redolent of DB.

(a) The Kanishka inscription was (it tells us) written in Greek and then put into Aryan or (on another understanding of the text) records the King's replacement of Greek by Aryan (Bactrian) as an official language, and tells a story which repeatedly locates the King's actions

[50] Plat. *Leg* 695D, *Ep*.332A (no *magus* or impersonation). Deinon: it is no more than a guess that his version is reflected in the distinctive mixture of Herodotean and non-Herodotean features found in Just.1.9–10.

in the first year of his reign. Scholars have been prepared to envisage indirect (perhaps oral) knowledge of DB (Sims-Williams and Cribb 1996; Fussmann 1998).

(b) Somewhat earlier, a second-century AD pseudepigraphic letter of Themistocles refers to bowls and censers 'inscribed with the old Assyrian letters, not the ones Darius recently wrote for the Persians'. This may reflect an idea that Darius invented Old Persian script—an idea that could derive from a reading of DB 70.[51] What the author's ultimate Greek source was is impossible to say; and there is little or no guarantee that the datum about *grammata* reached a Greek environment still attached to knowledge of the Behistun monument as a whole or the full content of its texts. It is worth noting that, whereas the Enthroned King icon from the Persepolis apadana generates reproductions and reflexes in the iconography of objects produced in the western part of the empire,[52] Behistun's Triumphant King appears to have no such resonance. (An image of captives roped together at the neck and with hands tied behind the back found on seals, including one inscribed with the name of Artaxerxes, is sometimes cited in this context. But it is an exception which proves the rule: the Persian figure in these scenes leads the captives by a halter rather than facing them, is sometimes spearing a further adversary, and does not depict the King.)[53] The stimulus for the pseudo-Themistocles story was the inscribed precious metal objects that did circulate within Greek horizons, and the explanation (to the ultimate Greek source) of the fact that different examples bore different types of script will have been oral.

[51] *Letter* 21 (762 Hercher). English translation: Lenardon 1978: 193. Nylander 1968 was the first to exploit this source fully.

[52] Dascyleion seal no.4: Kaptan 1996: 260 (fig. 1), reproduced in Briant 1997: 16 (fig. 2), Stronach 2002: 401 (fig. 9). (A less complete version appears in Miller 1997: pl. 28.) Painting inside a shield on the Alexander Sarcophagus: von Graeve 1987: 137, Briant 1996: 223 (fig. 9a) = Briant 2002: 209 (fig. 14). Pulydamas Base (Olympia): Demandt 1972: pl. xxiii.5. Darius Vase: Demandt 1972: pl. xxiii.6; Koch 1992: 218 (fig. 160), Moreno 2000: 115 (fig. 64). Satrap Sarcophagus (Sidon): Boehmer and Gall 1973: pl. 32.2. Payava sarcophagus: Demargne 1974: pls XXX and 42. Nereid Monument 879: Childs and Demargne 1989: pl. 57.2. Harpy Monument: Demargne 1958: pl. VIII. Louvre seal AO 223559: Koch 1992: 246 (fig. 174), Moorey 2002: 209 (fig. 2). Louvre seal AO 2405: Ward 1910: 338 no.119. Istanbul Arch.Mus. 7501: pelike (unpublished): AM 1975: 115; Miller 1988: 86. Vouni Lekythos 249 (ARV^2 1150 [27]): Schauenburg 1975: pl. 39.3–4. Various mythological scenes exploit the image: see LIMC s.vv. Alexandros (Paris), Busiris, Cepheus, Midas, Priam, Alföldi 1955, Miller 1988, 1995, 2000, DeVries 2000. The audience-scene icon is also reflected in a different format at Persepolis itself on PTS 26 (Schmidt 1957: 28, pl. 8 (no.26); Calmeyer 1977: 193 (fig. 1) = Calmeyer 1989: 52 (fig. 1)) and PTS 55 (Schmidt 1957: 36, pl. 13).

[53] Schmitt 1981: pl. 5 (SA^{3}b), Briant 1996: 227 (fig. 12c) = 2002: 215 (fig. 18c); Briant 1996: 227 (fig. 12b) = 2002: 215 (fig. 18b); PTS 28 = Schmidt 1957: 29, pl. 9.

The same, I think we must conclude, had been true of Greek engagement with DB all along. The contrast between this case and that of the two stelae Herodotus (4.87) says were erected on the Bosporus with Assyrian and Greek inscriptions listing the components of Darius' empire—a plausible evocation of a potentially real monument—is striking. So is the quandary we are in when asked by Herodotus (4.91) to believe in a stela erected on the Tearus in which Darius compared his own excellence and that of the waters of the river. We have no comparable royal inscription, but the King's delighted reaction to a well-watered site rings true, and there is evidence of a cuneiform inscription having once stood at a spot in this general vicinity (Jochmus 1854: 44ff; Unger 1915). When dealing with a real contemporary oriental empire it was *possible* to have comparatively serious reports of royal monumental writing (by contrast with fantastical rationalizations associated with Sesostris),[54] but this simply did not work with objects whose location lay far to the east and whose message was transmitted verbatim beyond the original monumental location, in languages which left Greek consumers at the mercy of the selectivity of oral go-betweens. Whether it would have made much difference if DB had had a different historiographical style, or if Darius and his successors had continued to produce texts which did record specific events in the real politico-military world even to the extent that (for all its symbolic character) DB did, is a question not perhaps as large as Cleopatra's Nose but, in its own way, quite as intriguing.

I do not know that there is much of an intersection between the new and the true in what I have said, and given the density of exposition the reader may be unable immediately to tell. I am probably on safer ground in claiming to have redefined the limits of ignorance—if only my own. But the issues raised—what counts as history, how and why one writes it—are of large importance and constitute significant cultural *differentiae*. As a classicist who developed a visitor's passion for some parts of the world of Assyriology I have for a quarter-century been asking Alan Millard questions to which his response has often properly been that there is no clear answer. In this paper I have offered some answers and some (I hope) proper evasions. Whether I have asked the right questions is another matter.

[54] Hdt. 2.102, 106. See Lloyd 1975/1988: ad loc., West 1985: 298–302, Pritchett 1993: 106–12, 181–82, 248–50. For recent important developments in study of the Karabel monuments see Hawkins 1998.

Bibliography

Ahn, G.
1992 *Religiose Herrscherlegitimation im Achämenidischen Iran* (Leiden).

Alföldi, A.
1955 'Gewaltherrscher und Theaterkönig', in K. Weitzmann, *Late Classical and Mediaeval Studies in Honor of A.M. Friend* (Princeton): 15–55.

Beaulieu, P.A.
1991 'UBARA (EZEN KASKAL)^{ki} = Udannu', *Act.Sum.* 13: 97–109.

Berger, P.R.
1975 'Der Kyros-Zylinder mit dem Zusatzfragment BIN II Nr. 32 und die akkadischen Namen im Danielbuch', *ZA* 64: 192–234.

Bivar, A.D.
1998 'Babylon or Persis? A crux of the Behistun inscription', *IrAnt* 33: 187–93.

Boardman, J.
2000 *Persia and the West* (London).

Boehmer, R.M., and H. von Gall
1973 'Das Felsrelief bei Batas-Herir', *BagM* 14: 65–77.

R. Borger, R.
1982 'Die Chronologie des Darius-Denkmals am Behistun Felsen', *NAWG* Phil.-Hist. Kl.: 105–31.

Briant, P.
1984 'La Perse avant l'Empire', *IrAnt* 19: 71–118.
1990 'Hérodote et la société perse', in *Hérodote et les peuples non-grecs* [Entretiens Hardt XXXV] (Geneva): 69–104.
1996 *Histoire de l'empire Perse* (Paris).
1997 'Bulletin d'histoire achéménide (I)', *Topoi* Suppl.1: 5–127.
2002 *From Cyrus to Alexander: A History of the Persian Empire* (Winona Lake). (English translation, by P.T. Daniels, of Briant 1996, with new introduction and some additional material.)

Brosius, M.
2000 *The Persian Empire from Cyrus II to Artaxerxes I* (LACTOR no.16) (London).

Calmeyer, P.
1977 'Zur Genese altiranischer Motive. V. Synarchie (Korrekturen, Nachträge)', *AMI* 10: 191–95.
1989 'Das Datum der Gründungsinschrift vom Apadana und die Krone der ältesten Bogenschutzen', *REA* 91: 51–59.
1996 'Die Landschaft Kambadene', in W. Kleiss and P. Calmeyer, *Bisutun* (Berlin): 13–14.

Cameron, G.
1960 'The Elamite version of the Bisitun inscriptions', *JCS* 14: 59–68.

Canby, J.V.

1979 'A note on some Susa bricks', *AMI* n.f. 12: 315–20.

Childs, W.A.P., and P. Demargne

1989 *Fouilles de Xanthos* VIII: *Le Monument des Néréides: le décor sculpté* (Paris).

Dandamaev, M.

1994 'The neo-Babylonian *zazakku*', *AOF* 21: 34–40.

Demandt, A.

1972 'Die Ohren des falschen Smerdis', *IrAnt* 9: 94–101.

Demargne, P.

1958 *Fouilles de Xanthos* I: *Les piliers funéraires* (Paris).

1974 *Fouilles de Xanthos* V: *Les tombes-maison, tombes rupestres et sarcophages* (Paris).

K. DeVries

2000 'The nearly other: the Attic vision of Phrygians and Lydians', in B. Cohen (ed.), *Not the Classical Ideal* (Leiden): 338–63.

Di Benedetto, V.

1993 'Dario e Artaphrenes in Aesch. *Pers.* 774–780', *Rivista di Filologia* 121: 257–71.

Fussman, G.

1998 'L'inscription de Rabatak', *JA* 286: 571–651.

Greenfield , J., and B. Porten

1982 *The Bisitun Inscription of Darius the Great: Aramaic Version* [CII I v.1] (London).

Grillot-Susini, F., C. Herrenschmidt and F. Malbrat

1993 'La version elamite de la trilingue de Behistun: une nouvelle lecture', *JA* 281: 19–59.

Handley-Schachler, M.

1998 'The *lan* ritual in the Persepolis Fortification texts', in M. Brosius and A. Kuhrt (eds), *Studies in Persian History: essays in Memory of David M. Lewis* (Leiden): 195–204.

Hawkins, J.D.

1998 'Tarkasnawa King of Mira: "Tarkondemos", Bogazköy sealings and Karabel', *AS* 48: 1–31.

Herrenschmidt, C.

1976 'Désignations de l'Empire perse et concepts politiques de Darius Ier d'après ses inscriptions en vieux-perse', *Studia Iranica* 5: 33–65.

1989 'Le paragraphe 70 de l'inscription de Bisotun', in *Etudes irano-aryennes offertes à Gilbert Lazard* (Paris): 193–208.

Hinz, W.

1968 'Die Entstehung der altpersischen Keilschrift', *AMI* n.f. 1: 95–98.

Hinz, W., and H. Koch

1987 *Elamisches Wörterbuch* (Berlin).

Huyse, P.
1999 'Some further thoughts on the Bisitun monument and the genesis of Old Persian cuneiform script', *BAI* 13: 45–66.

Jacobs, B.
1997 'Ein weitere Kopie des Bisutun-Reliefs? Zu einem Reliefziegel aus Susa', *AMI* n.f. 29: 303–8.

Joannès, F.
1994 'A propos du *zazakku* à l'époque néo-babylonienne', *NABU* 103.

Jochmus, A.
1854 'Notes on a journey into the Balkan or Mount Haemus', *JRGS* 24: 36–85.

Kaptan, D.
1996 'The Great King's audience', in F. Blakolmer *et al.* (eds), *Fremde Zeiten: Festschrift für Jörgen Borchhardt* (Vienna): 259–71.

Kent, R.G.
1953 *Old Persian: Grammar, Texts, Lexicon* (second ed.: New Haven).

Koch, H.
1992 *Es kündet Dareios der König... Vom Leben im persischen Grossreich* (Mainz).

Lambert, S.D.
1993 *The Phratries of Attica* (Ann Arbor).

Lecoq, P.
1997 *Les inscriptions de la Perse achéménide* (Paris).

Lenardon, R.
1978 *The Saga of Themistocles* (London).

Lloyd, A.B.
1975/1988 *Herodotus Book II* (Leiden).
1995 'Herodotus on Egyptian buildings: a test case', in A. Powell (ed.), *The Greek World* (London): 273–300.

Malbran-Labat, F.
1994 *La version akkadienne de l'inscription trilingue de Darius à Behistun* (Rome).
1998 'La trilingue de Behistun et les singularités de la version babylonienne', *Semitica* 48: 61–74.

Mayrhofer, M.
1978 *Supplement zur Sammlung der Altpersischen Inschiften* (Vienna).

Miller, M.C.
1988 'Midas as the Great King in Attic fifth-century vase painting', *AK* 31: 79–89.
1995 'Priam, King of Troy', in J.B. Carter and S.B. Morris (eds), *The Ages of Homer: A Tribute to Emily Townsend Vermeule* (Austin): 449–65.
1997 *Athens and Persian in the Fifth Century* BC*: A Study in Cultural Receptivity* (Cambridge).

Moreno, P.
2000 *Apelle: La Battaglia di Alessandro* (Milan).

Nylander, C.
1968 '*Assyrian gramma*: Remarks on the 21st "Letter of Themistokles"', *Op.Ath.* 14/15: 119–36.

Parker, R.
2002 'A new euphemism for death in a manumission inscription from Chaironeia', *ZPE* 139: 66–68.

Potts, D.T.
1999 *The Archaeology of Elam* (Cambridge).

Pritchett, W.K.
1993 *The Liar School of Herodotos* (Amsterdam).

Ramsay, W.M.
1895–97 *The Cities and Bishoprics of Phrygia* (Oxford).

Root, M.C.
1979 *The King and Kingship in Achaemenid Art* (Leiden).

Sancisi-Weerdenburg, H.
1999 'The Persian Kings and History', in C.S. Kraus (ed.), *The Limits of Historiography* (Leiden): 91–112.

Schauenburg, K.
1975 'ΕΥΡΥΜΕΔΩΝ ΕΙΜΙ', *MDAIA* 90: 97–121.

Schmidt, E.F.
1957 *Persepolis* II (Chicago).

Schmitt, R.
1980 'Zur babylonishcen Version der Bisitun-Inschrift', *AfO* 27: 106–26.
1981 *Altpersische Siegelinschriften* (Vienna).
1990 *Epigraphisch-exegetische Noten zu Dareios' Bisitum-Inschriften* (Vienna).
1991 *The Bisitun Inscription of Darius the Great: Old Persian Text* [CII I i.1] (London).

Seidl, U.
1999 'Ein Monument Darius' I. aus Babylon', *ZA* 89: 101–14.

Sims-Williams, N., and J. Cribb
1996 'A new Bactrian inscription of Kanishka the Great', *SRAA* 4: 75–142.

Stolper, M.W.
1985 *Entrepreneurs and Empire* (Leiden).

Streck, M.
1996 Review of Malbran-Labat 1994, *ZA* 86: 275–84.

Stronach, D.
1990 'On the genesis of the Old Persian cuneiform script', in F. Vallat (ed.), *Contributions à l'histoire de l'Iran: Mélanges offerts à J. Perrot* (Paris): 195–204.
1997a 'Darius at Pasargadae: a neglected source for the history of early Persia', *Topoi* Suppl.1: 351–63.
1997b 'On the interpretation of the Pasargadae inscriptions', in B. Magnusson *et al.* (eds), *Ultra Terminum Vagari: Scritti in onore di Carl Nylander* (Rome): 323–29.

2000 'Of Cyrus, Darius and Alexander: a new look at the "epitaphs" of Cyrus the Great', in R. Dittmann *et al.* (eds), *Variatio Delectat: Iran und der Westen. Gedenkschrift für Peter Calmeyer* (Münster): 681–702.

2002 'Icons of dominion', *IrAnt* 37: 373–402.

Tadmor, H.

1981 'History and ideology in the Assyrian Royal Inscriptions', in F.M. Fales (ed.), *Assyrian Royal Inscriptions: New Horizons* (Rome): 13–34.

Trümpelmann, L.

1967 'Zur Enstehungsgeschichte des Monumentes Dareios' I. von Bisitun', *Arch.Anz.* 82: 281–98

Tuplin, C.J.

1997 'Achaemenid arithmetic', *Topoi* Suppl.1: 365–421.

Unger, E.

1915 'Der Dariusstele am Tearos', *Arch.Anz.*: 3–17.

Vargyas, P.

2000 'Darius and Oroites', *AHB* 14: 155–61.

Vogelsang, W.

1986 'Four short notes on the Bisutum text and monument', *IrAnt* 21: 121–40.

Voigtlander, E.

1978 *The Bisitun Inscription of Darius the Great: Babylonian Version* [CII I ii.1] (London).

von Graeve, V.

1987 'Eine Miszelle zur griechische Malerei', *IstMitt* 37: 131–44.

Ward, W.H.

1910 *The Seal Cylinders of Western Asia* (Washington DC).

West, S.R.

1985 'Herodotus' epigraphical interests', *CQ* n.s. 35: 278–305.

West, S.R., and M.L. West

1991 'Sham Shahs', in M. Flower and M. Toher (eds), *Georgica* (London): 176–88.

Westenholz, J.

2000 'The king, the emperor, and the empire: continuity and discontinuity of royal representation in text and image', in S. Aro and R. Whiting (eds), *Heirs of Assyria* [MELAMMU Symposia I] (Helsinki): 99–125.

Zadok, R.

1977 'Iranians and individuals bearing Iranian names in Achaemenid Babylonia', *IOS* 7: 89–138.

Zawadkzi, S.

1994 'Bardiya, Darius and Babylonian usurpers in the light of the Bisitun inscription and Babylonian sources', *AMI* 27: 127–45.

1995 'Chronology of the reigns of Nebuchadnezzar III and Nebuchadnezzar IV', *NABU* 55.

'HAZAEL, SON OF A NOBODY': SOME REFLECTIONS IN LIGHT OF RECENT STUDY[1]

K. Lawson Younger, Jr.

With the discovery and publication of the fragments of the Tel Dan inscription in 1993 and 1995, scholars were confronted with what appeared to be a new source for the reign of Hazael of Aram-Damascus (Biran and Naveh 1993; 1995). Not many years earlier one of the short 'booty inscriptions' of Hazael was published (Röllig 1988; Bron and Lemaire 1989; Eph'al and Naveh 1989). In 1996, A.K. Grayson published an important critical edition of the inscriptions of Shalmaneser III; and in 2000, S. Yamada published a full-length monograph devoted to the study of Shalmaneser's inscriptions, as well as Peter Hulin's hand copies of some of Shalmaneser's texts including that of a broken statue from Nimrud which contains a passage preserving information about Shalmaneser's 838 BC campaign against Hazael (Yamada 2000a; 2000b). Finally, recent excavations at Tell eṣ-Ṣāfī (Gath) seem to supply evidence of Hazael's activity there (Ehrlich 2002).

All of these publications have re-energized the study of the Aramean king of Damascus, Hazael. But they have also introduced a number of interpretive problems. In particular, due to its fragmentary nature, the Tel Dan inscription has presented a number of challenges to epigraphists and historians. But Hazael's booty inscription also presents a difficulty that interpreters have not always addressed. This essay will investigate and evaluate some of these difficulties in order to clarify the important historical issues.[2]

The Tel Dan inscription

It has been a decade since the initial discovery and publication of the Tel Dan inscription. As of the writing of this article in Autumn 2003, 95 articles in journals or books, and one entire monograph have been devoted to its

[1] It is a great pleasure to offer this study to one of my mentors and friends, Alan Millard, who has done so much to advance the study of the Assyrians, Arameans and Israelites.

[2] For a more comprehensive study of all the issues concerning Hazael, see the still very useful article by Lemaire (1991), although the Tel Dan material was, of course, unknown to him at the time.

discussion. Of these, approximately 37 have been specifically or significantly devoted to the exposition of the phrase in line 9: *bytdwd*. This is truly disproportionate in that this is not the kind of interpretive problem deserving such attention. An elementary application of Ockham's razor deduces that *bytdwd* is a simple metonymy put for the kingdom of Judah.[3]

The inscription is generally dated, on paleographic grounds, to the last quarter of the eighth century BC (Schniedewind 1996: 78; Lemaire 1998: 11). Although it does not preserve the name of its author, a general consensus has emerged that the inscription belongs to Hazael, the king of Aram-Damascus (*c*. 844/843–803/802 BC). This seems to be the best fit historically, since the restoration of '[Jo]rom, son of [Ahab] king of Israel' in lines 7b–8a seems virtually certain (see discussion below).[4]

The Assyrian and biblical texts declare that Hazael was a usurper. But if Hazael was a usurper on the throne of Damascus, and if he was the author of the Tel Dan stela, why does he talk about his 'father' at the beginning of the inscription (*ʾby* is used three times in lines 2, 3, 4)? In a recent article, P. E. Dion argues:

> It is important to realize, in this matter, that our previous sources about the accession of Hazael were not all that clear. In most of the Assyrian documents that usher him onto the historical scene, including the most detailed of those [Calaḫ Bulls—*RIMA* 3: 42–48, A.0.102.8: 1″–27″], his power in Damascus is simply taken for granted, without any hint at his being a usurper. Only one text [Assur Basalt Statue—*RIMA* 3: 118, A.0.102.40: i.25–ii.6], always quoted, calls Hazael a 'son of a nobody', and even this text falls short of saying explicitly that he killed or overthrew his predecessor, the soul of the Qarqar alliance.
>
> On the biblical side, most scholars believe that 2 Kgs. 8:7–15 tells how Hazael murdered his predecessor by smothering him with a pillow, during a visit of the prophet Elisha; but serious doubt has been cast on this interpretation (Lemaire 1991: 95–96). Even if one does not follow Lemaire, it remains that

3. The best recent study addressing *bytdwd* is the thorough study of Couturier 2001. See also Dion's study of the formula *bīt X* (1997: 225–32); and Millard's comments on *bytdwd* (2000b: 166, n. 11). In his recent monograph, G. Athas (2003: 223–24) argues that *bytdwd* is the Aramaic equivalent of Hebrew *ʿyr dwd*; and therefore, *bytdwd* is best understood as a geographical name for Jerusalem; and from this, that 'at the time that the Tel Dan Inscription was written, Jerusalem was a city-state rather than the capital of a much wider regional state'. There is not one bit of evidence that Jerusalem was called *bytdwd*, and the monograph is poorly researched at virtually every point. Forty of the 95 bibliographic items devoted to the Tel Dan inscription are missing from the volume, including the important studies of, to name a few, Couturier, Dietrich, Dion, Emerton, Kottsieper, Lemaire, Lipiński, Müller, Naʾaman, and Naveh (all of which should have been known to Athas).

4. Most scholars accept the placement of the fragments by the *editio princeps* (Biran and Naveh 1995) with perhaps the slight modification proposed by Schniedewind 1996.

the evidence branding Hazael as a usurper is not very convincing, all the more so since it originated in the enemy camp. It may well have developed somewhat belatedly, and for propaganda purposes (Dion 1999: 153–54).

Methodologically, this approach is problematic since it takes the fragmentary and difficult passage in the Tel Dan Stela, which well may be more propagandistic than the other sources, and uses that passage to evaluate clear passages from two different sources. In the case of the Assyrian source, the Assur Basalt Statue (*RIMA* 3: 118, A.0.102.40: i.25–ii.6) states:

Hadad-ezer (Adad-idri) passed away. Hazael, son of a nobody (DUMU *la ma-ma-na*), took the throne. He mustered his numerous troops; (and) he moved against me to do war and battle. I fought with him. I decisively defeated him. I took away from him his walled camp. In order to save his life he ran away. I pursued (him) as far as Damascus, his royal city. I cut down his orchards.

'Son of a nobody' (*mār lā mammāna*) is a term referring to a usurper or upstart. This strongly suggests that Hazael was not the first in line of succession and had seized the throne in an unusual manner (Yamada 2000a: 189). The expression, common in historical documents from Assyria and Babylonia, indicates someone whose father was not a legal member of the major branch of the contemporary royal family, and expresses a value judgment with negative connotations, i.e. 'usurper' or 'an upstart'.[5]

The phrase is used in the Assyrian King List with this nuance. For example, the section devoted to describing the reign of Aššur-dugul states (Grayson 1980–83: 106, §14):

^{m}*Aš-šur-du-gul* DUMU(*mār*) *la ma-ma-na la* EN(*bēl*) GIŠ.GU.ZA(*kussê*) 6 MU.MEŠ LUGAL(*šarru*)-*ta* DÙ-*uš*(*īpuš*)
Aššur-dugul, the son of a nobody, not suitable to the throne,[6] ruled for six years.

While a propagandistic motive in the Assur Basalt Statue is possible, it cannot simply be assumed without some grounds. The fact that the passage is found in the context of a very concise summary of Shalmaneser III's western campaigns (lines i.10b–ii.6) and is otherwise a parallel to the other Hazael passages in Shalmaneser's inscriptions seems to argue against a specific propagandistic motive here. In line 25, the text, in a matter-of-fact fashion, records the death of Hadad-ezer (Adad-idri) (^{md}IŠKUR-*id-ri* KUR-

[5] For the attestation of the term, see Seux 1980–81: 150–52.

[6] Following Yamada 1994: 26, n. 47. He states: 'This phrase clearly expresses a value judgement with negative connotations, as seen in a sentence well attested in omen texts: *lā bēl kussî kussâ iṣabbat* "one who is not suitable to the throne will seize the throne."'

šú e-mi-id)[7] who had been the subject of lines 14–24. It then notes that Hazael seized the throne and that Shalmaneser attacked him. There is no apparent reason to doubt the general veracity of the Assyrian statement that Hazael was the 'son of a nobody', i.e. a usurper.

Even though the biblical text is part of a prophetic tradition concerning the work of Elisha, many critics and commentators have accepted the general historicity of the passage that states that Hazael usurped the throne of Damascus.[8] Further, it is not necessary to accept all the detail of the story in order to recognize a base tradition that Hazael was a usurper. Finally, it is hermeneutically sounder to reconstruct the historical events on the clear claims preserved in two different sources from different parts of the ancient Near East than to reconstruct the historical events on the basis of an interpretation of a fragmentary inscription (an interpretation that may or may not be correct), and then make the two sources fit that reconstruction.

In another recent article, through the aid of computer techniques of image enhancement and matching, W.M. Schniedewind and B. Zuckerman (2001: 88–91) have suggested the reading [*b*]⌜*rqʾl*⌝ . *ʾby* '[Ba]⌜raqʾel⌝, my father'. If their restoration is correct, then this Baraq-El would have been Hazael's father who was king of Damascus before him and whose land the king of Israel invaded (see lines 3–4: *wyʿl . mlky*[*ś*]⁽⁴⁾*rʾl . qdm . bʾrq . ʾby* 'And the king of I[s]rael formerly invaded the land of my father'). But the *resh* and the *qoph* are very doubtful, as also the *beth*. In fact, there is no compelling reason that there must be a proper name preceding *ʾby*.[9] Until another fragment is discovered, it seems best to refrain from accepting this reading.

Lemaire, who accepts that Hazael was a usurper, 'the son of a nobody', suggests that in calling Hadadezer/Adad-idri his father Hazael was following an ancient Near Eastern historiographic tradition: kings of a new dynasty might refer to the previous king as 'father'. He cites for examples Tiglath-pileser III and David, who once calls Saul *ʾābî* 'my father' (1 Sam. 24: 11 [Eng 12]). Thus Lemaire concludes:

> one should not be surprised that Hazael, whose father is not known, could call Hadadezer: 'my father'. It was a traditional way to present oneself as a legitimate successor (Lemaire 1998: 6).

[7] KUR-*šú e-mi-id* / *šadāšu ēmid* 'he disappeared forever', lit. 'he reached his mountain.' The phrase is simply a euphemism for 'to die' and, in and of itself, does not specific whether the death was due to natural or unnatural causes. See *CAD* E 138–47, esp. 140, 1.d.3N.

[8] Noth 1960: 248.

[9] Their speculation, based on this almost entirely restored name Baraq-El, that there was some kind of religious rivalry and tension within Aram-Damascus between the adherents of El versus the adherents of Hadad, makes little sense in that Hazael (an adherent to the 'El-clan') gives his son a name with a Hadad theophoric—'Bar-Hadad, son of Hazael, king of Aram' (see the Zakkur Inscription, line 4).

But there are some difficulties with Lemaire's examples. In the case of David, Saul is not dead and David is attempting to convince Saul that he is not a usurper and is, in fact, a member of Saul's family. In the case of Tiglath-pileser III, matters are complicated by the Assyrian King List which attributes Tiglath-pileser's filiation to his immediate predecessor Aššur-nērārī V,[10] while on two inscribed enamelled bricks, Tiglath-pileser declares that he is the son of Adad- nērārī III.[11] The filiation in the Assyrian King List is most likely wrong. As Yamada[12] has rightly observed this incorrect filiation is not the result of a lack of information (since it is highly unlikely that the editor would not have accurate information for the next to last entry in the King List, who reigned not all that long before this edition [the SDAS list] was written); but rather is probably due to a miscopying of the original on account of the graphic similarity between the two royal names, Adad-nērārī and Aššur-nērārī. Yamada notes: 'When the right half of the IM sign is ignored, ^{d}IM = *Adad* is similar to *Aš-šur* and identical to AN.ŠÁR, the common Sargonid spelling of *Aššur* (the SDAS list is a product of the Sargonid period)'.[13] Therefore it is very likely that the scribe miscopied the original ^{d}IM-*nērārī* as *Aš-šur-nērārī*.

Tiglath-pileser's claim on the enamelled bricks to being the son of Adad-nērārī III, could, of course, be taken literally. As Tadmor (1994: 212–13) points out, Adad-nērārī was young when he ascended the throne in 811, and he died in 783 after a 28-year reign. If Tiglath-pileser was about 50 when he ascended the throne in 745, then he could have been born around the turn of the century. On the other hand, it is quite possible that he was Adad-nērārī's grandson.

However, Tiglath-pileser III's filiation is curiously not indicated in his other inscriptions. Moreover, he substituted the typical royal parentage formula (i.e. 'king X, son of king Y, grandson of king Z') with the phrase *pir'i Bal-til*(BALA.TIL)^{ki} 'precious scion of Baltil', an apparent reference to the oldest part of the city of Assur (Tadmor 1994: 41). Tadmor argues that 'by tracing his descent to the seat of the ancient dynasty, Tiglath-pileser, who obviously was not in the direct line of succession, emphasizes his claim to the throne' (ibid). Consequently, many scholars believe that Tiglath-pileser III deposed his predecessor Aššur-nērārī V in the rebellion of 746 BC and set

[10] Grayson's edition reads: [^{m} ^{g}]^{iš}*Tukul-ti-apil*-É-*šár-ra mār* ^{m}*Aš-šúr-nērārī* 18 MU.MEŠ *šarru$_2$-ta īpuš*^{uš} 'Tiglath-pileser (III) son of Aššur-nērārī (V) ruled for 18 years'. See Grayson 1980–83: 115; Millard 1997: 465.

[11] Tadmor 1994: 212–13; Messerschmidt 1911: 21: Assur 918 and 1559. Tadmor's transliteration reads: (1) *ekal* ^{m}*Tukul-ti-apil*-É-*šár-ra* (2) *šar$_4$ māt Aš-šur apil* ^{m}*Adad*(x)-*nērārī* (ÉRIN.TÁḪ) *šar$_4$ māt Aššur* (3) *ša ki-gal-li ša bīt Aš-šur* 'Palace of Tiglath-pileser (III), king of Assyria, son of Adad-nērārī (III), king of Assyria, from the platform of the temple of Aššur.'

[12] Yamada 1994: 34, n. 78.

[13] Ibid. It is also possible that the scribe accidentally copied Aššur-nērāri from the previous line.

himself on the throne (745 BC).[14] Hence, while complicated, the case of Tiglath-pileser III supports Lemaire's contention regarding the use of the term *ʾby* 'my father' in the Tel Dan stela.

Some scholars believe that there is further evidence of the illegitimacy of Hazael's accession within the Tel Dan inscription itself. In 1995, Biran and Naveh noted that the end of line 4 and the first word of line 5, [*w*]*yhmlk* . *hdd* . *ʾ*[*yty*] [(5)]*ʾnh* '[but] Hadad made me, myself, king', may hint that the succession between Hazael and his predecessor was not natural (1995: 15). Lemaire (1998: 6) reinforces this view arguing:

> Zakkur I, line 3, Panamuwa lines 6–7 and several biblical texts (1 Sam. 8: 22; 15: 11–35; 1 Kgs. 1: 43; 12: 1–20) show clearly that in ancient North-West Semitic historiography, the factitive of *mlk* was generally introduced when the succession was unusual and, somehow, problematic.

Naveh himself has published two articles (1999: 119–20; 2002: 240–41) asserting that in the Hebrew Bible, the *hiphʿil* is used 'in those instances in which the king ascending the throne is not the legitimate heir or in which there is dissension concerning the throne' (2002: 241). He claims: 'It is reasonable to assume that making somebody king (and anointing which was part of the ceremony) was not practiced when the king was the undisputed legitimate heir' (1999: 232*). 'Whenever the legitimate heir ascends the throne, neither *mšḥ* nor *hmlk* is used in the biblical or epigraphic texts' (2002: 241).

While the Zakkur inscription certainly supports this assertion (using the *haphʿel* just like in the Tel Dan stela), the Panamuwa inscription does not. Panamuwa is the legitimate heir being restored by the king of Assyria. While the *haphʿel* of *mlk* in the Tel Dan stela might indicate some irregularity in the accession, it does not prove that Hazael was illegitimate.[15] His status as a usurper comes from the Assyrian and biblical sources discussed above.

Lines 7–9a present a number of challenges to interpreters. Table 1 lists some of the more important suggested restorations and translations.

Biran and Naveh (1995: 9) correctly observe: 'The only king, either of Israel or Judah, whose name ends with *resh* and *mem* is Jehoram'. In this light, the restoration *br* . [*ʾḥʾb*] 'son of [Ahab]' seems very likely. Schniedewind (1996: 80) points out that the Arameans would most likely spell the name as Joram (*ywrm*), according to the northern Hebrew orthography, without the *he* found in the Judahite dialect (*yhwrm*).[16]

[14] For example, Tadmor 1981: 25–30. See the Eponym Chronicle for years 746–745 (Millard 1994: 43, 59).

[15] The argument based on the usage of the *hiphʿil* in the Hebrew Bible would be more convincing if the *hiphʿil* were used in every instance where an usurpation takes place; but it is not (e.g. Baasha, Athaliah, Shallum, Menahem, Pekah, etc.).

[16] This is further supported by the analogy of spelling of the name of Joash/Jehoash

Table 1. *Suggested Restorations and Translations*

Scholar	Restoration and translation
Biran and Naveh 1995: 12–13	*[qtlt .ʾyt . yhw]rm . br . [ʾḥʾb] mlk . yśrʾl .* *wqtl[t . ʾyt . ʾḥz]yhw . br [. yhwrm . ml]k . bytdwd* [I killed Jeho]ram son of [Ahab] king of Israel, and [I] killed [Ahaz]iahu son of [Jehoram kin]g of the House of David
Schniedewind 1996: 77	*[wqtlt . ʾyt . yw]rm . br . ʾ[ḥʾb] mlk . yśrʾl .* *wqtl[t . ʾyt . ʾḥz]yhw . br [. ywrm . ml]k . bytdwd* [And I killed Jo]ram, son of A[hab,] king of Israel, and [I] killed [Ahazi]yahu, son of [Joram, kin]g of the House of David
Lemaire 1998: 4	*[qtlt . ʾyt . yw]rm . br . [ʾḥʾb] mlk . yśrʾl .* *wqtl[t . ʾyt . ʾḥz]yhw . br [. ywrm . ml]k . bytdwd* [I killed Jo]ram son of A[hab] king of Israel, and I killed [Achaz]yahu son of [Joram, kin]g of the House of David
Kottsieper 1998: 478	*[wʾqtl . ʾyt . yw]rm . br . [ʾḥʾb] mlk . yśrʾl .* *wqtl[t . ʾyt . ʾḥz]yhw . br [. ywrm . ml]k . bytdwd* [Dann tötete ich Jo]ram, den Sohn [Ahabs], den König von Israel. Und ich töte[te Ahas]jahu, den Sohn [Jorams, den Kön]ig vom Haus Davids.
Dion 1999: 148–49	*[wʾky . ʾyt . yw]rm . br . [ʾḥʾb] mlk . yśrʾl .* *wqt?l[qtlh .ʿbdh] . yhw . br [. nmšy .]* *[wyh]k . bytdwd* and [I struck Jo]ram, son of [Ahab,] king of Israel; and [his servant] Jehu, son of [Nimshi], killed [him]; [and walk]ed away the House of David.
Millard 2000b: 162 and n. 10	*[ ]rm . br .[ ] mlk . . yśrʾl .* *wqtl[ ]yhw . br [.]* *[wʾhp]k . bytdwd* [ ]rm son of [ ] king of Israel and kill[ed]yahu son of [ ] [I overthr]ew the house of David.

Scholar	Restoration and translation
Rainey 2003	[*wqtyl .yhw*]*rm . br .* [*ʾḥʾb*] *mlk . yśrʾl .* *wqty*[*l .ʾḥz*]*yhw . br* [*. yhwrm . ml*]*k . bytdwd* [so that then was killed Jo]ram son of [Ahab] king of Israel, and [was] killed [Ahazi]yahu son of [Joram kin]g of the House of David [*wqtlw .yhw*]*rm . br .* [*ʾḥʾb*] *mlk . yśrʾl .* *wqtl*[*w .ʾḥz*]*yhw . br* [*. yhwrm . ml*]*k . bytdwd* [so that then they killed Jo]ram son of [Ahab] king of Israel, and [they] killed [Ahazi]yahu son of [Joram kin]g of the House of David

The beginning of the sentence, however, is more difficult. As can be seen in Table 1 above, most scholars restore some form of the verb *qtl*, although there may be a problem with there being enough room for a form of this verb. As a reasonable alternative, Dion (1999: 148) has proposed restoring [*wʾky*]. Thus the restoration and translation of this sentence would be either: [*qtlt . ʾyt . yw*]*rm . br .* [*ʾḥʾb*] ⁽⁸⁾*mlk . yśrʾl* '[I killed Jo]ram, son of [Ahab], king of Israel', or [*wʾky . ʾyt . yw*]*rm . br .* [*ʾḥʾb*] ⁽⁸⁾ *mlk . yśrʾl* '[And I struck Jo]ram, son of [Ahab], king of Israel'. The former seems preferable.[17]

Lines 8–9a present perhaps some of the greatest difficulties in the inscription. The first word appears to be *w*⌜*qtl*⌝[ ]. A common restoration has been: *w*⌜*qtl*⌝[*t . ʾyt . ʾḥz.*]yhw . *br* [*. yw(h)rm . ml*]⁽⁹⁾*k . bytdwd* 'and I killed Ahaziah, son of Je(ho)ram, king of Beth-David' (Biran and Naveh 1995: 12–13; Schniedewind 1996: 77; Lemaire 1998: 4; Kottsieper 1998: 478). While the restoration of the verbal form as a first person common singular makes logical sense in light of the clear reading of *wʾqtl* in line 6, it is not, of course, certain. Recently, Rainey (2003) has suggested that the indeterminate third person plural *wqtl*[*w*] '[they] killed' may be the correct restoration.[18]

(*ywʾš/yhwʾš*) in Neo-Assyrian without the *h* being represented: ᵐ*Iu-ʾa-su* in Adad-nērārī III's Tell al-Rimah Stela (*RIMA* 3: 211, line 8).

[17] Since the next verbal form in line 8 is a *waw* plus suffix conjugation (*wqtl*), it is most likely that the form in line 7 is a simple suffix conjugation form (*qtl*). In the Hebrew Bible, in a narrative context, a *waw* plus prefix conjugation (*wyqtl*) followed by a *waw* plus suffix conjugation (*wqtl*) only occurs in 1 Sam. 1: 4 where the first verbal form is in a subordinate clause to the second verbal form. Thus a suffix conjugation (*qtl*) followed by a *waw* plus suffix conjugation (*wqtl*) used to coordinate the actions is most likely.

[18] A second suggestion made by Rainey to read *wqtyl*, while syntactically possible, seems unlikely since there does not appear to be a *yod* after the *taw* and before the *lamed*. I would like to thank Professor Rainey for sharing an earlier version of this article with me.

This restoration is, of course, possible since the suffix to *wqtl* is unfortunately not preserved. However, the flow of the narrative in this part of the inscription would seem to necessitate a first person verbal form.

But there are two other problems with the common restoration as pointed out by Dion: (1) the spelling of Ahaziah: one would expect a northern spelling *ʾḥzyw* without the *he*, as with Joram (*ywrm*) above; (2) there is a grammatical problem with *mlk bytdwd*. Only Millard and Dion have noted the grammatical problem with the restoration of [*ml*]*k bytdwd*. Millard (2000b: 166, n. 9) states:

> A restoration '[Jeho]ram son of [Ahab] king of Israel and killed [Ahaz]iah son of [Jehoram kin]g of Beth-David' is attractive historically (Kitchen 1997: 32–34), although 2 Kgs. 9: 14–28 names Jehu as the killer and the expression 'king of the House of PN' has grammatical problems. Possibly Hadad was the subject here, for the first person ending of the verb is not preserved. The number of missing letters is impossible to calculate with certainty, for, even if only one is to be restored at the end of the third line, there is no proof that the stele was symmetrical, or that the lines were of equal length.

Instead of reading [*ml*]*k bytdwd*, Millard suggests a restoration: [*wʾhp*]*k*, 'and I overthrew' (2000b: 166, n. 10). He notes the usage in Sefire IC 19, 21 (*ʾhpk*) (see Fitzmyer 1995: 54) and 2 Sam. 10: 3 (*wlhpkh* 'and to overthrow it [the city of Rabbath-Ammon]').

Dion is more specific about the problem:

> In Old Aramaic as in Hebrew and other Northwest Semitic languages, *mlk* never is followed by 'the house of So-and-so', and the rule is the same in the Assyrian inscriptions when they refer to smaller neighbours and vassals, in contrast, say to Ambaris, King of Tabal (Luckenbill 1927: §§ 24–25). In biblical Hebrew and in Ammonite inscriptions, *mlk bny ʿmn*, for instance, is very well documented; but one never encounters *mlk byt ʿmn*. In Aramaic, the normal pattern is represented by phrases like *mlk yśrʾl* in the Dan Stele, or *mlk ʾrpd* in the Sefire inscriptions. The kingdom of Arpad could be called *byt gš* as the kingdom of Judah is called *bytdwd*; but one never finds *mlk byt gš* (Dion 1999: 152).

Dion (1999: 148) proposes the reading: *wqtl* [*qtlh . ʿbdh* .] *yhw . br* [*nmšy* .] [*wyh*]*k bytdwd* – 'and [his servant] Jehu, son of [Nimshi], killed him; [and walked away] the House of David'.

As seen in this restoration, Dion's solution to the spelling of Ahaziah is to suggest reading the name, not as Ahaziah, but as Jehu. But there are two problems with this. First, the name Jehu is consistently spelled *yhwʾ* in the Hebrew Bible. There is always an *aleph* at the end of the name; it is never spelled: *yhw*. Second, in the Neo-Assyrian spelling, it is important to note that the name of Jehu is consistently spelled: ^{m}*Ia-ú-a* (Calaḫ Bulls, Kurbaʾil Statue, and Black Obelisk).[19] Thus the final *aleph* is preserved in the Assyrian writing of the name. We could rightly expect this to be the case in the Aramaic spelling of the name too.

It is not impossible that the scribe of the Tel Dan Stela simply chose to use the southern spelling of *ʾḥzyhw*, if the reference is to the king of Judah. Also there is no attestation of spelling the name as *ʾḥzyw* in biblical or extra-biblical texts (whether in reference to the northern or southern kings who bore this name or anyone else). The attestations of the name in Neo-Assyrian evince the spelling *ʾḥzyhw* – ^{m}*ạ-zi-iá-a-u* and ^{m}*ạ-zi-i[a-a-u]*.[20]

Concerning the grammatical problem with the restoration *[ml]k bytdwd*, there is one example of *mlk* before *byt* in the Hebrew Bible. Interestingly, it is found in a statement made by the counselors of Ben-Hadad of Aram-Damascus in 1 Kgs. 20: 31a:

> שָׁמַעְנוּ כִּי מַלְכֵי בֵּית יִשְׂרָאֵל כִּי־מַלְכֵי חֶסֶד הֵם
> ‘we have heard that the kings of the house of Israel are merciful kings’.

Although in this context *mlk* is a plural construct, there is no reason it could not be used as a singular in a construct chain by *byt* X. Thus there is a possibility that the inscription originally read *mlk bytdwd*, and that further evidence in support of this reading may come forth in the future. Such a restoration has great appeal because of the resultant parallel structure:

> I killed A, son of B, king of Israel;
> and I killed X, son of Y, king of Beth-David (Judah).

Nevertheless, two facts are important to remember: (1) *mlk* is not the preserved reading (only a *kaph* is preserved), and (2) the evidence argues strongly that one does not normally find the construction *mlk byt X*. Hence one should be cautious in positing the restoration: *[ml]k bytdwd*. In light of these points, Millard’s suggestion may be preferable: *[wʾhp]k bytdwd*, ‘[and I overthr]ew Beth-David (Judah)’. Such a restoration certainly fits the historical context since the death of Ahaziah of Judah threw the country into chaos with Athaliah seizing power. Consequently, it seems best to read the two sentences: *w⌜qtl⌝[t . ʾyt . ʾḥz]yhw . br [ywrm] [wʾhp]*$^{(9)}$*k . bytdwd* ‘And [I] ⌜killed⌝ [Ahaziah], the son of [Joram, and overthr]ew Beth-David (Judah)’.

19 *RIMA* 3: 60 (29); *RIMA* 3: 149; and *RIMA* 3: 54 (iv.11) respectively. See Brinkman and Schwemer 2000. The only exception is the Marble Slab where it is spelled ^{m}*Ia-a-ú* due to scribal error (*RIMA* 3: 48, 26′′).

20 Selz 1998. In the Hebrew Bible the name is most often spelled אֲחַזְיָהוּ and occasionally אֲחַזְיָה.

Since the author of the stela (Hazael) appears to claim '[and I killed Jo]ram, son of [Ahab], king of Israel ...', there seems to be a contradiction to 2 Kgs. 9 which narrates Jehu's murder of both Joram of Israel and Ahaziah of Judah. A number of scholars have attempted to explain this by appealing to such claims by kings of the ancient Near East, in particular a passage in Shalmaneser III's inscriptions that describes the killing of a certain Giammu. Thus Lemaire (1998: 10–11) notes:

> One should note here, after B. Halpern and W. H. Schniedewind, that we have a very interesting parallel double claim in contemporary Assyrian royal inscriptions. In the Kurkh Monolith again, it is said that nobles, 'with their own weapons', killed Giammu, their lord (on the Baliḫ), but in the Marmorplatte, about fifteen years later, Shalmaneser III claims to have killed Giammu himself. This parallel gives us another hint that Hazael is boasting here and that the Dan stela was probably not engraved immediately after 841 but several years later, at least late enough in Hazael's reign, when he controlled Israel, Judah and most of the Transeuphrates.

But scholars have not paid close enough attention to the cuneiform texts.[21] Table 2 shows all the texts of Shalmaneser III which contain the Giammu episode and their precise wording concerning his death.

Michel's edition of Shalmaneser's Marble Slab inscription reads:

> ᴵ*gi-am-mu* ⁽¹⁵⁾*bēl āli-šú-nu adūk*
> 'Giammu ⁽¹⁵⁾ihren Stadtherrn tötete ich' (Michel 1954: 32–33, ii.14b-15a)

However, Grayson's edition of this text reads:

> ᵐ*gi-am-mu* ⁽¹⁵⁾EN URU-*šú-nu* GAZ
> 'They killed Giammu, their city ruler' (*RIMA* 3: 52; A.0.102.10, ii.14b–15a)

Michel normalized the logogram GAZ as *adūk*, believing that the context demanded a first common singular verb form. Michel's edition is the one that Lemaire, Halpern and Schniedewind have used. But W. Schramm (1973: 77) noted in his study that GAZ in line ii.15 should be understood as *idūkū* on the basis of comparison with the Black Obelisk (line 55). To this, one can now also add the text of the Broken Kalḫu Stone Statue (828–827 BC).[22] The reading is clear in P. Hulin's copy published by Yamada:[23]

[21] At this point, N. Na'aman's explanation is unnecessary. He argues that the Giammu episode was an insignificant, marginal episode in Shalmaneser's inscriptions, while this dual killing in the Tel Dan inscription is central. Therefore, since the Tel Dan inscription is closer in time to the events, it is more reliable than the 'prophetic narrative'. 'Hazael's contemporary inscription should be accorded primacy over the biblical prophetic narrative' (2000: 104).

[22] See *RIMA* 3: 75, A.0.102.16, 29a.

[23] Yamada 2000b: 77, line 29 of transcription.

Table 2. *Texts Describing the Death of Giammu*

	RIMA 3	Text	Translation
Kurkh Monolith (853–852 BC)	A.0.102.2 (ii.79b–80a)	*ina* GIŠ.TUKUL *ra-ma-ni-šú-nu* ^{m}*gi-am-mu* EN-*šú-nu i-du-ku*	'With their own weapons they killed Giammu, their lord.'
Annals: Assur Clay Tablets (842 BC)	A.0.102.6 (ii.21b)	^{m}*gi-am-mu* EN URU-*šú-nu i-du-ku*	'They killed Giammu, the lord of their city.'
Bulls from Kalḫu (841 BC)	A.0.102.8 (13b)	^{m}*gi-am-mu* E[N *ālīšunu idūkū*]	'[They killed] Giammu, [the lo]rd [of their city].'
Marble Slab (839 BC)	A.0.102.10 (ii.14b-15a)	^{m}*gi-am-mu* EN URU-*šú-nu* GAZ	'They killed Giammu, the lord of their city.'
Black Obelisk (828–827 BC)	A.0.102.14 (55)	^{m}*gi-am-mu* EN URU-*šú-nu* GAZ-*ku*	'They killed Giammu, the lord of their city.'
Broken Kalḫu Stone Statue (828–827 BC)	A.0.102.16 (29a)	^{m}*gi-am-mu* EN URU-*šú-nu* GAZ-*ku*	'They killed Giammu, the lord of their city.'

> (29)^{m}*gi-am-mu* EN URU-*šú-nu* GAZ-*ku*
> 'They killed Giammu, their city ruler'.

Thus the Marble Slab's reading is not *adūk* 'I killed' but *idūkū* 'they killed'. Therefore this text from Shalmaneser III does not support the contention that Shalmaneser claims to have killed Giammu as well as stating that the citizens killed him.

This does not mean, however, that double claims are not found in ancient Near Eastern texts. Perhaps a better example can be seen in the claims of 2 Kgs. 15: 30 and the inscriptions of Tiglath-pileser III concerning the death of Pekah and the accession of Hoshea.

2 Kgs. 15: 30 states:

> וַיִּקְשָׁר־קֶשֶׁר הוֹשֵׁעַ בֶּן־אֵלָה עַל־פֶּקַח בֶּן־רְמַלְיָהוּ וַיַּכֵּהוּ וַיְמִיתֵהוּ וַיִּמְלֹךְ תַּחְתָּיו
> Then Hoshea son of Elah made a conspiracy against Pekah son of Remaliah, attacked him, and killed him; he reigned in place of him.

Tiglath-pileser III states (Summary Inscription 4, lines 17′b-18′a) (Tadmor 1994: 141):[24]

[24] See also Summary Inscription 9:r.10–11 and Summary Inscription 13:18′ (Tadmor 1994:188–89 and 202–3).

m*Pa-qa̯-ḫ̯a* LUGAL(*šarru*)-*śú-nu* [...]-*du*-x_1-x_2-*ma*
m*A-ú-si-ʾi* (18′) [*a-na* LUGAL(*šarru*)-*ti i*]-*na* UGU(*muḫ̯ḫ̯i*)-*šú-nu áš-kun*
[I/they killed] Pekah, their king, and
I installed Hoshea [as king] over them.

The restoration of the verb describing Pekah's fate is uncertain. The possible restorations include: [*i*]-*du*-[*ku-ma*] 'they killed' or [*a*]-*du*-[*uk-ma*] 'I killed' (Tadmor 1994: 141, n. 17′). But the first person singular verb *aškun* clearly indicates Tiglath-pileser's claim of involvement in the events that brought Hoshea to the throne in Israel. Similarly, Hazael could be claiming a role in the removal of the Israelite king Joram that brought Jehu to the throne.

Hazael's booty inscriptions

There are four very short booty inscriptions from Hazael's reign. The first two contain duplicate texts engraved on bronze horse trappings. Both of these were discovered in Greek temples. They were probably looted from somewhere in Syria, perhaps the temple of Hadad in Damascus and passed through several hands to Greece. The third and fourth inscriptions are fragmentary and incised on ivory.

Inscription 1

This is a horse's nose-piece in the form of a trapezoidal bronze plaque cast with figures in relief. It was excavated in the Hera temple at Samos in 1984 (Kyrieleis 1988). It contains one line of Aramaic letters incised in the field. The text of this bronze piece established the reading of number 2, since they are, in fact, duplicates.

Inscription 2

This is a bronze horse's cheek piece which was discovered years earlier in the area of the temple of Apollo Daphnephoros in Eretria, Euboea (see Charbonnet 1986). The established reading of the text of inscriptions 1–2 reads:[25]

zy ntn hdd lmrʾn ḥzʾl mn ʿmq bšnt ʿdh mrʾn nhr

[25] Röllig (1988: 62) read the inscription: *zy ntn hdr lmrʾn ḥzʾl mn ʿmq bšn tʿrh mrʾn nhr* '(Das ist es) was HDR gab unserem Herrn Haza'el von der Ebene von Basan. "Stirnbedeckung" unseres erhabenen Herrn'. Röllig understood HDR as the name of the one dedicating the object to Hazael.

The translation of this reading, however, presents three difficulties for interpreters. First, some interpreters have suggested that *hdd* is not the deity Hadad, but a personal name. For example, Bron and Lemaire (1989: 38) translate the text 'Ce qu'a donné Hadad à notre seigneur Hazaël, depuis ʿUmq, dans l'année où notre seigneur a traversé le fleuve', and argue that *hdd* is the name of the dedicator of the object to Hazael (i.e. the divine name is used as a hypocoristicon, cf. the Edomite prince and king[26] in Gen. 36: 35–36 [= 1 Chr. 1: 46–47]; 1 Kgs. 11: 14–22). They speculate that this Hadad may have been king of ʿUmq in the latter part of the 9th century BC (1989: 43). Naʾaman (1995: 383) translates 'That which Hadad gave our lord Hazael from ʿAmqi in the year that our lord crossed the River'. Likewise, he argues that Hadad is a personal name of one of the 'officers or dignitaries in the court of Hazael, who offered gifts to their lord on the occasion of his victorious campaigns.'

While Ephʿal and Naveh (1989: 193) translate the text similarly ('That which Hadad gave our lord Hazael from ʿUmqi in the year that our lord crossed the river'), they feel that, while Hadad could be a personal name, it is more probable that it is the divine name. They argue that 'in Old Aramaic Hadad should first of all be considered as a divine name' (1989: 194). 'As the national deity played an important role in wars fought by the kings in antiquity (both in the Bible and in ancient Near Eastern sources), it appears that booty taken by Hazael from ʿUmqi was considered as a gift of Hadad.' Two biblical passages illustrate that booty from war was considered a gift from the deity: Deut. 20: 14 and 1 Sam. 30: 22–23.

Naʾaman, however, argues against this understanding of the inscription on the basis of genre. He sees this text involving the dedication of an object to a deity (Naʾaman 1995: 383). Thus he feels that 'Ephʿal and Naveh failed to appreciate properly the type of the inscription and their interpretation must therefore be abandoned'. Naʾaman is quite correct that this is a votive text, but as Millard has pointed out such booty objects were often selected and then inscribed as votive offerings in accordance with the common practice of giving the deity part of the spoils of war (Gen. 14: 20; Num. 31: 25–54; 1 Chr. 18: 11) (Millard 2000c: 162). He sums it up this way:

> '... it is preferable at present to treat them (the bronze duplicates) as celebratory notices, marking booty as the gift of the god Hadad to Hazael following an incursion across the Orontes into Umq' (Millard 1993: 176*)

Thus on this type of booty object, the inscription would function as a registration of its origin similar, for example, to the Black Stone Cylinder inscription of Shalmaneser III (*COS* 2.271).

[26] Lemaire feels that the name is Aramaic, not Edomite. See Lemaire 1988.

A recent and independent study by Amadasi Guzzo (1996) greatly reinforces Millard's conclusion. She notes that in theory a human named Hadad could have given the harness to Hazael. But, on the basis of a thorough investigation of Old Aramaic dedicatory inscriptions, she observes that if this were the case, the subject would have had a title or at least a patronym (1996: 331–34). Moreover, the verb *ntn* is not used in Old Aramaic for a person dedicating an object whether to another human or to a deity (rather it is used of deities granting things to humans), and the appellation 'our lord' (*mr'n*) is wrong, if a vassal king is donating the harness to Hazael (it should be 'my lord' or 'his lord', i.e. a singular suffix, not a plural suffix) (1996: 334–36). She concludes, therefore, that Hadad must refer to the deity and that the inscription is a type of label, tag or registration (1996: 336).

Concerning Bron and Lemaire's proposal that Hadad was the name of a ruler of ʿUmq during the latter part of the 9th century BC, this seems very unlikely since the known rulers of Patina during the 9th and 8th were Neo-Hittite (Hawkins 2000). Moreover, the probability that there was an Aramean dynasty between Sasi (829 BC) and Tutamuwa (738 BC) that had a king with an Aramaic personal name 'Hadad' reduced to the sole theophoric element is very low (Lipiński 2000: 388, n. 222), especially since the archaeological evidence points to Neo-Hittite cultural continuity until the campaign of Tiglath-pileser III in 738 BC (Harrison 2001). Therefore, it is most likely that *hdd* refers to the deity Hadad, whom Hazael credited with making him king and going before him in battle in the lines 4b-5a of the Tel Dan Inscription.

The second difficulty for interpreters has been the geographic identification of *ʿmq*. While most scholars have understood this to be a reference to the state of ʿUmq/Unqi/Patina, Na'aman (1995: 381–94) understands *ʿmq* as Amqi, a geographic name for Bīt Reḥob. However, Lipiński (2000: 389, n. 227) disagrees stating: 'There is not the slightest evidence that ʿAmqi was a geographical name for Bēt-Reḥob, and the construction *ntn* - subject - *l* + complement - *mn* + complement perfectly corresponds to the use of *mn* in connection with verbal forms indicating acquisition and related concepts'.

The third difficulty has been the interpretation of the referent of *nhr* 'the river'.[27] Dion (1997) and other scholars understand the reference to be to the Euphrates and reconstruct a historical context in which Hazael crosses the Euphrates to take advantage of Assyrian weakness in the last days of Shalmaneser III. 'The river' is understood to be the Euphrates in many biblical and cuneiform texts. Nevertheless, in conjunction with *ʿmq*, there is a high probability that *nhr* here denotes the Orontes River (see Millard 1993:

[27] A related question is whether the clause *bšnt ʿdh mr'n nhr* constitutes a 'year name.' See the discussion of Harrak 1992; and esp. Amadasi Guzzo (1996: 334–36) who concludes: 'l'expression *bšnt* + complément de spécification était un formulaire de type historiographique plus répandu qu'on ne le supposait et qu'il n'était pas employé seulement à Damas' (contra Bron and Lemaire 1989: 41).

175*–76*; Amadasi Guzzo 1996: 334). Lipiński notes concerning this 'crossing of the river' by Hazael:

> This river might be the Euphrates, but the mention of ʿUmq rather suggests a crossing of the Orontes. The word *nāru*, 'river', often occurs in Assyrian correspondence without any qualification and may designate any river, according to various contexts. Also in Hebrew 'the river' must be identified sometimes with the Jordan, as in Numb. 22, 5. Therefore, there is no stringent reason why *nhr* should be the Euphrates in Hazael's inscriptions (2000: 389).

Y. Ikeda (1999: 291) dates this campaign of Hazael against Unqi (Patina) some time after the Assyrian intervention led by Dayān-Aššur in 829 BC.

Inscription 3

This is a fragmentary ivory plaque discovered in 1928 at Arslan Tash, ancient Hadatu, that some scholars believe to be from the edge of a bed. Winter (1981: 123) suggests that it may have been carried to the Arslan Tash as booty by Shamshi-ilu after the capture of Damascus in 773 BC. From the time of the inscription's discovery, three fragments have been attributed to it, with the second and third obviously joining one another. The first fragment may not belong to the beginning of the inscription, but to its end (since Puech 1981, most scholars have understood this order for the fragments). Only the upper half of the first two letters of the second fragment are preserved. Thus the beginning of the inscription is very uncertain. Nevertheless, an array of suggested restorations have been given, none of which is compelling. In this light, the preserved part of the inscription reads:

> [ ]?? *ʿmʾ* . *l//mrʾn* . *ḥzʾl* . *bšnt* //[.]*zt* . *ḥ*[…?][28]

The two partially preserved letters before the term *ʿmʾ* have been read as *br* ('son'), [*q*]*rb* ('offered') or [*h*]*dd* ('Hadad') (*KAI* #232; *SSI* 2: 4–5; Puech 1981; Bron and Lemaire 1989: 37; Naʾaman 1995: 382–83; Lipiński 2000: 388).[29] The term *ʿmʾ* has been often understood as a personal name, ʿAmma, although some scholars have seen it as the noun 'people' (e.g. Millard 2000c: 163). Lipiński (2000: 388) is unique in understanding it as a toponym: ʿImma. The middle of the inscription clearly reads: *l//mrʾn* . *ḥzʾl* . *bšnt* 'to our lord Hazael in the year'. In recent years, the restoration of [*ʾḥ*]*zt* has been proposed by a number of scholars, but the restoration of the geographic term following it is very difficult since only one letter is preserved: *ḥ*[…?]. Puech

[28] The // represent the division points between the fragments.

[29] Perhaps the two words *br* and *ʿmʾ* should be read as one: *brʿmʾ*, a proper name Bir-ammâ (*PNA* 1/1: 345).

(1981) restores *ḥ*[*wrn*?] 'Ha[wran?]'. But Bron and Lemaire (1989: 37)[30] reject Puech's idea of an annexation of Hauran, arguing that [*ʾḥ*]*zt* speaks of the capture of a city (cf. Mesha 11, 14, 15–16, 20) and that one could restore *ḥ*[*sr*] 'Ḥ[azor]', *ḥ*[*mt*] 'Ḥ[amath]', *ḥ*[*zrk*] 'Ḥ[azrak]', or *ḥ*[*zz*] 'Ḥ[azazu]'. Without the discovery of another fragment the restoration must remain uncertain. Thus, due to its fragmentary nature and highly uncertain readings, this booty inscription of Hazael offers very little for historical reconstruction.

Inscription 4

This is a very fragmentary ivory strip discovered at Kalḫu (Nimrud)[31] that provides little in the way of historical information (Millard 1966: 598; Röllig 1974 2: 37–64, esp. 48, number 6; Lemaire 1991: 92; Millard 2000c: 163). It reads:

> [*mr*]*ʾn ḥzʾl*
> [our lor]d Hazael.

The broken statue from Nimrud

In his critical edition of 1996, A. K. Grayson published two texts that added information concerning Shalmaneser III's campaign against Hazael in 838 BC. In the case of the first text, the Assur Stone Slab (*RIMA* 3.13, pp. 61–62) had not been published before, although E. Weidner may have mistakenly used part of it as a variant of a text of Shalmaneser I. In the case of the second, the Broken Statue from Nimrud (*RIMA* 3.16, pp. 72–84) had been published before by Laessøe (1959), but Grayson's edition of the inscription was based on Peter Hulin's unpublished copy and transliteration that deciphered much more than Laessøe's work. In 2000, S. Yamada published Hulin's hand copies (Yamada 2000b), as well as a monograph that discusses all these texts concerning Shalmaneser's 838 campaign.

Before these publications, the only text which gave any information about this campaign was Shalmaneser's Black Obelisk (*RIMA* 3.14, lines 102b–104a) which rather simply states:

> In my twenty-first year (*palû*), I crossed the Euphrates for the twenty-first time. I marched to the cities of Hazael of Damascus. I captured four of his important cities (*māḫāzīšu*). I received the tribute of the Tyrians, the Sidonians, and the Byblians.

[30] See also Ephʿal and Naveh (1989: 197, n. 24)

[31] More precisely Fort Shalmaneser room T 10. See Oates and Oates 2001: 181.

But the Eponym Chronicle hinted at more. It records the destination for 838 as *a-na* KUR ⸢*ma*⸣-⸢*la*⸣*ḫ-i* 'to Malaḫi', (Millard 1994: 29; Reade 1978: 254), and for 837 as *a-na* KUR *da-na-bi* 'to Danabi' (Millard 1994: 29). Since both toponyms are cities that belonged to Aram-Damascus, it appears that the 21st *palû* account of the Annals conflates the incidents of the two successive years into a single account (Yamada 2000a: 206).

The Broken Statue from Nimrud (*RIMA* 3.16: 152′–162′a) preserves the names of two of the four cities which happen also to be the two toponyms in the Eponym Chronicle.

> [In] my [twenty-first regnal ye]ar, [I crossed] the Euphrates [for the twenty-first time]. I received the [trib]ute of all the kings of the [land of Ḫat]ti. I departed from [the land of Ḫatti?]. I took the route (along) the [Leba]non, trave[rsed] Mt. Saniru (and) I descended to the cities [of] Hazael of Damascus. The cities [...] feared (and) they took to the difficult mountains. I conquered the fortified cities of Ya[...], [...], Danabu, Malaḫa, by means of [mine, battering]-rams and towers. I defeated and plun[dered] them. The [cit]ies I razed, I destroyed, I burned with fire.
>
> Ba'il (*ba-a'-il*) of G/Q/Z[i-x-r]a seized my feet. I received his tribute. I placed my royal image in the temple in Laruba (URU *la-ru-ba*), his fortified city.
>
> Moreover, I received the tribute of the Tyrians, the Sidonians and the Byblians. I went as far as the land of Muṣuruna (KUR *mu-ṣu-ru-na*).[32]

Unfortunately, the names of the first and second cities are not preserved. The locations of the two preserved city names Danabu and Malaḫa are uncertain. Scholars have generally suggested possible identifications in the area around Damascus or the Hauran area. The city of Danabu has been identified with the modern town of Sedanayā/Ṣeidnāyā (20–30 km north of Damascus) (Pitard 1987: 150; Sader 1987: 265–66).[33] Another suggestion has been to identify it with Duneibeh/Dhunaybah (in the region of Nawa, i.e. Bashan) (Dion 1997: 198, n. 120; Sader 1987: 265–66; Lemaire 1991: 100; Röllig 1988: 73; Na'aman 2002: 205). A different proposal has recently been given locating the site in the Beqa valley at Ḏunaiba (modern) (52 km east of Damascus) (Parpola and Porter 2001: 8, map 8).

The city of Malaḫa is also mentioned in the Black Stone Cylinder (*RIMA* 3.92, p. 151). The short inscription reads:

> Booty from the temple of the god Šēru (Aram. *šhr*) of the city of Malaḫa, a royal city of Hazael of Damascus, which Shalmaneser, son of Aššur-naṣir-pal,

[32] Location uncertain, but most likely on the Phoenician coast.

[33] Pitard quotes Porter 1855: 1.346 '...Saidnâya ... its ancient name being Danaba.' But see Dion's objection (1997: 198, n. 119).

> king of Assyria, brought back inside the wall of the Inner city (Assur) (*COS* 2: 271).

Unfortunately, its location remains uncertain.[34] In the Damascus area, Almalīha, several kilometres east of Damascus has been suggested (Sader 1987: 266). In the Hauran region, the sites of Malīḥat al-ʿAṭāš (*Tübinger Bibelatlas*, TAVO B IV 14) and Safiyet-Melah (17 km east of Ṣalhad (Sader 1987: 266) have been proposed. Just to the west, the site of Malaḥ ez-Ezraʿ/Malaḥ d'Ezraʿa has been proposed (Lemaire 1991: 100–1; Dion 1997: 198; Yamada 2000a: 207–8; Parpola and Porter 2001: 13, map 8); Naʾaman 2002: 205). Finally, Lipiński (2000: 350–51) has recently argued that Malaḫa was the Aramaic name for the city of Hazor, but this is very doubtful.

Following the destruction of these cities of Hazael, Shalmaneser received the tribute of a certain Baʾil, whose name is probably a hypocoristic form of a personal name that has the divine name Baʿal as its first element. Yamada (2000a: 208) argued that the passage concerning Baʾil

> is connected by the conjunction *u* with the following sentence: 'and I received the tribute of the people of Tyre, Sidon and Byblos' (ll. 161′b–162′a). This implies the closeness of the country of Baʾil to Tyre, Sidon and Byblos. On these grounds, it seems safe to regard Baʾil as a ruler on the south Phoenician coast.

But *u* may often be rendered 'and also, moreover, furthermore, additionally, as well' (Huehergard 1997: 50), especially in such a narrative context. Besides, the episode involving Baʾil follows on the heels of the description of the campaign against Hazael east of the Anti-Lebanon mountains. Therefore, a location on the Phoenician coast is not demanded by the syntax.

The name of Baʾil's country is not fully preserved. The text reads: ⸢KUR⸣ Z/G/Q[I](?)-[*x*]-[*r*]*a-a-a* (text has 2) (note Hulin's copy, Yamada 2000b: 80).[35] It is tempting to read the ZI sign as *ṣí* and identify this Baʾil with the Baʾali-manzēri of Tyre attested in year 18 of Shalmaneser's texts. In fact, Grayson (1996: 79) tentatively translated 'Baʾal, the man of [*Tyr*]*e*', and Yamada (2000a: 206–9) seemed to favour this explanation. However, in a note, Grayson observed the problem of reading '*ṣurrāiia* at the beginning of line 160′'. Moreover, contextually why would the text mention Baʾil of Tyre

34 Malaḫa is identified as a royal city of Hazael (URU MAN-*ti-šú*) (*RIMA* 3.92, line 3), one of the fortified cities (URU.MEŠ-*ni dan-nu-te*) (*RIMA* 3.16, line 157′), and one of his important cities (with a cult centre) (*ma-ḫa-zi-šú*) (*RIMA* 3.14, line 103). In the Eponym Chronicle, it is preceded by the determinative KUR.

35 The following are the proposed readings: Grayson (*RIMA* 3:79): ⸢KUR⸣ x-[x x-*r*]*a*?-*a-a*(*); Lipiński (1999: 242): ⸢KUR⸣ [*ṣi-mir-r*]*a-a-a*; Yamada (2000a: 206): ⸢KUR⸣ Z[I](?)-[x]-[*r*]*a-a-a* (text: II); Yamada (2000b: 80): ⸢KUR⸣ *Ṣ*[*i-mir-r*]*a-a-a* (text: 2); Naʾaman (2002: 205): ⸢KUR⸣ *G*[*i-šu(r)-r*]*a-a-a*.

and his tribute only to mention the tribute of the Tyrians (along with Sidonians and Byblians) a few lines beyond?

Lipiński has suggested reading the toponym as Ṣimirra (1999: 242; 2000: 385). Yamada (2000b: 80) notes that this suggestion is quite possible since Hulin's hand copy seems to preserve the traces of the *ṣí* and *ra* signs. Thus one can better read the text ⸢KUR⸣ [í-*mir-r*]*a-a-a* (text has 2).

While this seems on the surface a good possibility, Na'aman has recently shown the impossibility of this understanding. He argues:

> The suggested restoration '[Ty]re' (*Ṣ*[*urr*]*aya*) is unlikely in view of the recently published facsimile of the inscription (Yamada 2000a: 206–7, and n. 449). Lipiński (1999) suggested restoring it 'Ṣimirra' (*Ṣ*[*í-mir-r*]*a-a-a*). However, not only does Ṣimirra always appear as a city and not as a land (with one exception written long after it became an Assyrian province), but its name is consistently written with the ṢI-sign and never with the ZI-sign. Moreover, Ṣimirra does not fit the route of a campaign conducted east of Mt. Anti-Lebanon (2002: 205).

Na'aman is correct that Ṣimirra is never spelled with the ZI-sign read as ṢÍ. It is important to note that Lipiński (1999: 242) suggested reading the ṢI-sign. However, what can be seen in Hulin's copy (Yamada 2000b: 80) cannot be a ṢI-sign. ZI, GI and RAD are the only possibilities. RAD does not bear any good toponymic possibilities, nor does ZI. On this basis, Na'aman has proposed 'restoring the land's name as Geshur: *G*[*i-ū(r)-r*]*a-a-a*'. This is a possibility, although the only occurrence of the writing of Geshur in cuneiform comes from the Amarna period (EA 256: 23) where it is spelled in an emended text: GA-<ŠU>-RI. Thus the reading *G*[*i-šu(r)-r*]*a-a-a* is not problem free. One cannot help but think of the reading KUR *gi-di-ra-a-a* found in line 11 of a Neo-Assyrian letter from Nimrud (ND 2773, see Saggs 2001: 160–61). Such a reading would fit quite well here. But this letter has its own interpretive difficulties, not the least of which is the understanding of KUR *gi-di-ra-a-a*. In any case, the city of Laruba was a fortified city (*āl dannūti*) of Ba'il, though unfortunately its identity is uncertain.[36]

Archaeological evidence from Tel eṣ-Ṣafi

In recent years, excavations at a number of sites in northern Israel have produced evidence that may point to the activities of Hazael. Space does not

[36] Yamada's suggestion (Yamada 2000a: 209) to emend the text to read *Ma-ru-ba*, understanding a scribal error of the LA sign for the MA sign, appears to be premature. Na'aman tenatively suggests identifying Laruba with 'En Gev (2002: 207) but, of course, there is no evidence to support this.

allow for a discussion of the complexities related to this issue here. Rather I will only look at the evidence from Tell eṣ-Ṣafī (Gath) since the excavators have uncovered a unique piece of evidence that may relate to Hazael's capture of that city.

The biblical text in 2 Kgs. 12: 18 notes that Hazael captured Gath (cf. Amos 6: 2). One of the major difficulties facing historians was the identification of Gath, but the arguments in favor of Gath being located at Tell eṣ-Ṣafī are strong (see Rainey 1975; Schniedewind 1998; Maeir and Ehrlich 2001; Ehrlich 2002). The renewed excavations at the site have uncovered a siege moat of significant size that dates to the time of Hazael (Ehrlich 2002: 63–67). While the siege moat could be the product of some other force attacking Gath, the interesting parallel from the Zakkur inscription which notes that Bar-Hadad (son of Hazael) during the siege of Hazrach 'dug a ditch deeper than [its] ditch' (Millard 2000a: 155) seems to point in Hazael's direction. While hardly definitive proof, this does lend support to the excavators' interpretation that this siege moat was the work of Hazael in his conquest of the city of Gath.

Conclusion

This essay has attempted to assess the recent evidence concerning Hazael, the most enigmatic, yet interesting of the kings of Aram-Damascus. This evidence has helped clarify certain aspects of his reign, but has also raised new problems. In this respect, even the biblical record sounds an ambivalence: Hazael was anointed by the prophet Elisha through the command of Yahweh, yet he was the one who would 'set Israelite fortresses on fire, kill their young men with the sword, dash in pieces their little ones, and rip up their pregnant women' (2 Kgs. 8: 12).

BIBLIOGRAPHY

Amadasi Guzzo, M.G.

1996 'Le harnais des chevaux du roi Hazaël', in L. Bacchielli and M. Bonanno Aravantinos (eds), *Scritti di antichità in memoria di Sandro Stucchi*, 2 vols, Studi Miscellanei 29 (Rome: 'L'Erma' di Bretschneider): 1:329–38.

Athas, G.

2003 *The Tel Dan Inscription: A Reappraisal and a New Interpretation*, JSOTSup 360 (Sheffield: Sheffield Academic Press).

Biran, A., and J. Naveh

1993 'An Aramaic stele fragment from Tel Dan'. *IEJ* 43: 81–98.

1995 'The Tel Dan Inscription: a new fragment'. *IEJ* 45: 1–18.

Brinkman, J.A., and D. Schwemer
2000 'Iāū(a) (Jehu)', in S. Parpola and H. Baker (eds), *The Prosopography of the Neo-Assyrian Empire* 2/1 (Helsinki: The Neo-Assyrian Text Corpus Project): 496–97.

Bron, F., and A. Lemaire
1989 'Les inscriptions araméennes de Hazaël', *RA* 83: 35–44.

Charbonnet, A.
1986 'Le dieu au lions d'Erétrie', *AION, Archeologia e Storia antica* 8: 117–56.

Couturier, G.
2001 'Quelques observations sur le *bytdwd* de la stèle araméenne de Tel Dan', in Daviau, Wevers and Weigl: 2001, JSOTSup 325: 72–98.

Daviau, P.M.M., J.W. Wevers and M. Weigl (eds)
2001 *The World of the Aramaeans*, 3 vols, JSOTSup 324–26 (Sheffield: Sheffield Academic Press).

Dion, P.-E.
1997 *Les Araméens à l'âge du fer: histoire politique et structures sociales*, Études bibliques, nouvelle série no. 34 (Paris: J. Gabalda).
1999 'The Tel Dan Stele and its historical significance', in Y. Avishur and R. Deutsch (eds), *Michael*: *Historical, Epigraphical and Biblical Studies in Honor of Prof. Michael Heltzer* (Tel Aviv/Jaffa: Archaeological Center Publications): 145–56.

Ehrlich, C.S.
2001 'The *bytdwd*-inscriptions and Israelite historiography: taking stock after half a decade of research', in Daviau, Wevers and Weigl: 2001, JSOTSup 325: 57–71.
2002 'Die Suche nach Gat und die neuen Ausgrabungen auf Tell eṣ-Ṣāfī', in U. Hübner and E.A. Knauf (eds), *Kein Land für sich allein*: *Studien zum Kulturkontakt in Kanaan, Israel/Palästina und Ebirnâri für Manfred Weippert zum 65. Geburtstag*, OBO 186 (Freiburg: Universitätsverlag): 56–69.

Eph'al, I., and J. Naveh
1989 'Hazael's booty inscriptions', *IEJ* 39: 192–200.

Fitzmyer, J.A.
1995 *The Aramaic Inscriptions of Sefire* (rev. ed.), Biblica et Orientalia 19/A (Rome: Pontifical Biblical Institute).

Grayson, A.K.
1980–83 'Königlisten und Chroniken B. Akkadisch', *RlA* 6:86–135.
1996 *RIMA* 3.

Halpern, B.
1994 'The stela from Dan: epigraphic and historical considerations', *BASOR* 296: 63–80.

Harrak, A.
1992 'Des noms d'année en araméen?', *WO* 23: 68–73.

Harrison, T.P.
2001 'Tell Taʿyinat and the kingdom of Unqi', in Daviau, Wevers and Weigl: 2001, JSOTSup 325: 115–32.

Hawkins, J.D.
2000 *CHLI* 1/2: 361–65.

Huehergard, J.
1997 *A Grammar of Akkadian*. HSS 45 (Atlanta, GA: Scholars Press).

Ikeda, Y.
1999 'Looking from Til Barsip on the Euphrates: Assyria and the West in ninth and eighth centuries BC', in K. Watanabe (eds), *Priests and Officials in the Ancient Near East: Papers of the Second Colloquium on the Ancient Near East—The City and its Life held at the Middle Eastern Culture Center in Japan (Mitaka, Tokyo)* (Heidelberg: Universitätverlag C. Winter): 271–302.

Kitchen, K.A.
1997 'A possible mention of David in the late tenth century BCE and deity *Dod as dead as the dodo?', *JSOT* 76:29–44.

Kottsieper, I.
1998 'Die Inschrift vom Tell Dan und die politischen Beziehungen zwischen Aram-Damaskus und Israel in der 1. Hälfte des 1. Jahrtausends vor Christus', in M. Dietrich and I. Kottsieper (eds), *'Und Moses schrieb dieses Lied auf'. Studien zum Alten Testament und zum Alten Orient: Festschrift für Oswald Loretz zur Vollendung seines 70. Lebensjahres mit Beiträgen von Freunden, Schülern und Kollegen*, AOAT 250 (Münster: Ugarit-Verlag): 475–500.

Kyrieleis, H.
1988 'Ein altorientalischer Pferdeschmuck aus dem Heraion von Samos', *MDAIA* 103: 37–61.

Laessøe, J.
1959 'A statue of Shalmaneser III from Nimrud', *Iraq* 21: 147–57, pls xl–xlii.

Lapinkivi, P., and K. Radner
1999 'Gē-ammu'. *PNA* 2/1: 422.

Lemaire, A.
1988 'Hadad l'Edomite ou Hadad l'Araméen?', *BN* 43:14–18.
1991 'Hazaël de Damas, roi d'Aram', in D. Charpin and F. Joannès (eds), *Marchands, diplomates et empereurs: Études sur la civilisation mésopotamienne offertes à Paul Garelli* (Paris: Éditions Recherche sur les Civilisations): 91–108.
1998 The Tel Dan Stela as a piece of royal historiography', *JSOT* 81: 3–14.

Lipiński, E.
1999 'Baʾalu', *PNA* 1/2: 242–43.
2000 *The Aramaeans: Their Ancient History, Culture, Religion*, OLA 100 (Leuven: Peeters).

Luckenbill, D.D.
1927 *Ancient Records of Assyria and Babylonia. Volume 2* (Chicago: University of Chicago Press).

Maeir, A.M., and C.S. Ehrlich
2001 'Excavating Philistine Gath: have we found Goliath's hometown?', *Biblical Archaeology Review* 27/6: 22–31.

Mallowan, M.E.L.
Nimrud and Its Remains (London: John Murray).

Messerschmidt, L.
1911 *Keilschrifttexte aus Assur historischen Inhalts. Volume 1*, Wissenschaftliche Veröffenlichung der Deutschen Orient-Gesellschaft 16 (Leipzig: J.C. Hinrichs).

Michel, E.
1954 'Die Assur-Texte Salmanassars III. (858–824) 6. Fortsetzung', *WO* 2/1: 27–45.

Millard, A. R.
1966 in Mallowan 1966 2: 598-599, number 582.
1993 'Eden, Bit Adini and Beth Eden', *EI* 24: 173*–177*.
1994 *The Eponyms of the Assyrian Empire 910–612 BC*, SAAS 2 (Helinski: The Neo-Assyrian Text Project).
1997 'Assyrian king lists', *COS* 1: 463–65.
2000a 'The inscription of Zakkur, King of Hamath', *COS* 2: 155 (2.35).
2000b 'The Tell Dan Stele', *COS* 2: 161–62 (2.39).
2000c 'The Hazael booty inscriptions', *COS* 2: 162–63 (2.40).

Na'aman, N.
1995 'Hazael of 'Amqi and Hadadezer of Beth-rehob', *UF* 27: 381–94.
2000 'Three notes on the Aramaic inscription from Tel Dan', *IEJ* 50: 92–104.
2002 'In search of reality behind the account of David's wars with Israel's neighbours', *IEJ* 52: 200–24.

Naveh, J.
1999 'Marginalia on the inscriptions from Dan and Ekron', in B.A. Levine *et al.* (eds), *Frank Moore Cross Volume*, EI 26 (Jerusalem: Israel Exploration Society [Hebrew]): 119–22.
2002 'Epigraphic miscellanea', *IEJ* 52: 240–53.

Noth, M.
1960 *The History of Israel*, 2nd ed. (New York: Harper & Row).

Oates, J., and D. Oates
2001 *Nimrud: An Assyrian Imperial City Revealed* (London: British School of Archaeology in Iraq).

Parpola, S., and M. Porter
2001 *The Helsinki Atlas of the Near East in the Neo-Assyrian Period.* Helsinki: The Casco Bay Assyriological Institute/The Neo-Assyrian Text Corpus Project.

Pitard, W.T.
1987 *Ancient Damascus: A Historical Study of the Syrian City-State*

from Earliest Times Until its Fall to the Assyrians in 732 BCE (Winona Lake, IN: Eisenbrauns).

Puech, É.
1981 'L'ivoire inscrit d'Arslan-Tash et les rois de Damas', *RB* 88: 544–62.

Rainey, A.F.
1975 'The identification of Philistine Gath: a problem in source analysis for historical geography', *Eretz Israel* 12:63*–76*.
2003 'The suffix conjugation pattern in ancient Hebrew tense and modal functions' in *ANES* 40: 3–42.

Reade, J.
1978 'Assyrian campaigns, 840–811 BC, and the Babylonian frontier', *ZA* 68:251–60.

Röllig, W.
1974 'Die Amulette von Arslan Taş', *Neue Ephemeris für semitische Epigraphik* 2: 37–64.
1988 'Die aramäische Inschrift für Haza'el und ihr Duplikat', *MDAIA* 103: 62–75.

Sader, H.
1987 *Les états araméens de Syrie depuis leur fondation jusqu'à leur transformation en provinces assyriennes*, Beiruter Texte und Studien 36 (Wiesbaden: Steiner).

Saggs, H.W.F.
2001 *The Nimrud Letters, 1952*, CTN 5 (London: British School of Archaeology in Iraq).

Schniedewind, W.M.
1996 'Tel Dan Stela: new light on Aramaic and Jehu's revolt', *BASOR* 302: 75–90.
1998 'The geopolitical history of Philistine Gath', *BASOR* 309: 69–77.

Schniedewind, W.M., and B. Zuckerman
2001 'A possible reconstruction of the name of Haza'el's father in the Tel Dan Inscription', *IEJ* 51: 88–91.

Schramm, W.
1973 *Einleitung in die assyrischen Königsinschriften*, II (Leiden: Brill).

Selz, G.J.
1998 'Aḫzi-Iāu', in S. Parpola and K. Radner (eds), *The Prosopography of the Neo-Assyrian Empire* 1/1 (Helsinki: The Neo-Assyrian Text Corpus Project): 88–89.

Seux, M.-J.
1980–81 'Königtum B. II. und I. Jahrtausend', *RlA* 6: 140–73.

Tadmor, H.
1981 'History and ideology in the Assyrian royal inscriptions', in F.M. Fales (ed.), *Assyrian Royal Inscriptions: New Horizons* (Rome): 13–34.
1994 *The Inscriptions of Tiglath-pileser III King of Assyria* (Jerusalem: The Israel Academy of Sciences and Humanities).

Winter, I.J.

1981 'Is there a south Syrian style of ivory carving in the early first millennium BC?', *Iraq* 43: 101–30.

Yamada, S.

1994 'The editorial history of the Assyrian king list', *ZA* 84: 11–37.

2000a *The Construction of the Assyrian Empire: A Historical Study of the Inscriptions of Shalmaneser III (859–824 BC) Relating to His Campaigns to the West*, SCHANE 3 (Leiden: Brill).

2000b 'Peter Hulin's hand copies of Shalmaneser III's inscriptions', *Iraq* 62: 65–87.

4Q341: An Exercise for Spelling and for Spells?[1]

George J. Brooke

Amongst the hundreds of fragmentary manuscripts from cave four at Qumran on the north-west shore of the Dead Sea there is a single piece of leather, 77 x 58 mm, inscribed on one side only in a square Herodian script which has been catalogued as 4Q341 and labelled as Exercitium Calami C. First published by J.M. Allegro in 1979,[2] it was identified by him as some kind of medical text. The continuous form of the presentation of some of the words on the fragment enabled Allegro to apply word-division so as to suit a reading of the text as a mixture of diagnosis and prescription. J.H. Charlesworth was taken by Allegro's reading and attempted a more elaborate interpretation, fitting the text into what might be reconstructed of the history of medicine in Palestine in the late Second Temple period (Charlesworth 1985). Before long, J. Naveh presented a short reconsideration of the fragment which seemed to demonstrate conclusively that it contained nothing more than a scribal exercise.[3] This interpretation has been repeated in the official publication of the *editio princeps* of the fragment in the series Discoveries in the Judaean Desert (=DJD).[4] However, Naveh's presentation of the text is confined to the bare minimum of observation and it seems appropriate that at least a few further questions should be asked of this text to see whether it might be possible to suggest what kind of scribal exercise it could be.

[1] I am delighted to offer this short study in honour of Alan Millard who has in many places carefully presented the scholarly world with detailed information on writing habits in antiquity; see, especially, Millard 2000.

[2] Allegro 1979: 235–40; pls 16–17. From the archives in the Manchester Museum it appears that J.T. Milik agreed to Allegro publishing this fragment in a preliminary edition. In return Allegro handed back to Milik a large piece of what is now known as fragment 6 of 4Q252 (see Brooke 1996: 205–6). As a result Allegro's volume of principal editions (1968), did not include the principal edition of what Allegro had called 4QPatriarchal Blessings, though he had been responsible for its preliminary edition in Allegro 1956: 174–76.

[3] Naveh 1986: 52–5, pl. II. Charlesworth states that, after studying the actual fragment in Jerusalem, in a letter dated 5th September 1986 he retracted any support he had given to Allegro's identification; see Charlesworth 1987: 2.

[4] Naveh 2000: 291–93, pl. xviii. Cf. enlarged photograph in E. Tov 2004: pl. 2 (Pam 43. 407), and descriptive caption.

I represent the text as it is in its *editio princeps* in order to make my brief discussion of this fragment all the more accessible.

1 לבעפסאצגדהו[ooo]טיכל
2 סחרה א[ooo]אoסooסooסo
3 תירקוס [ ]א בי[ ]ק
4 שרחסי מגנס מלכיה מניס
5 מחתוש מקליח מפיבשת
6 [ ]לגוס בניבן ם בסרי גדי
7 דלוי הלכוס הרקנוס וני ז
8 זוחלזלפ
9 זכריאל יoי
a יתראיתישילא
b יטריסיסי
c עקילא
d עלי עדפי

In the right margin of lines 1–5 [ ]מריאל קפ is written vertically. Naveh presents the text like this, reckoning that at the bottom of the fragment the two words זוחלזלפ and זכריאל were written one under the other to the left (his lines 8 and 9); subsequently the words on a–c were written to the right of those two names beginning with zayin, and the two names beginning with ʻayin were added at the bottom. If the name written vertically also begins with an ʻayin as was proposed by Allegro[5] and as is endorsed by Naveh,[6] then it would not represent anything more special than the continuation of the list of names beginning with ʻayin which has run from c and d at the bottom of the fragment.

As pointed out by Naveh (2000: 291), a remarkably similar composition has been published by E. Puech (1980: 118–26). It is an ostracon containing the alphabet from ʼalep to taw in the first two lines, followed by a series of personal names in alphabetical order (lines 3–8). Of particular note are the names דליה, הודיה, וני and זכריה. Two fragmentary ostraca from Masada contain the same list. Naveh concludes that ʻthe Masada ostraca were writing exercises of beginners who did not deviate from the prescribed formula, while the much more skilled scribe from Qumran permitted himself variations on the same theme' (Naveh 2000: 291).

Despite these parallels, or indeed because of them, it is necessary to ask just what might be taking place in this scribe practising in the way he does. It seems clear that the manuscript contains a combination of the practice of letters, many of which are in alphabetical order, and the listing of various proper names and other words, some of which seem nonsensical, which

5 Allegro 1979: 236 (in his line 10a).

6 Naveh 2000: 293: ʻOn the right side the writer wrote a personal name, presumably [ע]מריאל (Omriel) or the like, and two letters, *qop* and *pe*, perpendicular to the main text.'

appear in groups and are also arranged alphabetically. It would thus seem that it is the combination of alphabet and alphabetically ordered names which should be the focus of investigation. In this short study I do not wish to describe both kinds of writing practice in any detail, since I am more concerned to ask some questions than to provide any definitive answer about 4Q341. The descriptions in the next few paragraphs will of necessity use broad brush strokes for setting the scene for raising those questions.

Texts from antiquity which contain alphabets are not uncommon.[7] As is well known, the late second millennium Ugaritic alphabet tablet attests to the conscious scribal presentation of an alphabet in a North-west Semitic setting. The clearest early examples of compositions which reflect the Hebrew alphabet and its order are the alphabetic acrostic compositions found almost exclusively in the Writings. Psalms 111, 112, 119, Proverbs 31:10–31 and the first four chapters of Lamentations all contain complete alphabetic acrostics. Incomplete alphabetic acrostics occur in Psalms 9–10, 25, 34, 37, 145,[8] and Nahum 1:2–9. Of note is that ʻayin and pe appear transposed in Lamentations 2:16–17, 3:46–51 and 4:16–17, and may have been the original order of Psalm 34:15–16 and Proverbs 31:25–26 (because of the evidence of the LXX).

Naveh is of the opinion that the skilled scribe of 4Q341 from Qumran permitted himself variations on the alphabetic theme (2000: 291). That may indeed have been the case[9], but it is also possible that the skill of the scribe of 4Q341 rested in part on his knowledge of alternative orders for the alphabet, or parts of it. Intriguingly, the order of the letters of שרהסי at the start of line 4 is somewhat close to that of the Qatabanian alphabet known from the discovery made at Hajar Kohlan in the Wadi Beihan (ancient Timna), the capital of the Qatabanian kingdom of S. Arabia, of a set of *c.* 300 BCE paving stones laid out sequentially as marked alphabetically by masons. Part of the order is š, r, ġ, s.[10] Perhaps other orders were also known.

Although it is unlikely that the acrostic use of the Hebrew alphabet in scriptural compositions has any magical significance,[11] it is clear that the use of the alphabet exercises a dominant structural control over the compositions where it is used in this way. In addition to such use of the Hebrew alphabet, one can readily imagine other uses for which alphabets were needed in the composition of all kinds of lists and catalogues. Amongst the most intriguing

[7] On the history of the alphabet in general the landmark study is by D. Diringer (1947). In several places he comments on the magical significance of the alphabet in a range of cultures, notably the Mandaeans (p. 291). A recent example of the discussion of the magic of writing is by D. de Smet (2002: 51–60).

[8] The nun verse is present or supplied in the 11QPs^{a} copy of the psalm.

[9] See the comments on the varied use of the alphabetic structure of multiples of 11 in D.N. Freedman and D. Miano 2005: 87–96.

[10] See the brief description by T.O. Lambdin (1962: 1.89–96 and the bibliography there).

[11] As was argued, e.g., by M. Löhr (1905: 173–98).

is the medico-magical catalogue of the first book of Cyranides.[12] Arranged alphabetically, each entry in this first or second century CE magico-medical composition is also a mnemonic catalogue of what natural resources might be used for various ailments.

The theological significance of the alphabet is readily apparent in several medieval Jewish compositions, especially Sefer Yetzirah.[13] How early such traditions of its mystical use go back is difficult to determine, but the symbolic use of alpha and omega in the Jewish Christian writing, the Book of Revelation (Rev. 1:8; 22:13), representing the first and the last, the beginning and the end, is an indication that the significance of the letters and their position was almost certainly not lost on scribes of the late Second Temple period.

The second feature of 4Q341 is the list of words which appear in some lines to be arranged alphabetically too. As Allegro and Naveh have both pointed out it is clear that this list contains several proper names. Naveh has noted too that some of these names also appear on what are classified as scribal exercises from Masada, which suggests that there was a set pattern of scribal practice, though the question still remains concerning precisely for what purpose or purposes the scribal exercises were performed.

In 4Q341 the list of names seems to be catalogued in two ways. On lines four and five all the names begin with a mem. On lines six to nine, there seems to be a list of names which run in alphabetical order from aleph to zayin, with one or two names written for each letter. It is also important to note that the words and names are laid out in an intriguing fashion at the bottom of the piece of leather. In effect the words are set out in two columns, though the shape of the leather forces the diagonal layout of the names in the last three lines (b–d). Naveh comments that 'at first the right sides of lines 8 and 9 were left blank for some reason. The writer subsequently filled in this space in a more condensed manner' (2000: 293).

The reason for the layout at the bottom of the fragment may lie in any one of several directions. Perhaps the matter is to be explained by the character of the surface of the leather, so that the poorer surface was only used last. Perhaps the scribe temporarily forgot or did not realize at the outset that he was supposed to practice more words and names than could fit in the space he was using by only writing at the left side of lines 8 and 9. Or, it could be that there was a more sophisticated reason, such as the need to practice the writing of a word square using such proper names. In line 8 the two names beginning with zayin have virtually no space between them as if the scribe is anticipating the length of the word he is to include in line 9. Are these

[12] See the edition and commentary by Waegeman 1987.

[13] See the classic descriptions of Jewish traditions, especially Sefer Yetzirah, in Dornseiff 1922: 133–42; on Sefer Yetzirah see the introductory comments in Alexander 2002: 708–10 and the bibliography there.

features of the construction of a list of names in a neat arrangement, perhaps eventually a square? Perhaps it is also notable that these words and names are of four or five letters, with two of six letters. Does that suggest that some of these names might have been used in the construction of word squares made up of four-letter or five-letter words which could be constructed into a word square of sixteen, twenty-five or more characters? Such a word square might then be presented as an amulet of some kind.

The existence of word squares in antiquity involving proper names is neatly exemplified for our discussion through the consideration of the list of the proper names of the fallen angels in 1 Enoch 6:7. A. Lods demonstrated long ago that the differences in the order between the various manuscript representations of the names could be explained if they were set out as a word square (Lods 1892: 106–7). At least in the archetype of the Greek version the list 'was arranged in four columns beginning with the third name, but instead of reading the names from left to right, the scribe of G read from top to bottom, column by column'.[14] What may also be significant for our interrogation of 4Q341 is that this list of proper names in 1 Enoch 6 occurs within a context that a few verses before has described the oath that these Watchers have taken with regard to descending to earth to take wives from amongst the daughters of men. The list of names is immediately followed by a passage concerning the actions of the Watchers: they 'took for themselves wives from all whom they chose; and they began to cohabit with them and to defile themselves with them, and they taught them sorcery and spells and showed them the cutting of roots and herbs'[15] (1 Enoch 7:1). Perhaps the list of angels names had once existed separately as an amulet arranged as a word square.[16] M. Schwartz has argued that the names of the fallen angels and accounts of their evil giant progeny were widely circulated by the Manichaeans; he has provided evidence that the names of various of these evil angels and giants passed, via Manichaean Middle Persian, into a Manichaean Arabic translation, and that these names were used in magic, eventually becoming part of Islamic Arabic magico-medical traditions (Schwartz 2002: 231–38).

But let us return to the more basic question: Why should a scribe practice writing proper names? C. Schams has recently argued convincingly that in the Second Temple period the designation 'scribe' could refer to a large number of different roles, so that not all scribes can be lumped together as a single class or group for social analysis (Schams 1998). She outlines the range of possibilities for the scribe. On higher levels of administration, scribes would have had a variety of functions including the drafting of laws, and they would

14 Black 1985: 118. The square is conveniently set out in Milik 1976: 154.

15 Trans. Black 1985: 28.

16 A list of angels occurs in the non-Jewish apotropaic prayer found on a silver phylactery in Therasos (3rd C. CE): see Kotansky 1994: 206–10, No. 38, ll. 6–8; as used by Eshel 2003: 70.

have lived up to their reputation as wise scholars and intellectuals; at a lower level, scribes would have exercised their skills 'in reading and writing and their responsibilities included the reading and writing of correspondence and records, supervising functions and sometimes legal matters', they 'occupied administrative functions, dealt with financial matters, and were responsible for all kinds of records' (Schams 1998: 310–11). In addition some scribal functions must have been exercised in the Temple in the distribution of tithes to the priests and the Levites (Neh. 13:13). Schams argues that the sophisticated administration put in place by Ptolemy II Philadelphus (285–46 BCE) resulted in a few scribes being present as part of 'a new rural elite' (1998: 312) in towns and villages throughout Palestine. The military also required specialist scribal administrators.

Against this varied set of job descriptions, what kind of scribe might have been trying his hand in an exercise like 4Q341? It seems to me that at least four settings might explain the need for this kind of practice. First, it is well known that lists of names occur on legal documents as witnesses; is the scribe practising to be a legal notary? Second, amongst the scrolls from Qumran there are other lists of names which seem to belong to genealogies or significant figures in historical sequences; is the scribe practising for a career as an historiographical archivist? Third, some texts refer to names being inscribed in a book; amongst such practices could be the enrolment of new members to the community, the recording of those being promoted up the hierarchy, or the listing of those who have appeared before a community hearing of some sort. Perhaps the scribe was to function as a recorder. Fourth, names are recognized as carrying the character of a person, they are truly representative, and represent ways in which individuals can be controlled. Was the scribe practising so as to operate some such system of control, perhaps through the writing of incantations or spells?

It is difficult to know whether there any grounds for thinking that it is at all possible to decide what kind of scribe was indeed being trained through an exercise such as is extant in 4Q341. However, rather than paying attention discretely either to the alphabetical characteristics of the manuscript or to the word-list and its proper names, it could be important to ask what kind of composition might have contained both elements and have required some practice. Whereas on the one hand archivists, cataloguers, poets and wisdom instructors might be particularly interested in alphabets, on the other hand genealogists, lawyers, civil servants, military bureaucrats and tax-collectors could all have been concerned with proper names. Tantalizingly, however, it seems as if scribes concerned with the production of the realia of what may be broadly termed 'magic'[17] might have been distinctively interested in both.

[17] On the problem of the use of this term, especially in relation to the finds from Qumran, see Lyons and Reimer 1998: 16–32. Hereafter I use it in inverted commas to indicate its problematic character, especially in relation to Jewish texts.

If such is the case, then the combination of both items in a scribal exercise might suggest that this scribe was practising in order to equip himself for writing 'magical' texts. As already mentioned, one of the clearest examples of a composition which is nearly contemporary with 4Q341, and which uses both the alphabet for its organization and also lists key terms in alphabetical groups, is the First Book of Cyranides, described as 'a medico-magical treatise based on the magic of letters and words' (Waegeman 1987: 7).

In general it is clear from a number of sources that a wide range of written materials for 'magical' practices were required in the Mediterranean world of the Hellenistic period.[18] In many of these it was required that a key term or a proper name should feature.[19] Even in the general description of Paul in Ephesus it appears that there are books of magic to be destroyed, and it is intriguing to note that the incident of the burning of such books (Acts 19:19) occurs in a pericope which speaks of how the evil spirit can recognize the names of Jesus and Paul but not the use of the name of Jesus by the seven sons of Sceva.[20] In Jewish Palestine, as attested by the fragments from the Qumran caves, such written materials could have included physiognomies,[21] tefillin and other apotropaic texts,[22] exorcisms, blessings and curses, and possibly even brontologies and zodiologies.[23] For the finds from Qumran, I. Fröhlich is a lone voice in commenting on the role of the scribe in the transmission of exorcistic practice (2001: 73–81), though she says little more than that he may be identified with the *maskil* ('wise man') or a sage of some kind. There is more work to be done on the types of scribe whose practice exercises and written works are represented in the Qumran caves.[24]

The combination of playing with letters of the alphabet and the construction of word squares is further exemplified in its most well-known form in the ROTAS/SATOR five-letter word square, the earliest datable example of which is to be found in a public exercise square at Pompeii and therefore must predate 79 CE. Several interpreters of the square have been inclined to conclude that it represents the opening two words of the Lord's Prayer in Latin, together with the surplus alphas and omegas, though others disagree,

[18] As is most clearly attested by the Greek magical papyri: Preisendanz 1973–74; Betz 1992.

[19] For brief comments on such magical texts and on the other realia of antiquity, see Graf 1997: esp. 127–28, 218–20.

[20] For a description of the elements of magic in Acts 19, see Klauck 2000: 99–102.

[21] On 4Q186 and other texts, see the important study by Alexander 1996: 385–94.

[22] See Eshel 2003: 69–88.

[23] Various survey articles on 'magical' texts at Qumran are now available: see, e.g., Alexander 1997: 318–37; Alexander 2000: 502–4; García Martínez 2002: 13–33.

[24] E. Tov has produced several studies on the scribal practices to be observed in the various manuscripts, especially the so-called 'biblical' ones; see recently, Tov 2002: 139–66 and Tov 2004. A more general study on literacy and scribal practices is Alexander 2003: 3–24.

offering a Mithraic interpretation.[25] Two features deserve particular comment. First, if the Pater Noster interpretation is correct, then the word square could be deemed to preserve precatory incantation; perhaps the word square functioned apotropaically. Second, it seems as if the double use of the first and last letters of the alphabet may be a reference at least to the power of the alphabet itself; such a reference was readily taken over by the early church communities, as the Book of Revelation amply attests.

By taking this brief fresh look at 4Q341 I have not been concerned to demonstrate that it is indeed an amulet or set of spells. Rather, I have attempted to indicate that the kind of scribal exercise which the text represents may lead us towards recognizing that some scribes were being trained with a view to providing the realia of magical practices, whether these be charms or amulets, or apotropaic psalms, or texts which could be used as blessings or curses, or some other 'magic books'. Very little is known for late Second Temple Palestinian Judaism about the kind of religious practices which modern interpreters might be tempted to label 'magic', whether these were based in popular religious culture or in the more specialist practices of experts.

The manuscripts and artefacts from Qumran have provided us with a glimpse into the lives of some Jews from the time. Although strict adherents to the Torah,[26] those who lived and worked at Qumran seem to have had access to lots for casting and to a wide range of texts which can be understood as relating to a world view which took the spirit world seriously. Amongst these texts are so-called horoscopes, physiognomies, blessings and curses, and tefillin (phylacteries). In some cases it was a matter of observations made by experts being recorded accurately, but in others the writing itself actually required an expertise which is sometimes really quite remarkable, as in the cases of the very small writing on the Qumran tefillin or the cryptic scripts of the physiognomy (4Q186).

In sum, in light of other contemporary texts, 4Q341 certainly seems to have the character of being some kind of scribal exercise, an abecedary as well as an introduction to the appropriate spelling of various proper names. However, the text seems to suggest more than that the writing is being practised for its own sake. The distinctive combination of alphabet and proper names, a few of which may be arranged in columns, can be set alongside such works as the medico-magical treatise of Cyranides, the lists of the names of the fallen angels of 1 Enoch 6:7 arranged as a word square, and the apotropaic quality of the Sator square, to lead to the suggestion that

[25] See the concise discussion in Millard 2000: 58–60, together with the bibliography cited there, to which can be added the recent essay by Thierry 2002: 267–73.

[26] They do not seem to have thought of themselves as in any way in breach of the prohibitions of Deuteronomy 18: see Brooke 2003: 66–84.

the scribe of 4Q341 was being trained or was training himself so as to be able to provide 'magical' texts. What was the writing in 4Q341 being practised for? What might have been the professional interest of the scribe trained in the way 4Q341 tantalizingly implies? Perhaps the way in which the alphabet is presented and the distinctive character of many of the proper names suggests that 4Q341 was a scribal exercise with elements of training for magical practices. Perhaps this fragment displays training in both spelling and spells; 4Q341 is possibly an abecedary with hints of abracadabra.

BIBLIOGRAPHY

Alexander, P.S.

1996 'Physiognomy, initiation, and rank in the Qumran community', in H. Cancik, H. Lichtenberger and P. Schäfer (eds), *Geschichte–Tradition–Reflexion: Festschrift für Martin Hengel zum 70. Geburtstag*. Band I: *Judentum* (Tübingen: J.C.B. Mohr [Paul Siebeck]).

1997 '"Wrestling against wickedness in high places": magic in the worldview of the Qumran community', in S.E. Porter and C.A. Evans (eds), *The Scrolls and the Sriptures: Qumran Fifty Years After* (JSPSup 26; Sheffield: Sheffield Academic Press).

2000 'Magic and magical texts', in L.H. Schiffman and J.C. VanderKam (eds), *Encyclopedia of the Dead Sea Scrolls* (New York: Oxford University Press).

2002 'Mysticism', in M. Goodman (ed.), *The Oxford Handbook of Jewish Studies* (Oxford: Oxford University Press).

2003 'Literacy among the Jews in Second Temple Palestine: reflections on the evidence from Qumran', in M.F.J. Baasten and W.Th. van Peursen (eds), *Hamlet on a Hill: Semitic and Greek Studies Presented to Professor T. Muraoka on the Occasion of his Sixty-Fifth Birthday* (Orientalia Lovaniensia Analecta 118; Leuven: Peeters).

Allegro, J.M

1956 'Further Messianic references in Qumran Literature', *JBL* 75.

1968 *Qumrân Cave 4.I (4Q158-186)* (DJD 5; Oxford: Clarendon Press).

1979 *The Dead Sea Scrolls and the Christian Myth* (Newton Abbot: Westbridge Books).

Betz, H.D. (ed.)

1992 *The Greek Magical Papyri in Translation Including the Demotic Spells* (Chicago: University of Chicago Press).

Black, M.

1985 *The Book of Enoch or 1 Enoch: A New English Edition with Commentary and Textual Notes* (SVTP 7; Leiden: Brill).

Brooke, G.J.

1996 '252. 4Q Commentary on Genesis A', in G. Brooke *et al.* (eds), *Qumran Cave 4.XVII: Parabiblical Texts, Part 3* (DJD 22; Oxford: Clarendon Press).

2003 'Deuteronomy 18.9–14 in the Qumran scrolls', in T. Klutz (ed.), *Magic in the Biblical World: From the Rod of Aaron to the Ring of Solomon* (JSNTSup 245; London: T & T Clark International).

Charlesworth, J.H.

1985 *The Discovery of a Dead Sea Scroll (4QTherapeia): Its Importance in the History of Medicine and Jesus Research* (Lubbock, TX: Texas Tech University).

1987 'A misunderstood recently published Dead Sea scroll', *Explorations* 1/2.

Diringer, D.

1947 *The Alphabet: A Key to the History of Mankind* (London: Hutchinson's).

Dornseiff, F.

1922 *Das Alphabet in Mystik und Magie* (Stoicheia: Studien zur Geschichte des antiken Weltebildes und der griechischen Wissenschaft 7; Leipzig/Berlin: Teubner).

Eshel, E.

2003 'Apotropaic prayers in the Second Temple period', in E.G. Chazon, R. Clements and A. Pinnick (eds), *Liturgical Perspectives: Prayer and Poetry in Light of the Dead Sea Scrolls: Proceedings of the Fifth International Symposium of the Orion Center for the Study of the Dead Sea Scrolls and Associated Literature, 19–23 January, 2000* (STDJ 48; Leiden: Brill).

Freedman, D.N., and D. Miano

2005 'Non-acrostic alphabetic psalms', in P.W. Flint and P.D. Miller (eds), *The Book of Psalms: Composition and Reception* (VTSup 99; Leiden: Brill).

Fröhlich, I.

2001 'Demons, scribes, and exorcists at Qumran', in K. Dévényi and T. Iványi (eds), *Essays in Honour of Alexander Fodor on his Sixtieth Birthday* (Budapest Studies in Arabic 23; Budapest: Eötvös Loránd University and Csoma de Kőrös Society).

García Martínez, F.

2002 'Magic in the Dead Sea scrolls', in J.N. Bremmer and J.R. Veenstra (eds), *The Metamorphosis of Magic from Late Antiquity to the Early Modern Period* (Groningen Studies in Cultural Change 1; Leuven: Peeters).

Graf, F.

1997 *Magic in the Ancient World*, trans. F. Philip (Cambridge, MA: Harvard University Press).

Klauck, H.-J.
2000 *Magic and Paganism in Early Christianity: The World of the Acts of the Apostles* (Minneapolis: Fortress Press).

Kotansky, R.
1994 *Greek Magical Amulets: The Inscribed Gold, Silver, Copper, and Bronze Lamellae, Part I: Published Texts of Known Provenance* (Papyrologica Coloniensia 22; Opladen: Westdeutscher Verlag).

Lambdin, T.O.
1962 'Alphabet', in G.A. Buttrick, *et al.* (eds), *The Interpreter's Dictionary of the Bible* (Nashville: Abingdon Press).

Lods, A.
1892 *Le livre d'Hénoch: fragments grecs découverts à Akhmîm (Haute-Égypte), publiés avec les variantes du texte éthiopien, traduits et annotés* (Paris: E. Leroux).

Löhr, M.
1905 'Alphabetische und alphabetisierende Lieder im AT', *ZAW* 25.

Lyons, W.J., and A.M. Reimer
1998 'The demonic virus and Qumran studies: some preventative measures', *Dead Sea Discoveries* 5.

Milik, J.T.
1976 *The Books of Enoch: Aramaic Fragments of Qumrân Cave 4* (Oxford: Clarendon Press).

Millard, A.R.
2000 *Reading and Writing in the Time of Jesus* (Biblical Seminar 69; Sheffield: Sheffield Academic Press).

Naveh, J.
1986 'A medical document or a writing exercise? The so-called 4QTherapeia', *IEJ* 36.
2000 '341. 4QExercitium Calami C', in S.J. Pfann, P.S. Alexander *et al.* (eds), *Qumran Cave 4.XXVI: Cryptic Texts and Miscellanea, Part 1* (DJD 36; Oxford: Clarendon Press).

Preisendanz, K. (ed)
1973–74 *Papyri Graecae Magicae: Die griechischen Zauberpapyri*, ed. A. Heinrichs (Stuttgart: Teubner; 1st ed. Leipzig/Berlin: Teubner, 1928–31).

Puech, E.
1980 'Abécédarie et list alphabétique de noms hébreux du début du IIe s. A.D.', *RB* 87.

Schams, C.
1998 *Jewish Scribes in the Second Temple Period* (JSOTSup 291; Sheffield: Sheffield Academic Press).

Schwartz, M.
2002 'Qumran, Turfan, Arabic magic, and Noah's name', in R. Gyselen (ed.), *Charmes et sortilèges, magie et magiciens* (Res Orientales

14; Bures-sur-Yvette: Groupe pour l'Étude de la Civilisation du Moyen-Orient).

Smet, D. de
2002 'L'alphabet secret des Ismaéliens ou la force magique de l'écriture', in R. Gyselen (ed.), *Charmes et sortilèges, magie et magiciens* (Res Orientales 14; Bures-sur-Yvette: Groupe pour l'Étude de la Civilisation du Moyen-Orient).

Thierry, N.
2002 'Le devenir du carré magique "sator" en Cappadoce dite "archaïque"', in R. Gyselen (ed.), *Charmes et sortilèges, magie et magiciens* (Res Orientales 14; Bures-sur-Yvette: Groupe pour l'Étude de la Civilisation du Moyen-Orient).

Tov, E.
2002 'The biblical texts from the Judaean desert—an overview and analysis of the published texts', in E.D. Herbert and E. Tov (eds), *The Bible as Book: The Hebrew Bible and the Judaean Desert Discoveries* (London: British Library; New Castle: Oak Knoll Press).
2004 *Scribal Practices and Approaches Reflected in the Texts Found in the Judean Desert* (STDJ 54; Leiden: Brill).

Waegeman, M.
1987 *Amulet and Alphabet: Magical Amulets in the First Book of Cyranides* (Amsterdam: J.C. Gieben).

The Origins of the Inscribed Greek Stela

John Davies

For two interlocking reasons it is both a pleasure and a privilege to have been asked to contribute to this volume. The first stems from the history of scholarship, for as seen from the perspective of Alan Millard and of most other contributors, my scholarly business has lain wholly on the other side of a long-standing cultural and linguistic divide. On one side of it lies that version of Antiquity access to which comes first and foremost via texts written in alphabetic Greek and Latin, on the other that version which is accessible only via the languages and physical antiquities of the whole complex of cultures which were eventually encompassed by the Achaimenid Persian Empire. That divide, as we all know, is deeply entrenched, fostered by the privileged educational status which was long accorded to Latin and Greek, and ostensibly but disastrously legitimized by 'Western' 'European' constructions of everything east of Rhodes as the 'Oriental' 'other'. It is a matter of profound institutional satisfaction to me, as the first Head of School, that in Liverpool we managed to create and to foster an academic entity, in the form of the School of which Alan Millard and I have long been senior colleagues, part of whose mission is to bridge—indeed to abolish—that divide: the Liverpool contributions to this volume are some token that we have succeeded. Here, my first reason becomes my second, for he, with others, has been a consistent ally in attempting to forward that mission. In that and in many other ways, ever since I joined Liverpool in 1977, he has been a figure whom it has been a privilege to have next door as a close colleague and friend. (That we now, in retirement, share an office is itself symbolic.) By teaching and writing of the whole of Antiquity as a continuum, by seeing it as an intrinsic part of an academic's mission to reach out to the people at large, and by focusing so constructively on the craft of writing in Antiquity, he has been a constant stimulus and example to me, for whose presence and goodwill I shall always be deeply grateful.

It is therefore appropriate that my contribution[1] should both attempt to strengthen the bridge and to focus specifically on an aspect of the earlier

[1] This chapter owes much to the scholarship and sane judgement contained in *LSAG*² 50–63 and 429–30, and also to Ben Millis, Graham Oliver, and especially to Stephen Lambert, whose

stages of the use of the alphabet to write Greek: all the more because the interests of recent scholarship have been curiously lop-sided. On the one hand the debate about the date, region, purposes, and mental modalities of those early stages of transfer continues to be intense.[2] Very briefly, and without joining any of the arguments, the *communis opinio* continues to see *c.* 850–800 BCE as the likely horizon of the adaptation of the Phoenician alphabet for Greek, though advocates of (much) earlier dates are not lacking (e.g. Bernal 1990; Naveh 1982 and 1991). There is much less unanimity about location, reasoned cases having been advanced for Crete in general (e.g. Guarducci 1967–78 I: 67–70; Duhoux 1981) and Kommos in particular (cf. *SEG* XLVIII 2101; Lazzarini 1999: 55), for Cyprus (Johnston 1983; Woodard 1997), for North Syria (Jeffery 1990: 1–12; Lipiński 1988), for Euboia (Lazzarini 1999), or for a plurality of places in the Semitic world (Isserlin 1991), not least Byblos itself (Guarducci 1969–87 I: 64). Equally, there is no consensus about purpose, for the views which see the Greek alphabet as an instrument forged to record Greek hexameter poetry (Wade-Gery 1952: 11–14; Powell 1991a; Robb 1994) or to help communication with colonies (Harris 1996: 65–67) contrast with the commoner view that it emerged from trading and mercantile activities (Harris 1989: 45–48).

However, notwithstanding such disagreements, the debate has shown one uniformity, that of focusing almost entirely on letter forms and phonology, on what was being written, and on levels of literacy, while saying far less about the objects and the surfaces on which Greek words were being written. The bias is understandable, for surfaces can be regarded as non-problematic, being those which were suitable and easily available such as potsherds or rock outcrops, while, though all scholars accept that much early Greek alphabetic writing will have been on wholly perishable materials, the arguments have to start from what can be seen and touched. Yet the 'placing' of inscriptions constitutes a trace element which is informative in two related but separable ways. First, if understood as their location in a human landscape, their appearance in non-domestic or non-private domains has to be seen, not just as 'publication' or 'publicity', but as the outcome of processes of definition of public space and public interest,[3] irrespective of how many or how few

comments and suggestions transformed an earlier draft out of all recognition: to them and to him my profound and grateful thanks. Omissions and foolishnesses remain mine.

[2] Among useful surveys are *LSAG*[2] 1–42 and 425–27; Powell 1991a: 123–80, Marek 1993, Harris 1996, and Ghinatti 1999. Almost every year since 1976 the 'Varia' section of *Supplementum Epigraphicum Graecum* contains summaries or notices of work on the alphabet. The most important are XXIX 1740–41, XXXI 1636, XXXII 865, XXXIII 1555, XXXVIII 1935 and 2036, XXXIX 1764, XL 1633, XLIII 1205, XLV 2208 and 2262, XLVI 2309, XLVII 2238, and XLVIII 2101.

[3] Such a process must emphatically be seen as conceptually separate from, and unfolding much later than, the adoption of alphabetic script to denote Greek. The formulation of Vernant, 'The purpose of writing was no longer the production of archives for the king's private use

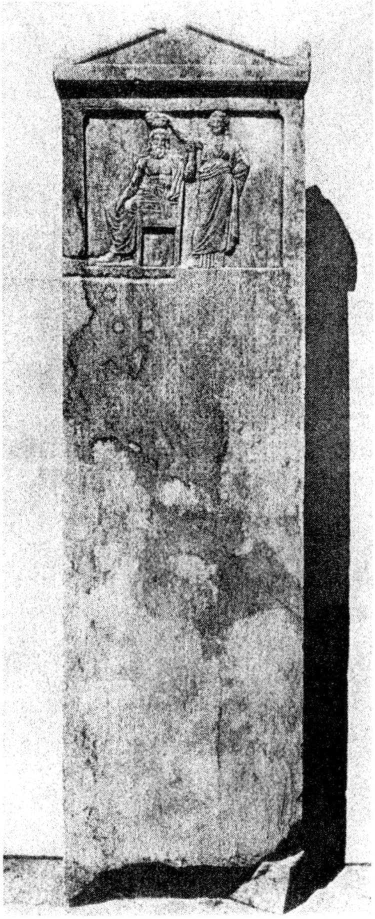

Fig. 1. The Athenian law against tyranny. After Hesperia *21 (1952), pl. 90(a).*

persons were able to read them or of whether each individual inscription was meant to function as text or as symbol. Secondly, and more relevantly to the present argument, in any context where a ready-made surface was unavailable, 'placing' as understood as the need to find or to create usable surfaces generated expedients of various kinds. Eventually, that process yielded, as the predominant (but far from the only) solution, the standard Greek inscribed stela, normally inscribed on one side only, slightly tapered, with a

within the palace. Now it served a public purpose: it allowed the various aspects of social and political life to be disclosed to the gaze of all people equally' (cited by Powell 1991a: 115), unhelpfully telescopes several very different phases into one.

thickness:width:height ratio approximating to 1:4:9.[4] Above the inscribed surface there frequently came to be a pediment, sometimes carrying acroteria, and/or a bas-relief bordered by antae. The stela carrying the Athenian law against tyranny of 337/6 may serve as a model (Fig. 1), though one should think in terms of a family of variations rather than of a uniformly followed archetype. The question which this paper addresses is the origin of this format: specifically, whether it reflected native inventiveness or adapted existing, even remote and non-Greek, monumental forms via direct or indirect awareness. I add 'non-Greek' since the need which generated it gathered force in the eighth and seventh centuries BCE, i.e. during the very period when Greeks were moving fastest to reach out towards, and to adopt or adapt, a huge range of cultural goods from Anatolia, Egypt, Balkan Europe, and the Levant;[5] an imitation of formats then current in the Eastern Mediterranean has to be at least a possibility. I return to the topic towards the end of this paper.

Though there is a real risk of starting from the wrong end, and therefore of offering a tidy linear developmental model rather than a more realistic shambles of short-term expedients, it may therefore be worth trying to map those expedients in an unorthodox way, by reviewing Greek alphabetic inscriptions primarily in terms of the physical format of the object on which they are written. The task is intractable for two reasons. First, though indeed the alphabet came as an indivisible package (Bourdreuil, this volume), the idea was given practical form through a range of local alphabets which showed substantial differences throughout the archaic period and beyond. It is these alphabets, rather than the objects which carried them, which have therefore come to be the primary basis of classification and study, as exemplified alike in the standard textbooks (Guarducci 1967–78 and *LSAG*²) and in the regional divisions of material which have long been adopted by the authoritative publication format of *Inscriptiones Graecae* and its avatars. Secondly, both within the corpus of each local script and over the broader canvass of epigraphic study as a whole, the ordering of documents has been carried out by genre, typically comprising civic decrees, royal letters, accounts, dedications, gravestones, and manumissions,[6] while more recently the perceived need to study the inscriptions of major sanctuaries as bounded wholes has introduced a further level of fragmentation. Hence, though it would not be true to allege that questions of material and placing have been neglected,[7] any approach such as the present one engenders a sense of having to abandon the roads and cut across country.

[4] References in Lawton 1995: 11 n. 28.

[5] This is not the place to spell out the obvious heavy-handedly. It suffices to cite Dunbabin 1957; Szemerényi 1974; West 1997.

[6] Cf. the format of Guarducci 1967–78, or the recent handbook of McLean 2002.

[7] Cf. Detienne 1988b; Hölkeskamp 1992: 99–102, Hölkeskamp 1994: 135–64; Harris 1996: 69–70. The fullest review remains that of *LSAG*² 50–58 and 429–30.

This brief essay, therefore, merely reports a first reconnaissance of what is almost virgin territory. To this end, in order to create a first sketch map, I begin by eschewing approaches by genre (thus Guarducci 1967–78) or by region (thus *LSAG*²), at least for the initial stages of attested Greek alphabetic writing, and by focusing instead on the media used. Significantly, no collection known to me organizes itself by that criterion, but fortunately, at least for illustrative purposes, and with no pretence of independent judgement or completeness, the catalogue of Powell (1991a: 119–80) provides a usable initial collection, for (accepting that all dates for early Greek inscriptions are approximations with a considerable margin of error) its cut-off date of *c*. 650 BCE allows us to review the first century of alphabetic writing as a whole. His 68 examples are revealing. A large majority of them are graffiti on pottery sherds,[8] whether (when the genre is discernible) they are votive, erotic, labels of ownership, abecedaria, or poetic in content. The next largest group, albeit with only 11 items, comprises rock-cut inscriptions, mostly from Thera and either funerary or erotic (Powell 1991a: nos 13–16, 39, and 63–68). Then come five dipinti, three metal objects, a writing-tablet,[9] a scrap of flat stone from the Athenian Akropolis relegated by editors to the *Incerta* in despair,[10] and a mere five stone stelae, votive and funerary. Since it is this last medium whose fortunes are primarily being tracked here, two points are relevant. First, though they, like the rock-cut inscriptions, may have been visible and therefore in that minimal sense 'public', none of them—and still less any of the other exhibits—can plausibly be deemed to pertain to any civic or communal activity.[11] Secondly, though even in these early stages alphabetic writing was being used for a wide variety of purposes, the format of the inscribed

[8] Nos 1–9, 11–12, 17–32, 34, 36, 42–43, 49–54, 56–60. The publication of Powell's book coincided with that of what is currently thought to be the oldest Greek alphabetic inscription, a graffito from Osteria dell'Osa at Gabii 19 km east of Rome dated by archaeological context to *c*. 770 BCE (*SEG* XLIII 646; XLV 1429; XLVII 1478; XLVIII 1266; XLIX 1353; cf. also Lazzarini 1999: 51).

[9] Respectively Powell 1991a: nos 10, 33, 35, 44, 46; 41, 61 (and *IG* I³ 584, not cited by Powell); 55.

[10] *Inscriptiones Graecae* I³ 1418 (= Powell 1991a: 150 no. 47).

[11] In chronological order of dates suggested in *LSAG*², they are: (a) Gravestone of Ankylion, Anaphe, early seventh century. *IG* XII, 3, 255 = *LSAG*² 324 no. 23 = Powell 1991a: 144 no. 40. (b) Limestone stela once holding a spit dedication, Perachora, *c*. 650? *LSAG*² 131 no. 7 = Powell 1991a: 147–48 no. 45. For problems of dating etc. see *LSAG*² 122–24. (c) Grave-stela of Dwenia(s), Korinthiad, *c*. 650? *IG* IV 358 = *LSAG*² 131 no. 6 = Powell 1991a: 142–43 no. 38, there misleadingly dated '*c*. 700?'. (d) Daidalic statue of Artemis dedicated to her on Delos by Nikandre of Naxos, *c*. 650? *IG* XII 5, 2 p. xxiv = *LSAG*² 303 no. 2 = Powell 1991a: 169–71 no. 62. (e) Grave stela, Thera, 'seventh c.?'. *IG* XII 3, 781 = *LSAG*² 323 no. 3 and pl. 61 = Powell 1991a: 142 no. 37 ('impossible to date accurately but perhaps reaching back into our period').

In addition (f) (g) two other grave stelae from Thera, *IG* XII 3, 765 and 771, are grouped in *LSAG*² with (e) as *LSAG*² 323 no. 3.

stela was being seen, for easily understandable reasons which reflect pre-literate practice,[12] as appropriate above all for grave markers and some dedications.

If now we move into the second century of alphabetic use in Greece, it will be recalled that the first known 'public' inscription on stone, a law from Dreros in Crete, is commonly dated *c.* 650[13] and was gradually followed by others. Most scholars would probably agree that this development reflects a significant horizon not just of effective literacy but also of communal atmosphere and institutions, in that it was from that epoch onwards that public utterances (laws, decrees, dedications by magistrates) gradually established themselves as genres distinct from those of private utterance (dedications, gravestones, graffiti, etc.). From this point onwards, therefore, as public written documents began to proliferate, each issuing authority had to decide how and where to display them.

On the available evidence, stela form was not the preferred format. Instead, inscriptions meant to be seen in public (even if not read)[14] took four main forms. In very rough chronological order of appearance, the first was to use a surface which had already been created for other purposes. Especially in Crete, the region which generated by far the majority of early public inscriptions, the preferred medium comprised course blocks or orthostats which formed part of a temple wall. When, as at Dreros and Gortyn, the temple was that of Apollo,[15] the surface was appropriate as well as convenient, since it linked the text thus promulgated with the god whose role as the god of *Nomos* ('measure', 'due order', hence 'law') made him the obvious patron and protector of such utterances, but the walls of shrines of Artemis and Athene were also used.

Next in time, on conventional chronologies in the 620s and the 590s, came two sets of texts, the laws of Drakon and of Solon at Athens, the medium and most of the content of which are known only from a sadly confused literary tradition. Fortunately, this is not the place to reopen the never-ending debate about how to interpret that tradition,[16] since what is agreed as common ground is enough for present purposes. It is clear that media were designed and created specifically and uniquely to carry text, that the texts were first written (carved? painted?) on wood and perhaps later transferred to bronze, that the text-bearing components were termed *axones*

[12] As in the Geometric cemetery at Corinth (Blegen *et al.* 1964: 16). My thanks to Dr Merriss for this reference.

[13] *LSAG*^{2} 315 no. 1a = ML^2 2, inscribed on the wall of the temple of Apollo Delphinios.

[14] Cf. Stoddart and Whitley 1988 and especially Whitley 1997.

[15] The Pythion (Ricciardi 1986/87 and Sporn 2002: 152–56). Sporn 2002: 153 n. 1039 warns against following Guarducci's assumption that all these texts came from the Pythion itself rather than from another public building, but the essential point still stands.

[16] See instead Dow 1961b, Stroud 1979 and the references in *LSAG*^{2} 52–55 and 429–30.

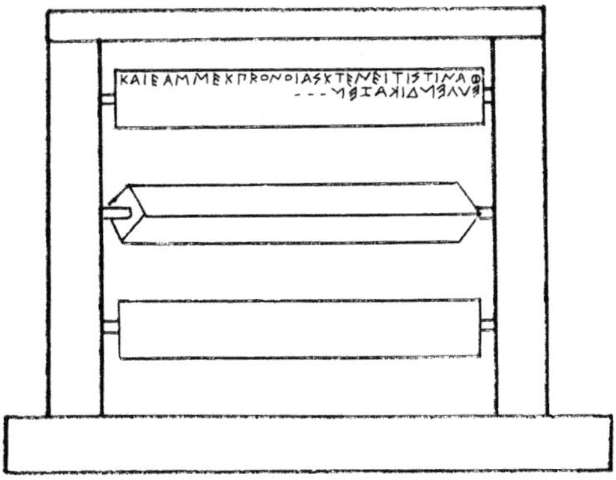

Fig. 2. Reconstruction of wooden axones. *After Stroud 1979: 46, fig. 1.*

and *kyrbeis* (the difference, if any, between the two being disputed), that they may have been 'large rectangular four-sided [or three-sided] pieces of wood mounted in an oblong frame....by means of pins at each end which permitted them to be rotated by the reader in such a way that the text inscribed on each of the four surfaces was legible' (Stroud 1979: 41, with his fig. 1, reproduced here as Fig. 2), that the mounting may have initially been horizontal, later vertical, and that they were first set up on the Akropolis before being transferred at a disputed date to the Agora.[17]

With this expedient one major Greek community was already well down the road of creating specific text-carrying objects.[18] (Whether other Greek micro-states used wood in comparable ways to carry text is unknown but is likely enough.) What is known is that Athens was not alone in using bronze, for a third format, the bronze plaque, came to be widely used from the early sixth century onwards, especially at Olympia and in the Greek west in Sicily and South Italy[19] but also at Argos.[20] Since the nail-holes which many surviving examples carry indicate that they were intended to be fixed to buildings, and especially (as find-spots make clear) to temples, this third format is not so different a style of medium from the inscribed wall-block as might appear: while the relative availability of good-quality stone surfaces and of sheet bronze will have determined the choice, the idea underlying the choice of location remained much the same.

[17] A number of the stone bases in which one (three-sided) version of the text-bearing components was set up survives from the Agora: see Stroud 1979: 49–60.

[18] Not that all communities moved in a uniform direction: the rock-cut Schlangenschrift inscription from Tiryns of *c.* 600–550 (*LSAG*² 443 no. 9a, pl. 74) is a healthy reminder of diversity.

[19] Numerous examples can be found in *LSAG*² and *Nomima*: a full list would be more tedious than helpful.

[20] *Nomima* I 100, from the Heraion.

The archaic period also created a fourth format, which approaches that of the classical stela but still shows significant differences: a pillar, inscribed on several faces with lettering which ran vertically. In very approximate chronological order (dates as per *LSAG*²), some of the clearest examples[21] are the following:

(a) *LSAG*² 150 no. 8, pl. 25, and 443: *lex sacra*, Kleonai (note Jameson 1974: 70 for the reattribution), *c*. 600–550?;
(b) *IC* I xxxviii 7 = *LSAG*² 315 no. 12: legal code, Rhizenia (Prinias) in Crete, 'early sixth c.?';
(c) *CIL* I² 1 = *ILLRP* 3 (the *lapis niger*), with *LSAG*² 52 no. 2: *lex sacra* from the forum, Rome, early sixth century?;
(d) *IG* IV 1607 = *SEG* XXV 358 = *LSAG*² 150 no. 6, pl. 25 = *Nomima* II 79: purification law, Kleonai, *c*. 575–550?;
(e) *LSAG*² 343 no. 41 = ML² 8 = *Nomima* I 62: constitutional law, Chios? (or Erythrai, cf. ML² pp. 17 and 309), *c*. 575–550;
(f) *LSAG*² 372 no. 51, pl. 72 = *Nomima* I 32: honorary decree, Kyzikos, *c*. 525–500 (not yet republished in *IK Kyzikos*);
(g) *IG* I³ 1 = ML² 14 = *Nomima* I 6: Salamis decree, Athens, 510–500.

Again, one must think of a family resemblance rather than of uniformity, the main features being that the text is set out vertically along the stone, not horizontally across it, that the format remained stark and unadorned,[22] and that the five earlier texts spread over several faces of the stone.[23] Small though the sample is, I suspect it is not chance that the two latest texts, (f) and (g), show text on one side only and are decrees rather than laws, while (f) is explicitly termed a stela within its surviving text. Moreover, if one follows the course of Athenian public documentation down to *c*. 450, what we may call by 500 the older pattern, viz. the practice of creating text-carrying blocks meant to carry text on several sides, clearly continued and was evidently thought particularly appropriate for texts (by far the majority) which were

[21] The list could be expanded, but not much. The treaty between the Lakedaimonians and the Erxadieis (*LSAG*² 447, G) is eccentrically dated at the end of the sixth century in *Nomima* I 55, but probably belongs a century later. However, Guarducci rightly discerned that *IC* I ix 1, the ephebes' oath from Dreros, cut in the late third century BCE on all four sides of a tapered pillar, reproduced both the text and the format of a much older document, the original of which could certainly have been added to the list.

[22] Text (e) is a possible exception, since its top is reported to show a cutting for a crowning member.

[23] Text (a) is on at least two sides (since Werner Peek, the first editor, reports 'Schrift auf Oberseite, Schrägkante, und Vorderseite' (*AM* 66 (1941), 198), it must remain moot whether the Schrägkante ('bevels') count as separate 'sides'). Texts (b) and (d) are on three, (e) on four, and (c) on five sides.

concerned with cult.[24] It is not until the 460s and especially the 450s, when more directly political decrees begin to be cut on stone and set up, that the single-sided 'standard' stela becomes the norm.

Yet, even then practice remained stark, far removed from the developed and decorated form of documentary stela exemplified by the tyranny law, and even further removed from the elaboration and grandeur which dedications and gravestones had widely taken on in the course of the sixth century. In fact, the later ornamented stela took a surprisingly long time to emerge. I consider briefly date, location and function, and possible influences. First, date. Two recent detailed studies (Meyer 1989; Lawton 1995), one of which (Meyer's) includes non-Attic material, agree in beginning their catalogues of dated and datable examples in the 420s, though two disputed examples[25] preclude certainty that the custom had not started in the 450s. However, once the prolonged controversy over the existence or non-existence of a crowning member for the First Stela of the Tribute Lists ended fairly decisively with the discovery and publication of a new fragment which showed 'a weathered and pockmarked <top> surface from long exposure to the elements', that Stela, erected in 454/3, offers firm negative evidence, as also does the Second Stela, set up in 439/8.[26] Likewise, the Treasurers' records for the Pronaos of the Parthenon, set up in 434/3, show a smooth but unadorned top.[27] It will be wise to hold firm to the horizon of the 420s for the start of the spasmodic addition of bas-relief or pediment.

Secondly, location and function. Again, a *praeteritio* is unavoidable, for the role of inscriptions in the process of the emergence of public archives in Classical Greece has aroused recent discussion[28] which cannot be advanced here. Relevant considerations include the absence (in Athens after 480) or

[24] Thus, with the *leges sacrae*, though nothing can be asserted about *IG* I^3 230 and 235 and though 231 (500s: altar?) was single-faced, 232 ('510–480'; an altar?) has text on three of its four sides, 233 has text on at least two sides, and 234 is inscribed on front and back ('opisthographic'). Cult-active demes followed suit, 243 (Melite, 480–450), 244 (Skambonidai, *c.* 460) and 246 (unknown body, 470–450) having text on four sides, with only 245 (Sypalettos, 460s) being certainly single-faced. Likewise, of early decrees *IG* I^3 4 (485/4, Hekatompedon decree) is opisthographic, 5 (*c.* 500) is single-faced but cut on an altar, 6 (Eleusinian Mysteries, *c.* 460) has four faces, while the single-sided sequence begins with 7 (Praxiergidai, 450s). One stone, indeed, *IG* I^3 3–4, shows the change eloquently, the text cut first (*IG* I^3 3, *c.* 500, uncertain content) being cut vertically top-down, while the text added on the reverse in the 480s (*IG* I^3 4, Herakleia at Marathon) is cut horizontally. Moreover, as Dr Lambert reminds me, the opisthographic blocks which carried Nikomachos' republication of the law-code between 410 and 399 (Dow 1961a) are evidence that the older pattern continued to be thought appropriate for laws, especially *leges sacrae*.

[25] *IG* I^3 21 (Miletos decree: Meyer 1989: A 1 = Lawton 1995: no. 63) and *IG* I^3 28 (decree for the sons of Iphiades: Lawton 1995: no. 64; absent from Meyer 1989).

[26] For bibliography see lemma to IG I^3 259–72; quotation from Meritt 1972: 403.

[27] IG I^3 292–316, with photograph in Guarducci 1967–78: II 232 fig. 52.

[28] *Inter alios* Thomas 1992; Robb 1994; Sickinger 1999; Davies 2003.

unavailability (as perhaps at Gortyn) of suitable temple walls;[29] the proliferation of documents, which (as the endless sockets for stela-bases on the Athenian Akropolis make clear) either gradually generated a thick maquis of marble surfaces or (as at Delphi) overran every available surface; the need to be able to identify particular documents (a need which painted individualized[30] reliefs would help to meet); or the need to be able to obliterate, annul, and reuse out-of-date stelae.

Lastly, and in order to return to the wider theme of adoptions and adaptations, the question of influences may usefully be broached.[31] Since even early examples of documentary stelae show variation, the relief being placed above the taenia and cyma reversa in one case[32] but integrated with the text field in another,[33] no one model was being followed or imposed, so that we should be looking towards a context where such variation was normal. The obvious short-range derivation or correlation, at least in Attika, is with the re-emergence of relief gravestones in the 430s after the hiatus which began in the very late sixth century.[34] Now that the documentary reliefs cannot be safely taken back beyond the 420s, it becomes possible to postulate that the designers and cutters of documentary stelae in the 420s and subsequently were influenced by the contemporary revival in funerary sculpture. Nor is the route of adaptation hard to follow, for all that was needed was to shift the balance between text and relief, by confining the latter to the top register and allowing the greater part of the body of the stela to carry text. Moreover, as Lawton's plates make clear, there was nothing to stop a mason from adding a pediment above the tainia or from filling an enlarged pediment with sculpture. As a sample, and without claiming a mastery of either genre, I juxtapose as Figs 3 and 4 two *dexiosis* scenes which

[29] Hence perhaps the physical format of the Great Code on a specially created surface, its layout on the stone (as with so many inscriptions, as Dr Lambert reminds me) reflecting that of the lost holograph master text, whether on a papyrus roll (Davies) or wax tablets (Millard 1991 and pers. comm.).

[30] Dr Lambert notes 'the immense scope for variety' available in spite of 'the essentially homogeneous…. nature of stelai', and reports that hardly ever are two reliefs identical.

[31] Unfortunately, neither Meyer nor Lawton goes beyond questions of stylistic analysis to seek the origins of the format.

[32] IG I^3 68 = Meyer 1989: A 3 = Lawton 1995: no. 1.

[33] IG I^3 61 = Meyer 1989: A 4 = Lawton 1995: no. 2.

[34] Neither the hiatus nor its end can be discussed here: see *inter alios* Diepolder 1931: 7–8; Richter 1944: 119–24; Johansen 1951; Richter 1961: 53–55; Kurtz and Boardman 1971: 121–24. To an outsider the striking feature of the discussion is the degree to which the two genres, the documentary relief and the funerary relief, have been studied as if they were being created in separate worlds. Honourably, and exceptionally, Johansen did link the two, by briefly canvassing the idea that the *dexiosis* scene which is a recurring theme on classical grave-reliefs was taken over from the documentary reliefs, the start of which, following Binneboessel 1932 and Schweitzer 1943, he dated *c.* 450 (Johansen 1951: 149–51). Though the idea now falls in its original form, it is tentatively inverted in the text above.

Fig. 3. Relief surmounting the dossier of decrees for the Samians, passed in 405/4 and 403/2. After Lawton 1995: pl. 7.

Fig. 4. Relief surmounting the funerary stela (IG I³ 1283bis) for Aristeas of Iphistiadai and his family, c. 430–390. After Diepolder 1931: taf. 3,2.

have some chance of being roughly contemporary:[35] that there has at least been a convergence of genres seems to me inescapable.[36] However, even that hypothesis does not provide a complete explanation, for the pediment itself, normally a flat isosceles triangle, may convey a message. As Dr Lambert points out to me, it may deliberately reflect in miniature the shape and content of a Greek temple pediment, a suggestion all the more plausible since the 'sacral' nature of such relief-bearing stelae should not be underestimated: set up mostly in sanctuaries, with sculpture which echoes divine iconographies, and with the divine invocation '*Theoi*' ('Gods') commonplace in the prescript, they are protected citizens of sacred space, not just components of a secular archive (Lawton 1995: 14–15 and 40–55; Pounder 1984).

Such considerations point firmly towards indigenous development. The initial presentation of this chapter did indeed toy with the notion that since the decorative motifs which adorned both archaic and classical funerary stelae—lions, palmettes, sphinxes, sirens, etc.—have long been traced back to models available in, and adopted and adapted from, Eastern Mediterranean cultures from the eighth century onwards, the case could be argued for a comparable adaptation of the stela itself from Near Eastern examples which will have been visible to visitors from Greece. On reconsideration, it will be wise to scout that idea firmly. There are certainly superficial resemblances, but at the Greek end they involve gravestones and dedications, not the acts of states or rulers. Indeed, though the plates in *LSAG*² have to be viewed via the awareness that the authors were concerned with letter-forms first and foremost, not with the objects which carried them, yet even a rapid scan brings out forcibly how unmonumental, not to say scruffy and mean, most Greek public documentation was until well after the Persian Wars. Moreover, though kings and tyrants littered the political landscape of archaic and classical Greece far more comprehensively than current obsessions with the canonical republican Kleinstaat are willing to admit, the genre of royal *res gestae*, as exemplified by Kilamuwa at Zinjirli or by Azitawada at Karatepe, or later by Nabonidus in Babylon (Schaudig 2001), Dareios at Behistun or Yehaumilk at Byblos, had no correlate whatever in Greece. Likewise, no custom developed of displaying documents at or on city gates: virtually universally, it was the sanctuaries which were seen as the appropriate locations.

35 (a) the relief (Meyer 1989: A 26, taf. 10,1: Lawton 1995: no. 12, pl. 7) which surmounts the dossier of decrees for the Samians, passed in 405/4 and 403/2 (ML² 94 = *IG* I³ 127: *IG* II² 1) (Fig. 3). (b) the scene (Diepolder 1931: taf. 3,2: Clairmont 1993: III 61 no. 3.075) on a funerary stela for Aristeas of Iphistiadai and his family (*IG* I³ 1283*bis*) which in spite of debate over detail (references *ap. IG*) seems to be agreed to date to the first generation of renewed production in the genre, i.e. to 430–390 (Fig. 4).

36 G. Davies 1985. Funerary formats are discussed in much greater detail in Clairmont 1970 and 1993.

We are therefore left with an interesting and complex divergence of practice. Of course, as always with the artefacts of any culture, it was a matter of selecting from a variety of known or unknown sources those components which met the needs of the time, the genre, and the patron. While for privately sponsored inscribed artefacts practice in archaic and classical Greece continued to parallel, and to be influenced by,[37] practice in the other literate cultures of the Eastern Mediterranean, public documentation, increasingly shaped by considerations of access and accountability, created its formats with reference to locally-defined spaces and buildings, and took such ornament as was felt appropriate from within specifically Greek architectural and iconographic traditions. No simple formulation will do.

Bibliography

Amadasi Guzzo, M.G.
1991 '"The shadow line". Réflexions sur l'introduction de l'alphabet en Grèce', in Baurain *et al.* 1991: 294–311.
1999 'Sulla formazione e diffusione dell'alfabeto', in Bagnasco Gianni and Cordano 1999: 27–51.

Bagnasco Gianni, G., and F. Cordano (eds)
1999 *Scritture mediterranee tra il IX e il VII secolo a.C: Atti del Seminario, Milano, 23–24 Febbraio 1998* (Milano).

Baurain, C., C. Bonnet and V. Krings (eds)
1991 *Phoinikeia grammata: Lire et écrire en Méditerranée.* Actes du colloque de Liège, 15–18 November 1989 (Namur).

Bernal, M.
1990 *Cadmean Letters: The Transmission of the Alphabet to the Aegean and Further West before 1400 bc* (Winona Lake, Ind.).

Binneboessel, R.
1932 *Attischen Urkundenreliefs* (Kaldenkirchen).

Blegen, C.W., H. Palmer and R.S. Young
1964 *Corinth XIII: The North Cemetery* (Princeton, NJ).

Boegehold, A.L., *et al.* (eds)
1984 *Studies Presented to Sterling Dow on his Eightieth Birthday* (Durham, NC).

Bradeen, D.W., and M.F. Mcgregor (eds)
1974 *ΦΟΡΟΣ. Tribute to Benjamin Dean Meritt* (Locust Valley, NY).

[37] Cf. Miller 1997 for belated appreciation of the continuing debt of Greek luxury culture to Near Eastern fashions, materials, and symbolisms.

Brosius, M. (ed.)
2003 *Ancient Archives and Archival Traditions: Concepts of Record-Keeping in The Ancient World* (Oxford).

Börker-Klähn, J.
1982 *Altvorderasiatische Bildstelen und vergleichbare Felsreliefs*, I: Text, II: Tafeln, *Baghdader Forschungen* 4. (Mainz).

Clairmont, C.W.
1970 *Gravestone and Epigram: Greek Memorials from the Archaic and Classical Period.* Mainz.
1993 *Classical Attic Tombstones*, I–V with Supplements (Kilchberg).

Davies, G.
1985 'The significance of the handshake motif in classical funerary art', *AJA* 89: 627–40.

Davies, J.K.
2003 'Greek archives: from record to monument', in Brosius 2003: 323–43.

Détienne, M.
1988a *Les savoirs d'écriture en Grèce ancienne* (Lille).
1988b 'L'éspace de la publicité: ses opérateurs intellectuels dans la cité', in Détienne 1988a: 56–64.

Diepolder, H.
1931 *Die attischen Grabreliefs des 5. und 4. Jahrhunderts v. Chr.* (Berlin).

Dinsmoor. W.B.
1922 'A new type of Attic grave stele', *AJA* 26: 261–77.

Dow, S.
1961a 'The walls inscribed with Nikomakhos' law code', *Hesperia* 30: 58–73.
1961b 'The "Axon", Inscriptiones Graecae I^2 2', *AJA* 65: 349–56.

Duhoux, Y.
1981 'Les Étéocrétois et l'origine de l'alphabet grec', *AntClass* 50: 287–94, planches I–VI.

Driver, G.R.
1948 *Semitic Writing: From Pictograph to Alphabet* (Oxford).

Dunbabin, T.J.
1957 *The Greeks and their Eastern Neighbours: Studies in the Relations between Greece and the Countries of the Near East in the Eighth and Seventh Centuries BC JHS* Suppl. Paper 8 (London).

Gehrke, H.-J. (ed. with E. Wirbelauer)
1994 *Rechtkodifizierung und soziale Normen im interkulturellen Vergleich* (Tübingen).

Ghinatti, F.
1999 *Alfabeti greci* (Torino).

Gibson, J.C.L.
1971 *Textbook of Syrian Semitic Inscriptions, I: Hebrew and Moabite Inscriptions* (Oxford).

1975 *Textbook of Syrian Semitic Inscriptions, II: Aramaic Inscriptions* (Oxford).

1982 *Textbook of Syrian Semitic Inscriptions, III: Phoenician Inscriptions* (Oxford).

Guarducci, M.

1969–87 *Epigrafia Greca,* I (1967), II (1969), III (1974), IV (1978) (Roma).

Hägg, R. (ed.)

1983 *The Greek Renaissance of the Eighth Century* BC: *Tradition and Innovation. Proceedings of the Second International Symposium at the Swedish Institute in Athens, 1–5 June 1981* (Stockholm).

Harris, W.V.

1989 *Ancient Literacy* (Cambridge, MA/London).

1996 'Writing and literacy in the archaic Greek city', in Strubbe *et al.* 1996: 57–77.

Hitzl, I.

1991 *Die griechischen Sarkophage der archaischen und klassischen Zeit* (Jonsered).

Hölkeskamp, H.-J.

1992 'Written law in archaic Greece', *PCPhS* 38: 87–117.

1994 'Tempel, Agora und Alphabet: Die Entstehungsbedingungen von Gesetzgebung in der archaischen Polis', in Gehrke 1994: 135–64.

Isserlin, B.S.J.

1991 'The transfer of the alphabet to the Greeks', in Baurain *et al.* 1991: 283–91.

Jacobsthal, P.

1911 'Zur Kunstgeschichte der griechischen Inschriften', *Χάριτες Friedrich Leo zum sechzigsten Geburtstag dargebracht* (Berlin): 453–65.

Jameson, M.H.

1974 'A treasury of Athena in the Argolid (*IG* IV, 554)', in Bradeen and McGregor 1974: 67–75.

Jeffery, L.H.

1990 *The Local Scripts of Archaic Greece*, second ed., edited by A.W. Johnston (Oxford).

Johansen, K.F.

1951 *The Attic Grave-Reliefs of the Classical Period: An Essay in Interpretation* (Copenhagen).

Johnston, A.

1983 'The extent and use of literacy: the archaeological evidence', in Hägg 1983: 63–68.

Kurtz, D.C., and J. Boardman

1971 *Greek Burial Customs* (London).

Koeferd-Petersen, O.

1948 *Les stèles Égyptiennes* (Copenhagen).

Lawton, C.
1995 *Attic Document Reliefs: Art and Politics in Ancient Athens* (Oxford).
Lazzarini, M.-L.
1999 'Questioni relative all'origine dell'alfabeto greco', in Bagnasco Gianni and Cordano 1999: 53–66.
Lipiński, E.
1988 'Les Phéniciens et l'alphabet', *Oriens Antiquus* 27: 231–60.
LSAG[2]: see Jeffery 1990.
Marek, Chr.
1993 'Euboia und die Entstehung der Alphabetschrift', *Klio* 75: 27–44.
McLean, B.H.
2002 *An Introduction to Greek Epigraphy of the Hellenistic and Roman Periods from Alexander the Great down to the Reign of Constantine (323 BC–AD 337)* (Ann Arbor).
Meiggs, R., and D.M. Lewis
1988 *A Selection of Greek Historical Inscriptions to the End of the Fifth Century BC*, second ed. (Oxford).
Meritt, B.D.
1972 'The tribute quota list of 454/3 BC, *Hesperia* 41: 403–17.
Meyer, M.
1989 *Die griechischen Urkundenreliefs. Athenische Mitteilungen, Beiheft* 13 (Berlin).
Millard, A.R.
1991 'The uses of the early alphabets', in Baurain *et al.* 1991: 101–14.
Miller, M.C.
1997 *Athens and Persia in the Fifth Century BC: A Study in Cultural Receptivity* (Cambridge).
ML[2]: see Meiggs and Lewis 1988.
Möbius, H.
1968 *Die Ornamente der griechischen Grabstelen klassischer und nachklassischer Zeit.* Second, enlarged ed. (München). (First ed. Berlin-Wilmersdorf, 1929.)
Naveh, J.
1982 *Early History of the Alphabet: An Introduction to West Semitic Epigraphy and Palaeography* (Jerusalem). (Second ed. with additions and corrections, 1987.)
1991 'Semitic epigraphy and the antiquity of the Greek alphabet', *Kadmos* 30: 143–52.
Nomima I–II: Van Effenterre, H., and F. Ruzé
1994–95 *Nomima: Recueil d'inscriptions politiques et juridiques de l'archaïsme grec,* I–II (Rome).
Palaima, T.G.
1990–91 Review article, *Minos* 25–26: 434–54.

Pounder, R.L.

1984 'The origin of θεοί as inscription-heading', in Boegehold *et al.* 1984: 243–50.

Powell, B.B.

1989 'Why was the Greek alphabet invented?', *ClassAnt* 8: 321–50.

1991a *Homer and the Origin of the Greek Alphabet* (Cambridge).

1991b 'The origins of alphabetic literacy among the Greeks', in Baurain *et al.* 1991: 357–70.

Pritchard, J.B.

1969 *The Ancient Near East in Pictures*, second ed. with supplement (Princeton, NJ).

Ricciardi, M.

1986–87 'Il tempio di Apollo Pizio a Gortina', *ASAtene* 64/65: 7–130.

Richter, G.M.A.

1944 *Archaic Attic Gravestones*. (*Martin Classical Lectures*, X) (Cambridge, MA).

1961 *The Archaic Gravestones of Attica* (London).

Robb, K.

1994 *Literacy and Paideia in Ancient Greece* (New York and Oxford).

Schaudig, H.

2001 *Die Inschriften Nabonids von Babylon und Kyros' des Grossen, samt den in ihren Umfeld entstandene Tendenzschriften. Textausgabe und Grammatik. AOAT, 256* (Münster).

Schweitzer, B.

1943 'Urkundenreliefs', in *Festgabe z. Winckelmannsfeier des archäologischen Seminars der Universität Leipzig.* [Non vidi.]

Sickinger, J.P.

1999 *Public Records and Archives in Classical Athens* (Chapel Hill, NC).

Sporn, K.

2002 *Heiligtümer und Kulte Kretas in klassischer und hellenistischer Zeit. Studien zur antiken Heiligtümer,* Bd. 3 (Heidelberg).

Stewart, H.M.

1976 *Egyptian Stelae, Reliefs and Paintings from the Petrie Collection* (Warminster).

Stoddart, S. and J. Whitley

1988 'The social context of literacy in archaic Greece and Etruria', *Antiquity* 62: 761–72.

Stroud, R.S.

1979 *The Axones and Kyrbeis of Drakon and Solon*, University of California publications: Classical Studies, 19 (Berkeley, Los Angeles, and London).

Strubbe, J.H.M., R.A. Tybout and H.S. Versnel (eds)

1996 *ΕΝΕΡΓΕΙΑ. Studies on Ancient History and Epigraphy Presented to H.W. Pleket* (Amsterdam).

Svenbro, J.

1993 *Phrasikleia: An Anthropology of Reading in Ancient Greece*, tr. J. Lloyd (Ithaca, NY).

Szemerényi, O.

1974 'The origins of the Greek lexicon: *Ex Oriente lux*', *JHS* 94: 144–57.

Thomas, R.

1992 *Literacy and Orality in Ancient Greece* (Cambridge).

Wade-Gery, H.T.

1952 *The Poet of the Iliad* (Cambridge).

Watzinger, C.

1929 'Die griechische Grabstele und der Orient', in *Genethliakon Wilhelm Schmid, Tübinger Beiträge zur Altertumswissenschaft*, Heft 5 (Stuttgart): 141–67

West, M.L.

1997 *The East Face of Helicon: West Asiatic Elements in Greek Poetry and Myth* (Oxford).

Whitley, J.

1997 'Cretan laws and Cretan literacy', *AJA* 101: 635–61.

Woodard, R.D.

1997 *Greek Writing from Knossos to Homer* (New York and Oxford).

Woodhead, G.

1959 and reprints *The Study of Greek Inscriptions* (Cambridge).

Only Fragments from the Past: the Role of Accident in our Knowledge of the Ancient Near East

Alan Millard

The role of accident in archaeological discoveries deserves more attention than it is usually given, for most of the objects in our museums, most of the evidence for material culture and most of the documents for reconstructing the course of ancient Near Eastern history have survived by accident and have been discovered by accident. Although this may be stating the obvious, yet it has consequences which are not always recognized.

The accident of discovery

Chance finds by local people have revealed Ugarit, Mari and other sites, duly excavated and now prominent on maps of the ancient world. Archaeological excavations today are undertaken to rescue threatened sites or for 'scientific' reasons—although one may suspect some are begun out of a passion for digging or for prestige and some in the same spirit as mountaineers climb upwards, just because the site is there. The specific aims at the outset may be frustrated by heavier remains of later periods than expected, or by misleading information from earlier surface surveys. At the beginning of Assyriology, when the first man to excavate, Paul Emile Botta, found Nineveh unrewarding because of the heavy overburden of Parthian remains, he turned to a nearby site where local people had been digging out ancient sculptured slabs to burn for lime, and thus he discovered the capital city of Sargon II of Assyria, Dur Sharrukin, now Khorsabad. A few years later, Henry Layard was working at Nimrud. He made amazing discoveries, but almost missed one of his best known. He described what happened one November morning in 1846 when he had almost stopped the work in one place.

> 'The trench was carried in the same direction for several days; but nothing more appeared. It was now above fifty feet in length, and still without any new discovery. I had business in Mosul, and was giving directions to the workmen to guide them during my absence. Standing on the edge of the hitherto unprofitable trench, I doubted whether I should carry it any further:

> but made up my mind at least not to abandon it until my return, which would be on the following day. I mounted my horse; but had scarcely left the mound, when a corner of black marble was uncovered, lying on the very edge of the trench. This attracted the notice of the superintendent of the party digging, who ordered the place to be further examined. The corner was part of an obelisk, about six feet six inches in height, lying on its side, ten feet below the surface.
>
> An Arab was sent after me without delay, to announce the discovery; and on my return I found the obelisk completely exposed to view'.

The men had found what is now famous as the Black Obelisk of Shalmaneser III (Layard 1850: I, 346).

In a different region, the late Yigael Yadin's extensive investigations at Hazor from 1955 to 1958 revealed a Late Bronze Age occupation that extended across the enormous Middle Bronze Age enclosure at the foot of the tell.[1] There were shrines, houses, burials, with quantities of local wares and imported Cypriot and Mycenaean pottery. In 1928 John Garstang had declared the great area was only a camping ground (1931: 184, 382–83), after his small-scale trenches failed to find anything, notably no Mycenaean sherds, accidentally hitting patches apparently unoccupied!

Most amazing of all accidental discoveries in Near Eastern archaeology are, surely, the Dead Sea Scrolls. There is no need to rehearse the story of the goat-herd who threw a stone into a cave intending to frighten out a missing animal, was himself frightened by the clatter of the stone breaking pottery, then returned with his brother hoping to find treasure and was initially disappointed with the frail leather rolls inside pottery jars, the most complete of the hundreds of rolls to survive from one 'library' in first century Palestine.

The accident of survival

The child visiting a museum asks, 'Why did they bury all those things?' Of course, the ancients did not bury any material for inquisitive generations aeons afterwards to exhume! Deliberate burial was made for one of three reasons: firstly, safe keeping, a temporary burial, where there was an intention to recover the treasure; secondly, the most common, funerary ritual; thirdly, the rarest, foundation deposits, which were usually made by royalty. There was no intention that tombs be opened and burial goods removed, although the risk of that happening was very real and recognized, as the curses written in some tombs demonstrate. It is hard for modern minds to conceive that all the equipment Tutankhamun needed for living, wealth befitting a pharaoh, was

[1] Yadin 1972: 18–20, 27, 28, cites Garstang's unpublished notes.

locked away for ever at his death. Its discovery was the result of six seasons of determined searching by Howard Carter, its preservation the result of the accident that Egyptians built over the forgotten entrance in the Twentieth Dynasty. Other pharaohs of the Eighteenth and Nineteenth Dynasties were buried with equal or greater splendour and all were robbed within a few decades. Recently the tombs of eighth-century Assyrian royal ladies at Nimrud have astonished the world with their golden treasures—hitherto scholars had lacked the imagination to credit the witness given by the written records and stone reliefs. These riches had escaped the Median and Babylonian looters in 612 BC and were found initially by workmen tidying the palace (see Damerji 1998; Oates 2001: 78–90). Again, the tombs of the great kings of Assyria surely contained equal or richer treasures but all that remained in burial vaults at Ashur were a few stone sarcophagi shattered by looters (Haller 1954: 170–81).

Foundation deposits were placed principally by kings for their successors to find when they repaired the buildings and some report how they did so.[2] Royal monuments were carved on stone blocks which have sometimes remained where they were placed, like the stela of Ashurnasirpal commemorating the banquet he held for 69,574 people at Nimrud, although such stones were often smashed, or reused in later buildings. Kings also left monuments on cliffs and rock faces, saying, in effect, 'I was here', and those may endure weathering and human interference to last until today. Such large royal monuments may also survive because they were carved on rock surfaces in inaccessible places, such as the narrow pass by the Nahr el-Kelb, the Dog River, near Beirut, or the rock of Behistun. In recent years hitherto unknown inscribed reliefs of Sargon II of Assyria and of, probably, Nabonidus of Babylon have been located in Iran and Jordan, respectively (Frame 1999: 31–57; Dalley and Goguel 1997: 169–76). It is unlikely those kings envisaged scholars three or four thousand years later carefully editing their boastful memorials—but surely they would have been pleased!

Apart from those three categories, most of the things archaeologists find, buildings, tools, pots, inscriptions, have been buried by accident and survive by accident. The circumstances of burial affect the survival. Perishable materials, wood, cloth, leather, survive only in exceptional conditions, such as the charred woodwork from Ebla, or the dehydrated leather and papyrus manuscripts, basketry and fabrics from caves near the Dead Sea. Occasionally the form of the lost material can be discerned from impressions in clay (e.g. of papyrus fibres on the reverse of clay sealings) or metal fittings which remain. A remarkable example is the imprint of the side of Marduk's throne at Babylon fallen on to the bitumen floor in Esagila.[3]

[2] E.g. Merodach-Baladan II, see Frame 1995: 136–38, referring to Shulgi.

[3] Koldewey 1911: 43; cf. Barnett 1950: 1–43, especially 40–43.

Misleading conclusions

Unless this accidental element is fully recognized, interpretations of the surviving evidence may be skewed or wrong. Two examples from the interpretation of material remains illustrate the point. In 1979 there was published, posthumously, the fourth edition of Kathleen Kenyon's textbook, *Archaeology in the Holy Land.* In the chapter on the Chalcolithic Ghassulian culture, she described the site of Tell Abu Matar, near Beersheba, where, in subterranean chambers, people smelted copper ore for manufacturing. She wrote, '...the evidence shows that the use of metal had not yet become a dominant factor. The tools and implements of the inhabitants of Tell Abu Matar were still of flint. The manufactured copper objects found were maceheads (which probably had a ceremonial rather than a warlike significance), pins, rings, ornamental cylinders, and handles. The metal was still regarded as far too precious for rough, everyday use'. Those words were carried unchanged from the first edition of the book (Kenyon 1960: 80), but by the time Kenyon was preparing the fourth edition she knew about the remarkable 'treasure' Israeli archaeologists had found in a cave in Nahal Mishmar in the Judaean desert. She gave a brief account of it, mentioning the 'most exciting objects were in copper, with in addition to many maceheads, chisels, and axes, objects which most certainly can be identified as ceremonial...' (Kenyon 1979: 61–62). The chisels and axes were almost certainly not ceremonial but utilitarian, although probably offered as gifts at a shrine where the treasure had originally been stored. Other examples of such axes have since come to light on other sites. Kathleen Kenyon's earlier verdict that 'the metal was still regarded as far too precious for rough, everyday use' is seen to be mistaken, the result of the accidents of discovery. Roger Moorey observed of this hoard, 'It spectacularly illustrates the recurrent restriction of the surviving material record as evidence for ancient metallurgy and dramatically reinforces the dangers of assuming, for any material so readily recycled, that poverty of evidence is evidence of poverty of production, even at an early stage of metalworking'.[4]

The second case is rather similar. In 1983 Michael O'Dwyer Shea published a paper discussing and cataloguing 'The Small Cuboid Incense-burners of the Ancient Near East'.[5] He established that these objects were most widely used from the Neo-Babylonian period onwards across the Fertile Crescent, listing scores of examples, reaching in date to Roman times. In his survey he noted sixteen examples which had been found during Sir Leonard Woolley's excavations at Ur. Three of these the excavator claimed belonged to

[4] Moorey 1988: 171–89, see 171.

[5] O'Dwyer Shea 1983: 76–109. For descriptions and catalogue of these objects, see Zwickel 1990: 62–109.

the second millennium BC, one in the first half of that millennium, two in the latter half. O'Dwyer Shea argued that all three should be redated to the Neo-Babylonian or Persian periods, in keeping with the other examples he studied. He rightly noted uncertainties about Woolley's attribution of earlier dates to two of the pieces and the third cannot be said to be securely dated. Whatever doubt may be thrown on Woolley's dating of the Ur pieces, as that study was being written evidence was becoming available to demonstrate that such incense burners could belong to the second millennium. French excavations at Meskeneh, ancient Emar, produced more than forty fragments, practically identical with those already known from Ur and other sites, yet indubitably from a Late Bronze Age context. At another site on the mid-Euphrates, Tell Kannas, Belgian scholars found more examples, and they date from the Middle Bronze Age, perhaps even before 2000 BC (Millard 1984: 172–73). Here the danger of trying to make all cases fit the same pattern is evident. The fact that many specimens of a type of object can be set in one age does not mean that every one belongs to it. In making this observation, the writer noted the appearance of the eight-sided clay prism for recording the extensive 'annals' of Tiglath-pileser I of Assyria about 1100 BC No other Assyrian king is known to have used that form of document until Sargon II (721–705 BC), so had prisms from the reigns of Sargon and his successors alone survived, no one would have imagined they were current five centuries before.

The contribution of written documents

The survival and discovery of cuneiform tablets illustrates this phenomenon of accident well and gives precision to another aspect of archaeological discovery. With the thousands of cuneiform tablets in modern museums and private collections, it is tempting to suppose that knowledge about the ancient Near East is very extensive and those sources thoroughly exploited. That is far from the case. Large proportions of major tablet collections remain to be studied intensively and there are periods of time and areas of activity in Mesopotamia and beyond which remain almost blank. Moreover, the majority of the documents written in antiquity were thrown away or reused and so are beyond recovery; we should never forget that those remaining, numerous as they are, are a tiny percentage of all that were written.

Cuneiform tablets have been found strangely isolated and in unexpected places. At Tell al-Rimah a Neo-Assyrian land exchange deed dated in 777 BC lay alone in debris washed from higher up the mound, while excavators at Tawilan in Jordan unearthed a tablet of the Persian period, written far away at Harran, in a post-occupation fill.[6] A Kassite house at Ur yielded an archive

[6] Postgate 1970: 31–35; Dalley 1995: 67–69, cf. 102.

covering the years 1267–1166 BC, 'approximately the last 140 years of the Kassite dynasty', yet containing one tablet from a century later.[7] In the first case the tablet is evidently a stray from a hoard long destroyed or yet to be excavated; it does not signal the amount of writing or the business transactions at that place in the eighth century. The Tawilan tablet, unique in its provenance, was apparently carried from Harran and could be the only cuneiform document its owner possessed, the only tablet ever to reach the site, or, again, it could be a relic of a larger deposit. Similarly, the eleventh-century tablet from Ur is a lone witness to legal activity in the city at that date. Baskets of old tablets were sometimes tipped as rubble in building works[8] and so are found out of context, occasionally providing information about unexplored phases, while others were uprooted from their primary locations in antiquity.[9]

The majority of cuneiform tablets, however, belong to archives or libraries found in temples, palaces, administrative buildings and private houses. Although the collections were deliberately formed, they remain by accident. Distinguishing the reasons for the ruin of the places where they are found is important. Were they abandoned peacefully? In such cases, the inhabitants are likely to have removed everything they wanted and left only tablets they did not value, or that were out-of-date, so the texts that are unearthed may not necessarily be those from the last days, or even years, of occupation, as at El-Amarna (see below). Where there was violent destruction, by nature, by accident, or by enemies, time will have prevented removal of documents, or all but the most vital, as at Ugarit or Emar. Surveying the groups of tablets known from about 2000 BC onwards reveals an overall wave-like pattern of survival; from some centuries there are many documents, from others few, or none at all. There are peaks shortly before 2000, in the eighteenth and seventeenth centuries, in the fourteenth and thirteenth and in the seventh. For the second half of cuneiform writing's life-span, Olof Pedersén has compiled a comprehensive catalogue of all known groups of tablets and other texts which illustrates this pattern (Pedersén 1998).

The administrators of the Third Dynasty of Ur (*c.* 2112–2004 BC) produced more tablets than any others, so far as the numbers in modern collections show. The list of published tablets dated by regnal years of the dynasty mirrors the known history, with a tremendous increase from year thirty-two of Shulgi's reign, following the reorganization of the revenue system, and continuing in the reigns of Amar-Sin and Shu-Sin. Under Ibbi-Sin, the last king, who ruled for about 23 years, the numbers decline rapidly until there are tablets from Ur alone after his eighth year, and their numbers

[7] Gurney 1983: see pp. 13, 14; no. 13 is dated *c.* 1079 BC.

[8] For example, a group of tablets found in Ur, Woolley and Mallowan 1976: 80, n. 1.

[9] At Assur several dozen fragmentary Middle Assyrian administrative texts and letters lay in a post-Assyrian fill, see Pedersén 1985: 53.

are small, except for year 15, soaring to some 400, and year 16, with 74. The reforms Shulgi made to the administration of his kingdom are assumed to have generated these myriads of documents, and their number contrasts strikingly with the list of tablets dated in the first 20 years of his reign and the 17 named years of the reign of his father, Ur-Nammu. Only 15 tablets carry year-names of Ur-Nammu and about 120 the names of Shulgi's first 20 years; for some of those years there are no dated tablets at all.[10] Years 21 to 31 of Shulgi have between one and 113 tablets each. Does this mean there was little or no bureaucratic activity in those years prior to the reorganization, even if at a lower level than we see later? Surely not!

In the Old Babylonian period the pattern of a growing volume of texts towards the end of a phase can be observed at several places. Overall, the number of documents extant for the later part of the period is greater than for the earlier, as a glance at the collections of dated texts put together in the 1950s by Barbara Morgan will show.[11] Later publications augment the figures without changing their shape. At individual sites where excavators have recorded the circumstances of discovery more details of distribution can be established. At Ur, Sir Leonard Woolley's records of the tablets recovered show a spread through the Isin-Larsa dynasties, increasing markedly towards the end of that time and all but ending with the attack by Samsuiluna of Babylon in his eleventh year, *c.* 1737 BC. There is a small cluster of 20 to 30 tablets each from the reigns of Gungunum, Abisare and Sumuel of Larsa (*c.* 1932–1865), few from the next 30 years, then 40 or so from Warad-Sin's reign (*c.* 1834–1823) and upwards of 300 from the long reign of Rim-Sin which was ended by Hammurabi's conquest (*c.* 1822–1763). There is a trickle of texts from the later years of Hammurabi himself (less than a dozen), a handful from the brief rule of Rim-Sin II of Larsa and a couple of dozen from the early years of Samsuiluna. The tablets dated nearer the beginning of the period, such as most of those concerned with offerings for the Ningal temple, 'are but the remnants of larger archives', and do not present an even distribution, for 'The bulk of ... tablets, i.e., 57, was written in the first 50 years of this period, and within the last 32 years we find the remaining 10 tablets; thus for about 20 years in between, there are no tablets at all'.[12] Where there is a sufficient range of tablets from other towns of the period, the picture they give is comparable; Mari's plentiful documents belong mainly to the reign of Zimri-Lim, who fell to Hammurabi.[13]

[10] Information taken from Sigrist and Gomi 1991.

[11] Morgan 1953: 16–22, 33–41, 56–79, set out 'to supply references to all dated texts under the respective reigns' (p. 16, n. 1). M.J.A. Horsnell 1999, adds many texts, but they do not change the overall picture

[12] Figulla 1953: 88–122, 171–92, see 184.

[13] Charpin 1995: 29–40. For other sites, see the charts drawn up by Stone 1977: 267–89, especially p. 271, fig. 2, and Stone 1987: 34, 109–11.

The centuries of Kassite rule—about 1595 to 1155 BC—form one of the less well-known periods of Babylonian history. Very few documents are extant from the first two centuries, that is earlier than the mid-fourteenth century BC, the reigns of Kadashman-Enlil II (*c.* 1374–1360) and his son Burna-buriash II (*c.* 1359–1333). They corresponded with the pharaohs Amenophis III, Akhenaten and Tutankhamun, and Burna-buriash refers to messages which had passed between kings of Babylon and the pharaohs half a century earlier. El-Amarna Letters 9 and 11 mention Kurigalzu, probably his predecessor but one; Letter 10 names Karaindash, who flourished *c.* 1413 BC. At the same time, Ashur-uballit of Assyria (*c.* 1363–1328, Letter 16) refers to his predecessor Ashur-nadin-ahhe writing to a pharaoh, probably meaning Ashur-nadin-ahhe II (*c.* 1400–1391), less likely Ashur-nadin-ahhe I (*c.* 1440). Although letters from Kadashman-Enlil, Burnaburiash and Ashur-uballit are preserved among the El-Amarna Letters (nos 2–5, 6–11, 15, 16), there is only one possible example of a royal letter concerning any of these kings that has been found in Babylonia itself, a tablet from Dur-Kurigalzu which had apparently been sent to Kadashman-Enlil.[14] From his reign 54 economic texts can be listed, from Burna-buriash's reign over 80. The increased distribution of economic texts among the subsequent kings is:

Kurigalzu II (*c.* 1332–1308)	167
Nazi-Maruttash (*c.* 1307–1282)	387
Kadashman-Turgu (*c.* 1281–1264)	119
Kadashman-Enlil II (*c.* 1263–1255)	54
Kudur-Enlil (*c.* 1254–1246)	202
Shagarakti-Shuriash (*c.* 1245–1233)	301
Kashtiliash IV (*c.* 1233–1225)	177[15]

The last king's reign ended when the Assyrian, Tukulti-Ninurta, invaded Babylonia. J. A. Brinkman observed, 'seven kings, spanning slightly more than a century, account for the vast majority of texts of the dynasty'. Thereafter the number of deeds dated by any of the remaining kings of the Kassite era is very small: 'for the final period of the dynasty (1216–1155) economic texts slow to a mere trickle', that is, 'approximately 35 spread over 62 years' and all are from Babylon, Ur and Dur-Kurigalzu (Brinkman 1976: 39, n. 30). Brinkman commented that the accidental discovery of archives might explain the decline, rather than the pattern being 'a measure of the rise and fall of legal or economic activity in the city' (1976: 39, n. 11).

In the same period, the genealogies reconstructed from the various archives of Nuzi cover five generations, the size of the archives increasing

[14] Gurney 1949: 131–49, see 131–41.

[15] This information is taken from Brinkman 1976.

markedly with the last two generations prior to the moment when the town was sacked in the mid-fourteenth century (see Lion 1995: 77–88).

Turning from Mesopotamia to the contemporary Levant, we note that the archives of over one thousand tablets from Emar cover three generations, but that the Late Bronze Age town may not have existed longer. It was destroyed early in the twelfth century.[16]

Ugarit did not have such a short life-span. There, tablets in Akkadian and in Ugaritic run from the reign of Niqmad III, about 1350, down to the fall of the city about 1180. However, texts dated in the fourteenth century are few and they are the particularly important agreements between the Hittite Great King, Shuppiluliuma (*c*. 1344–1322 BC), and his vassal of Ugarit, Niqmad, and their renewal by Murshili II (*c*. 1321–1295 BC) with Niqmad and his successor Ar-Halba (Nougayrol 1956: 35–37, 85–101). The palace ruins yielded a few royal letters from the time of Niqmepa (*c*. 1324–1274 BC), no legal deeds earlier than his reign and no general administrative documents older than the period of Ammishtamru II (*c*. 1274–1240). In his detailed examination of the archives of Ugarit, W. van Soldt observed, 'Only those documents which bore significant information for future generations were kept on file', especially treaties, legal deeds and related texts. He then noted that 'all the economic and administrative texts are to be dated to the ca. 50 years directly preceding the seizure and sacking of the city around 1175 BC' (van Soldt 1991: 230, 231). Recent discoveries have shown that the famous Ugaritic literary tablets with colophons placing them in the reign of a king Niqmad should not be associated with Niqmad III of the mid-fourteenth century, as had long been supposed, but rather with Niqmad IV, who ruled about 1230 BC, a dating which also applies to some other documents.[17] There is a handful of tablets gleaned from various parts of the site which can be placed in the earlier part of the fourteenth century, before the Hittite conquest about 1340, and these, van Soldt concluded, had been thrown out as rubbish.[18]

It is to that earlier period that the El-Amarna Letters belong. Five of them may have been sent from Ugarit, in the reigns of Ammishtamru II and Niqmad II (before 1360–1330; nos 45–49),[19] the earliest period from which any documents have been found in Late Bronze Age Ugarit. The El-Amarna Letters as a whole are an instructive example of an accidental survival. We may assume they were left in the city of Akhetaten when the court moved back to Memphis in the third or fourth year of Tutankhamun (*c*. 1336–1327 BC), left, presumably, as dead letters, an unwanted file, and so not likely to be

16 See principally Arnaud 1985–87; 1991; Beckman 1996.

17 Bordreuil 1995: 427–49, see pp. 446–49; Dalix 1997: 819–24; and 1998: 5–15. The dating to the reign of Niqmad IV had been suggested earlier, Millard 1979: 613–16.

18 van Soldt 1991: 140, n. 150.

19 Translations: Moran 1992: 117–21.

the most recent correspondence of the Egyptian Office of Foreign Affairs. Only one letter can be dated certainly in Tutankhamun's reign (no. 9), the others were sent to or by his predecessors, Amenophis III and IV (=Akhenaten). At least 46 of them were sent from towns of Canaan (excluding what became Phoenicia) and it is revealing to set beside them the rather smaller number of cuneiform tablets, or fragments of tablets, from the Late Bronze Age found at sites within the country. The total overall is under three dozen.[20] Single tablets might be brought from one site to another, so the Megiddo fragment of Gilgamesh could be a 'visitor'; the letter found at Aphek appears never to have reached its destination, and the one inscribed on a small clay cylinder from Beth-Shean may also have been stopped on its way. That is less likely for the others which are mostly letters and administrative texts and probably also for the lexical pieces excavated at Aphek and recently at Ashkelon (Huehnergard and van Soldt 1999: 184–92). Plotting these discoveries gives a meagre distribution map—nine places (excluding Pella in Transjordan). Plotting the places known to have sent letters to El-Amarna produces a slightly different pattern: 11 towns can be identified with assurance and others may be currently unrecognized or uncertain. Here is an excellent demonstration of the difference a single discovery can make to our knowledge. In place of the nine sites where local finds attest the practice of cuneiform writing, combining the lists yields at least 17. Although some local princes may have shared the services of a single scribe (Campbell 1964: 112f.), there is no reason to suppose that was normal. Other places mentioned in the Letters may also have been in correspondence with the pharaoh or with each other. The total of 17 places now known to have used Akkadian cuneiform in Late Bronze Age Canaan is the minimum, therefore. Over a century of familiarity with the El-Amarna Letters makes it easy to overlook their importance in this respect.

Documents from the Middle Assyrian kingdom attest some activities of the central government in Assur and of provincial administration and reflect the rise and fall of its power. Several sites in the north-west flourished under Shalmaneser I (*c.* 1274–1245) and Tukulti-Ninurta I (*c.* 1243–1207), namely, Tell Chuera, Tell Fekheriyeh, Tell al-Rimah, Tell Sabi Abyad, Dur-Katlimmu, and in Assyria, Admannu (Tell Ali, near Kirkuk) and Shibaniba (Tell Billa). At Assur itself, tablets in Pedersén's *Archives* nos 4, 8, 10–14 belong mostly to the same reigns, 10–14 being from private houses.[21]

Assyrian tablets of the first millennium are especially significant for this inquiry because the dates of so many of them can be fixed precisely thanks to the eponym system. Tables produced a few years ago show the distribution of dated texts from Assyrian sites and demonstrate a great increase in the number

[20] For details in this paragraph see Millard 1999: 317–26. The tablets are listed in Horowitz, Oshima and Sanders 2002: 753–66.

[21] For details see Pedersén 1998, 80–103.

of dated documents from the eighth century to the seventh and a great variety in the numbers available from different years.[22] Thus between 750–701 BC there are three years for which we have no dated legal or administrative texts, only literary or historical ones, and in the next half century the years 691, 662, 656 or 655 are without any dated tablets. There is no reason to suppose that business stopped in those years or that scribes ceased to copy works of literature, rather for that period we face the results of chance survival. The deeds that do reach further back are the records of royal grants, existing in originals from the time of Adad-nirari III onwards (Postgate 1969). This group has the appearance of an archive or dossier carefully preserved for reference as the benefactions of the royal house, re-copied from time to time.

In Ashurbanipal's Library at Nineveh most tablets were fresh copies; ancient scribes usually preferred new copies to old. There was a group incorporated from the collection of the Nabu-zuqup-kena family of Kalah made in the last years of the eighth century, but hardly any clearly older ones. Palaeographical examination may yet identify a few, like the fragment of the Dream Book bearing a date in the time of Ashurnasirpal and perhaps a piece of an incantation series.[23]

At Kalah, survey of the smaller quantity of tablets discloses a more or less parallel distribution. The majority of the economic and legal deeds was written in the late eighth and the seventh centuries. Administrative documents from Fort Shalmaneser which date from Adad-nirari III onwards remain within the last century of the arsenal's heyday (Kinnier Wilson 1972; Postgate 1973), and although the royal letters from the reigns of Tiglath-pileser III and Sargon do not belong to the final decades of the city, those were the last monarchs who used Kalah as their capital. However, the handsome hemerology from the Temple of Nabu was inscribed by a scholar working for Ashurnasirpal II and one royal deed can be attributed to the same reign on palaeographical and contextual grounds (Deller and Millard 1993: 219–42; Hulin 1959: 42–53). The temple library contained omen tablets dated in 787 BC and the handwriting may indicate others are as early (see Wiseman and Black 1996).

Literary tablets of the Neo-Assyrian period are available in considerable numbers from Ashur. They include the collection of over 600 belonging to Nabu-bessun, his associated exorcists and his family, his son, Kisir-Assur, writing one tablet in 658 BC, while others are half a century older (see Pedersén 1986: 41–76). Again, there are a few with earlier dates, one copied by the same scribe as the Nimrud hemerology and one ritual from Middle Assyrian times.[24] Although there is a slightly larger quantity of older literary

[22] The following paragraphs draw from Millard 1997: 207–15.

[23] Oppenheim 1956: 322, K.14884; Nougayrol 1947: 329–36, if it was found at Nineveh.

[24] Pedersén 1986: 44; hemerology: 55, 70, no. 455 (*KAR* 147); Middle Assyrian ritual: 57, 70, no. 472 (*KAR* 139).

tablets in two of the Assur collections than clearly identifiable at Nineveh or Kalah, the result is the same: texts from the last century of Assyrian power predominate. Legal and business documents show exactly the same pattern.

Other Neo-Assyrian sites tell the same story. At Sultantepe the oldest dated literary tablet was written in 718 BC, the few other dated documents in the seventh century (Gurney and Finkelstein 1957: iv). At Balawat the temple of Mamu was founded by Ashurnasirpal II in the ninth century and he and his son, Shalmaneser III, had the famous gates erected, richly decorated with bronze reliefs, yet the majority of the deeds found there belong to the years after 697 BC, three are slightly earlier (from 734, 719 and 710 BC), and none survive from the reign of the founder or of his son (Parker 1963: 86–103). One of the two groups of Assyrian tablets found at Tell Halaf comes from the seventh century, again. The other group was written about 800 BC and was apparently part of a fill for a later structure (Friedrich *et al.* 1940). The tablets from Tell Billa, ancient Shibaniba, all deal with affairs in the reign of Shalmaneser III, although the site was occupied into the Sargonid era.[25] It is possible they were left forgotten after the widespread revolt at the end of that reign, which included the town. The discovery of a single Neo-Assyrian deed of 777 BC at Tell al-Rimah, mentioned above, presents another exception, contrasting with a large number of Middle Assyrian ones thought to have been thrown out by looters from their storage place and with various Old Babylonian archives found at the same site.[26]

Conclusion

The enormous increase in tablets dated in the seventh century is parallel to the hoards of tablets from the last half century of Ugarit, and points to the conclusion that the bulk of the texts that survive belong to the last few decades of life or occupation in a town. In sites where life continued without major interruption over many generations, little will be left from any but the last two or three. That is the principle this paper is trying to emphasize, with the assertion that it does not apply to written documents only but may also affect most other objects found at a site. Of course, where there have been many centuries of occupation, there will be material from all periods, yet it is the last phases of the occupations, the phases prior to destruction or desertion that will offer the largest amount of material remains to the archaeologist.

The Neo-Assyrian tablets substantiate this. Before 750 BC the number of dated texts of all kinds is only 90 in the 160 years from the start of the Eponym List and that number includes several duplicate copies of building

[25] Finkelstein 1953: 111–76; Neo-Assyrian texts pp. 111–76.

[26] Postgate 1970: 31–35; Saggs 1968: 154–74; Wiseman 1968: 175–205; Dalley *et al.* 1976.

inscriptions. Relatively few cuneiform tablets have been recovered from the ninth century and the first half of the eighth, whether dated by eponyms or undated. That is surprising when we recall the period in question covers the decades of Ashurnasirpal II and Shalmaneser III who have left inscriptions on stone reliefs and stelae, statues and foundation tablets which spread over 375 pages of text and translation in two volumes of A.K. Grayson's *Royal Inscriptions of Mesopotamia Project* (Grayson 1991, 1996). Were all the scribes so busy preparing the royal monuments that they had little time for more mundane texts, for the adminstration or for private citizens? Some modern writers might give that impression! Now on several occasions when an Assyrian king died, the palace he had created ceased to be a royal residence because his successor built a new one. Although the stone reliefs might survive, furniture might be removed and any current records be carried to new offices, ready for royal consultation. While old furniture might be stored if it was valuable, as the ivory furniture was at Nimrud, out-of-date documents would be discarded, thrown into the river, on to a rubbish heap, or used as rubble in construction work. Occasionally, as at El-Amarna, some might be overlooked or simply left in a corner, perhaps in a basket or jar. The majority of the archives from past reigns would be jettisoned.

The rule of the survival of only the latest documents can be applied to areas where documents have survived which cannot be so precisely dated as the Assyrian ones. The most numerous type of ancient Hebrew documents is the ostraca. They have varied provenances, but the best known groups, from Arad and from Lachish, clearly belong to the final stratum at each site, destroyed by the Babylonians. At Arad another group lay in an earlier stratum which is believed to have been destroyed by the Assyrians in 701 BC Although these ostraca belong to the last days of the respective occupations, the analogies from cuneiform-using regions show that they are likely to be the latest products of long-established scribal habits. And there are a few examples of ostraca from earlier strata to substantiate that. Most of the ostraca are administrative notes or messages, but there are rare cases of literary texts.[27] It has been supposed that writing literature only occurred when a culture felt itself to be threatened, as if, when the enemies were advancing, the scribes hastily asked their grandfathers to dictate the family traditions to them![28] When judged in the overall context of this study, that idea cannot be supported. It is worth observing that a similar situation applies to the vast quantities of Greek papyri from Oxyrhynchus and adjacent settlements in Egypt. The greater numbers from the second and third centuries AD, according to W. H. Willis, 'must be due in large measure to...the general economic decline and failure of the irrigation system' at the end of

[27] For the ostraca, see Renz and Röllig 1995; for the literary texts see Millard forthcoming.

[28] Nielsen 1954: 60–61.

the third century, which 'caused progressive abandonment of outlying villages, so that papyri abandoned to drought..were likely to be the most recent till then in use'.[29]

The role of accident in our knowledge of the ancient Near East should have become clear from the variety of examples given. It means that speaking of a 'dark age' at a certain period, for example the eleventh and tenth centuries BC in Assyrian history, indicates that it is only dark to us through the accidents of survival and discovery. That may have been a period of Assyrian weakness, yet the ninth century, a period of power, would be almost as dark to us had the sculptured and inscribed stone sculptures of Ashurnasirpal and Shalmaneser not been discovered. Where the evidence available is meagre, ancient life was not necessarily poorer, less organized or less literate, as the case of the ninth century shows.

The overview of the survival pattern of cuneiform tablets points to two conclusions which deserve wide recognition.

1. Texts found on a site do not necessarily relate to the whole period of life of a building or town in any particular phase. Where a place has been occupied continuously for a long period, texts that are discovered will usually belong to the last century or so of occupation, and there may be no texts from its beginning. Furthermore, if the place has been deliberately abandoned, the texts found may not indicate the time of its end precisely, the latest documents having been removed.
2. The presence of quantities of texts from one century and few from the previous century is no measure of growth in scribal activity. Unless there is strong internal evidence, or there are indications of a different sort, the existence of more texts in one period than in another cannot be used as a pointer to increased economic activity or prosperity, or to greater attention to legal and administrative matters. The recovery of numerous literary texts from the end of the Larsa period, from later in the First Dynasty of Babylon, from the reign of Tiglath-pileser I, or from late eighth and seventh century Assyria does not of itself mark those decades as moments of greater literary creation or more intensive copying. It is an accident that the cuneiform tablets studied today have often survived in clusters, an accident that should be understood lest the very existence of those clusters lead to distortion of their value.

The significance of this discussion of texts can be applied to all archaeological deposits. A plethora of objects from one period preceded by a minimal

[29] Willis 1968: 205–41, see 211.

harvest need not mean the earlier phase was poorer or less active. It is factually correct to state 'there is little archaeological iron from Assyria predating the late eighth century' (Philip 2000: 154–55), yet the statement has to be qualified by recognition that much iron is mentioned as tribute or booty in the previous centuries. The absence of earlier ironwork from excavations is an example of this principle that things from earlier phases of a continuing occupation will not usually be found in any quantity because they will have been discarded or, in some cases, recycled. Understanding these factors will lead to a better balance in reconstructions of the ancient cultures and history of the Near East.

BIBLIOGRAPHY

Arnaud, D.
1985–87 *Emar VI: Textes sumériennes et akkadiennes* 1–4 (Paris: Recherches sur les Civilisations).
1991 *Textes syriens de l'âge du bronze récent. Aula Orientalis*, Supplementa 1 (Barcelona).

Barnett, R.D.
1950 'The excavations of the British Museum at Toprak Kale near Van', *Iraq* 12.

Beckman, G.
1996 *Texts from the Vicinity of Emar in the Collection of Jonathan Rosen* (Padua: Sargon).

Bordreuil, P.
1995 'Les texts alphabétiques', in M. Yon, 'La Maison d'Ourtenou à Ougarit', *CRAIBL*.

Brinkman, J.A.
1976 *Materials and Studies for Kassite History* (Chicago: Oriental Institute).

Campbell, E.F.
1964 *The Chronology of the Amarna Letters* (Baltimore: Johns Hopkins University Press).

Charpin, D.
1995 'Le fin des archives dans le palais de Mari', *RA* 89.

Dalix, A.-S.
1997 'Ougarit au XIIIe siècle av. J.-C.: nouvelles perspectives historiques', *CRAIBL*.
1998 'Suppiluliuma II(?) dans un texte alphabétique d'Ugarit et la date d'apparition de l'alphabet cunéiforme', *Semitica* 48.

Dalley, S.
1995 'The cuneiform tablet', in C.-M. Bennett and P. Bienkowski, *Excavations at Tawilan in Southern Jordan* (Oxford: Oxford University Press).

Dalley, S., and A. Goguel
1997 'The Sela' sculpture: a Neo-Babylonian rock relief in southern Jordan', *ADAJ* 41.

Dalley, S., C.B.F. Walker and J.D. Hawkins
1976 *The Old Babylonian Tablets from Tell al Rimah* (London: British School of Archaeology in Iraq).

Damerji, M.
1998 'Gräber assyrischer Königinnen aus Nimrud', *Jahrbuch des Römisch-Germanischen Zentralmuseums, Mainz* 45.

Deller, K.-H., and A.R. Millard
1993 'Die Bestallungsurkunde des Nergal-apil-kumuja von Kalhu', *Baghdader Mitteilungen* 24.

Figulla, H.H.
1953 'Accounts concerning allocation of provisions for offerings in the Ningal-Temple at Ur', *Iraq* 15.

Finkelstein, J.J.
1953 'Cuneiform tablets from Tell Billa', *JCS* 7.

Frame, G.
1995 *Rulers of Babylonia: From the Second Dynasty of Isin to the End of Assyrian Domination (1157–612 BC), The Royal Inscriptions of Mesopotamia, Babylonian Periods*, Vol. 2 (Toronto: University Press).
1999 'The inscription of Sargon II at Tang-i Var', *Orientalia* 68.

Friedrich, J., G.R. Meyer, A. Ungnad and E.F. Weidner
1940 *Die Inschriften vom Tell Halaf, AfO* Beiheft 6 (Berlin: E.F. Weidner, repr. Osnabrück: Biblio-Verlag, 1967).

Garstang, J.
1931 *Joshua-Judges* (London: Constable).

Grayson, A.K.
1991/1996 *The Royal Inscriptions of Mesopotamia. Assyrian Rulers of the Early First Millennium I (1114–859 BC), II (858–745 BC)* (Toronto: University Press).

Gurney, O.R.
1949 'Texts from Dur-Kurigalzu', *Iraq* 11.
1983 *The Middle Babylonian Legal and Economic Texts from Ur* (London: British School of Archaeology in Iraq).

Gurney, O.R., and J.J. Finkelstein
1957 *The Sultantepe Tablets*, 1 (London: British Institute of Archaeology at Ankara).

Haller, A.
1954 'Die Königsgrüfte von Assur', in *Die Gräber und Grüfte von Assur* (Berlin: Mann).

Horowitz, W. Oshima, T and Sanders, S.
2002 'A bibliographical list of cuneiform inscriptions from Canaan, Palestine/Philistia, and the land of Israel', *JAOS* 122.

Horsnell, M.J.A.
1999 *The Year Names of the First Dynasty of Babylon*, Hamilton, Ont., McMaster University Press.

Huehnergard, J. and W. van Soldt
1999 'A cuneiform lexical text from Ashkelon with a Canaanite Column', *IEJ* 49.

Hulin, P.
1959 'A hemerological text from Nimrud', *Iraq* 21.

Kenyon K.M.
1960 *Archaeology in the Holy Land* (London: E. Benn; New York: W.W. Norton).
1979 *Archaeology in the Holy Land*, 4th ed. (London: E. Benn; New York: W.W. Norton).

Kinnier Wilson, J.V.
1972 *The Nimrud Wine Lists. Cuneiform Texts from Nimrud* 1 (London: British School of Archaeology in Iraq).

Koldewey, R.
1911 *Die Tempel von Babylon und Borsippa* (Leipzig: Hinrichs).

Layard, A.H.
1850 *Nineveh and Its Remains*, 5th ed. (London: John Murray).

Lion, B.
1995 'Le fin du site de Nuzi et la distribution chronologique des archives', *RA* 89.

Millard, A.R.
1979 'The Ugaritic and Canaanite alphabets — some notes', *Ugarit Forschungen* 11 [C.F.A. Schaeffer volume].
1984 'The small cuboid incense-burners: a note on their age', *Levant* 16.
1997 'Observations from the Eponym Lists', in S. Parpola and R.M. Whiting (eds), *Assyria 1995* (Helsinki: University Press).
1999 'The knowledge of writing in Late Bronze Age Palestine', in K. van Lerberghe and G. Voet (eds), *Languages and Cultures in Contact: At the Crossroads of Civlizations in the Syro-Mesopotamian Realm. Proceedings of the 42th RAI* (Leuven: Peeters).
in press 'Books in Ancient Israel'.

Moorey, P.R.S.
1988 'The Chalcolithic hoard from Nahal Mishmar, Israel, in context', *World Archaeology* 20.

Moran, W.L.
1992 *The Amarna Letters* (Baltimore: Johns Hopkins University Press).

Morgan, B.
1953 'Dated texts and date-formulae of some First Dynasty kings', *MCS* 3.

Nielsen, E.
1954 *Oral Tradition* (London: SCM Press).

Nougayrol, J.
1947 'Un texte inédit du genre Šurpu', *JCS* 1.
1956 *Textes accadiens des archives sud. Le Palais royal d'Ugarit* IV (Paris: Imprimerie Nationale).

Oates, J. and D.
2001 *Nimrud: An Assyrian Imperial City Revealed* (London: British School of Archaeology in Iraq).

O'Dwyer Shea, M.
1983 'The small cuboid incense-burners of the ancient Near East', *Levant* 15.

Oppenheim, A.L.
1956 *The Interpretation of Dreams in the Ancient Near East* (Philadelphia: American Philosophical Society).

Parker, B.H.
1963 'Economic tablets from the Temple of Mamu at Balawat', *Iraq* 25.

Pedersén, O.
1985 *Archives and Libraries in the City of Assur*, 1 (Uppsala: Almqvist & Wiksell).
1986 *Archives and Libraries in the City of Assur,* 2 (Uppsala: Almqvist & Wiksell).
1998 *Archives and Libraries in the Ancient Near East, 1500–300 BC* (Bethesda, MD: CDL Press).

Philip, G.
2000 'Iron', in P. Bienkowski and A. Millard (eds), *British Museum Dictionary of the Ancient Near East* (London: British Museum Press).

Postgate, J.N.
1969 *Neo-Assyrian Royal Grants and Decrees* (Rome: Pontifical Biblical Institute). [Re-edited in L. Kataja and R. Whiting, *Grants, Decrees and Gifts of the Neo-Assyrian Period, SAA* 12, (Helsinki: University Press, 1995).]
1970 'A Neo-Assyrian tablet from Tell al Rimah', *Iraq* 32.
1973 *The Governor's Palace Archive. Cuneiform Texts from Nimrud* 2 (London: British School of Archaeology in Iraq).

Renz, J., and W. Röllig
1995 *Handbuch der althebräischen Epigraphik*, I. *Text und Kommentar* (Darmstadt: Wissenschaftliche Buchgesellschaft).

Saggs, H.W.F.
1968 'The Tell al Rimah tablets, 1965', *Iraq* 30.

Sigrist, M., and T. Gomi
1991 *The Comprehensive Catalogue of Pubished Ur III Tablets* (Bethesda, MD: CDL Press).

Stone, E.C.

1977 'Economic crisis and social upheaval', in L.D. Levine and T.C. Young (eds), *Mountains and Lowlands: Essays in the Archaeology of Greater Mesopotamia, Bibliotheca Mesopotamica* 7 (Malibu: Undena).

1987 *Nippur Neighbourhoods* (Chicago: Oriental Institute).

van Soldt, W.

1991 *Studies in the Akkadian of Ugarit: Dating and Grammar. Alter Orient und Altes Testament* 40 (Neukirchen: Neukirchener Verlag).

Willis, W.H.

1968 'A census of the literary papyri from Egypt', *Greek, Roman and Byzantine Studies* 9.

Wiseman, D.J.

1968 'The Tell al Rimah tablets, 1966', *Iraq* 30.

Wiseman, D.J., and J.A. Black

1996 *Literary Texts from the Temple of Nabû, Cuneiform Texts from Nimrud* 4 (London: British School of Archaeology in Iraq).

Woolley, C.L., and M.E.L. Mallowan

1976 *The Old Babylonian Periods, Ur Excavations* 7, ed. T.C. Mitchell (London: British Museum).

Yadin, Y.

1972 *Hazor: The Head of All Those Kingdoms* (London: British Academy).

Zwickel, W.

1990 *Räucherkult und Räuchergeräte, Orbis Biblicus et Orientalis* 97 (Freiburg: Universitätsverlag).